SAWDUST CAESAR

SAWDUST CAESAR

THE UNTOLD HISTORY OF MUSSOLINI AND FASCISM

BY

GEORGE SELDES

AUTHOR OF "WORLD PANORAMA"
"THE VATICAN: YESTERDAY—TO-DAY—TO-MORROW" ETC.

LONDON
ARTHUR BARKER LTD.
21 GARRICK STREET, COVENT GARDEN

First Published 1936

PRINTED IN GREAT BRITAIN BY
MORRISON AND GIBB LTD., LONDON AND EDINBURGH

CONTENTS

PART I

THE FORCE OF DESTINY

		PAGE
CHRONOLOGY		vii
CHAP.		
I. TIDE . . . TAKEN AT THE FLOOD . . .		1
II. THE ROMANTIC REBEL		11
III. "DIEU N'EXISTE PAS"		22
IV. COMRADE ANGELICA AND COMRADE BENITO .		36
V. A MIRACLE IS EXPLAINED . . .		42
VI. A POLITICIAN GOES TO WAR . . .		52
VII. FIUME OR DEATH !		60
VIII. THE SECRET OF 1920		72
IX. FASCISM CONQUERS MUSSOLINI . . .		86
X. PRIEST *VERSUS* POLITICIAN . . .		94

PART II

THE CONQUEST OF POWER

XI. THE GLORIOUS MARCH ON ROME . .		101
XII. THE VICTOR IN SEARCH OF A PROGRAMME .		117
XIII. PERSONAL VENDETTA		128
XIV. THE ASSASSINATION OF MATTEOTTI . .		137
XV. BLOOD AND IRONY		157
XVI. THE SONS OF BRUTUS		168
XVII. PURGE OF THE FREEMASONS . . .		176
XVIII. MUSSOLINI CONQUERS THE MAFIA . .		189

CHAP.   PAGE
XIX. Cheka—spelled Ceca or Ovra   .   .   . 193

XX. The Fate of Heroes   209

XXI. "'Live dangerously' is my Motto"   .   . 216

XXII. The Silent Revolution   226

PART III

MUSSOLINI VICTORIOUS

XXIII. Mussolini *versus* The Pope   .   .   . 235

XXIV. Diplomacy: Corfu to Ethiopia   .   .   . 254

XXV. The Corporate State: People under Fascism 270

XXVI. Fascism Finance   293

XXVII. A Journalist suppresses the Free Press   . 309

XXVIII. Let there be Culture!   328

XXIX. The Imperialist Road to War   .   .   . 345

XXX. Ave Caesar!   364

Appendices—

The Fascist Decalogue   383

The Fascist Ten Commandments.   .   . 383

The Foreign Policies of Fascism   .   .   . 384

"Dieu n'existe pas"   388

Bibliography   393

Index   397

CHRONOLOGY

1883	July 29	.	Mussolini born at Dovia, commune of Predappio, province of Forli.
1901	. .	.	Obtains teacher's licence; first post at Gualtieri, in Reggio Emilia.
1902	Jan. 3	.	Went to Switzerland in search of work and to escape military service.
,,	July .	.	Arrested at Lausanne for vagabondage.
1903	Sept. .	.	Expelled from Berne. Went to Geneva. Called for military service.
1904	March 6	.	Debate with Tagliatelli : "God does not exist."
,,	April .	.	Declared deserter at Forli.
,,	,, .	.	Arrested in Geneva for falsifying passport; expelled.
,,	Dec. 31	.	Presented himself at Forli for military service in the 10th Bersaglieri regiment.
1906	Nov. 27	.	Schoolmaster at Tolmezzo.
1908	Feb. 25	.	Schoolmaster at Oneglia.
,,	July 22	.	Sentenced at Predappio to eight months' imprisonment and 200-lire fine for " armed revolt."
,,	Sept 10	.	Sentenced by the municipal judge of Mendola to 100-lire fine for revolutionary expression.
1909	March	.	Went to Trento, Austria, to work on the *Avvenire* ; secretary of the Socialist Party local.
,,	Sept. .	.	Expelled from Austria for revolutionary writing.
,,	Oct. .	.	Became leading Socialist at Forli.
,,	Nov. 10	.	Arrested and imprisoned ten days for radicalism.

1910 Jan. 2 . Published *La Lotta di Classe* (The Class Struggle).

,, April 14 . Paid secretary of Forli Socialist local.

,, Sept. 17 . Represented local at Florence Socialist Congress.

1911 Sept 25 . Organized armed uprising against Tripoli war.

,, Sept. 28 . Sentenced to five months' imprisonment.

1912 March 14 . Approved the attempted assassination of the King.

,, July . . Socialist Congress at Reggio Emilia ; Mussolini becomes nationally known ; becomes director of Socialist Party.

,, Dec. 1 . Editor of *Avanti* ; extreme radical Socialist.

1913 . . . Publishes *John Huss*, with preface attacking Catholic Church.

,, Oct. . . Defeated candidate for the electoral college.

1914 April . . Ancona Congress ; proposes expulsion of Freemasons from Socialist Party.

,, June 7 . Mussolini " patron saint " of the Red Week, revolutionary attempt to seize and occupy the factories.

,, Aug. 4 . Socialist Party declares for Italian neutrality.

,, Sept. 9 . Mussolini denounces Belgian sentimentality.

,, Oct. 13 . Prezzolini in *La Voce* notes Mussolini has changed his anti-interventionist policy.

,, Oct. 25 . Socialist Party accuses Mussolini of treason. Deputy Treves accuses Mussolini of selling out to France.

,, Nov. 15 . Mussolini issues the *Popolo d'Italia* with funds supplied by the French propaganda department.

,, Nov. 23 . Mussolini expelled from the Socialist Party " for moral and political betrayal."

1915 April 19 . Arrested in Rome for organizing interventionists.

,, April 29 . Wounded by Treves in duel.

1915	May 15	.	Italy declares war on Austro-Hungary.
,,	Sept. 1	.	Mussolini called to the colours.
,,	Dec. 9	.	Taken to hospital, suffering from gastro-enteritis.
1916	March 10	.	Fights duel with General Count Spingardi.
1917	Feb. 23	.	Taken to hospital for removal of shell splinters.
,,	Aug. .	.	" I took my place as a fighter in my newspaper office."
,,	Oct. .	.	Italy defeated at Caporetto.
,,	Nov. .	.	Organization of Fasci di Resistenza.
1918	Oct. .	.	Victory of Vittorio Veneto.
,,	Nov. .	.	Armistice.
1919	Jan. .	.	Organization of Partitio Popolari (Catholic Party).
,,	March 23	.	Mussolini, Marinetti, Cesare Rossi and others found the Fascio Italiani di Combattimento in accordance with the suggestions of d'Annunzio.
,,	March 24	.	" We are for a Republic ; we are absolutely against dictatorship."
,,	Sept 12	.	D'Annunzio occupies Fiume.
,,	,,		Mussolini defeated for Chamber of Deputies.
,,	Nov. 10	.	" We will accept no dictatorship."
1920	April 20	.	Fascist programme includes confiscation of war profits ; confiscation of lands, etc.
,,	Sept. 1–19 .		Occupation of the factories by workmen ; approved by Mussolini.
,,	Dec. 22–26 .		Allies bombard d'Annunzio.
,,	Dec. 29	.	D'Annunzio quits Fiume.
,,	Dec. 31	.	Mussolini writes, "Bolshevism has been dyked."
1921	Jan. .	.	Socialist Congress at Livorno expels Communists.
,,	May 15	.	Mussolini elected Fascist deputy.
,,	Aug. 3	.	Makes peace pact with labour and Socialists.
,,	Nov. .	.	Partito Nazionale Fascista formed.

1922	Aug. 3	.	Fascist armed mobilization and violence destroys attempt at general strike protesting Fascist violence.
,,	Oct. 24	.	Fascist Congress at Naples.
,,	Oct. 27	.	Mussolini returns to Milan.
,,	Oct. 27–29	.	Mussolini barricades his office while Fascisti " march " on Rome.
,,	Oct. 29	.	King calls Mussolini to premiership.
,,	Oct. 30	.	Mussolini arrives in Rome *via* Pullman train ; reviews victorious Fascisti with King.
,,	Nov. 16	.	Mussolini demands dictatorial powers.
,,	Nov. 19	.	Abolishes commission exposing war profiteers (Decree No. 487).
,,	Dec. .	.	Massacre of working-men in Turin.
1923	Feb. .	.	Creation of Fascist militia.
,,	Aug. 23	.	Murder of Father Minzoni.
,,	Aug. 27	.	Five members of Italian delegation assassinated on Albanian side of Albano-Greek border.
,,	Aug. 31	.	Mussolini occupies Corfu ; massacre of children in American orphanage.
,,	Sept. 3	.	Mussolini refuses League of Nations intervention.
1924	Jan. .	.	Treaty with Yugoslavia.
,,	March	.	Democrats and Socialists quit government.
,,	April 4	.	Fascisti win elections through terrorism ; Brianza sacked.
,,	June 11	.	Assassination of Matteotti.
,,	Aug. .	.	Abolition of free press.
1925	June .	.	Augusteo speech : " Violence is profoundly moral."
,,	Nov. 4	.	Attempted assassination by Zaniboni ; abolition of Freemasonry.
1926	April 7	.	Attempted assassination by Miss Gibson.
,,	Aug. 30	.	Podestá system ; municipal elections abolished.

1926 Sept. 11 . Attempted assassination by Lucetti.

,, Oct. 31 . Bullet fired at Mussolini ; Zamboni, Fascist youth in uniform, lynched by Mussolini's entourage.

,, Nov. 4 . General Ricciotti Garibaldi and Colonel Macia arrested in France ; Garibaldi confesses receiving large sums as Fascist *agent provocateur.*

1927 Jan. 5 . Mussolini announces " end of epoch of reprisals, devastations, and violence. Squadrismo must disappear."

,, Jan. 24 . Pope dissolves Catholic Boy Scouts and protests Fascist monopolization of youth.

,, April 21 . Fascist Labour Charter abolishes strikes.

,, July 2 . Mont Blanc christened Monte Mussolini by Fascisti.

,, Oct. 22 . Manhood suffrage abolished by decree.

,, Oct. 27 . Decree justifying crimes committed for nationalistic purposes.

,, Dec. 21 . Stabilization of lira on gold basis announced.

1928 Jan. 23 . Fascist arms for Hungary and Hitler found at St. Gothard.

,, March 30 . Mussolini abolishes Catholic Boy Scouts and other non-Fascist youth organizations.

,, ,, Fascism celebrates first anniversary of Corporate State.

,, April 14 . Mussolini tells peasants price outlay not equalled by crop in " Battle of the Grain."

,, June 2 . Mussolini expelled from National Press Club, Washington, in resolution charging suppression of the press and denial of personal liberty.

,, Sept. 21 . Fascism made permanent government ; Grand Council, not King, to appoint future premiers.

1929 Feb. 11 . Mussolini and Cardinal Gasparri sign Vatican peace treaty.

1929 March 24 . Italy votes Fascist majority ; opposition
                  parties not permitted to name candi-
                  dates.

  ,, April 10   . Corporate State announced in force.

  ,, June 7   . Pope becomes ruler of Vatican State.

1930 June .   . Mussolini tours North Italy, making mili-
                    taristic speeches against France.

  ,, July 23   . Writes article favouring revision Versailles
                    Treaty in favour of Germany and
                    Hungary.

  ,, Oct. .   . New Fascist criminal code abolishes jury
                    system.

  ,, Nov. 20   . Military training for youth extended.

  ,, Dec. .   . In Christmas broadcast Mussolini says,
                    " Italy will never take the initiative of
                    starting a war. Italy needs peace."

1931 Jan. 26   . Major-General Butler, U.S. Marines, tells
                    Contemporary Club, Philadelphia, Mus-
                    solini ran over child ; Ambassador de
                    Martino protests.

  ,, Feb. .   . International Committee for Political
                    Prisoners, Civil Liberties Union, Ligue
                    des Droits d'Hommes, Oxford and Cam-
                    bridge professors protest arrest of intel-
                    lectuals in Italy.

  ,, March 6   . Grand Council extends O.V.R.A. (Fascist
                    Cheka) for another five years.

  ,, April 27   . Zamora, President Spanish Republic, cables
                    anti-Fascist organizations offering Spain
                    as refuge.

  ,, June 29   . To avoid censorship, Pope smuggles en-
                    cyclical to Paris denouncing Fascist
                    " irreverencies, indecencies, destruction,
                    confiscation, and vandalism . . ." ; de-
                    clares Fascism and Catholicism incom-
                    patible.

1932 June 30   . Mussolini announces Fascism has support
                    of entire population ; secret tribunal
                    announces results February 1927, to
                    date : 9 sentenced to death, 257 to
                    6076 years' imprisonment ; 1391 to
                    4040 years ; 584 awaiting trial ; total
                    arrests and tried, 12,000—for political
                    offences.

1932 Aug. .   . Marriage and birth-rate reach lowest point.

  ,,   Oct. .   . Domenico Bovone and his mistress, Margharita Blaha, charged with plotting assassination of Mussolini. Angelo Sbardellotto accused of attempting assassination, admits plot as revenge for execution of Michele Schirru, recently executed for similar offence. Bovone and Sbardellotto executed.

1933 Jan. .   . Preliminary budget report, 1933–1934, shows deficit 2,900,000,000 lire ; with losses in movement of capital, deficit of 3,088,000,000 lire foreseen, or double deficit current year.

  ,,   Feb. 11   . Italian army planes sold Hungary in violation of treaty.

  ,,   Sept. 19   . Mussolini announces for German re-armament.

1934 March   . Mussolini announces " a plan, not for five years or ten years, but for sixty years . . . at which time Italy will have the primacy of the world. . . . Our future lies in Asia and Africa. . . ."

  ,,   June .   . Corporative State voted.

  ,,   ,,   .   . Italians kill ten Greeks in Rhodes uprising.

1935   .   .   . Encounter at Ual-Ual ; Mussolini refuses arbitration by League of Nations, and moves troops to Ethiopia for war of conquest.

PART I

THE FORCE OF DESTINY

CHAPTER I

TIDE . . . TAKEN AT THE FLOOD

WHEN the European War crisis came to Italy, as it was to come to America two years later, all the parties of the Left, the radicals, the liberals, were joined by the Democrats, the Centre, and elements of the Right in denouncing the war mongers who favoured the Triple Entente or the Triple Alliance. So long as the powerful Socialist Party remained integral, intelligent, and determined in its opposition to war, so long as its official organ, *Avanti*, and its courageous editor, Benito Mussolini, united in labouring masses to the policies of the party, the war makers dared not move.

On July 27 Mussolini wrote the decisive editorial of the time, under the startling headline, " Our Neutrality Must Be Absolute." It was more than an abrogation of Italy's contract to fight with Germany and Austro-Hungary; it was a threat of revolution at home. The government realized that *Avanti* had struck the popular tune. The Nationalists still raged patriotically about the nation's duty to Germany, and Albertini of the *Corriere della Sera* and Bergamini of the *Giornale d'Italia* coined pre-Wilsonian phrases about saving Democracy and preserving Civilization by joining the Allies, but realistic politicians knew Italy was out of the war.

Officially on August 4 the Socialist Party voted for neutrality.

Loudest and most violent of the strict neutralitarians, militant pacifists, die-hard Socialists, was the white knight

I

of peace-at-any-price and the Red Internationale, the editor of *Avanti*.

Magnificently he met the challenge. His editorials were heavy with sarcasm, his phrases reeked of the Milan political gutters, he used words rarely if ever seen except on fences, but his pacifist violence was absolutely bloodthirsty. He even mocked the Belgian atrocities which were breaking the heart of the world, and he sneered at the pretensions of Republican France, which, he said, was born in revolution, consecrated to the glorious future of humanity in the bloody days of the Commune, and had now become a militaristic, capitalistic, exploiting, and suppressing nation. Austria he hated with a national hatred. Through his months of fury there ran this leitmotif : Revolt ! Let the proletarians of all the nations, French, German, and Russian, and Austrian too, arise and smite the bourgeoisie on both sides who were bathing the world in blood for their own financial profits ; smite them, destroy them, and establish the dictatorship of the working-class. Thus he echoed Lenin in nearby Switzerland.

But the German Socialists, with the exception of such men as Liebknecht, the French with the exception of the Rolland-Juarez group, and the liberals and radicals of many other countries, suddenly became patriots, voted war credits, and rallied round flags, leaving to Italy and Mussolini only one honourable open road—strict neutrality. Late in August 1914, Mussolini was attacking the " delirium tremens of the Nationalists " whose " scandalous opportunism " favoured intervention. " Italy," reiterated the editor of *Avanti*, " must remain neutral. We Socialists, tenacious enemies of war, are partisans of neutrality."

He saw the war as the " crisis of capitalist society " ; unable to exploit it for revolt, he urged sabotage, but at least neutrality. His old editor in Italian Austria, Cesare Battisti, who wanted Italy to free the Trentino and Venetia Guilia, the *irredenta* provinces, became his enemy. On September 4, under the headline " Italian Proletariat, Resist the War Menace," Mussolini continued : " We are invited to weep over martyred Belgium. We are in the

presence of a sentimental farce staged by France, and
Belgium herself. These two old gossips would exploit the
universal credulity. For us Belgium is nothing but a
belligerent power just like the others . . . all the powers
at war are guilty in the same degree, and it is our right,
our duty, to cause a revolution of the working class against
them."

On September 21 Mussolini arose to new pacifist heights
of violence. The Socialist Party assembled in Bologna
under the eyes of the belligerent world. The editor of the
party organ was given the floor. He began with an oration
for neutrality, which was expected, but suddenly launched
into an attack on his colleagues, the comrades of the party,
saying their anti-war effort was infantile, useless ; they
must become revolutionary, follow him, preach and work
for the new Commune in France and Belgium, in Germany
and Austria, and in Russia, smashing Tsardoms and re-
publics in all the countries at war, and establishing the
utopian dictatorship of the proletarian masses. It was
Mussolini at his best.

On September 24, four days later, this same wild,
impassioned pacifist issued a call to all Italy to come to
arms, to join him and march to the front, to take the side
of ravished France and martyred Belgium, and " to drown
the war in its own blood."

What had happened in those four days between September 21 and 25 ? Nothing short of a miracle, say all the
laudatory biographers of the present Duce. He " weighed
the situation," says one ; " Illumination came to him,"
says another ; and still a third informs this unbelieving
world that " he miraculously changed his opinion and
founded the *Popolo d'Italia* as a clarion call to all Italy
to take up arms on the sides of the Allies." Mussolini
himself is silent, half-hearted at best, usually mysterious
and vague when this question of the miracle confronts
him.

But in all the political cafés of the kingdom long-bearded
ministers of state, emotional waiters and angry working-
men, discussing the situation, asked only one question :

2

" *Chi paga ?* " (" Who has paid for it ? ")   The whispers
rose ; the tumult eventually reached the ears of the persons
most concerned.

Mussolini was still editing the Socialist daily.   On
October 10 his leading editorial was entitled, " From
Absolute Neutrality to Active and Operating Neutrality."
The government took this as a sign that the whole Socialist
movement was wavering, that it could go ahead with its
plans, certain that the Mussolini wing would no longer make
its promised revolutionary troubles.   But Mussolini's first
assistant editor, Angelica Balabanoff, said to him :   " When
you write as you do, it seems you go either to a madhouse
or to the trenches ; you must be prepared to take the
consequences ; there is no place in Socialism for you now."

" You will see," replied Mussolini, " that the whole
executive committee will declare its solidarity with
me."

He spoke in such a grandiloquent, theatrical voice that
Dr. Balabanoff had the feeling he was suffering either from
delusions of grandeur or actual insanity.   She informed
him of the table-talk in all the cafés, asking him for a
straight answer.   All she got were shouts of denial and
threats of revenge.

Then suddenly, early in November, Mussolini resigned
as editor of *Avanti*.   His associate had begged him to stay,
and asked him how he would make his living.

" Five lire a day are enough for me," he replied, " and
I can earn them as a mason.

" I will never write another word.

" And of this you can be assured : I will never write a
word against the Socialist Party."

Just eight days later, on November 15, 1914, there
appeared a new journal on the streets of Milan.   It was
called *Il Popolo d'Italia* and underneath the title were the
words :   *Quotidiano Socialista* (Socialist Daily).   In its
right ear appeared the quotation " *La rivoluzione é un'idea
che ha travato delle baionette* : Napoleone " (" Revolution
is an idea which has obtained bayonets ").   In the left ear
of this new " Socialist " newspaper was the quotation from

the rebel leader, Blanqui, " *Chi ha del ferro ha del pane* " (" Whoever has a weapon has bread ").

The feature of the first issue was a large editorial with the heading " Audacia." It concluded :

" I shall produce a daily which shall be independent, liberal in the extreme, personal. My own. . . . For I shall be answerable to my own conscience and nothing else. I have no aggressive intentions towards the Socialist Party, in which I propose to remain. . . .

" Continuing my march after a brief repost, I fling to you my call, O Youth, Youth of Italy, youth of the workshops and universities, whose hearts and souls are young, who belong to the generation which has to make the future according to the command of destiny—my call, which will resound in History.

" This appeal, this cry, is a word that I would never have uttered in normal times, but which I give out to-day, clearly and vigorously, without reservation, and I give it with full confidence—that one rebellious and terrifying word, WAR ! "

The leading pacifist of Italy now essayed the rôle of leading interventionist. But he still called his a Socialist newspaper, and proclaimed his adherence to the Socialist Party and its major doctrines.

Led by Serrati, Mussolini's boyhood friend and teacher, the Socialist Party now took action. A general assembly was called in Bologna for November 25, at which the former editor accepted the invitation to defend himself.

As Mussolini entered the excited hall the congress shouted as one man : " *Chi paga ?* "

The general assembly became a trial for treason. Mussolini accepted the challenge. Immediately Serrati and the remaining editorial board of *Avanti* demanded Mussolini's political life. (In time to come all men and newspapers which now attacked him were to feel the clubs, the bullets, and the flames of an old-fashioned Italian blood vendetta.)

" *Chi paga ?* " thousands of voices shouted, " *Traditore ! Venduto ! Sicario !* "

The assembly, so members who participated recount,

was tumultuous and bellicose. There was difficulty in
finding a president, a personality strong enough to calm
the angry accusers and permit the defendant to speak,
explain. It seemed impossible. The assembly became
unruly, infuriated, vociferous in its insults. Judging by
the shouting, one would have believed it wanted to beat the
accused to death. Serrati arose, begging that he be allowed
to speak in perfect quiet. Utopia ! For a minute the
pacifists were pacific. Mussolini was called to the platform.
Suddenly all his enemies decided to hear him. " Louder !
Louder ! " The orator's voice was lost in the uproar.

But it was none the less stirring. " You are more
implacable," Mussolini cried, " than the bourgeois judges
who leave the right to the defence. If you have decided
that I am unworthy of fighting amongst you . . ."

" Yes, yes ! " shrieked the audience.

" Expel me, then, but I have the right to demand an
act of accusation in good form. . . . I will not be guillotined
with a motion that doesn't mean anything. As far as the
moral question is concerned, I repeat once more that I am
ready to submit to any commission of inquiry whatsoever.

" You think you are destroying me, but I tell you that
you are mistaken. *Voi mi odiate perchè ancora mi amate !*
(You hate me to-day, because you still love me.) But you
will not ruin me. . . . My twelve years of party life are,
or should be, a sufficient guarantee of my Socialist faith.
Socialism is something which is rooted in the blood. . . .
What separates me from you now is not a petty matter ;
it is a question which is dividing all Socialists. Amilcare
Cipriani himself has declared in speech and in writing, that
if his seventy-five years would permit it, he would be in the
trenches to-day fighting against the European militaristic
reaction which is stifling our revolution.

" But I tell you," continued Mussolini, " that from now
on I shall have no mercy, no pity for all those who in this
tragic moment do not speak their minds, for fear of being
either hissed or cried down. I shall have no mercy, no
pity, for those who are reticent, hypocritical, vile. . . .
And you shall yet see me at your side. You need not

believe that the bourgeoisie are enthusiastic in favour of our intervention. They are gnashing their teeth, they are accusing us of temerity, and are afraid lest the proletariat, armed with the bayonet, may use it for its own purpose.

" Don't think that by tearing up my card you will deprive me of my Socialist faith, and that you will keep me from fighting for the cause of Socialism and the revolution."

In spite of this stirring self-vindication, Mussolini was struck from the party. Thus it is recorded that " the first responsibility for Fascism falls to Socialism."

Mussolini, raging, ran to his paper, the *Popolo d'Italia*, and, between shouting and waving his arms, wrote the following reply :

" EXPELLED

" Had I wanted to stand on a question of procedure, I should have the right to challenge the legitimacy of the vote, and even to demand whether a true and proper vote had taken place, given the manner in which this discussion developed from beginning to end, directed by the shameless partiality of the assessor Schiavi. But I accept the *fait accompli*. I consider myself expelled. The history of Italian Socialism does not record in its more or less glorious pages a more summary execution, a more Inquisition-like, a more bestial one than the one that trapped me. De Marinis, Bissolati, and the others were subjected to exclusion from the big debates of the congress, and were accorded very broadly the right of defence ; and their accusation was carried to the tribune, with documents, and exhaustively gone into.

" For me, nothing of the sort. The trial was conducted in the shortest possible way. Some one presented the most radical motion without even sustaining it by argument ; after much hesitation, I was allowed to expose my thought ; then Lazzari [a Socialist], instead of bringing up an act of accusation, repeated the usual low insinuation. The political question was not even touched upon, the moral question not examined. If that is Socialist justice, truly one should prefer that of Magistrate Allara. But the breed which dominates the party wished to conquer, and conquer it did.

" I am expelled, but not tamed ! If they think me dead, they will have the terrible surprise of finding me alive, implacable, intent upon combating them with all my strength. That is why I have forged for myself a weapon with which to enlighten the proletariat and to remove it from the sad influence of these false preachers. And I hope that in the proletariat of the simple and upright souls, the light will be seen promptly.

" It is not against the proletariat—it is not against the sacred principles of the proletariat—that I am fighting. The proletarians know well that when it was a matter of assuming responsibility for the uprisings, for the lawsuits in the Court of Assizes, for the campaigns of the party, I gave freely of myself out of an irrepressible need of action, without worrying about the danger, without measuring my fatigue. But you, gentlemen, who form the directing élite of the party, you who speak when you should be silent, or who are silent when you should speak ; you with the medals, you who have preferred to hide your votes in the amorphous and tempestuous hand-raising, you who, however, owe something to the ' Barbarossa ' of June, you will have to pass under the Caudine forks. I understand the hatred, the exasperation of the proletarians ; but your reticences constitute a document of a baseness which dishonours Italian Socialism to the extreme point. But I am precisely here to spoil your little party.

" *The Mussolini case is not over, as you think. It is just beginning. It is becoming complicated. It is taking on vaster proportions. I am openly raising the flag of schism.* I am not becoming appeased—I am crying out. I do not bend ; I am revolting.

" All the Socialists who claim for themselves the right to live, and to think ; the proletarians who refuse to bend to the wishes of a coterie which pretends stupidly to stay the course of history and to dictate an eternal and universal law, must gather around this paper, a free arena for free minds, a pure standard which the infamous insinuation of a damaged breed will never succeed in soiling. A party which ' carries on ' in this fashion is a party into which men worthy of the name cannot enter—or, once inscribed, cannot, must not, remain. I invite them to leave, to seek more liberty, more air, more light, more humanity, and more Socialism.

" And now, driving into the depths of my soul all sadness and all complaint, I gather together my weapons, all my weapons. For Socialism ! and against the obvious enemies, and the occult enemies of Socialism ! "

Looking back to that great crisis which was to lead so quickly to Fascism and to dictatorship, Mussolini says of his expulsion and of his raising the banner of schism : " I felt lighter fresher. I was free."

He was free.

The turn in his life had been taken. Our Caesar had crossed his Rubicon. He was now editor and owner of a paper ; he was becoming feared and respected and followed ; moreover, he was no longer held by party lines and rules and the ideas of dead men. He was free !

This was the moment for which he had waited. Out of biographies and histories he had made a pattern for his own life and built a world-empire for himself, which he ruled with appropriate magic words. Denying in childhood and youth the power of men and gods, he had spoken always of his Star of Destiny, repeating Napoleon's favourite phrase until he believed he was its author; and always he had cultivated not only the historical but the Shakespearean Julius Caesar in word and look.

In his youth he had announced sententiously his belief in both Free Will and Predestination, and, unlike his fellow-men who drifted where tide and wind fantastically veered, the young editor of the Socialist *Avanti* felt that a crisis would one day arise, that he would master it, and then achieve that satisfaction which a magnificent egotism, chained in childhood by poverty and misfortune, in youth by the dead hand of Karl Marx and the pressure of political organization, had rendered inevitable for him.

As a good European, he realized early in life that the

road to power led directly through the doors of a newspaper office. He had before him the picture of the first and third Napoleons, the later Bismarck, the contemporary North-cliffe. He had already tasted the surprise and satisfaction in the effects of his amateur writings on the mass mind, both in Switzerland and in his native province, and his elevation to *Avanti* had confirmed every thought about the power of the press. He was free. He was independent.

And yet, there was that childhood in Socialism and that manhood suffering for " the cause " which could never be forgotten. " Socialism is something which is rooted in the blood." It was to appear time and time again in the black blood stream of Fascism.

He had raised the flag of schism, but the old ideals which he had absorbed with his mother's milk and his father's sweaty bread were still beneath the banner. He had been horribly wounded, but he still believed it was he who was the great hero, the noble patriot, and although the Italian world shouted " Traitor " for many years, he tried more than once to return to that paternal heaven under which he was born and raised to leadership.

And again the cry " *Chi Paga ?* " would be raised, the charge of betrayal, the charge that he had sold the Socialist Party and peace for a handful of silver from a foreign country.

CHAPTER II

THE ROMANTIC REBEL

BY deserting the policy of neutrality and pacifism of his Socialist colleagues, young Benito Mussolini earned the immediate enmity of many million compatriots who, naturally accusing him of treason, suspected that the Allies had invested large sums in this secret business. Even to-day, reviewing the entire political career of the Duce, there are some who say that " he has raised betrayal to a mode of life," and who offer documentary proof of this appraisal.

As an action, of course, Mussolini's was not without parallel in past history, and it recurs in the lives of other notable living men. If, however, we accept the philosophy of the Gautama Buddha, if we desire to understand all so that we may forgive all, it is necessary first to review for a moment the childhood and youth of the man who has risen to such worldly eminence by following a course which to some may appear nothing but zigzags, retreats, and changes of face, but to others the straight and narrow path of a fierce and victorious will to power.

The great students of human behaviour agree that a human pattern is " set " before the fifth year ; the child grows to be a hero or a traitor, a racketeer or a statesman ; he becomes an artist, a leader, a neurotic, a madman, because of his treatment by his parents, his brothers and sisters, his companions ; because of his youthful sex life ; because of these and many other events or influences, and the environment of childhood.

" I was not a good boy." " I was a restless and pugnacious child." " I was an audacious *ladro campestre*," he writes at various times, the third confession translatable as " rural thief " according to the dictionary, but " young

buccaneer " by romatic lady biographers. He fought with
his hands and with stones, sometimes sharpened, and there
was blood spilled when young Benito engaged in battle
with peasant lads and schoolboys. When his younger
brother, Arnaldo, began to grow up he, too, was bullied
and hit by his senior. " I was a little rogue, restless,
exacting, passionate, pugnacious, and ever ready to fight.
Often I came home with my head broken with stones, but
I knew how to revenge myself."

The vendetta motif comes early. Life in that hard
countryside around Varano da Costa, where he was born on
July 29, 1883, was for children and men a constant struggle
amidst great poverty ; and where there is poverty and
desperation there is always vendetta and betrayal and
feuds and bloodshed, and a more violent outlook on life.
No wonder, then, that father Alessandro, an excellent man,
an honest man who lived and suffered for his socialistic
principles, and who had spent three years in prison for
having associated with the revolutionist Bakunin, when
it came to teaching his own son the rules for getting along
in a mean world, inculcated the policy of revenge, blow
for blow, blood for blood. It was the philosophy of survival.

In his passionate Socialist days when he published his
own little weekly, *La Lotte di Classe* (The Class Struggle),
Benito wrote of Papa Alessandro :

" My father was born in 1854 in Predappio. . . . He
became an apprentice in a smithy at Dovadola. Then he
went to Dovia and there opened a forge. I do not know
at what time and under what influences he became a follower
of the Internationale. But it is certain that when he
arrived at Dovia he was already carrying on a great propaganda, and had formed the first organization of the Internationale. He was thrown into prison. When he returned,
he remained under police supervision for forty-two weeks.

" His house always offered shelter and friendship to
those pursued by the authorities. Later, when the Socialists
had come to take part in municipal politics, my father
became mayor of Predappio. In 1892 he formed in Predappio the first labour union. . . . In 1902 he was again

arrested. . . . The clergy, the police, and the moderates persecuted him ceaselessly. . . .

" He left me no material heritage, but he left me a moral one—his treasure : the Ideal. . . .

" And after this sorrowful burial, I pursue my way, following in his footsteps."

The boy was named after Benito Juàrez, liberator of Mexico. Papa Alessandro chose the name for two reasons —anti-clericalism and rebellion ; he taught his firstborn to hate the Catholic Church and the Royal State, calling both the oppressors of the human spirit.

From his father Benito learned that intelligence and subtlety must be employed by the minority, if it was not to be for ever suppressed by those in power. In his father's fate Mussolini saw that failure came to those who knew and spoke intelligent plans for the remaking of the world, but who were weak in action. With every year of his childhood his confidence in himself increased.

The most characteristic of all the incidents which Mussolini himself recalled in the first days of his success, concerns his early oratory. His mother, terrified by tremendous noises and a locked door, said to him one day :

" Are you mad, my son ? Only lunatics talk to themselves. What is ailing you ? "

" Do not worry, dear mother," Benito replied simply. " I was practising oratory. Believe me, mother, the time will come when all Italy will tremble before me."

Friends and enemies alike have also drawn many morals from another youthful incident. Fear, betrayal, perfidy, treason, revenge, blows, bloodshed, all enter into it, and all are remembered throughout a lifetime, and satisfaction comes over the face of the dictator as he recounts, time after time, how, on his father's advice, he sharpened a stone, ambushed his enemy, cut open his face, and cursed him. He had earlier that day come naïvely forward to accept the other boy's invitation, and, if one is to believe the narrator, the neighbour lad, without provocation or warning, had smacked his face. That night he had had his revenge. But in the young mind the blow on the face remained for ever imprinted, warning the coming leader never to trust another man, never to surround himself with friends, never to put his trust in humanity, but to rely on the ethics of Schopenhauer, Nietzsche, and above all, of that Machiavelli who despised the mass of human beings.

He was sent to the cloister of the Salesian Friars at Faenza, his mother hoping that the atmosphere of order and piety and the companionship of a better class of children would have some effect in curbing that violent nature. But the boy continued to seek quarrels, to insult those smaller and weaker than himself, and to give the monks many uneasy moments.

" Your father is a rebel," they once said to him, " and you, you are turning into a young anarchist." If he did not change he would be expelled. Then another schoolboy fight, and more punishment. " Mussolini," the friar said, " your soul is black as hell. Confess your sins. Repent before it is too late. Confess or we expel you."

He fled from the school. He roamed, afraid of shadows, through the night, only to be caught and whipped and taken to confession. But instead of that being a lesson to him it only hardened him. The next time he got into a fight it was with an older boy. But young Mussolini knew now how to fight those physically stronger than himself. The world was civilized and there were weapons to be used. Mussolini gave his enemy what the Italians call a *temperinata* : he got out his penknife and stabbed the older boy.

Although, fortunately, the wound was not serious, the action was. The Salesian monks would stand for much ; they would preach, and they would use the rod, but they would not have bloodshed in their quiet walls. So Benito was sent home.

He had been a rebel. He had lived in solitude. From the first days he could not mingle with others, could not accept orders, could not follow. He walked alone. He sought trouble and it always led to more loneliness. " Who in my whole life," he burst out one day, years later, " has shown me tenderness ? Nobody ! Poor, dreadfully poor,

was my home, poor and bitter my life. Where could I
have learned tenderness ? Perhaps at school, in the cloister,
or in the world ? Nowhere. Then why do people wonder
that I am reserved, solitary, harsh, and stern ? "

At his next school at Forlimpopoli it is recorded by one
named Bonavita that Mussolini " got into a fight with three
fellow students ; he went beyond legitimate defence, and
he had to flee from the college." The weapon used is not
named. But it was always the same. From the first days
when he pulled the hair of little girls, climbed about on the
floor pinching bare feet, or bullying the children on the play-
grounds, to the days he drew a knife, it was always the
same rebellion against discipline, the rebellion of a spoiled
child, a beaten child revenging himself upon others for
youthful sufferings at home.

The father passed from blacksmith to tavern-keeper,
from tavern-keeper to mayor of the district. In the forge
he had pounded society as his anvil; his saloon, " l'Agnello,"
became a political centre in the countryside, and Alessandro
himself was always a politician. The young Benito, who
had been whipped for not minding the bellows, was now to
receive another sort of education. For now he lived in a
political café. Here was the place men came to drink and
talk, and to drink more and talk more wildly of the coming
revolution which would assert the rights of man. Socialism,
Karl Marx, the First Internationale, the Communist Manifesto, Syndicalism, direct action, and anarchism, those
were the subjects over which men drank and fought and
fought over again, night after night, while children stood
around in amazement.

Young Mussolini grew up a soap-box orator and a
sturdy brawler. Throughout his province there are many
alive to-day who fought with him, drank with him, gambled
with him, and sometimes engaged in bouts which led to
police interference. At Tolmezzo, and later at Pieve
Saliceto, in the province of Reggio Emilia, where he taught
in the elementary schools, there are strange tales about the
youth with the furious eyes and black temperament.

At Caneva, where he taught in 1905, an attempt was

made to discharge him on the ground of blasphemy in the schoolroom ; the teacher escaped the charge by protesting he was using the names of Oriental gods only ; the reason, however, of the town's dissatisfaction was the terror that ruled the children who were the innocent victims of Mussolini's hatred of the teaching profession. His eyes, his hands, his voice were continually in a state of violence ; he was impatient, would strike the children, and so thoroughly scare them that they would run home weeping and trembling.

In Italy Mussolini's first arrest occurred in Oneglia in 1908, when he marched at the head of a group of workingmen who insisted on their right to work and to strike, and who got into a fight with the authorities. The sentence was ten days in jail. In his home district, in Forli, Mussolini led a mob into the mayor's office : the price of milk was too high, and the way to cure that was to throw the mayor and his staff through the window, to injury or perhaps to death, it did not matter. Those were moments of direct action for the young man who had absorbed so many of his ideas around the wine-dripping tables of his father's saloon. The mayor capitulated, and the man of action was lionized.

No other leader of violence has led so violent a life. Lenin, Trotsky, Kemal Pasha, Pilsudski, in fact most of the modern dictators have a long police record ; but no history of stabbings, shootings, bar-room brawls, street fights, as well as political adventures, make up the youth of Mussolini's prominent rivals. It was the same in his birthplace, his Swiss exile, his first sojourn in Austria, his return to Italy, his editorship in Italia Irredenta, and finally his years of power as member of the directorate of the Socialist Party in Italy, immediately preceding the war. Almost every year is marked by a deed of violence.

From the earliest days of his life, Mussolini engaged in the most violent political activities. Frequently he went to jail. And it is in this record, perhaps, that the key will be found to his decisive action during the war, because it becomes obvious that it was a will to power, and not an idealism disciplined within party barriers, that animated the fiery revolutionary in his youth.

His *Lotta di Classe* pretended to be a Socialist organ at the time Social Democracy in Italy was about as radical as the Socialist Party in the United States now is, and even less so than the British Labour Party, or the Social Democrats of Germany in the early days of the Republic. But Mussolini's paper advocated syndicalism and direct action. " I understood now," the editor wrote, " that the Gordian knot of Italian political life could only be undone by an act of violence." And sadly, " The man who still cherishes ideals in his heart is rated an imbecile or a lunatic." It did not matter what the world called him, he still chose to belong to the Socialist Party and to proclaim ideals which the majority denounced as violent or called childish and Utopian.

The Socialist Party, however, did not know what to make of this super-enthusiastic adherent who preached and practised things it could never harbour nor endorse. Mussolini was for direct action and sabotage. " When I declare myself in favour of sabotage," he declared himself, " I mean in accordance with my theories, economic sabotage, which is not to be confused with *vandalismo*. . . . Sabotage according to me ought to have a moral bearing "—and this led to the July 1910 arrest. When Italy made war in Tripoli, Mussolini was the leader not only of those who opposed that war, but of the pacifists who were willing to spill blood in the name of peace at all costs.

An attempt was made to call a general strike. For three days in Romagna the proletariat became master of the streets. At Forli they occupied the railroad station, hindered the sending of troops, sabotaged the government in every way. Cavalry was sent. Mussolini and Nenni, destined later to be his successor on the *Avanti*, led the mob. Sticks and stones. A fence was destroyed. The strikers armed themselves with staves and the women shook them in the face of the sabres.

The cavalry charged. The women threw stones or placed themselves in front of the men, daring the horsemen to run them down or cut them with their swords. The cavalry charged again. There was confusion. The cavalry charged a third time, and there was the moaning of the wounded, the weeping of women, and the curses of Mussolini and his men followers. But they won. The strikers marched to the railroad station and tore up the tracks. A train had just arrived with soldiers, but they would not let it proceed.

The next day, martial law. Arrests everywhere. The hastily constructed barricades became again nothing but a lot of junk, and the might of law and order was felt. Mussolini sat in his prison cell meditating on the injustice of this world, and planning the liberation of mankind when he had risen to power. But with that feeling there was that other view, gained from his books, that distrust and disgust with his fellow-men. " Only twelve of us here," he said to Nenni amidst the dirt and vermin of the prison, " and the cowards ! they are not going out on a general strike."

He stayed in jail from that 16th of October to the 23rd of the next month, when he was tried on eight serious charges :

" Opposition to the supreme power and defiance of authorities.

" Attempt to prevent recruiting.

" Inciting to strikes and the stoppage of work at war factories.

" Violence in stopping street-car communications and damaging tracks.

" Cutting telegraph lines.

" Destroying a telegraph office.

" Violent seizure of a railroad locomotive.

" Laying telegraph poles across a railroad to derail an express."

On November 23, 1911, he was sentenced to seven months' imprisonment, which term was reduced to five on appeal. His opposition to the war, during the war, was almost treasonable. " Every honest Socialist must disapprove of this Libyan adventure," he had declared. " It means only useless and stupid bloodshed," and thousands had agreed with him. Were it not for this fact of public support his sentence would have been more severe. At the trial he denied only those acts which might have resulted in the deaths of innocent persons, such as the laying of telegraph poles on the railroad track. Before sentence, he said to the judge :

" Honourable Court, if you acquit me you make me rejoice ; for then I can return to work and the community of human society. If you sentence me you honour me, for then you will be condemning not a criminal, but a follower of the Ideal, an agitator according to his conscience, a Soldier of the Truth."

This Soldier of the Truth came out of prison the Hero of the Truth with the halo of a Socialist martyr about him. He had been the leader of a small branch of the party, the editor of only a little local weekly, but he had been noticed by the national leaders ; and his trial, related to a war which was going badly and which was unpopular, brought him some fame ; he stepped out of prison into the midst of an intense political campaign which came to a climax at the congress of his party in July 1912, at Reggio Emilia. It was this meeting which made Mussolini nationally known as a leader.

Some months before there had been an unsuccessful attempt on the life of the King. Congratulations were in order. Other crowned heads sent telegrams and ambassadors ; the President of the United States offered his felicitations ; the Senate of Italy and the Chamber of Deputies expressed their joy, and among those who subscribed to these sentiments were three Socialist leaders, Bonomi, Bissolati, and Cabrini.

It was the action of these three deputies which caused a crisis in the affairs of the Socialist Party : was it to remain Right and loyal and pacifist, or go Left, use violence, prepare for that bloodbath of the proletariat which the editor of The Class War was advocating ? Bissolati was for evolutionary legal progress ; Mussolini leaped into the discussion, demanding action.

" On March 14," cried the boyish demagogue, " a Roman mason fired a revolver against Victor Savoia "—there was a shout of joyful laughter when the orator thus labelled the King. " There have been precedents which ought to indicate the line of conduct for us Socialists. There has

3

already been strong criticism of the indescribable spectacle offered by subversive Italy after the *attentat* of Bresci at Monza. We had reason to hope that after ten years we would not again see flags hung in mourning and Socialist mayors sending telegrams of condolences and congratulations, and all democratic Italy subserviently on its knees at a given moment before the throne.

"It is very difficult to separate the political from the human question. It is very difficult to separate the man and the king. To avoid pernicious misunderstanding the Socialists have but one duty after the *attentat* of March 14 : to keep away.

"Attempted assassinations are the accidents of kings, just as falling chimneys are the accidents of masons. If we must weep, let us weep for the masons.

"Why weep for the King? Why this sentiment, hysterical, excessive, when it concerns crowned heads? Who is the King? He is by definition a useless citizen. There are peoples who have sent their kings for a walk, when they did not want to safeguard themselves better by sending them to the guillotine, and these peoples are the advance guard of civil progress.

"For us Socialists an *attentat* is a historical act or it pertains to the daily news according to the case. Socialists cannot associate themselves with mourning or with condemnation or with monarchist festivities."

The Socialist congress became a maddened crowd. Mussolini called for the expulsion of the three leaders of the moderate, pacifist, anti-violence Right wing of the party. Bissolati stood as their spokesman, a Socialist of the old school, an intellectual, a thinker, a man of the finest moral fibre and the highest ideals of humanitarian philosophy— and like many others of like character, a victim later of the universal war mania which engulfed Europe.

The Reggio Emilia congress was the prelude to the Milan meeting which decided Mussolini's lifetime direction. Here, as later, he felt *la forza del destino*, he displayed opportunism to its utmost, using the appeal to emotion to overcome the appeal to reason.

Ivanoe Bonomi was forced out of the party because he was not radical enough. Claudio Treves was dismissed from the editorship of *Avanti*, and his successor, Giovanni Bacci, six months later made way for that same Benito Mussolini who had defeated Leonida Bissolati at the Reggio Emilia meeting, and who had become, in addition to a director of the Socialist Party, one of its accepted leaders.

Direct action, sabotage, revolutionary tactics, the use of violence to establish philosophical ideas, in other words, the Mussolini programme, was victorious. He became not only the head of the party, but one of the men in control of Italian politics. Bonomi said of him, that he was " a revolutionary in whom the spirit of the barricades is stronger than Marxist discipline," and George Sorel, whose disciple Mussolini had declared himself to be, wrote [1] from Paris : " Our Mussolini is not an ordinary Socialist. It is my belief that some day we shall see him at the head of a mighty legion, saluting the Italian flag with his sword. He is a fifteenth-century Italian, a condottiere."

The Sorel prediction appears in all the early Fascist biographies, and in one instance was used as a triumphant book blurb, the publishers evidently being unaware that in the days of the free republican cities of Italy, in the time of the Renaissance, the condottieri were captains who bought and sold themselves and their soldiers to princes, and were hired for pay to wage the battles of other people.

Whether apocryphal or holographic, the Sorel letter and the judgment of Bonomi help to explain the character of the man and the force driving him into a career of power ; they forecast the decision of 1914 and illuminate the historical events of Mussolini's rule as a dictator.

In 1912, when Bonomi spoke and Sorel prophesied, Mussolini was one of the directors of the Socialist Party, and all the signs pointed to a Revolution, and to the editor of the *Avanti* as a duce, or leader, of a victorious proletarian uprising.

---

[1] No proof that the letter is genuine has ever been produced by the Fascist biographers, but the contents read more like an accusation than an endorsement.

CHAPTER III

" DIEU N'EXISTE PAS "

IF the episodes of his childhood furnish a clue to the man's behaviour in the critical year 1914, the *emigré* years in Switzerland provide the key to the actions and decisions of a whole lifetime.

The little violences of youth were now to be followed by violence in the political field, the little treacheries of boyhood, of which proud parents had boasted, were now to become a pattern of living, while the will to power, demonstrated at first by merely oral declarations, drove through opportunities in dynamic fashion.

Although we are told that love and hate are the opposite poles of the same emotion, we find evidences of the second the harder impulse, in this period of the hero's existence. We see him now as a complete rebel. But what had driven him into that position was not the usual humanitarian reaction. It was almost purely hatred. Mussolini hated the Church, religion, the rich ; he hated society and he hated the State, yet his was not the class hatred shared with Socialist, proletarian friends, it was a personal hatred, a desire for revenge, the result of what he himself, not his people, had suffered. He was not " class " conscious, Whenever he spoke of his childhood it was with bitterness, of his hunger years in Switzerland he spoke with a desire for revenge.

He joined and passed through anarchist, socialist, republican, and other groups, which opposed the state of things as they are, not with the ideal of hastening the day of Utopia, but in pursuance of a vendetta against elements and persons, the Church, society, on individuals he believed had wronged him. For the same reason he opposed Freemasonry, first as a Socialist and later as a Fascist, because its policy was incompatible with his personal programme of retaliation. He never acted from social consciousness as other radicals, but from individual necessity.

Now the State, which he had fought with the same fury as, later, was to mark his exaltation of it, was reaching out inexorably to subdue him, as it for generations had subdued all rebels. The time for compulsory military service was coming, and the eyes of the police were upon him. For as in all conscript countries, where the military age is twenty, the authorities began their watch a year or more before. Mussolini fled to Switzerland. Officially, on April 10, 1904, in his home judicial district, he was accordingly listed as *renitente di leva*—one who deserts before being called to the colours.

Switzerland was the second choice, the choice of economic necessity. He desperately wanted America, that still unrestricted land of opportunity where all his countrymen had relatives, where success was easy, opportunity more equal, gold and success to be had, where class barriers were more easily broken, where liberty and Italian dreams came true. Frequently during the exile years he thought of America with longing.

" Yes," he once said to the present writer, " I came very close to that decision on several occasions. Once it was in fact a 50-per-cent. chance. I was a political exile then, you know, and for us there were but two lands of freedom. Times were hard in Switzerland ; I thought I would try my fortune in America, as so many Italians did at that time.

" I knew I could get work in my line. I was a mason. Well, I tossed a coin." He was silent, meditating ; he seemed to follow that coin spinning in the air, falling, sending him to America, where he would have been swallowed, obliterated in the regiments of labour-union masons in New York.

" Youth, youth," he sighed, " a dream. A dream. I wonder what would have become of me in America. Had I gone over as an emigrant in 1904 what would I be now ? "

" Why did you go to Switzerland ? " I asked.

" Because my views conflicted with that of the Italian government. I was the victim of a love of freedom and individualism."

He hated the " cramped, confining atmosphere " of Italy ; he yielded to " his restless wanderlust " ; he decided " to seek his fortune in Switzerland, as it was the easiest country to be reached." So say the biographers ; and he himself declares in writing that " I did not want to go back to my family. There was a narrow world for me . . . one could neither move nor think without feeling at the end of a short rope. I became conscious of myself, sensitive to my future. I felt the urge to escape. . . . Courage was my asset. I would be an exile. I crossed the frontier. . . . It was the milestone which marked my maturity."

He telegraphed home and got the equivalent of nine dollars. At the frontier station he read in a Milan newspaper that his father, accused with others of smashing ballot-boxes to prevent the Catholics from winning the local elections from the Socialists, had been arrested. " This piece of news placed me in a dilemma. Was I to return or go on ? " He did not hesitate long. He had made his decision to escape the army and he took the first train, arriving at Yverdon, Switzerland, with just forty-two cents in his pockets, and the address of some one who might give him a job.

But it was neither fear nor cowardice, as his political enemies say, that drove Mussolini to Switzerland ; it was rather a deep belief in pacifism and individual defiance of the power of the State which he detested. It is only the fact that later he was to outpatrioteer all patriots in militaristic passion which makes the escape noteworthy. At that time thousands of Italians, pacifists who believed in sabotaging militarism, from principle and idealism, were refusing to train as soldiers and accepting the refuge which America and Switzerland offered them.

In those terrible and glorious years of his Swiss exile, those honest years of his life, he often boasted of his desertion. That act had been his passport into the hearts and homes of all the exiles and rebels of all the world, who were grouped in Geneva and Basle and Lausanne, reading Karl Marx, and plotting revolution and liberty for Russia and Finland and for Czechoslovakia, for suppressed nations and persecuted races. Men starved and struggled in those days, but kept alight the red beacon of revolutionary hope.

Young Benito went to Lausanne. Eye-witness accounts of his arrival present a human picture of almost irreconcilable contrast. We have already seen the violent child bending to the blows of his father's leather belt and attacking a weaker youth with a knife ; we have more than one occasion had a view of that future leader of men, that burning orator who could scatter his fire into weaker vessels, that proud, domineering boyish ego. How different he looks when hunger and poverty hold him a prisoner.

It was evening. At the Italian Socialist club of Lausanne which housed also the co-operative stores and the communal restaurant, many men, all of them rebels, some republicans, a few anarchists, a majority revolutionary Socialists and most of them refugees from the army and from the law, sat at their coffee and gesticulated about the future.

A colleague entered. "I want to introduce a compatriot who has left Italy to escape military service." He indicated a new face, a face sad and humble and somewhat starved.

Serrati, that same Serrati who was later to befriend more passionately and to forgive and aid more frequently the young radical Mussolini, and who was afterwards to feel more fully the power of the Duce's retaliation to the comrades of his youth, Serratti as secretary of the club arose, went to the stranger, gave him his hand, made him welcome.

Mussolini was modestly but somewhat flamboyantly dressed ; with his plain, commonplace iron-grey suit he wore an artist's hat of wide brim and an artist's large black tie, knotted at his throat, the wide silk ends flowing romantically over his bosom.

" My name is Benito Mussolini," he said in a low voice. " I am a school teacher, Born in Predappio. My father you may know, a pure Socialist, councillor of the Socialist minority of our commune." He was ingratiating.

" You may feel yourself at home here," replied Serrati. " Speak without shame and fear nothing. You are among your friends. Tell me frankly, first of all, have you eaten to-day, do you want food ? "

Every one had turned towards the new young man. He was agitated, embarrassed, he murmured something about hunger.

" *Allons !* Do not blush. We are among comrades," said Serrati, smiling encouragingly, and taking Mussolini by the arm and calling on Francesco Capassi, director of the co-operative restaurant, conducted the former to the dining-room on the second floor and ordered a plate of spaghetti. . . .

" When you've eaten, descend," said Serrati, " and we will talk. We will find a roof for you. We will find something for you."

To Capassi, Serrati gave the order that the meal should be paid for out of the Socialist Party funds. While the hungry man, the future Duce who had exactly one cent in his pocket that night, gorged himself on spaghetti and bread, the good comrades listened to the one who had found the wanderer at the Place Pépinette, where he had come after sleeping under a bridge of Lausanne. It was an unwritten law of the club that every one who flew to Switzerland to escape military service must be aided, because there was perhaps no better proof of class solidarity.

Mussolini descended with a full stomach. He was welcomed to a table, offered coffee, a glass of wine ; he asked advice about work and something to live on until he found it. Serrati, a sweet and sentimental soul, adopted him as a friend. He called on one Marzetto to give him a bed or a blanket on the floor, and that night when Karl Marx had been exhausted for the hundredth time, the leading old radical and the beginner of nineteen went out arm in arm to find their roofs.

What a different man he became when the dictates of his belly were satisfied ! Within a week from his hesitating

entrance into the club young Mussolini was arguing theories
with other members, almost as loud, as cocksure, as vehement as the rest, and in another week he was intimidating
them with his non-conformist attitude. He had claimed
he was a Socialist, but now, they said, he had proven
either that he knew very little about Socialism or that, if
he did, he was already too individualist to be a good party
member, to belong to either the left or the right wing, both
of which, whilst contending for the approval of the masses,
agreed, however, on the main Marxian tenets.

So long as Mussolini argued Karl Marx they could understand him. But the newcomer had new views almost every
week. If the book he happened to be reading was by
Nietzsche, he was a Nietzschean that week, full of phrases
about the will to power, the revaluation of all values, and
the whipping of women ; if, on the other hand, he became
interested in Sorel, why, it was all syndicalism that week
and the devil take more timid social philosophy ! Sometimes it was Schopenhauer, when he would enjoy a week of
misogyny, and again it would be Stirner, when the Ego and
its Own set him on fire with faith in himself.

He had a sick man's, a weakling's, belief in strength.
(He had not yet come upon Machiavelli, who, four or five
years later, was to make such an impression on him as to
rule his thoughts for ever after.) For him there never arose
the question which has troubled philosophers from Athens
to Harvard, the question of Free Will. "I have willed
this," "It is my will," are his favourite expressions. In
his childhood he had not been allowed any freedom, yet he
speaks of carrying out his " will " on certain occasions,
while in Switzerland his daily reference to his own strength,
his courage, his power, his " clear will " so impressed his
colleagues that, not seeking the psychological reasons which
force a sick, unhappy, suppressed individual to resort
almost daily to such terms, they accepted him at his own
estimation, as his party and the nation later were to accept
him, and as propaganda later was to exhibit him to all the
weak-willed people of a mediocre world.

New revolutionary vistas opened to Mussolini with every

book he found in Switzerland. After he had studied
Karl Marx's Communist Manifesto he became interested in
Babeuf, whose ideas Marx had studied, and in Blanqui,
the political heir of Babeuf, absorbing but not digesting
all these violent views, one after another. He accepted
Babeuf's statement that the French Revolution " is only a
forerunner of another, a greater, a more majestic revolution
which will be the last " and " it is our duty to set up a
dictatorship of the poor." Babeuf " conceived of revolution as an insurrection on the part of well-organized and
armed plotters," [1] and Mussolini, at Socialist gatherings,
where all spoke of peaceful changes, of philosophic progress,
of the education of the masses in preparation for taking
over power, advocated activity, not talk. He was young
and he was headstrong. Blanquism, " a synonym for
revolutionary adventure," was seized upon by Mussolini
and made his guide ; Blanqui's motto, *Chi ha del ferro ha
del pane*, became his motto.

Mussolini was developing into a fine soap-box orator.
He continued to make speeches, mocking the King of Italy,
defying the ruling powers everywhere, deriding parliaments,
and at times defying God. Because work was scarce,
he had to go from canton to canton, and there was no job
too humble for him. There were times when extreme
hunger drove him into the streets to accost some well-
dressed stranger, to beg for bread and money, and there
were grand days when he had enough to fill his stomach,
and his mind at one of the liberal universities. He worked
chiefly as a mason's assistant, but he was also a porter
once, and a butcher boy, delivering packages to the neighbouring bourgeoisie and envying their litres of wine and
their kilos of fresh meat.

He hated the rich. A murderous hatred. One hungry
day he crouched outside the iron railing of the Beau Rivage
Hotel—which later was to be the headquarters of dictators
and prime ministers of a League of Nations conference—
and listened to the orchestra. " The music comforts my
brain and my stomach. But the intervals are terrible,

[1] Isaac Don Levine, *Stalin*.

the cramp stabbing into my entrails like red-hot pins. . . .
The rustle of silks may be heard, and the murmur of languages which I do not understand. An elderly couple
pass me by. They look English. I would like to ask them
to give me money for a bed that night, but the words die
on my lips. The lady glitters with gold and precious
stones. I have not a cent, I have no bed, I have had no
bread. I make off, cursing. Ah, that blessed idea of
anarchy of thought and action. Is it not the right of the
man lying on the ground to murder him who crushes him ? "

He went again to his dirty resting-place under the
Grand Pont, that main bridge which breaks the cold wind
and shelters other beggars, where he met a man he recognized as an Italian. He hailed him in the native tongue,
asking for alms. " He laughs at me. I curse him. He
puts his hand in his pocket and gives me ten centimes. I
thank him. I hasten to the shop of a baker and buy a
piece of bread. . . . For twenty-six hours I had not eaten."

Occasionally the police clean out the beggars. One
morning he opened his eyes to find the helmeted face of a
policeman with a cynical stare. He is not beaten on the
shins nor clubbed on the head, his sure fate in the same
circumstances had the coin fallen otherwise and had the
bridge been Brooklyn. In Europe even policemen are men.
Instead there is a conversation.

The policeman says, " What are you doing here ? "

Mussolini replies, " I was just thinking of getting up."

" Then get up quickly, for I have been waiting for you."

" Very kind of you. Please tell my valet to bring me
my clothes and toilet requisites."

" Get up quickly or I'll help you up."

" Precisely what I want. Give me your hand."

The policeman gave the beggar his hand : " You are an
Italian ? "

" Yes. Of the extradition department " (army refugee).

" Follow me."

In this way Mussolini was taken to jail for the first time
in his life, and locked up for vagabondage.

Everything he did got him into difficulty with the

police. It could not be otherwise. With that anomalous upbringing, of whipping and pampering and the teaching of violent individualism, he had become a complete rebel. He accepted nothing. The gendarmes were for ever on the trail ; he was always denouncing the law and the petty agents who served as club-bearing symbols—he who could never conform and who was afterwards to organize next to the Russian Cheka and Hitler's Gestapo, the most all-invading police force of modern times, to destroy all non-conformity in the nation.

The Protestant evangelist, Alfredo Tagliatela, came to Lausanne preaching the goodness of God. But Christianity, too, with its vast organization of popes and tikhons and bishops and ceremonials and parades, Mussolini placed with all things bourgeois, like the military, the gendarmerie, the regimented passive minds of the masses who were not brave enough to accept his style of paradoxical individual Socialism. The evangelist challenged one and all to refute him.

Mussolini, who with a few working-men friends was sitting in the back of the hall, accepted the challenge. But not for debate. He arose, and his friends with him. Five or six in number, they rushed up the aisle, stormed the platform, and grappled with the speaker.

" God does not exist," shouted Mussolini. " Religion ! In science it is an absurdity ; in practice it is an immor-tality ; among men it is a malady."

The good Christian crowd now raised angry fists. While some howled down the blasphemers, others ran to the aid of the evangelist. Tagliatela was rescued. Turning to Mussolini, he said :

" You are the sort of atheistic fanatic who at the age of forty will turn reactionary and be a lickspittle of the Vatican."

Mussolini shouted back : " Bourgeois ! Renegade ! Slave ! "

A few days later, making an atheistic oration, Mussolini drew his watch from his pocket, placed it on the table, and defied God to strike him dead within five minutes.

No thunderbolt came.

This was the proof, the orator told his followers, that there was no God.

When this meeting ended, another Italian radical, Carlo Tresca by name, protested against this exhibition. He thought it unfair. Mussolini began an argument which lasted all night, and in the morning, when the two parted, one to return to demagogy, the other to try his fortune in the United States, the former said :

" Well, Comrade Tresca, I hope America will make you over into a real revolutionary."

" I hope," replied Tresca, " that you will quit posing and learn how to fight, Comrade Mussolini."

Commenting recently on this episode, Tresca said he had left Italy because he had been sentenced to eighteen months in jail or ten years in exile for an article he had published in his paper, *Il Germe* (The Seed). He found Mussolini " weak-tempered and vain, a man who would push himself forward, so that people applaud. He says he is a very radical man, an extreme Socialist, that I am not radical enough.

" Can you imagine ? I am an anarchist now and what is Mussolini, who was so radical ? A traitor. He remembers that incident ; if I go anywhere near Italy now I don't live long."

Within a few months after the Tagliatela encounter Mussolini published his first work. It is a pamphlet entitled *Dieu n'existe pas*, and its preface states :

" Besought by certain comrades, I publish to-day the development of my thesis, ' God does not exist,' and refute the principle arguments of the evangelist Tagliatela.

" The struggle against religious absurdity is more than ever a necessity to-day. Religion has revealed its soul in the full glare of the sun. To be still deluded would be cowardice. No matter what the adaptations of the Church to the new and inexorable necessities of the times may be— alas, it is to weep !—they are attempts, generally vain, to resuscitate the titles of the ' divine bank ' which already is on the road to failure.

" Confronted with the spread of free thought, Pope

Sarto,[1] fearful of the destinies of his domination, cried out :

" ' Faithful, the Antichrist is born ! '

" The Antichrist is human reason which rebels against dogma and a beaten god."

Switzerland is a Christian country but it grants religious liberty. Mussolini was safe in two heresies. But in June 1903, Mussolini organized a strike of some stoneworkers, and the authorities of the canton of Berne expelled him with promptness and smug satisfaction.

" My stay in Switzerland was a welter of difficulties. . . . I did whatever came to hand. . . . I knew hunger, stark hunger, in those days. . . . I took part in political gatherings. I made speeches. Some intemperance in my words made me undesirable to the Swiss authorities. They expelled me from two cantons. . . ."

They did more than that. They expelled him, as is the custom of the country, from canton after canton for violation of " State rights," but finally they expelled him from the whole of Switzerland.

When that order came, the Socialist Party of the confederated republic thought it time to protest against the persecution of one of its least important but loudest and most active personalities. In the Grand Council of Geneva,[2] the Socialist deputy Wyss denounced the government.

He demanded to know, first of all, why the government's order of expulsion indicated Chiasso as being obligatory as the frontier station. Chiasso was an Italian town, and Mussolini would find himself in the hands of the Italian police. Had the authorities forgotten that Switzerland was an asylum for deserters as well as for political rebels ? Why did the government act with cruelty, even if its charge was just ? Why not send the victim to France or Austria ?

But that was all secondary. Why were the bloodhounds of the government driving from canton to canton and finally out of the country a man who had committed no crime

[1] In those days Mussolini's sense of denunciation found satisfaction in calling kings and popes by their born names ; he here refers to Pius X.

[2] Parliamentary reports, session of May 11, 1904.

except that of being a Socialist ? True, he was more radical than most, he had spoken a little too freely, perhaps he had at certain moments, carried away by his own oratory, used some violent words, but no laws had been broken and the serenity of Swiss existence was untouched. Yet because he was a Socialist . . .

When Mr. Wyss had emptied himself of all invective, the Minister of State, M. Odier, responded to the interpellation :

" Mussolini had presented himself on March 9 at the office where the *permis de sejour* is granted and demanded an authorization.

" He supplemented his request with a French matriculation receipt which indicated that he had previously used a passport. The officials replied that the matriculation was not enough, and Mussolini was requested to present his passport, which he did and which at first sight seemed to be in order.

" It bore the date December 31, 1905 ; but traces were visible of a modification, and it related to the changing of a 3 into a 5."

Minister of State Odier further declared that while a provisional *permis de sejour* had been granted Mussolini, a request for information had been made to the Italian consul at Bellinzona, who confirmed the fact that the passport had been forged. On April 9, therefore, when Mussolini presented himself to receive the permanent card, he was arrested. Interrogated, Mussolini replied :

" I know that the date 1903 has been falsified into 1905, but I am not the author of this falsification. I admit that knowingly I have made use of a falsified passport."

In conclusion M. Odier said :

" Mussolini was a school-teacher in Italy ; here he has occupied himself with social-revolutionary propaganda. He was arrested in Lausanne for vagabondage : in Berne for a political crime. He was detained and expelled from the canton of Berne on June 19. He has been published by the federal authorities as an anarchist. I believe, however, that he would protest against this qualification as an anarchist and content himself with that of social-revolutionary. It is in effect in that quality that he has been presented to us. But can any one make a complaint against the State for having asked Mussolini to recross the frontier, when on the one hand, to remain among us he seeks to serve himself of dishonest means in falsifying an *acte de légitimation* which has been asked of him, and when on the other hand he has used words and developed his activity in a milieu essentially revolutionary and seeks with all his means to destroy the institutions of our Republic ? "

M. Odier said he understood quite well the purpose of the altered passport. Born in 1883, Mussolini would have had in his twentieth year to present himself for military service, and this he had not done, therefore he could never have had a passport legitimately prolonged after 1902— " except by a false act, which has now been discovered, to his dishonour."

In Germany, France, and Austria Mussolini saw the inside of prisons ; in Italy and Switzerland many times. " These bars and railings, I can't stand them. They torture me. I can't stand the feeling of being suffocated. Ah, yes, you others, you may laugh but you have never known what it is to have been in prison—eleven times in prison, my friends ! It is a feeling you can never get rid of."

In the police station of Zürich there existed for many years a dossier with the fingerprints of the present Duce neatly besmirching a white card. At Lausanne, and in the copies at Geneva and Zürich, the records of various imprisonments.

On Mussolini's arrival at the League of Nations in 1922, the Swiss president most considerately ordered his past to be removed from the public gaze. This was duly carried out.

Mussolini has only this to say : " To remain in Switzerland became impossible. There was the yearning for home which blossoms in the hearts of all Italians. Furthermore, the compulsory service in the army was calling me. I came back . . . I joined the regiment. . . ."

But not so fast as all that.

M. Wyss and the comrades were not without power. They could not maintain their request for Mussolini's freedom in the face of the charges against him, but they did insist that the Swiss law regarding Italian deserters applied to Comrade Benito and that the government must not deport the undesirable to his own country. Thus the frontier to Austria was opened.

Mussolini went to Ticino. At the frontier he was cheered as a Socialist hero and a martyr.

4

CHAPTER IV

COMRADE ANGELICA AND COMRADE BENITO

IN Switzerland Mussolini met a woman who more than
any other, except his mother, shaped his life. If at
one time the hero could quote Abraham Lincoln, as
he did, to the effect that all he was he owed to his mother,
so, at another moment, he could have said " and all I hope
to be I owe to Comrade Angelica."

She was not the fair-haired, light-eyed goddess, the
romantic inspiration of youth, which writers for the popular
magazines profess to have found in one or another of Mussolini's mistresses of a later period, and to whom in turn they
have given the title of " Joan of Arc of Fascism," or the
more commonplace one of " the woman who made Mussolini." Angelica Balabanoff was and remains to-day a true
Marxian Socialist, who naturally enough looks upon her
collaboration with the Fascist Duce as a regrettable waste
of time.

And yet it was she who picked him out of a dark corner
and made a man of him. For just ten years she ruled his
life. There is no mention of her in the Duce's autobiography.

Described by all as the " soul " and " the moving force "
of the Russian revolutionary movement in Switzerland,
which was in reality the mind and spirit of the Russian
revolution of 1917, this woman, whose life is a book of
amazement, occupied the unique position of comrade,
associate, fellow-worker, with the two most contradictory
dictators of this modern world, Lenin and Mussolini.

With Lenin and with Trotsky, and with other Red
leaders, Dr. Balabanoff sat as an equal, sometimes even
occupying a higher elected position, at conferences, Inter-
nationales, public meetings. She was part of the con-

spiracy to win freedom in Russia. With the Black leader the situation was different. It was she who took him in hand and began his education as a Red, teaching him the first principles of Karl Marx, whose follower she had always been.

The contrast between Balabanoff and Mussolini was extreme. He was the plainest of proletarians, she the daughter of a rich bourgeois merchant, brought up in a house of twenty rooms, surrounded by servants and luxury. But she, too, was born with the soul of a rebel, and in that they were alike. As a child Angelica fought her mother for maltreating the servants ; sometimes she would take her belongings and run down the street to give them to beggars who had been denied food or money at her home. When she grew up she gave away all she inherited, and to this day whatever she has above her needs, which are plain food and plain clothes, she gives away. A hater of property. A lover of humanity.

Lenin, Trotsky, Liebknecht, Rosa Luxemburg, idealists, radicals, exiles, revolutionaries from all of Europe, worked with Comrade Balabanoff and loved her. Mussolini could hardly believe his good fortune when she offered to help him. She was already famous as an international leader, a brilliant mind, a marvellous orator, a great force in all movements for freedom and liberation which at that time centred in Switzerland, and he was the lowest of nobodies.

There was terror in his eyes when Balabanoff first saw him that night in the small meeting-room of the Italians of Lausanne, more than thirty years ago. There were quite a few there, working-men and working-women, all very poor, all eager for the riches of a Socialist paradise, all at least washed and clean. But in the corner sat a man in filth. His face was unwashed, his clothes, which had been slept in, bore the traces of the sand and dirt of the little projections of land under the Grand Pont. He had flashing black eyes, a bulging jaw as well as bulging eyes, a bellicose bearing with a timid, cringing demeanour, nervous and restless. It was the first time he had come to hear the famous Russian speaker.

" Who is that strange creature ? " Dr. Balabanoff
asked a mason after she has finished speaking.[1]

" The most miserable being I ever met," the mason
replied. " He is an Italian, like us, and at home was supposed to be a school-teacher, but he was always getting
into a scrape, and he was said to drink too much. Then
when the time came to do his military service he fled to
Switzerland, and now he is a tramp. But he says he is a
Socialist, and I think he means well."

" A tramp ? Is he so poor ? "

" He sleeps under the bridge. Except when I take him
in and give him my bed when I am out at work. I feed
him when I can."

Another club member, also a mason, came up to
Balabanoff. " I have asked my wife to make him a shirt
and a pair of pants out of some old cloth," he said ; " next
time perhaps he will be better dressed."

Others came up and shook the speaker's hands, as was
the custom, they drifted out. Dr. Balabanoff went to the
unhappy vagabond and took his hand.

" I hear you have no job," she said kindly. " Can I
help you in any way ? " She had given away her fortune ;
she was always giving away every cent she had.

" No, nobody can help me," Mussolini replied in a
dramatic, almost tragic tone and without lifting his eyes,
" I am condemned to remain a wretched vagabond all my
life."

" Do not despair. Look at these men here. They are
all proletarians like you, but when they became Socialists
they found they had a great deal to live for, a great ideal."

" But *I* can't. My father was a drunkard, and besides,
I suffer from a congenital illness for which I have to thank
him. I can't work and I can't be militant. I will have
to die as miserably as I am living."

" No, no," replied the woman, " I will see that something
is done for you."

The man never looked up, never changed his blank

[1] The episode as here related was written by Dr. Balabanoff for this
book.

expression, but fidgeted endlessly, twisting his dirty black cap in his hands. Later he said, timidly :

" I have just had an opportunity to earn fifty francs, but I lost it, of course. I was not able to do the work. A Socialist editor offered me fifty francs if I would translate Kautsky's pamphlet, *The Coming Revolution.* But how could I ? I do not know German, and I do not know the Marxian terminology."

Dr. Balabanoff offered to help.

" You help me ? " he exclaimed, surprised, but still not looking up.

" Why not ? I am a Socialist and I find it quite natural. When I was young I had opportunities and privileges, while you lived in misery and could not study. It is not your fault."

This was the episode, a stepping-stone which became a turning-point. Dr. Balabanoff took the unkempt vagabond in hand and made a man, a radical, a revolutionary, out of him. She who had associated with Lenin and Trotsky as an equal leader, was intellectually head and shoulders above the youth of twenty with his weeping self-pity and his lackadaisical despair, his gauche manners, his embarrassed attitude, his masochistic satisfaction in proclaiming himself a lost soul.

After Mussolini's expulsion from Switzerland he wrote to Comrade Angelica frequently from Trento, telling of his activities and success as a journalist. He was meeting notable *irredenta* patriots who were to influence his actions in 1914, and a young woman named Irene Desler, who was to play a dramatic episode in his life. He was also aiming to write a history of philosophy.

One day in 1905 the King of Italy issued a birthday amnesty. Political refugees, provided they had committed no civil crime at home, were free to return to the fatherland and so were deserters who had fled to escape army service ; the latter must, however, come back to the colours.

Mussolini came back.

He went to Austria again after he had completed his military duty. Again he got into trouble with his political expressions which offended the authorities, and again he returned to Italy. He was now noted as both journalist and orator. In 1912, after the Reggio Emilia congress, a committee of directors of the Socialist Party, which included Comrades Balabanoff, Serrati, Vella, and Mussolini, was appointed to name a new editor for the party's organ, the *Avanti*. Most of Italy's leading journalists lived in Rome ; they sought a man from the industrial north. One of the central committee members mentioned Mussolini, and Balabanoff seconded the motion. With the exception of Vella the committee of directors voted for him. Mussolini at first objected, saying he lacked the ability, the information on politics, the knowledge of Marxism, the necessary background and culture of an editor, and above all, he did not want to assume so great a responsibility.

Comrade Balabanoff took Comrade Mussolini to lunch. There were hours of talk, argument, persuasion. The woman insisted it was the opportunity of a lifetime, and that the man must take it now or lose his chance for ever. The man wavered. He could not accept such a responsibility. Comrade Balabanoff insisted. She said she would help.

In the afternoon Mussolini conferred with other members of the committee. They, too, urged his acceptance.

" I agree, but on one condition," Mussolini said that evening. " That Comrade Balabanoff must work with me on the newspaper as my assistant editor."

It was then almost ten years from the day Dr. Balabanoff had picked the vagabond out of his dark corner and started him on the road to dictatorship. She, of course, had meant to do nothing of the kind. If there was any dictatorship idea in her mind, it was that of a class, the mass, the proletariat, the common people, the workers, the suppressed, the suffering, the miserable have-nots of this world. For ten years she taught Mussolini the doctrines of Karl Marx, hoping he would some day join with many others, with her colleagues in another part of Switzerland, Lenin and Trotsky, in a world-wide economic and political war of the classes.

They collaborated for about a year and a half, during the greater part of which they had desks side by side and worked their editorials together. Not a single decision of importance was taken by him without consulting his guiding star ; to every objection she made he quickly acquiesced, recognizing her intellectual and moral superiority.

" Rarely in my life," she records, " have I seen a human being dependent so on others as Mussolini was. His characteristics at that time were a lack of independent courage and an incredible physical fear. When leaving the headquarters of *Avanti* at night, or rather in the early morning, he would always ask me to accompany him. After my own work was finished, I had to wait for him.

" When he learned that we lived in the same street, he asked me to take him to his very door. I was surprised. I asked him what was the matter.

" ' It bores me to go home alone,' he replied. ' One never knows . . .'

" ' What are you afraid of ? '

" ' What am I afraid of ? Myself. A dog. A tree. My own shadow."

CHAPTER V

A Miracle is Explained

THERE were riots in the vineyards of France, and Mme Caillaux shot M. Calmette, the editor of *Figaro*. In Ireland seven hundred years of strife were again accentuated in a civil war; patriots fell in the streets of Dublin and British soldiery prepared for fire and blood. The Balkans were enjoying temporary peace, armed peace, reeking with plans of revolt and assassination. And in Italy there occurred a revolutionary outbreak of national importance. All these facts the German general staff noted with utmost satisfaction. The omens were good. The Central Powers, whose policy was Discipline, Order, Hierarchy, goose-stepped to world empire.

The Settimána Rossa, or Red Week, of 1914, was Italy's prelude to battle. A decade of strife between workers and employers was to have its test in a general strike which began that 7th of June. All the elements which were anti-government or anti-ruling-class, from the Liberals and Democrats to the Socialists and Radical-Socialists, and even the anarchists, were joined against the forces of law and order—and oppression.

This general strike, like the World War, was held to be inevitable, and a simple incident which paralleled the assassination of the Austrian archduke at Serajevo ignited the spirit of Italy. A conscript soldier had fired at his colonel. The case became national, a symbol. When the government sought the easy way out by declaring the would-be assassin insane, condemned to prison for life, the masses screamed for his freedom, and Mussolini, in the *Avanti*, joined. At first it was decided that there should be one day of national protest in honour of Masetti; later, a general strike was declared. Mussolini not only participated, but suggested revolution. One of his collaborators and admirers, Rossato, calls him " the Lenin of the Red Week, the originator of the idea of a Romagnole Republic." Mussolini hoped to turn the general strike into a national uprising. He made speeches, wrote articles, and one day, June 10, led his followers into the Cathedral Square of Milan as the first move to occupy the town and eventually seize power in all of Italy.

There are two versions of what followed. One, the Fascist, has Mussolini first to arrive and last to go ; he stood his ground, " heedless of cavalry charges," as his passionate biographer, Mme Sarfatti, more recently has it, " erect, motionless, his arms folded, hurling forth his invectives with eyes ablaze." On the other hand, all contemporary reports state merely that " when the mounted police arrived the demonstration was broken up," while still other testimony, from an eye-witness participant, relates that " we acted like human beings, we fled."

It is of little importance. The Settimána Rossa was a fiasco. What is important is that it confirmed Mussolini as a revolutionary Socialist, taught him that without violent leadership and organized violence there would be no success, and inspired him with the idea of armed leadership.

" The attempt at revolution—the Red Week—was not revolution as much as it was chaos. No leaders ! The middle class and the bourgeoisie gave us another picture of their insipid spirit." But the idea itself he defended, likening the event to the French Commune, " a magnificent insurrection of the Paris populace presenting all the characteristics of a revolutionary movement. . . but when the Commune was crushed by the bayonets of Thiers, a man, an immortal master for us all, arose to defend it. Karl Marx justified all the measures taken by the Commune and also many measures initiated by persons unknown. He justified the incendiarism and also the shooting of hostages ; he celebrated the flame and the blood and the deaths ; he raised on high the cry, ' Long Live the Commune ! ' in the face of that European bourgeoisie which with a ferocity made hundredfold by fear, prepared itself for its great revenge." Prophetic words !

The World War came almost immediately after this attempt at Italian revolution. The Socialist Party on July 29, 1914, issued its proclamation :

" It is to the interest of the proletariat of all nations to impede, circumscribe, and limit as much as possible the armed conflict, useful only for the triumph of militarism and parasitical business affairs of the bourgeoisie.

" You, the proletariat of Italy, who, in the painful period of crisis and unemployment of the recent general strike have given proof of your class consciousness, or your spirit of sacrifice, must now be ready and not let Italy go down into the abyss of this terrible adventure."

The phrasing of the proclamation was Mussolini's ; his name was signed with that of other leaders. One day earlier, he had written in *Avanti*, " The proletariat must no longer temporize, it must express immediately its desire for peace. If the government does not heed unanimous public opinion but enters into the new adventure, the ' truce of arms ' declared by us at the close of the Red Week will be ended." And another day : " In the case of a European conflagration Italy does not want to precipitate itself into the ultimate ruin, but has one attitude to take —neutrality."

Thus July 1914 passed into history and August found all the pledged nations of both armed camps, with the exception of Italy, at war.

The Nationalist Party, under Federzoni, who later sat symbolically at Mussolini's right hand in the first Fascist triumvirate, demanded that the government join Germany and Austria. The patriotic Socialists under the expelled leader, Bissolati, tried to drag the party towards the Allies. Mussolini and Bissolati met in furious debates which always ended in the triumph of the former.

Then came the mysterious September when Mussolini made the decision of his life and, as first payment on it, surrendered his membership of the party. In the new freedom which began for him he was better prepared, he wrote later, " to fight my battles than when I was bound by the dogmas of any political organization. But I understood that I could not use with efficient strength my convictions if I was without that modern weapon, capable of all possibilities, ready to arm and to help, good for offence and defence—the newspaper.

" I needed a daily paper, I hungered for one. I gathered together a few of my political friends who had followed me in the last hard struggle, and we held a war council. When money alone is concerned, I am anything but a wizard. When it is a question of means or of capital to start a project, or how to finance a newspaper, I grasp only the abstract side, the political value, the spiritual essence of the thing. To me money is detestable ; what it may do is sometimes beautiful and sometimes noble."

While Mussolini sat in the office of the *Popolo*, writing his harangues in favour of the noble Allied cause, the whispers of the cafés and the rumours throughout the land were investigated by the party he had left.

It was soon learned that many elements were buying public opinion in Italy. The Germans were represented by Prince von Bülow, ambassador to Rome, from whose immune offices agents operated in much the same manner as they did in neutral America at the same time. In New York, it will be remembered, the Germans succeeded in buying up only one important newspaper, the *Evening Mail*, whose unfortunate Dr. Rumeley went to prison when the United States some time later decided to join the war, but on the side opposed to Rumeley's masters.

In America, in Italy, in Spain, in Switzerland, Holland, and Scandinavian countries the subsidizing and purchase of public opinion was largely a Franco-British enterprise. In fact, a large part of the world was divided into so-called spheres of influence. Despite *The Secrets of Crewe House* and the French *Behind the Scenes in War-time Journalism*, the world still knows little of an effort which compares relatively with the slaughter at the front. The poisoning of the world mind is just as necessary for a successful war as the murder of millions of deluded subjects.

Secret as these efforts were, a few facts became known and were published in Italy in 1914 and 1915. The Socialist press began to answer the ominous question of the cafés and the party congresses—*Chi paga ?* Without fear of libel suits or contradiction, the secret of Mussolini's change from the advocate of proletarian revolution against the French government to an ally of the French army, was soon known throughout Italy.

The " miracle " of the days between September 21 and 25, 1914, was manipulated by the *Resto del Carlino*, which from the first days of the war was publicly charged with having been subsidized by the French government along with dozens of smaller publishers.

The people were prepared for the " conversion " of Mussolini with the publication of two articles by Libero Tancredi (Massimo Rocca), the first headed *Un Uomo di Ferro* (A Man of Iron), the other *Un Uomo di Paglia* (A Man of Straw). There was no secrecy in the *Resto del Carlino* office about its being an agency for Italian intervention on the side of France.

Among that nation's foremost agents in this patriotic business was a member of the Chamber of Deputies, Marcel Cachin, one of that considerable group of Socialist deputies who had been pacifist until the first shot was heard on the Alsace-Lorraine frontier, and who from that moment became enthusiasts for war, calling upon the enemies of bloody conflict to support it under the banner of The Sacred Union (*l'Union Sacrée*). This is the same Marcel Cachin who was later to edit *l'Humanité*, to become the leader and the inspiration and the occasional martyr of the extensive French postbellum Communism. To Naldi, editor and publisher of the *Resto del Carlino*, Cachin confessed his desire to win many political leaders and journalists over to the French side. He was especially anxious to gain the support of men like himself, Socialists who had seen the light of nationalist patriotism. Mussolini filled all his requirements.

In Bologna, one of those mysterious miraculous days, Mussolini confessed to Naldi his aforementioned " mortal desire " to edit his own newspaper. A newspaper, he said, was a fulcrum on which to rest a lever to move the world. He must have his own press. On its quick wheels one rode to power. One had to force ideas upon the masses ; they were so stupid, such cowards, and the Nationalists, the bourgeoisie as well as the Socialists, all of them were doing one thing or another, and everything wrong, because one and all they were afraid to listen to a bright new intelligence. Yes, the Socialists, too, his own people, they restrained him, they bossed him, possessed him ; they overpowered him in the central committee, issuing orders which he had to carry out in his newspaper office, which was their office, and every time he swerved, every time he changed a comma, there would be an uproar ; his associate editors would shout he was betraying the Socialist cause, they would expose him, drive him out of the party. He was a man born to live and act independently ; he hated restraint of any kind ; he needed a newspaper to show the world what he could do.

Naldi did not quite understand. He himself had no such ambitions. He was the typical continental European newspaper owner. He was, however, ethically on a par with the greatest of all French newspapers, *Le Temps*, and twenty other French newspapers, all of which had received several millions of gold francs from the Tsar for the purpose of propaganda and news suppression from the time of revolution, 1905, to the Russian collapse of 1917.[1] Now it was France who was paying money to editors. Naldi knew where the French funds were and the man to be " seen " ; when Mussolini was through talking, Naldi made him a promise. But in return he demanded of Mussolini an earnest of good faith.

Returning to Milan, the editor startled Italy with a leading article, sensational for the official Socialist paper, the first appeal against neutrality.

Quite sure of his future, no longer caring whether or not the party would accuse him of betrayal, nor fearing

[1] Documents from the Russian War Archives published in France as *L'Abominable Venalite de la Presse*.

the criticism of fellow-editors, Mussolini did not hesitate to gain his end by using as a means the very official organ of the pacifist party, and in it proclaiming a policy which the paper, the fellow-editors, and the party stood pledged to denounce with all their strength. The office became an uproar. There were angry scenes. Day and night fists were shaken and loud voices penetrated into the streets to the amazement of strangers. What was "relative neutrality"? Nothing but a step to "no neutrality, to war." "Who authorized the editorial?" "How dare you publish it without consultation?" But Mussolini had made his bid to the French representatives, sitting lightly on their money-bags, in the hotels of Geneva. He had shown them he was willing to be approached. He had taken the first step.

Then news came from Naldi that the financial negotiations were satisfactory.

Mussolini rushed from the *Avanti*, travelled the short distance to Switzerland secretly, came back quickly, and just fifteen days later, "starting with empty hands," as his admirers so quaintly put it, he produced the first number of the *Popolo d'Italia*, a French newspaper organ, a long but strong finger of the Quai d'Orsay. Polemic after polemic against the Socialist Party, against last month's friends on the *Avanti*, against the atrocities committed by the Central Empires, filled the new journal.

A complete *volte face*. But Mussolini's feet were now on wheels, and the wheels were turning out newspapers, and every edition was a challenge for power. It filled his own ears, leaving no room for the cries of protest. He did not hear, because he did not want to hear, the accusation of a former colleague—"If the Kaiser had offered you a double sum you would have defended neutrality." He immediately made his newspaper the organ of the Fasci, a little interventionist group which had been founded in July 1914, months before his "conversion," and which had from its origin been his enemy. He became its patron.

Returning from Geneva, several weeks later, Marcel Cachin took into confidence the Chamber of Deputies [1]

[1] *Journal Officiel.*

and, burning with pure passionate patriotism, he spoke of glorious achievements for the French cause.

"*Voyez*," he cried, "that which has happened in the Italian section ! *Voilà* Mussolini who in the *Popolo d'Italia*, to-day in its fortieth number, has had a great success, declaring that the revolution is an idea which has found bayonets. We register with joy the happy and concordant symptoms. Everything presages the inevitable intervention of Italy. She will help us finish the war, assuring victory against the militarist reactionaries, the Hapsburgs and the Hohenzollerns." France applauded Mussolini and Cachin.

The miracle of Mussolini's acceptance of Allied patriotism was finally explained in a famous case in the courts of Paris in 1926. The name of Charles Dumas, secretary to Minister Guesdes, as the actual bearer of the money was given and the sums specified. It was during the trial of one Bonomini for the murder of Buonservizi, friend and colleague of Mussolini on the *Popolo*. Maître Torrès, a French lawyer of renown, always the defender of victims of injustice, personal and political, pleaded for Bonomini. Maître Gautrand represented the *partie civile*, on behalf of the Italian embassy. The Italian government and its newspapers were demanding the guillotining of Bonomini, and were bringing intimidating pressure upon France.

Maître Gautrand resorted to that commonest of all commodities, wartime patriotism. Italy, " blood sister of France," had stood by her ; Italy had helped win the war. Fascism was the patriot of Italy. Mussolini was the chief of Fascism. Buonservizi was the colleague of Mussolini. It was all very simple. A political crime had been committed. The victim was a great patriot. Patriotic France and Patriotic Italy demanded the death of Bonomini !

Maître Torrès arose.

Italy, he said, it was true, had entered the war on the side of the Allies, Italy had done so because the Allies had made a financial and territorial deal with Italy. And as for Mussolini, it was the pure result of a plain business transaction on the part of the French government. It was a matter of dollars and cents, not sentiment.

Maître Gautrand was outraged.   He demanded instructions from the Italian embassy in Paris.   The embassy
cabled to Rome.   But to this very day no action has been
taken against the accusation.   In fact, Maître Torrès was
willing to amplify his charges in print.   In Stockholm, and
in the Italian newspapers published in Paris, he tells the
story of how the Allies won Mussolini :

" There had been a moment, the first moment, in which
the Italian Socialist Party was unanimous against the
intervention of Italy in the war.   The situation preoccupied
the French government.   The problem was examined at
a council of the Ministers.   The question was taken up,
how to convert some one leader for the war, with the aid of
money, and the name of Mussolini was suggested.   The
first sum was 15,000 francs ($3000) and it was followed by
monthly payments of 10,000 francs.   The man who actually
carried the money was M. Charles Dumas, secretary of the
Department of War Propaganda to Minister Guesdes.
Thus was born *Il Popolo d'Italia*, immediately interventionist.   This is the precise history to which no one could dare
bring any denial for fear of a documentation more crushing."

There was a time when the history of the " miracle "
was common knowledge, when the opposition press referred
to it as merely one of hundreds of similar wartime episodes
which fill many a dossier in the British and French Foreign
Offices.   To-day all the documents, the books, pamphlets,
and the newspapers dealing with this subject, have disappeared.

In 1924, when they were still in circulation, the present
writer asked Mussolini a question touching on this dramatic
and decisive moment of his life.   He replied :

" The turning-point in my life was the war.   The war
showed the world plainly, I think, the utter bankruptcy
of internationalism.   We had been fighting for a hollow
fraud.   I had fought for internationalism all my life,
preached it, gone to prison for that same cause, and suddenly the war came and I realized first that internationalism
was dead because it had never really lived, and that I had
a real duty in life, and that was to my country."

But if a man's life story, his childhood, the making of his behaviour pattern and the evidences of its fulfilment in youth, mean anything at all, they indicate that beyond patriotism and duty, there is a stronger force tugging at his vitals.

Mussolini was " condemned " to march towards power. As he so readily admits, he needed most of all a daily newspaper. To the shouts of treason and betrayal he can always reply he did no more or less than hundreds of others highly respected gentlemen, the leading patriots, the numerous editors and publishers throughout the world who took up either the side of France and England, or that of Germany and Austria, because in some way or another, it paid.

Luckily for him, he had chosen the winning side. In America, in a similar situation, Dr. Rumeley, the editor who chose the loser, paid for his error by a term in prison.

5

CHAPTER VI

A Politician goes to War

THE purchase of newspapers and editors is a small thing compared with the purchase of nations. Usually the first is the necessary prelude. And so it proved in Italy. That nation officially renounced the Triple Alliance on April 30, 1915, and amidst the applause of half the world joined the forces of Democracy, Humanity, Liberty, and commercial penetration on the following 15th of May. It was not until the days of the peace-making in Versailles that the secret of Italy's noble act became known.

In April 1915, according to the treaty signed by France, Britain, Russia, and Italy and presented to an incredulous and angry world by the Russian Soviet government, which had opened the Tsarist archives in 1917, Italy was bribed by the Allies with a promise of plunder equal to that which they themselves as victors had planned to share. Italy, too, was to receive lands and populations to which she had no moral, ethical, geographical, or ethnological claim.

In that same April of 1915 Benito Mussolini was arrested in Rome for violation of law and order in his activities in the interventionist movement. Thus was the spectacle of strict neutrality maintained publicly. Incidentally, on the 29th of the month, Mussolini fought a duel with the pacifist anti-interventionalist Socialist leader, Claudio Treves, the latter wounding the patriot, but not severely.

Mussolini left for the front to the accompaniment of journalistic fireworks. He was himself made into a patriotic symbol for a nation which needed enthusiasm badly. Early in December we find him in a hospital suffering from gastro-enteritis. In 1916 there is a period of intensive training, another trip to the hospital, recovery, a duel with General Count Spingardi, a series of articles in his newspaper telling about life near the front, a brief period in the trenches.

It was a quiet sector where the enemies had by a routine of action established a code of ethics. Every soldier who has ever kept his head down in the trenches knew and respected it. It was simply a live-and-let-live system by which firing was done at certain known intervals and a large part of the training-time was devoted to strictly human civilized activities. It made life possible—for a little longer for some men, the allotted peaceful span for others.

The leading editorial warrior came to the trenches full of the fury he had preached in print. He demanded, first of all, why the sector was so quiet, why the Italian army didn't advance, why the war was not being fought as it should be. The replies did not satisfy him. One night of his first week at the front he was looking over the trenches, himself an easy mark for any Austrian sniper, when he beheld a soldier in the enemy line lighting a match. In a flash Corporal Mussolini had removed the pin from a hand grenade and thrown it in the direction of the smoker opposite him. The crack-boom and a small flame broke the quiet monotony of the sector.

" Why did you do that, my son ! " the captain, who was making his rounds, asked of his corporal. " They were sitting peacefully and not doing us any harm. They were smoking their pipes in silence and perhaps talking of their brides. Have you no heart ? Why was it necessary to send them to death ? "

" If that is so, my captain," replied Mussolini in the account which his worshipping admirers tell to emphasize his patriotism, " then perhaps we had all better go for a little promenade on the Milanese Corso, a more agreeable occupation, certainly."

With great satisfaction the corporal learned the next day that his lucky grenade had killed two men and wounded five. But the established code also had been broken, and in retaliation the Austrian snipers picked off many Italians during food-delivery time and other previously peaceful hours, and the act of heroism resulted in useless deaths on both sides.

Fortunately for our hero, he had little time in the front line, although many months at the front. He frequently had his photograph taken sitting or standing on top of a parapet, which he sent back for publication in the illustrated weeklies. They were marked by him " front-line trenches." No British, French, or American soldier in the Great War was able to equal this photographic feat.

In December 1916 Mussolini recorded in his dairy that a cat was scratching about in the Italian wire, and that, taking advantage of the first rainless evening, " I wandered about the battlefield a little." Again, no Allied or American soldier can boast of such a deed. A few days later he is visited by Fasciolo of the staff of his *Popolo*, now a captain of artillery, and de Ambris, a naval officer, and he reports seeing them walking on the road. It must have been indeed a strange front when men photographed each other on parapets, strolled for their health in No Man's Land, and could see friends coming and going on a public road.

New Year's Day our hero was marching ; from January 10 to 20, 1917, he "rested in the hutments of Santo Stefano." In February he notes the formation of a second section of the Bettica trench mortars of which he has been placed in command, then " practice in the Polygon of Ronchi."

On the afternoon of February 23 " we were engaged in trial-firing with a trench mortar on Hill 144. . . . The firing went off without the least incident until the last round but one. But this round—and we had fired two casefuls— exploded in the barrel. I was hit by a shower of splinters and hurled several yards away. I cannot say any more. . . ."

Thus ended the war career of the hero.

But not the history of myth and oratory.

When the senior corporal was taken to the hospital it was found that the mortar splinters were imbedded in what the Germans unromantically call the *Sitzfleisch*. From the bed of pain, on which Mussolini lay on his stomach, rose the deep cry :

" I shall not die, because I *will* not to die.

" I shall not die even if all the doctors explode with fury.

" No doubt medical science says that I cannot remain alive, but I snap my fingers at medical science."

Thus, and thus only, can a man of destiny speak.

Many years later journalists seeking biographical details of the career of the Duce obtained from the press department of the Italian Foreign Office, notably from Baron Valentino and Barone Rosso, stories which made of Mussolini the bravest soldier in all the Allied and enemy armies. He had been wounded in battle, and no less than thirty times. Thirty wound stripes ! This was indeed a record few if any soldiers could surpass. Nungesser, the aviator, shot down time after time, alone could equal it.

But in the war histories published before the advent of censorship there are other pictures of the event. For instance, there is the story written by de Ambris, who later became premier of Fiume, which is simply this : " Mussolini preferred to wait until his class was called. Once at the front, he passed almost all his time in the special school, the school for officers, and in the hospital. In the trenches he stayed a total of thirty-eight days, and never took part in action. The wounds on which he prides himself, thanks to which there was an end to the brilliant career as warrior, were received during grenade practice, in a training-school, miles to the rear. It was an accident, nothing heroic. The gravity of the wounds was due to the fact that a disease had poisoned his blood. When healed, this thundering warrior stayed in Milan until all danger of a return to the front had passed. This is the entire glorious history of the participation in the war of Mussolini, who had preached intervention with fervour."

It is really amazing how facts known to so many men can be blurred, romanticized, mystified, turned into propaganda in this enlightened age of a free press and free opinion. This epiphenomenal Mussolini myth has grown so quickly.

We find the *Morning Post* saying : " Signor Mussolini fell
on the Italian front with as many wounds as Caesar " ;
the *English Review* : " He received forty-two wounds " ;
G. M. Godden's biography : " Mussolini, on leaving his
hospital bed at Ronchi after he had been wounded, literally
with a hundred wounds " ; Jeanne Bordeux : " On the
hills of Monte Nero they at last took their stand. In the
hell-fire of the fighting Mussolini was always in the first
line, ready and willing to face any and all danger. On
February 23, 1917, about two o'clock, he was wounded.
There were forty splinters in his body " ; Vladimir Poliakoff
in the *Fortnightly Review* : " After months of hard cam-
paigning he was dangerously wounded, and carries unto this
day in his body splinters of an Austrian shell " ; Sir Percival
Phillips, of the *Daily Mail* : " Mussolini fought with conspicuous bravery, was hit by shrapnel which made, literally,
a hundred wounds."

The sweetest of all worshippers, Mme Sarfatti, declares
that " he took part in a terrific bombardment, overwhelming the enemy with a rain of bombs. The trench-mortars
became almost red-hot. [The mortar burst.] Those
around were killed or maimed. Mussolini, terribly lacer-
ated, was hurled some distance away and stunned. I
remember the terrible shock when the news that he was
wounded reached Milan. What fearful details ! Forty-two
wounds. He seemed like San Sebastian, his flesh pierced
as with arrows, scarred with wounds, and bathed in blood."

And finally there is the soldier's own story :

" Almost at once I was, to my great relief, dispatched to
the thick of the fighting on the high Alps. For a few months
I underwent the hardest trials of my life in mountain
trenches. I amused myself by joining the most dangerous
reconnoitring expeditions. It was my will and my wish.
After one week of leave I went back to the trenches, where
I remained for months. We lived only a few dozen yards
from the enemy, in a perpetual and, it sometimes seemed,
an eternal atmosphere of shell-fire and mortal danger that
would be our life for ever. I was compelled from time to
time to give out in the newspapers news concerning myself.

This was in order to dispel the suspicions of those persons who thought me hidden in some office, distributing mail, and entertaining in my mind doubts of the possibility of our winning the war. I was then corporal of the Bersaglieri and had been in the front line trenches from the beginning of the war up to February 1917, always under arms, always facing the enemy without my faith being shaken or my convictions wavering an inch. From time to time I sent articles to the *Popolo d'Italia* exhorting endless resistance. On the morning of February 22, 1917, during a bombardment of the enemy trenches in Sector 144—the sector of the hard-pressed Carso under the heaviest shell-fire—there happened one of those incidents which was a daily occurrence in trench life. One of our own grenades burst in our trench among about twenty of us soldiers. We were covered with dirt and smoke and torn by metal. Four died. Various others were fatally wounded. My wounds were serious. The patience and ability of the physicians succeeded in taking out of my body forty-four pieces of grenade. Flesh was torn, bones broken. I faced atrocious pain ; my suffering was indescribable. I underwent practically all my operations without the aid of an anæsthetic. I had twenty-seven operations in one month ; all except two were without anæsthetics."

There is, it is evident, less myth in Mussolini's own story than in those of his admirers. And no less honour for a soldier in being wounded by one of his own shells. How many of our own dead were victims of our own guns no one can tell, and an accident at the front is no less painful than a sniper's well-directed bullet. The number of wounds was forty-four, not thirty, and not an even hundred, and a soldier hit by one shell or bullet or burst of gas is entitled to *one*, not forty-four wound stripes. There is no evidence, however, that the corporal was ever in a real battle, but that, too, is of no serious importance ; he was a soldier and he was wounded at the front.

Mussolini, however, was a politician gone to war. When he left Milan he was already well known as a rabid patriot and his officers were told to keep him out of real danger, since he was more valuable as a journalist writing propaganda good for the civilian morale, than as a common soldier. In a much smaller degree Mussolini was in the position of ex-President Theodore Roosevelt, had President Wilson permitted him to go to France. The American military establishment, it was revealed after the war, had asked Wilson to refuse the request because it feared Roosevelt would play the politician in the trenches. It thought he would be running for President while fighting the Germans, and for a like reason General Leonard Wood, another strenuous militarist with political ambitions, was also kept at home.

When Mussolini was wounded, considerable propaganda was made out of this unforeseen accident. It is true that his own newspaper, the *Popolo*, on February 24 was able to print the comforting announcement that the wound were not serious, but the process of creating a hero was well begun. When Mussolini wrote from his hospital that " I am proud in the fulfilment of duty, perilous duty, to have contributed to the opening of the road to Trieste with my own blood," these noble if not quite truthful but nevertheless magic words caused a considerable burst of patriotic hysteria in newspaper offices. The time of the singing of hymns had come.

The importance of hero-making in war-time cannot be overestimated. From a purely military viewpoint it must be said that Mussolini's wounds, accidental as they were, had a moral value surpassing perhaps the capture of a large section of enemy trenches or several hundred prisoners. In a manner it was like the battle of Cantigny which the American First Division fought, a minor episode in military history, but a tremendously invigorating force throughout France, because it was the first appearance of Yankee soldiers in a successful action.

While Mussolini lay in hospital the King of Italy came to visit the little corporal.

He progressed to crutches, to a cane. He then " asked exemption from further military service as being indispensable in the management of the *Popolo*."

Returning to Milan, he records, " I took my place as a fighter in my newspaper office."

After Caporetto, that defeat of defeats of the Allies, Mussolini, who had played his part in bringing Italy into the war, exerted himself to maintain her there. And so long as the Allies and the Associated Power, which is the United States of America, can believe that the World War was justified slaughter, that it helped civilization, that it was blessed by Almighty God, as thousands of preachers once declared, so long must they confess their gratitude to Benito Mussolini for his work in helping the victory.

General Cadorna did not think the corporal rated elevation to a sub-lieutenancy. As for himself, he records in his autobiography, " I was a good soldier."

CHAPTER VII

Fiume or Death!

Il Generale Cadorna
Scrive alla Regina :
Se vuol Trieste,
Compra la cartolina!

IT was treason to sing this song : General Cadorna wrote to the queen : " If you want to see Trieste, buy a picture postcard." But the soldiers sang it, and a volunteer ambulance driver named Ernest Hemingway composed another stanza about the regiment being decimated, the colonel being decorated, and hurrah for the cannonade ! The soldiers sang and shouted, " We want peace," and, " Long live the Pope," who on August 1, 1917, had sent a peace plan to all the nations.

October 17, 1917 : Caporetto. The retreat. The Germans announced the collapse of Italy.

Gabriele d'Annunzio suggested to Editor Mussolini that he form an organization of all patriots whose work would be to restore the civilian and military morale. Mussolini and many other patriots did so. It was called the Fascio di Resistenza.

From that day on, through the Vittorio Veneto of the following year when Italy triumphed, and in time of armistice and peace conferences, the two men were joined in many activities. One was the leading politician, the other the leading poet. They came back two of a triumvirate of acclaimed heroes. Benito Mussolini, Gabriele d'Annunzio, and Raffaele Rossetti shared many honours. The politician had played his part well, even if he was not long at the front ; the poet had flown in the back seat of an airplane which bombarded Vienna with leaflets of warning, and the third was an engineer who had, single-handed, ridden a torpedo into an Austrian harbour and destroyed the flagship of the navy. Rossetti was Italy's Sergeant York. Of the three, one rules, another does strange mystic rites on a battleship fastened down in his front yard, wearing the collar of the Annunziata, and answering to the title of Prince, while the third is a working-man in Paris, a refugee, a rebel.

All three were participants in the Fiume adventure. D'Annunzio led it ; Mussolini gathered the funds, and Rossetti one day, overcome by Mussolini's editorials, went into the office of the *Popolo* and presented to the sacred cause a small fortune which the nation had given him for his exploits. In exile he has time to think and regret.

D'Annunzio marched on September 12, 1919, a time of chaos and peace conferences. "We had won the war," wrote Mussolini, "but were utterly defeated in the diplomatic battle. We were losing—except Zara—the whole of Dalmatia, our land by tradition and history, by manners and costumes [*sic*], by language spoken and by the ardent and constant aspirations of the Dalmatians towards the mother country. Fiume, most Italian of cities, was contested."

Mussolini had been appointed "consul-general" by d'Annunzio, who gathered about him the Arditi, the ardent young veterans, many officers, some peasants, many socialists, some roustabout boys and adventurers. The march on Fiume was the forerunner of the march on Rome. Both were the poet's ideas. He marched, and he was met by General Pittaluga, commander of the port, peacemaker for the Allies.

"Thus you ruin Italy ! " he declared.

"It is you who ruin Italy by opposing Fiume's destiny," replied d'Annunzio.

"I must obey military orders," countered the general.

"What ? You would fire upon your brothers ? " cried the poet. "Then fire first upon me."

With a noble gesture d'Annunzio tore open his military tunic, exposing his undershirt.

Pittaluga was overcome.

" With you I cry, ' Viva Fiume ! ' " he cried.

" Evviva Pittaluga ! " cried d'Annunzio.

So they embraced and, crying together, led the march
into Fiume. The forty trucks started their motors. The
general advanced very militarily. D'Annunzio did his
best in a bow-legged way. The next morning he put on a
field-marshal's uniform.

Comic opera as this may seem to-day, the attack and its
success led directly to the making of the Fascist movement
and the advent of Mussolini in Rome. The poet had supplied the black shirts, the black fezzes, the slogans, the spirit
of armed adventure, the ideal of force triumphant and the
salutes, yells, and claptrap of Rome of the time of the
Caesars. A shrewder man knew how to employ them on
a national scale.

Italy, the people of Italy, cheered the *coup d'état* as an
act of justice. Mussolini editorially proclaimed that " the
government of Italy is not in Rome, but in Fiume. It is
that government which we must obey," a declaration of
pure patriotic treason which Premier Nitti promptly
denounced. He also saw with alarm that sedition for
the first time had entered the Italian army.

Every evening the victorious poet held an oration and
listened to the cheers of his men ; several times a week he
led parades, and again listened to shouts, watched the
waving of stilettos, the shaking of muskets, and found it
all magnificent. He gave Fiume a charter full of romantic
poetry . . . " to instil into the daily life a sense of that
virtuous joy which ought to revive the spirits of a people
liberated at last from the yoke of restraint and falsehood."
He also created ten classes of men, in ten corporations, the
ninth for seafaring men, the tenth for the intelligentsia.
" Its coming is expected like that of the Tenth Muse. It
is reserved to the mysterious forces of the people in toil and
attainment. It is almost a votive figure . . . to the complete liberation of the spirit over pain and agony, over
blood and sweat." The corporations, circumcised of
poetry, remain in the present Fascist state.

To the people of Fiume the poet said : " I shall not leave

here alive, nor shall I leave here when I am dead, for I shall be buried here, to become one with the sacred soil."

Always d'Annunzio dramatized himself. One day he strutted about like Napoleon, a bow-legged Napoleon it is true ; another day he was Lenin ; and again he would become Captain Kidd and organize expeditions to raid the main, board ships, steal cargoes of food. Twice his men raided and annexed islands. Frequently they brought prize ships and much booty into port. Sometimes d'Annunzio would play the part of field-marshal in resplendent uniform. Frequently he assumed his favourite rôle, which was that of Prince of the Renaissance.

Every day he held a ceremony of the Arditi. He concluded by asking : " To whom does Italy belong ? "

" A noi (To us) ! " shouted the trained Arditi.

" Who are our enemies ? "

" They disgust us ! " replied the Black Shirts, and with a superior smile the commandante, field-marshal, Napoleon, and Prince would dismiss his cohorts.

Frequently he called for the Socialists and Communists to come to the governor's palace to discuss revolution. In a strange muddled way he believed himself a rebel, therefore akin to the Bolsheviki, who in those days were enjoying the hatred of the universe. In that, too, he felt himself a kindred victim and flooded his emotions with self-pity while he made a grandiose gesture of dictatorship. I can still hear him talking in dactylic hexameters in answer to my simple journalistic questions.

" Our cause is the greatest and the most beautiful that to-day is opposed to the dementia and to the vileness of the world," he said. " It extends from Ireland to Egypt, from Russia to America, from Rumania to India ; it gathers together the white races and coloured races, reconciles the Gospel and the Koran, Christianity and Islam, rivets in one sole will as many peoples as possess in their bones and in their arteries salt and iron sufficient to feed action. We shall be victorious. All the rebels of all races of mankind will gather under our banners. And the weaponless shall be armed. And violence shall oppose violence. There shall be a new crusade of all the poor and impoverished nations, of all poor men and all free men against the nations, against the caste of usurers which yesterday made the profits out of the war and to-day profit by the peace ; and we shall re-establish the true justice which a cold and foolish man, with a hammer borrowed from a former German chancellor, crucified with fourteen nails."

He demanded an insurrection of the spirit, " against the devourers of raw flesh, and against the exploiters of weaponless peoples," and he called upon all the victims of their own or foreign governments to come to him in Fiume and conspire with him for revolt and rebellion and violence and insurrection everywhere and at once. As for himself, he intended to march on Rome. He had already arranged for that with his close associate, Benito Mussolini, the patriotic journalist, who in Milan was acting as his " envoy to Italy," and collecting three million lire from sympathizers. He would await the troops which Mussolini was arming for him, join them to the Arditi, land at Rimini or Ravenna, receive the acclamations of liberated Italy, and with thousands upon thousands joining him at every footstep, march victoriously into the streets of Rome, dissolve parliament and declare the dictatorship of the patriots.

Every evening he made an oration. He spoke with poetry and fire and beauty against the wrongs of Versailles ; with irony and fire he lashed Clemenceau and Woodrow Wilson and all the betrayers of the cause of Fiume, the Fiume of Italy and d'Annunzio. He spoke as if he were not merely the governor of a seized seaport, but the Messiah of all the downtrodden of the earth, a Messiah in a military uniform, but holding aloft a flag which all the unhappy and idealistic could see from their unfortunate parts of the world.

At the end of every evening's oration the same ceremony :

" For Gabriele d'Annunzio ! "

" Ayah ! ayah ! ayah ! Alala ! "

" For the people of Fiume ! "

" Ayah ! ayah ! ayah ! Alala ! "

" What is our slogan ? "

" *Me ne frego !* [We don't give a damn !] "

The Arditi in unison lifted their stilettos and the Prince smiled.

Twice or three times a week, according to the state of morale of his own troops, who were not getting enough to eat, and the Yugoslav population, who were enemies, there would be a full-dress parade of the Fiumian Legion, which the commandante would lead up to the main square, where he would mount a tribune and hold a review. There would be fanfares and loud and continued " Ayahs " and " Alalas." Salutes and poses. Frequently there were ceremonials, and always there were new ribbons, new medals for bravery, new victories to be celebrated. It was, in short, a carnival which was to end in bloodshed.

Among the important factors contributing to the final slaughter were the arrangements which the government was able to make with Mussolini, which resulted in his withdrawal of support, moral, financial, military, and of all supplies. Starvation and lack of new troops defeated d'Annunzio.

Almost from the first days trouble arose. Thousands of lire for Fiume came from all over Italy, but the big sums outside Rossetti's contribution were sent by Italian-Americans ; it is estimated that £10,000 came from the United States in the first three months, following on Mussolini's appeal for funds " to feed the starving babies of Fiume," and to aid the poet in other ways. In November 1919, after Mussolini had run for parliament and received almost no votes, he was publicly accused and tried by the journalists' association for using the Fiume fund to run his own election campaign.

This charge Mussolini denied, but admitted " diverting " some of d'Annunzio's money.[1] He admitted that two of his assistant editors resigned after accusing him of helping himself to Fiume money for political purposes, he admits he appeared for " trial," and adds that " my justification

[1] *Popolo d'Italia*, February 20, 1920.

was ample and precise. The board was forced by the acts to do me justice. As for the disposition of the funds for the Fiume campaign and other unworthy calumnies, I published in my newspaper documents and testimony which could never be refuted. The conclusion arrived at then has been and always will be the same until I cease to exist : on the score of integrity no attack can be made upon me. My political work may be valued more or less, this way or that, and people may shout me up or howl me down, but in the moral field it is another matter. Men must live in harmony with the faith by which they are driven ; they must be inspired by the most absolute disinterestedness. I am proud to know myself as one not to be suspected—even by myself—and so feel that my inmost moral fibre is invincible."

Against these lovely and noble words we have the testimony of the prime minister of Fiume, Alceste De Ambris, the man who was the practical strategist of the adventure, who was one of the original legionaries of d'Annunzio, who marched and fought, held the highest political office, and who later at the risk of his life came to Milan as the poet's personal representative to negotiate for Mussolini's aid.

" I was at that time," states De Ambris, " chief of the cabinet of the provisional government of Fiume, and I recall with what repugnance d'Annunzio received Mussolini's request for aid.

" D'Annunzio had large ideas, but at that moment the legionaries who occupied Fiume were suffering literally from hunger, and d'Annunzio found it strange that Mussolini should be taking the bread from the mouths of the soldiers and inhabitants of Fiume for the purpose of electoral ambitions, and for personal expenses.

" Nevertheless, d'Annunzio did send a letter which would help Mussolini to give a public denial of the grave charges made against him by the *Avanti*. Later, what gratitude Mussolini would repay him."

The two editors of the *Popolo* who resigned and brought charges against their duce were Capodivacca and Rossato ; the trial was begun on February 3, 1920 ; Mussolini wrote :

" The Fascist election bloc fought with its own money, exclusively its own, and not with that of Fiume. Of the sums received, several thousands of lire were used to pay the salaries of legionaries coming to Milan from Fiume and other Italian towns, who formed the armed bands at my orders."

The accusation declared that these " armed bands " were in fact the beginnings of the Fascisti, or of Mussolini's private militia, which were armed and fitted out by him, to be used by him to help in the election, and never to be sent as reinforcements to Fiume. Mussolini replied :

" We must distinguish two periods, the period of April 15 to May 15, and that which is truly the period of the ' bands ' of the *Popolo d'Italia*. It concerns the group of twenty to twenty-five Arditi who stood guard at my papers. Now we come to the other ' bands.' The fact is, as I have told the judge, that during the most important week of the election campaign, several dozens of Arditi, officers and sailors, came from Fiume. There were in all several hundred men divided into squadrons commanded by officers, and naturally all owning allegiance to me. It is perfectly true that they were paid ; they were given 20 to 25 lire a day."

It was this confession, incidentally, which caused Premier Nitti to act, because obviously the arming of several hundred men to use at an election, was the formation of a small professional army by a candidate for parliament, and a breach of the constitution ; it was no concern of the government's whether the men were paid out of the Fiume fund or not. About this time Mussolini was taken to the prison of San Fedela for a short sojourn, when Nitti feared a *coup d'état*.

When Giolitti came into power he devoted himself to two problems, the industrial revolution in the north, and the Fiume question. At Rapallo, September 20, 1920, he signed a treaty renouncing all Dalmatia except Zara, and returned to Yugoslavia a part of the port of Fiume. Premier Giolitti and Count Sforza, Minister for Foreign Affairs, heard from Mussolini that he would accept this arrange-

6

ment, although d'Annunzio refused. Mussolini had again turned his coat.

Moreover, d'Annunzio informed Mussolini he knew of a letter containing a secret codicil, giving the Yugoslavs port rights in Fiume ; but the agent sent with this news to Milan came back to say that Mussolini, who was now writing editorials praising the peaceful conclusion of the affair, had refused to change his attitude.

De Ambris then invited Mussolini to visit Fiume at the end of October, where a final meeting with d'Annunzio was arranged. But at the last hour Mussolini refused, going to Rome instead on political errands of his own. D'Annunzio at last began to suspect treason. Early in December it was apparent that the loyal royal Italian troops were concentrating for a march on Fiume. It was then, according to De Ambris, that d'Annunzio sent his ultimatum to Mussolini, asking for " an act of solidarity," and for money and more troops which Mussolini had promised for just such an emergency. Mussolini replied :

" The commandante wants me to start a revolution. But can he be sure that the workmen will work again twelve hours a day ? "

D'Annunzio's representative did not understand.

It is true that the question of a revolution in Italy had been discussed by the two leaders of the Fiume adventure. Much later, in self-defence, when accused of betraying d'Annunzio, Mussolini in a public speech declared :

" Let no one reproach me because I have not made that little, easy, cheerful, pleasant thing called a revolution. The Fascisti have never promised to make a revolution in Italy in the event of Fiume being attacked. I personally have never written to d'Annunzio to make him believe that a revolution in Italy depended on my inclinations. I do not bluff or talk hot air.

" Revolution is not a surprise packet which can be opened by all. I do not carry it in my pocket. Revolution will be accomplished with the army, not against the army ; with arms, not without them ; with trained forces, not with undisciplined mobs called together in the streets.

It will succeed when it is surrounded by a halo of sympathy or by the majority, and if it has not all that, it will fail."

A fine prediction, the confession of a plan, as we shall see afterwards. At present the Machiavellian Mussolini, the practical gentleman who had collected the funds and had armed his own bands in Milan, was making cryptic remarks to d'Annunzio. The latter, however, replied that he was not asking that the revolution begin at once, but that troops and money for food be sent as promised. To this Mussolini did not reply.

Left alone in Fiume, the poet heard the government troops were on the march. General Caviglia surrounded Fiume and sent an ultimatum to d'Annunzio. This fact was communicated to Mussolini, who, however, just before the ultimatum expired and the bombardment began, was able to write :

" In the hour in which we find ourselves we cannot know what reply Gabriele d'Annunzio has given to the ultimatum sent by General di Caviglia which expired yesterday at 18 o'clock. On the other hand, a declaration made by the Honourable Giolitti to the Honourable De Nava, president of the parliamentary commission on foreign affairs, signifies that the affair will not have a tragic end. The Honourable Giolitti has declared that the Fiume situation is such as to give no one any worry.

" This optimism, veritably olympic, contrasts with the tone of the note sent by di Caviglia and with the ultimatum which has already expired at this hour."

No neutral could have written a more suitable editorial. This was from the pen of the man who was the principal backer of the movement.

On the night of December 24 the bombardment began. From Christmas Eve through four nights and four days there was small but effective shooting from land and sea, and blood was spilled in the houses and streets of Fiume, while in the *Popolo* not even a cry of indignation was raised by Mussolini.

When d'Annunzio gave up his command to a committee

of citizens and left Fiume, only then did the Fascist chief
utter a valedictory, which he proudly recounts to-day :

" Beneath all the verbosity and the shuttle of mere
words, the drama is perfect ; horrible if you choose, but
perfect. On one side is the cold Reason of the State determined to the uttermost ; on the other the warm Reason
of the Ideal ready to make desperate, supreme sacrifices.
Invited to make our choice, we, the uneasy and precocious
minority, choose calmly the Reason of the Ideal."

" The Reason of the Ideal," according to De Ambris
and to thousands of other politicians and leaders, was soon
apparent : the government and Mussolini had come to an
agreement by which Mussolini, in return for withdrawing
his support from Fiume, would be allowed a free hand with
the arming and organizing of the entire Fascist movement.

" We know now," states the former premier of Fiume,
" that the new phase of the political fortune of Mussolini,
and especially of Fascism, dates from the treason to the
cause of Fiume, after his negotiations with Giolitti. From
that moment one may date a different attitude of the
government vis-à-vis Fascism, and the rapid transformation
of it into a reactionary movement. From the end of 1920
the Fascisti were in effect armed by Giolitti and largely
paid by him.

" Giolitti had been called into power to solve two
problems, Fiume and Bolshevism. To solve the former he
obtained Mussolini's passive consent to the fratricidal
aggression of Christmas 1920 ; to solve the latter Giolitti
obtained Mussolini's active consent, and engaged himself
to furnish arms and other material means for the guerrilla
warfare against Socialism.

" Giolitti believed himself powerful enough to suppress
the Fascisti, after he had used them as an anti-Socialist
reactionary force, without compromising the Liberal state
directly in the civil strike. But the old fox fooled himself
and lived to regret it bitterly.

" Mussolini turned his treason into profit. I do not
know what thirty pieces of silver the Fascist Judas got
from Giolitti, but it is certain that between Giolitti and

Mussolini, after the Treaty of Rapallo, there was a pact, whereby Mussolini, abandoning Fiume to Giolitti, received in compensation the government's aid for the Fascist enterprise. And the treason was doubly completed by Mussolini, who, on coming into power, annexed Fiume, instead of letting it remain free as specified in the Treaty of Rapallo. Moreover, the Treaty of Nettuno, which Mussolini later signed with the Yugoslavs, surrendered more than was specified in the secret letter of Count Sforza. When Mussolini was confronted with this fact in the Chamber of Deputies, he replied by calling Sforza a 'traitor' and a ' liar.'

" But Count Sforza did not lie to any one and betrayed no one ; he merely executed his programme, which was inspired by the idea of a peaceful understanding with Yugoslavia, even at the cost of grave sacrifices.

" If there is a traitor and a liar in this affair, it is uniquely Mussolini. That is the truth which I, a legionary of Fiume, can repeat even if the other legionaries, now in the service of the traitor, have forgotten."

In January 1924, Italy and Yugoslavia in the hall of victory of the Chigi Palace, signed their peace pact. It was announced as a great Fascist victory. The terms are almost identical with those proposed years before by Sforza ; the organization of the port, the division of the harbour and docks, the free-port part as designated in 1921, were approved by Mussolini, and remain so to this day. But in 1921 he had said to Sforza :

" You are placing a knife at the throat of Fiume."

Both d'Annunzio and Mussolini had waved the banner " Fiume o Morte," over their ambition and their followers for more than a year. D'Annunzio had said : " Until that day when there are only three men left standing up, there will be one less shame in this world," but he had marched out peacefully at the head of thousands.

To the new commander, the podesta of Fiume, he said : " I confide to you my dead, my sorrow, and my victory. Italy is not worth dying for."

There was only one victor at Fiume. It was the man who built Fascism upon its sorrow, its ruins, and its dead.

CHAPTER VIII

The Secret of 1920

GABRIELE D'ANNUNZIO, like many another parent, soon experienced the disillusioning sensation of not knowing his own child. Born of his furious poetic brain in Fiume, it was a mad, reckless, violent, but romantic and idealistic infant given to heroic posturings, intriguing clothes, Roman gestures, and semi-communistic dialectics. A year later, in Milan, he found it brandishing blackjacks and revolvers and castor oil.

Mussolini, the new foster parent, as well as d'Annunzio, united in admitting Fascismo to be the stepchild of still another leader of that time. That man was Woodrow Wilson. It was the President of the United States who had journeyed to Rome at Christmas-time 1918, and who in Milan had been worshipped in the streets because Italy believed him to be the man who would grant the nation its political demands, and the people the same "new deal" which Lloyd George had just proclaimed in Great Britain.

But when the Allied nations exposed their secret treaties, and asked President Wilson to agree to them, he compromised on some, accepted others, and remained steadfast in his decision against Italy's claim to Fiume.

It was then that Mussolini in his paper and d'Annunzio among the soldiers began the campaign against Wilson. In Rome crowds demonstrated against the American embassy crying, "*Ridacci la Lupa*" (Give back our Wolf!" the gold wolf of Rome which had been Italy's contribution to the trunkloads of presents given the man who had saved the world for democracy and the Allied politicians.) The police charged the mob. D'Annunzio exploited the spirit of the nation. He organized the march on Fiume.

More recently still another stepfather has been added
to Mussolini's Fascismo. Granting that the idea was
d'Annunzio's, that the inspiration was inversely Wilson's,
and that the leadership was successfully Mussolini's, the
astute politicians in Rome knew that the movement was
deathly sick with the loss of blood at Fiume, and that
nothing but a transfusion would save it. And this was
supplied by the government itself, and more particularly
by the " sly fox " of the generation, the premier Giolitti,
who, as De Ambris has stated, at one and the same time
liquidated the uprising at Fiume and the uprising in the
factories in the north, ending social agitation and radicalism
and the revolutionary strikes and, as he believed, bringing
about a permanent era of goodwill in Italy in 1920.

From the end of the war until the seizure of the factories
in August of that year, things went from bad to worse in
Italy, and Mussolini vigorously approved this turn of affairs.

Every day or every week there was a new strike. There
occurred the greatest horror which the American tourist
has ever experienced, and about which to this very day he
speaks with emotion, thanking God and Mussolini—the
horror of tourist trains not running to time. That Mussolini himself backed the railroad strikers and that he urged
them to seize the railroads, are historical facts of no interest
to those who, armed with a rapid schedule, see the Sistine
Chapel on Monday, the Pitti and Uffizi on Tuesday morning,
St. Mark's on Wednesday, get romantic in a gondola that
night, and catch the 10.15 on Thursday for somewhere else,
as per orders of the clerk in the Express Company's office in
Paris. Had the railroad strikes something to do with the
social revolution ? Americans did not care to hear such
things discussed.

Besides the railroad workers, the iron workers of Genoa,
the post-office employees, the foundry workers, the agricultural workers of Novara, the street-car men of Genoa
and others struck. Soldiers were spat upon, and officers
were followed by crowds who insulted them because they
still wore uniform. They were sometimes attacked, forced
to run and barricade themselves. Honourable wound

stripes were torn off, and even the medals of bravery
ripped from brave breasts and trampled on. The government could do nothing. Parliament was a big talking-
affair, but law and order were paralysed while in a sort of
nebulous and oratorical chaos various elements, which
aimed at restoring liberty and justice to the masses, muddled
around helplessly.

More strikes. Metal workers, bread workers, waiters,
teachers. On May 4, 1919, Mussolini wrote : " Convinced that the strikers are right and have justice on their
side, we are lending them our disinterested support."
On June 7, he added : " The nation follows with sympathy
the strike of the teachers." Almost every day Mussolini
commented favourably on the moves of the unionists,
insulted the government, cursed the employers (Later,
on taking office, one of the first things this man, great
enough to change his mind and political party, said of the
strikes was that " they were the low acts of the Socialists,
against which the Fascist patriots had to fight " ; but
before, during, and after the strike Mussolini not only
supported it, but urged the semi-Bolshevik idea that the
railroad and other unionists seize and operate their own
industries.)

A prologue to the seizure of the factories in 1920 was the
episode at Dalmine, March 1919, when Fascist agitators
caused a strike at the Franchi-Gregorini plant, the workers
raising the national, instead of the red, flag, and demanding
participation in the operation of the factory which they had
seized and refused to leave.

Mussolini called this a " creative strike." He rushed
there to aid the Bolsheviki, addressed them, saying :
" To protect the interest of your class you could have called
a strike in the old style, the negative and destructive strike ;
on the contrary, thinking of the interests of the people,
you have inaugurated the creative strike, which does not
interrupt production." In another exhortation he exclaimed : " You have proved your Will, and I say to you
you are on the right road. . . . I say to you that your
gesture is new and dignified, by the motives which inspired

them, worthy of sympathy. Your rights are sacred, and I am with you."

Meanwhile, back in Milan his associate editors wrote : " To-day the masses at Dalmine have taken a significant action, have reaffirmed their rights, they have vibrated to the impetuous and incisive words of Benito Mussolini."

" At Dalmine," wrote one of Mussolini's colleagues, " he was the Lenin of Italy."

On March 23 the Fascisti, then organizing, sent their salutations to the men who had seized the factory, and to the workers of Pavia who had gone on a general strike. Said the future Duce : " Historically we are on the grounds of the revolution begun by us in 1915. We must go ahead of the workers. We must accept the postulates of the working-class. Do they demand the eight-hour day ? And the control of the industries ? We must support all these demands, especially because we want little by little to make the working-class capable of directing the works. Economic Democracy ! That is our banner.

" The Senate must be abolished. We want to erase from our constitutional organization this feudal organism. We demand proportional representation. We want a national assembly which will have to decide whether Italy is to be a monarchy or a republic.

" We reply now : A Republic !

" *We are absolutely against all forms of dictatorship.*"

Employers' associations and the trades unions kept up the war for another year. Italian money fell ; the cost of living mounted ; wages were never raised, except once in a while when a strike was successful. The war profiteers held on to their money. The workers were exploited. All the promises of better times which the government at war had made to the people were studiously forgotten. But eventually there were revisions of salaries made individually. Then the metal workers' association decided for a general revision of wages based on the cost of living. The employers objected. On July 29, 1920, they issued the statement " We cannot admit the possibility of fixing salaries in relation to the rising cost of living."

But public opinion forced the employers to agree to a conference. Mussolini backed it. Yet on August 12 the owners crushed the conference with the statement : " All discussion is useless. We make no concessions."

This challenge to battle was accepted. A few days later the programme of the trades union was announced. It was " Obstructionism." But it was not violence, nor was it sabotage. It did mean slowing up. There was to be no " goodwill " at the works ; the men were to work mechanically, to do just what they were told, never to use their judgment, even if work done in accordance with orders from the bosses led to the spoiling of goods and tools. The letter of the law was obeyed.

The employers did not like that at all. But they could do nothing to obtain healthy co-operation, enthusiasm, goodwill, from underpaid and sometimes starving employees. So they threatened the lock-out. The Alfa-Romeo automobile works was the first to drive out its workers. The manufacturers' association agreed to follow. In reply the trades unions then ordered the occupation of the factory and the continuance of work, or the " Creative strike " of Dalmine which Mussolini had favoured, on a large scale. There was no sabotage. On August 30, 500,000 men were ordered to occupy factories and they did so without any troubles worth recording. Two men were killed in Turin. About a million men joined in the movement, which, when it reached the bottom of Sicily, was turned into the seizure of land by dispossessed peasants. Not a safe was cracked. Not a skull.

But from Paris the word was flashed around the world that Italy had " gone Bolshevik." The workers had seized the factories. The peasants had taken the land. The red flag was flying and the people were shouting, " Viva Lenin." If there were no dead, well, there should be. So all the journalists of Europe came to Milan and Turin to participate in the revolution.

The excitement in Europe and America was unbounded. Russia and Hungary were red, there were communist troubles in the Balkans, Germany trembling on the verge

—(the German " verge " lasted more than a decade and
became a Fascist verge in the end)—and now Italy was
gone, and who knows, perhaps all of Europe would soon be
engulfed. Foreign offices kept open at night, and newspapers clamoured for lists of dead and wounded.

Commotion everywhere except in Italy. It is true that
day by day more and more factories were being occupied by
the workers. Soon the 500,000 " strikers " were at work
building automobiles, steamships, forging tools, manu-
facturing a thousand useful things, but there was not a
shop or factory owner to boss them or to dictate letters
in the vacant offices. Peace reigned.

A feeling spread throughout Italy that the great day of
liberation had arrived.

It was holiday. Crowds came in automobiles and
wagons or walked by the thousands to see the great sight.
What they saw was pure normality, but they got a thrill
out of it. Tourists, caught in the midst of the revolution,
when their first fears were over, and not a rifle-shot disturbed the sunny calm, ventured out, too, and saw nothing
unusual.

For us of the press it was a terrible disillusion. There
was simply no story. We did see the red flag waving from
the chimneys, but there was smoke issuing from them too,
and all the sounds from within were those of ordinary
industry and progress. Occasionally some one shouted,
" Viva Lenin," or, " Long live the revolution," and sometimes a patrol of working-men would go by. The police
let them alone even when they bore arms. There was
much joyful singing.

The nation awaited the outcome hopefully. Every
one was pleased that things were going so well. Labriola,
Minister of Labour, was the first to attempt a conciliation,
but it did not succeed. The state did nothing. The press
was fair. Mussolini's paper applauded. To satisfy our
own newspapers, which were demanding that something
happen to justify our presence during the " revolution,"
we rushed around from Milan to Turin and from Turin to
Genoa, chasing rumours, that some Fascist spies had been

caught and burned alive in a furnace or that " Mr. Fiat " had been murdered by his employees, and other timely lies. In order to get Bolshevik pictures we had to persuade the working-men and women to erect barricades, arm themselves, take up menacing positions, and act in a revolutionary manner, which they did with laughter and smiles, much to the chagrin of the newsreel men.

From our journalistic point of view the Italian Bolshevik revolution was such a complete fiasco that we looked for other news. I had arrived with Harry Greenwall of the *Daily Express*, who had a tip that the Emir Feisal, later King of Iraq, was stopping incognito in the Villa d'Este near Milan, *en route* for London, where he wanted to see Lloyd George about a throne. Accordingly, we went to interview the dark Lord and he told us he had made a secret treaty, thanks to Lawrence of Arabia, whereby the British Government had promised him a kingdom in return for his aid against the Turks. That was a fine news item. Then, most opportunely for the journalists, there was an earthquake in Vivizzano, somewhere north of Pisa, and off I went with Lieutenant Cleveland, U.S.N., to help pull men and women and children out of fallen houses and débris in wrecked towns on the vine-clad hillsides. That was a three-day story, too. All these news happenings were much more sensational than the peaceful occupation of the factories which Mussolini then supported, and which years later, for political purposes, he was to denounce.

The whole nation also approved the seizure of the land. Agrarian reform had long been promised. When Nitti was Premier he had a law passed giving land, paid for by the government, to ex-soldiers. During the war the troops were fed on the propaganda that all wrongs would be righted when they came home victorious, and the land workers, who were little better than Russian serfs, would be given farms. Now they were taking them. In every instance the revolutionaries who were dividing up the huge estates in the south were led by former soldiers, some of whom were Fascists, Mussolini having in 1919 declared for land seizure. (In fact, in 1923, nineteen months after he came into power, he let the Fascist syndicates seize ten properties in the province of Novare for division among war veterans.)

With the peaceful failure of the occupation movement, called Bolshevism abroad, but in fact a real attempt to establish a peaceful co-operative industrial commonwealth, came the gradual disintegration of radical labour hopes in Italy. This double movement, the building up of discipline, the restoration of confidence, reconciliation and pacification on one side, and the war against violence on the other, was the work of the liberal, democratic parties. It was the crowning effort of Premier Giolitti. At least it was so heralded in those forgotten days.

But time reveals many secrets.

In the middle of the great crisis of 1920 there was a meeting in the Hotel Lombardia, in Milan, between the Honourable Bruno Buozzi, secretary-general of the Federazione Italiani Operai Metallurgica, or Italian federation of metal workers, and the editor of the *Popolo d'Italia*. Signor Buozzi occupied a place and a reputation equal if not superior to that of Samuel Gompers in the American Federation of Labour, and the revelations which follow were made by him to the present writer and have been confirmed by other Italian leaders.

"I remember," Signor Buozzi says in a statement signed and authorized by him for publication in this book, "the social revolutionary Mussolini studiously and transcendentally dressed for the part, with his large black hat and his artistic necktie. When we met to talk politics in the old days he was always the one to assume studious attitudes of mystery, of a conspirator or of an agitator ; at a café table he would speak as if from a tribune haranguing the crowd of thousands of listeners, although we sat there four or five. I remember an evening in Turin in 1913, where we held a conference on 'The Commune of Paris' in the hall of the syndicates. Mussolini even then spoke as an consummate actor ; his histrionism carried away the least intelligent part of the auditors. He had a marvellous mobility in his face, he rolled his black eyes,

his shoulders moved energetically, he modulated his voice,
made long pauses, then suddenly burst out in the loudest
tones, sweeping the crowd with him. He exalted to the
point of hyperbole the heroism of the Paris communards,
but did not spare their leaders his acid criticism. He
denounced, for example, the stupidity which ordered the
leaders of the armed patrols to defend the Banque de
France.

" ' Money makes war,' cried Mussolini. ' If the communards had appropriated the gold contained in the vaults
of the Bank, and utilized it for their ends, history might
have had another face.'

" We all went to the hotel then and sat around a table
discussing the social revolution. It was lively. Some one
suggested that the social revolution presupposes a knowledge and a mastery of formidable political and economic
problems. Mussolini replied that for the true revolutionist
such problems were unimportant. To solve all problems,
' down with the bureaucracy ! ' The real political leader,
he said, needed nothing but action. He had studied the
essentials of romantic revolution and its prophet, Blanqui.

" At one turn of the conversation, attacking our social-
democracy, Mussolini arose, pointing his index finger at
us, and speaking in a cavernous voice, accentuating each
syllable :

" ' Italy is the only country,' he said, ' in all Europe
which in the past hundred years has had not a revolution.
L'Italia ha bisogno di un bagno di sangue [Italy has need of
a bath of blood], and you, social democrats and leaders of
the syndicalists, are the major obstacle to the accomplishment of such a fact. We ought to barricade for ten years
the doors of your organizations.'

" Mussolini had always said, and printed in the paper
which he directed, that programmes are obstacles under
the feet which impede the man who would go forward.
He said and wrote that the syndicates and the co-operatives
were developing among the people an unhealthy sense of
responsibility, they were checking the people from dedicat-
ing themselves to the fight on the barricades and to the

for the profound transformation of the country, know that
you can count on my support and that of my friends.' "

This was Mussolini's offer to return to Socialism. He
was willing to make Fascism, its newspaper and its armed
militia, a part of the workers' revolutionary movement to
capture the country.

The Socialists had torn up his red card in 1914 ; they
had called him traitor, " hired assassin of the bourgeoisie,"
expelled him from the party, and he had replied that " you
will not deprive me of my socialist faith . . . you will not
keep me from fighting for the cause of Socialism and the
revolution." He had cried out that " Socialism is something that is rooted in the blood," and now he was to prove
it by returning to the fold after five years' absence. He
believed he would be accepted as a hero.

But although he still called himself a Socialist, he was
really more of a Bolshevik and a revolutionary opportunist,
ready to engage in a civil war, to shed any amount of blood,
for the establishment of a proletarian dictatorship which
the occupation of the factories seemed to make imminent.
He frightened the Socialists and the trades unionists. The
Honourable Buozzi, realizing how useless was his mission,
took the proposals for Mussolini's return and the incorporation of the Fascist bands, to a congress of the metal workers
which, on hearing the plan to use an illegal militia, to wage
war, to use violence, to burn and to seize, in short to continue the campaign which the Fascisti were waging independently, refused indignantly to traffic with bloodshed.
They, so they replied to Mussolini, intended to conquer
legally ; they had no use for a condottiere or a modern
captain of racketeers.

They did not know at that time, however, that Mussolini
was merely offering Fascism for sale to the best bidder.

With the same proposal offered to Buozzi, Mussolini
approached the metal-works owners, the Milan bankers,
the large landed proprietors, the Lega Industriale of Turin,
the Associazione fra Industriale Generale dell' Industria,
or the entire ruling industrial and financial class of Italy.

" Several months after our interview," states Buozzi,

7

" speaking to one of the captains of industry, Signor Agnelli, head of the F.I.A.T. automobile works, I referred to the fact that Mussolini had offered to come over to our side. Signor Agnelli informed me that Mussolini, at the same time he was making me this offer, had been dealing with Signor Olivetti, secretary-general of the Confederazione dell' Industria.

" This is the secret : animated by an unhampered ambition, Mussolini sought to keep one door open, be it the Right or Left, so that no matter what would happen after the occupation of the factories, he would always be able to emerge, be it at the head of a revolutionary movement or of a reactionary movement. If the seizure of the factories ended with a victory of the workers in the economic field, a prelude to the conquest of power by the Socialist Party, Mussolini would be on the Left. Otherwise, on the Right. When he saw that the Socialist Party was torn by internal dissensions, that it could not march towards power, Mussolini threw into the sea his offer and his Left programme and dedicated himself to the arms of reaction. There was now no longer a question of a proletarian revolution— leadership would be too difficult and dangerous for him ; he realized how much easier it would be to arrive in power if he served the ultra-nationalistic banner, renounced his past, and betrayed his old companions."

The industrial and agrarian bourgeoisie, still scared and distrustful, desperate before the menace of the seizure of factories, and failing to realize that the collapse of that movement meant the end of radical danger, immediately accepted the Fascisti as its military weapon. The Confederazione Generale dell' Industria openly began paying money, and other organizations secretly subventioned Mussolini and his militia.

Immediately the deal was made, Mussolini turned the threat of the Fascisti away from the warehouses, the factories and the lives of the war profiteers, the industrialists, the big-business men whom he had been threatening with hanging on lamp-posts, and directed them against the Socialists, the working-men, the co-operatives, the clubs, and the newspapers of the proletariat. Just as in 1914 he took his revenge on those who did not follow him, so now he began on a large scale to accomplish his vendetta. From that day on bloodshed increased throughout Italy. The very same boys and men who had been attacking the bourgeoisie were used a day or a week later to attack the working-class.

" The victory of Fascism over the Socialist movement," says the pro-Fascist Prezzolini, " is due to the Fascists not fearing to employ violence which the extremist preached but had never succeeded in putting into action, and because the Fascists' offensive coincided with the disruption of the Socialist Party which began about this time. It was an ill-matched contest. . . .

" Mussolini realized . . . that strikes were no longer a weapon. The Russian revolution had proved that armed force alone could secure the reins of power. And in this lay the novelty of Fascism—in the military organization of a political party."

So now Mussolini, his militia sold to the ruling class, his moral support and financial security arranged, marched forward on the road to power with an army behind him.

CHAPTER IX

FASCISM CONQUERS MUSSOLINI

THIS new army's tactics became known as squadrismo. Flying detachments of Black Shirts, aided by the military supplies, guns, and transportation of the regularly constituted authorities, concentrated secretly, rode to given destinations and wrecked the Socialist and labour movement in villages or towns by destroying its newspapers, co-operative stores, headquarters, and meeting-halls. Frequently they killed.

In America the first mention of Fascismo occurs on the 18th of October 1920, when " armed radicals in black shirts " were reported attacking the offices of the newspaper *Il Lavoratore* in Trieste with bombs, hand grenades, and bludgeons ; it was an item worthy of publication, because it affected the lives of two American citizens. Twenty shots were fired at Joseph Emerson Haven, the American consul, who had his office in the newspaper building, and Lincoln Eyre, the representative of the *New York World*.

Consul Haven sent an indignant report to the State Department, while the even more indignant Mr. Eyre cabled that " this outrage is one of a long series committed by these bandits, these nationalist hoodlums, Fascisti, as they call themselves, the word meaning ' nearly-leaders ' (*sic*), or perhaps with greater precision ' gangsters,' who pretend to be inspired with patriotic devotion to Italian ideals. This sentiment translates itself in their strangely warped minds into a systematic oppression by the most brutal and cowardly means of all who venture to disagree with them. Militaristic nationalism is their creed, and d'Annunzio (*sic*) is their prophet."

In November occurred the first large scale military action of the newly armed illegal forces of the monarchy—the

sack of Bologna—when the Socialist town council was driven
out, the chamber of Labour wrecked, the trades unions and
co-operatives burned to the ground, the newspaper presses
smashed, and working-men found on the premises beaten
or murdered.

Between January and May 1921, the Fascist squads
destroyed 120 labour union headquarters, and invaded 243
Socialist centres, killing 202 working-men and wounding
1144. In 1921 and 1922 they burned 500 labour centres
and co-operatives, and forcibly dissolved 900 Socialist
municipalities. In almost all instances, the military,
the national and the local representatives of law and order,
were confederates of the Black Shirts. For 162 Fascisti
arrested during the first six months of 1921, the authorities
jailed 2240 working-men. Of this period of violence
Prezzolini, who at the time was neutral, wrote :

" They [the Fascisti] could organize themselves in armed
camps and kill right and left with the certainty of impunity
and with the complicity of the police. It is thus no over-
statement to recognize that the Fascists fought with 99
chances out of 100 of gaining the victory."

This guerilla warfare was waged chiefly against the
co-operative movement, the labour unions, the Social
Democrats, and the Catholics. It was not a war against
Bolshevism, because whatever remained of Bolshevism
after the 1920 factory-occupation episode was unimportant.
Despite a million repetitions made since 1925, the year
public relations counsel were engaged to help in floating
Italian loans, it is a historic fact that there was no Bolshevik
danger in Italy, and final proof can be found in the *Popolo
d'Italia* of June 2, 1921, when Mussolini himself wrote :

" The Italy of 1921 is fundamentally different from that
of 1919. . . . To say that the Bolshevik danger still exists
in Italy is equivalent to trying to exchange, for reasons
of self-interest, fear against the truth. Bolshevism is
conquered. More than that, it has been disowned by the
leaders and the people. "

Trains, which had not been running to time, improved
their schedules. Strikes, which had been daily occurrences,

became less frequent. Wages went up a bit. The cost of living went down. Exports and imports showed some satisfactory figures, and slowly Italy began lifting herself out of her despair. The best proof in the world was the rate of exchange. The dollar which had gone from 18 to 23 in 1920 came back to 20.15 for the first half of 1922.

Throughout Europe a rumour of optimism was spreading. For the first time since the war there was a small restoration of good feeling. In Italy the end of 1920, marking the liquidation of the insurrection of Fiume, was followed by the famous January 1921 Socialist Party congress in Leghorn, which drove out the Communists, emancipating itself from a programme of retaliatory violence and earning the support of organized labour throughout the world. Italy felt she was now convalescent from the wounds of the war and after-war.

With Bolshevism officially exiled and actually dying, there was now no reason for the continuance of the Fascist movement. But the price of the surrender of Fiume had been the semi-official recognition of the Black Shirts as collaborators of the forces of the State. Fascisti now carried arms openly. Meanwhile the country had grown so quiet that a general election was fought bloodlessly. It gave Italy a new parliament constituted as follows :

Democrats	195
Socialists	126
Catholics	91
Nationalists	40
Fascists.	32
Communists	18

For the Communists it marked a significant defeat. The Fascisti, who in 1919 had fared so badly, got some satisfaction out of their 32 delegates in 1921, and the Populari organized in 1919 with 91 members, became a national force to be reckoned with in any future struggle for the maintenance of the middle road. Most important of all was the great victory of the Democrats and the moderate Socialists. The election showed the world that Italy was getting on well politically, and would remain a peaceful democratic constitutional nation.

It was at this moment that Mussolini, as usual without a platform, but with many promises to draw the sympathy of the masses whose psychology he knew so well, began his republican movement. But it did not go far. Immediately he played still another trick out of his inexhaustible sleeve. To the astonishment of his followers, on the 23rd of July 1921, he announced a proposed truce between the Fascist Party and militia and of its enemies ; also close co-operation between himself and the Socialist and Catholic Parties, both of which represented the working-classes.

In August this truce was signed " for the realization of the return to normal conditions " and for the renunciation of violence. The simple yet amazing text of this document, which, if made in good faith and capable of being carried out without opposition to Mussolini, would have changed the course of Italian history, is given in full in the Appendix. The signatories pledged themselves to end " all menaces, all reprisals, all punishments, all vengeances, all personal violence " ; they were to respect the political insignias and economic organizations, and to submit all violations to a college of arbitrators and to co-operate for the restoration of peace within the nation.

The treaty was signed by Mussolini, De Vecchi, and Giurati for the parliamentary Fascist group, by Cesari Rossi and three others for the Fasci di Combattimento, by the Socialist Party, the Socialist parliamentary group, the General Federation of Labour, and by Enrico de Nicola, president of the Chamber of Deputies.

It may be noted that the first man to sign for the " Fighting Fascisti " was Cesare Rossi, he who was later to become head of the Cheka, to carry out all orders against opposition leaders, and finally to be implicated in the assassination which almost destroyed Fascism, a blow unforeseen by the disciple of Machiavelli.

With the ink hardly dry on the peace pact, Mussolini, who had, it must be truly admitted, initiated the conference, went to his desk and wrote the following declaration of reaffirmation and defiance to his own followers :

" I will defend with all my forces this treaty of peace,

which in my view attains the importance of a historic event on account of its ' singularity ' without precedent.

" For this purpose I will attempt to apply the old and very wise proverb, ' Whoever does not employ the rod hates his son.' Well ! If Fascism is my son—which every one has always known it to be—I swear with the rods of my oath, of my courage, of my passion, I will either correct him, or I will make his life impossible."

Can any one doubt the courage, the passion, with which these words are written ? Are they the expression of an honest man, or can they possibly be those of the deepest hypocrite and villain ? History alone can tell. Certain it was that in August 1921, the nation believed whole-heartedly that Mussolini with an outburst of frankness and honesty and fearlessness had done a great thing, had accomplished more than parliament and the polemics of the party press. This was the real peace of the people !

August passed in tranquility. But there were signs of trouble. All the forces of reaction, of private property, the bankers, the proprietors of the factories which had once been seized, the ship companies, the hotel keepers, and certain large landowners, who had once seen the menacing spectre of Bolshevism, now determined that Socialism, liberalism, democracy, despite their legality, their pacifism, their disorganization, and their weaknesses, must also be banished. These elements were the employers of Mussolini the condottiere. On the other hand, there were the liberals of the same propertied classes, who expressed their support of the Black Shirt leader orally.

With tremendous enthusiasm Mussolini, who again saw himself as a popular figure, attempted to curb the forces he had originated or encouraged. He thundered against the " hot heads," the " irresponsibles," the " violent elements," and he withdrew the radical pledges he had made. But it was useless. The times were out of joint for that sort of leadership. Tuscany, Emilia, and his own beloved Romagna refused to ratify the peace treaty.

Within the Fascist Party the movement against its duce grew in the cities and in the country. One of the most noteworthy breaches of the treaty occurred at Modena, September 24. The Po Valley Fascisti, who had refused all attempts at pacification, not only kept their squadristi on a war footing, but used their newly acquired guns to terrorize the Socialist co-operatives, the Catholic clubs, the labour organizations. The prefect of police of Modena had adopted measures to ensure public order. The Fascisti protested against this action. They marched into the public square opposite the prefecture, and began their orations. Every one who passed was forced, with clubs, to take off his hat during the speaking. The prefect, hearing the orators urge their followers to invade the police station, called for extra police, who, however, refused to obey the order.

Several excited persons rushed the commissary of police and his men, striking about with clubs. Soon the whole Fascist group in excitement turned against the police, who, believing themselves in danger, fired into the crowd. There were seven dead and twenty wounded.

In the same month the Fascisti organized the assassination of the Deputy Di Vagno and the anti-French demonstrations of Venice.

In Bologna the Fascisti sang anti-Mussolini songs. During a meeting of the local committee practically every one attacked the leader, and soon printed signs appeared on the streets : " Who has betrayed once will betray again." It was ominous.

Old friends, leaders, founders of Fascism deserted. Strangely enough, the one who stood steadfast was Cesare Rossi. Mussolini, seeing his followers in arms against him, said again : " If Fascism does not follow me, no one obliges me to follow Fascism. I am the duce, a leader, a word which does not especially please me, but which pleases others. We are numerous : schism is fatal. Let it come. The peace pact will have the reaction of precipitating the cleaning out of the party."

Bologna then voted against Mussolini.

Mussolini resigned.

For a moment a great change came over Fascism. In

all the industrial towns now and wherever there were large estates, the owners of land and factories became more active, disregarded Mussolini, organized their own clubs, rented headquarters, subsidized new branches about which Mussolini himself knew nothing. Among the 100,000 army officers or more whom peace had thrown out of work, many found employment in this new business. Arms were bought by the manufacturers and landowners ; when military supplies arrived, it was the duty of the officers to drill and train and finally to lead the Fascist squadristi who were receiving money, guns, and orders from their new masters.

Thus it came about that Mussolini, on seeing his life-work disintegrating, and himself disappearing as a national figure, reconsidered his resignation, and at the congress of the Fascisti in Rome, November 1921, made once more a complete *volte face*.

The pacifist of August, who had sworn to whip Fascism into shape as a peaceful legal weapon, was himself whipped by Fascism. At the congress of Rome, Mussolini accepted the incorrigibility of his " son," and became Fascism's follower, not leader. He declared publicly that the peace treaty was dead and buried. Suddenly he declared himself for violence, as a holy crusade against the Socialists and Liberals. He even included the Catholics and Democrats in his speech demanding reprisals, a renewal of bloodshed, the supremacy of the Fascisti, and for the first time in history shouts of " Down with parliament ! " and " Long live the dictatorship ! " were heard, shouts which were to lead within a year to just the event they presaged.

Thus passed another great crisis in the life of the child of Destiny. He had meant to conquer, had been conquered, and knew how to rise again, even if his new leadership was for a cause, a programme, an idea entirely opposed to the one for which he had a few weeks earlier announced himself prepared to risk his position, and perhaps his life. The honest and sincere man of August, who swore with " the rods of his courage and his passion," became in November an instrument for ruthlessness, violence, bloodshed—the programme which the proprietors of Fascism demanded, and which he humbly accepted, suddenly trying to make himself appear their leader again by being more extremist than the rest.

Mussolini was conquered by Fascism because more powerful forces had taken possession of his movement. In 1920 he had placed his forces at the disposal of certain industrialists, without realizing that in saving them he would make them his masters.[1]

Shortly after Mussolini's lieutenant (and later ambassador to the Vatican) De Vecchi had caused the Rome offices of the *Avanti* to be destroyed, he, a Torinese, was taken up by Com. de Bendetti and Avv. Ugo Cogogni of the Lega Industriale of Turin. Benni and Gino Olivetti, the directors of the Confederazione Generale dell' Industria, and Director Mazzini of the Associazione fra Industriali Metallurgici Meccanici ed Affini, who was later to succeed de Benedetti as chairman of the Lega Industriale, were not only collaborating with Mussolini, but with more trusted lieutenants who had less radical minds. These associations, corresponding to the various manufacturers' associations in America and the Stahlverein and other organizations which subsidized the Nazi movement in Germany, not only supplied the money for the Black Shirts, but succeeded easily in organizing the rebellion against Mussolini.

Whether or not he was previously aware of all the facts, he learned, at the Rome congress which ended the schism, that he could no longer defy the financial forces of which he was merely the political and military spearhead.

He now was given orders to destroy the labour movement. As the correspondent of the *Manchester Guardian* and *New York World* wrote at the time, " the enemy was not, however, the Communists," because they were unimportant : the enemy was the federation of labour, social democracy, and the newly arisen Catholic party of workingmen and peasants who were led by a priest, Don Sturzo, and who were demanding agrarian reform, social justice, and a share in the wealth of the nation.

[1] Bolitho was the first journalist to name the financial backers.

CHAPTER X

PRIEST VERSUS POLITICIAN

A T Argentina Altabella rebellious peasants, marching behind a priest who held a crucifix above their heads, occupied the fields of the wealthy landowners in the name of Christ and Christian Communism. The soil, rich and poor, was equitably divided among working-men, who, like their ancestors for a thousand years, had tilled it and built up the fortunes of the landlords while they themselves slaved and hungered. To each man was given land according to his ability ; from each was expected a contribution to the commonwealth according to his capacity.

> *" Avanti o popolo ! Con fede franca*
> *Bandiera bianco trionferà,"*

sang the rebel peasants, substituting only one word for the common song of the Bolsheviki, the word " bianca " for " rosso " (" white " for " red ") ; the " white flag of Catholicism will triumph." Throughout the south of Italy and notably in Calabria the emancipation of the peasantry gained enormously. The masses " hailed Don Sturzo as an apostle, obeyed him as a dictator."

Thus, rudely, Italy's attention was called to a new force in its national life, the marching Partito Popolare Italiano, the party organized on January 18, 1919, by the priest Don Luigi Sturzo, for perpetuating the ideals of Christian democracy. This was his stirring proclamation :

" To all men free and strong, who, in this grave hour, feel the high duty of co-operation for the supreme ends of the Fatherland. . . .

" . . . We uphold the political and moral programme, the patrimony of the Christian people. . . .

" . . . As the soul of the new society, the true sense of

94

liberty responding to the civil maturity of our people and the highest development of its energies; religious liberty not only for the individual, but also for the Church; for the unfolding of her spiritual mission in the world; liberty of teaching without a state monopoly; liberty of class organization without preference or privilege for any party; communal and local liberties in accordance with the glorious Italian traditions."

The men who joined the Popolari were mostly peasants and urban members of the Azione Cattolica, so it became known as the Catholic Party, although it was no more affiliated with the Vatican than the Centrum in Germany and Catholic parties in many other nations. Significant, however, is the fact that the *non expedit* of February 1868, which withdrew good Catholics from participation in elections, was cancelled ten months after Don Sturzo organized his party.

The leader in every way, character, appearance, action, appeared to be the opposite of Mussolini. He was a man from the south, a pacifist, a fanatic in his belief in human liberty, a radical social reformer like Savonarola, candid and frank and incapable of making compromises, lacking entirely in the urge to self-advancement. He was truly the shepherd of his flock, and his flock were all the poor and oppressed of the country. He loved them like brothers. Don Sturzo is an almost emaciated figure, the picture of asceticism, his gaunt eager, passionate, sincere face distinguished by a long narrow nose set between deep brown eyes, which seem to be afire with his great idea of Christian brotherhood.

He was forty just after the war, when he made his first political step by permitting his election as sindaco or mayor of his home town, Caltagirone, in Sicily. Here he collected a sum of money, bought 2000 acres of land, divided it among the poorest, and demanded that the agrarian reform, promised for decades, be accomplished without violent seizure and illegal confiscation.

> " Vogliamo le fabricce, vogliamo la terra,
> Ma senza guerra, ma senza guerra,"

sang Sturzo's adherents at the time the working-men had
seized the factories. " We want the factories ; we want the
land ; but without war," was their song and their policy.
On the occasion of the railroad, telegraph, and telephone
strike, Mussolini urging the men to use violent methods,
came face to face with Sturzo's party for the first time.
Sturzo denounced the strike because of its violence, and
helped the government to win.

In 1921, 1922, and 1923, as radicalism receded in Italy,
the Catholic Party grew in strength in parliament, and
eventually replaced Social Democracy as the chief opponent
of Fascism.

In these years Mussolini was still the anti-clerical of his
exile in Switzerland. In his public speeches he ridiculed
the Pope and made jokes about the size of Sturzo's nose.
In April 1921, he wrote : " Fascism is the strongest of all
the heresies that strike at the doors of the churches. Tell
the priests, who are more or less whimpering old maids :
Away with these temples that are doomed to destruction ;
for our triumphant heresy is destined to illuminate all
brains and hearts."

Don Sturzo, on the other hand, wrote of his chief
opponent : " Of mediocre culture and meagre political
experience, Mussolini has the brilliant qualities of the
extemporizer and none of the scruples of those who, convinced of an idea, fear to be false to it. . . . He can pass
from theory to theory, from position to position, rapidly,
even inconsistently, with neither remorse or regret. . . .

" Another quality which he possesses is his constant
ability to seize the moment, to profit by circumstances. . . .

" His friends and companions he holds in esteem so
long as they are useful to him ; he fears them when he
cannot do without them ; he abandons them to their fate
when they are in his way."

In February 1922, Don Sturzo was the leader of the most
powerful party in the Italian parliament. He was also
a great influence in the Church. In the conclave for the
election of a Pope in that month it was commonly said in
Rome that " Don Sturzo might in one day name his Prime

Minister and his Pope." But the priest had no such ambitions. Recounting the accomplishments of his party early
in 1922, he summarizes them in this way :

1. Entry of the Catholic masses into political life after
half a century of abstention.
2. Adoption of proportional representation in parliament.
3. Opposition to the Socialists, and to general political
strikes.
4. Collaboration with the Liberals and Democratic-
Liberals.
5. Bringing the question of freedom of schools to public
and parliament.
6. Contribution to the solution of agricultural and
economic problems.
7. Support of administrative decentralization.
8. Support of solutions of Yugoslav problem.
9. Early realization of the Fascist peril, and a stand
against armed violence.

On the debit side Don Sturzo wrote : " Strength wasted
in compromises with opposition and in collaboration with
the government ; lack of courage to take office when a
crisis arose."

The political war of 1922 was over proportional representation. " Here," commented Don Sturzo, " was a
source of friction between the old oligarchic currents and
the new wave of democratic life. The latter was therefore
labelled demagogy, or even, with the Russian term,
Bolshevism, and much was written against the Red
Bolshevism of the Socialists and the White Bolshevism
of the Popolari, and against their possible union.

" Therefore both Democratic Liberals and industrialists
and agrarians turned to Fascism as the force that could
save them. Thus was invented the fable that Fascism in
1922 saved Italy from Bolshevism. There was no peril of
Bolshevism in Italy, nor did Fascism save her from it. If
by Bolshevism is meant the agitations and disorders of
1919–20, up till the occupation of the factories, these were
already past history, and the general elections of May 1921

were evidence of the state of mind of the country and of its constitutional normality.

" There does not exist in Italian political life a more insincere phenomenon than the fear of Bolshevism on the part of the wealthy class in 1922 ; the latter had taken the offensive against the State by Fascist acts of violence, and had to justify both offensive and violence : this they could only do by crying out that there was peril of a Bolshevization of Italy in the near future."

In 1922 the Fascist squads attacked Catholic institutions with the same enthusiasm with which they had wrecked labour unions and co-operatives. The squadristi of Fascism stormed Catholic institutions, and murdered more than one parish priest ; but the Catholic leader insisted that violence should not be met with violence.

To conclude the tragic story of Don Sturzo, it is necessary here to disregard the chronology of the history of Fascism and its Duce. In April 1923, when, clubs and headquarters of the Popolari were again being looted and wrecked and burned, the party held its fourth congress in Turin, where it reaffirmed " its will to continue the fundamental battle for Liberty and against any centralizing perversion in the name of the pantheistic State or deified nation " ; it asserted its " solidarity with those who suffer for the idea and for internal peace, and invokes for the welfare of Italy respect for human personality and the spirit of Christian brotherhood." The party decided to remain independent, to protect individual liberty in Italy, to defend religion and the church.

Shortly afterwards Mussolini proposed a new election law. The " reform," as he so brilliantly called it, would give the party which obtained 25 per cent. of the total votes cast 66⅔ per cent. of the seats in the Chamber of Deputies, while the remaining 33⅓ per cent. would be divided among all other parties proportionately, thus making it possible for the Fascist minority to rule the anti-Fascist majority " legally."

Into the final struggle Don Sturzo put all his force ; while other parties still proclaimed liberty, his was the only

one which dared, in the face of Black Shirts armed with
rifles, bludgeons, and castor oil, openly to resist. But his
was passive resistance and his weapon chiefly an appeal to
reason and Christian morals.

His followers in hot-headed Calabria got out of control.
For every Catholic institution attacked they attacked a
Fascist institution, and in Naples and less important
centres the Catholics found that the employment of re-
taliatory violence was the one and only way to victory.
They beat Fascismo at its own game.

It was at this moment that Mussolini's envoys went to
the Vatican with a message which was also a threat. The
attention of the Pope was called to the fact that St. Peter's
and the Vatican were surrounded by Fascist bayonets,
and yet had not suffered harm. Unless pressure was
brought against Don Sturzo the Catholic churches and
the Catholic religion would suffer great harm.

On June 9, 1923, Don Sturzo sent his resignation to the
Pope, and on the 10th he departed for the monastery of
Montecassino and retirement. Some time later, no longer
sure of his safety, he went to London, where he is living
to-day, " recommended by Fascist newspapers to the
special attention of any assassin who happens to be idle
in England," according to Professor Gilbert Murray, who
befriended him.

That the Pope and the Catholic Church had been threatened with attack by Mussolini was admitted more recently,
when Don Sturzo wrote that " at the critical moment the
man who was believed by the Fascisti and philo-Fascisti
alike to be the pivot of the situation, the convinced adversary of Mussolini [meaning himself], left the leadership of
his party because of obscure Fascist threats of armed
reprisals against the Church. . . ."

In this way the last and most important political party
to dispute Mussolini's claim to dictatorship was eliminated
from public life. The epitaph was written by Don Sturzo :
" Fascismo came forward as an anti-constitutional and
revolutionary movement based on violence and direct
action. Popolarismo was law-abiding, constitutional, and

8

moral. Fascismo considers itself the absolute and sole manifestation of political life. Popolarismo looks on itself as a political party with rights and duties like any other party functioning in the plane of the modern state. Fascismo is against liberty, against democracy, against the parliamentary State. Popolarismo is for liberty, for democracy, for the parliamentary State. Fascismo upholds the nationalist, plutocratic, and imperialist State. Popolarismo upholds free trade, international co-operation, and peace. . . .

" The Popolari arose in the name of liberty, In the administrative and educational, in the social and religious, fields they fought for liberty in the teeth of the Democrats, the Liberals and the Socialists. . . . for liberty, based on the rights of human personality, is unalienable and cannot be surrendered for any material prosperity or alleged national right. . . ."

The unarmed prophet had failed, and the armed prophet again had won, as Machiavelli had informed Mussolini in his exile years.

PART II

THE CONQUEST OF POWER

CHAPTER XI

THE GLORIOUS MARCH ON ROME

AFTER the battle of Arques, which was fought through September and October of the year 1589, Henry, King of France, wrote to the Duke of Crillon : " Hang yourself, brave Crillon ; we have conquered at Arques and you were not there."

Just three hundred and thirty-three years later, almost to a day, occurred another great event, the glorious Fascist march on Rome, which has now become in the black-shirted minds of Italy, the noblest victory in all its history. Only a few years past, and in the memory of most men now living, this episode has become a marvellous myth. National hymns, popular songs, millions of photographs, hundreds of paintings, new sagas, and at least one made-to-order epic tell us how Mussolini led the Fascisti into Rome, and conquered Bolshevism.

The books of history are being rewritten. In Russia, Trotsky, the hero of the Bolshevik revolution, the military genius of the war with Poland, becomes in a decade a minor figure of no importance, if not an actual villain ; while in Germany a similar decade is wiped from the public mind to leave room for the inscription of the record of a new man. And so it has been done in Italy.

But if history has any value for the people who are its inheritors, it is indeed a simple task to right the record of which we ourselves are the witnesses and at times the participants. Was Trotsky a nobody ? Are a dozen years of the German Republic to be regarded solely as the story of Hitler's rise ?   Did Mussolini really slay the Red Dragon, and was he even present at the Arques of 1922 ?

That year opened for the European world with another of its supplementary conferences, which, despite a denial to Russia's claim to participation, and America's refusal to participate, was hopeful of accomplishing something in righting the wrongs of the Versailles congress.   Here in Cannes, on the French Riviera, hundreds of journalists of many lands were almost as important as the diplomats of the great nations.

Benito Mussolini came to Cannes as the representative of his own newspaper.   But neither he nor Fascism were at the time interesting enough to warrant attention from the American, British, or other noted journalists who had accompanied Lloyd George and Briand, and the premiers of Belgium and Italy and Czechoslovakia, and the sensational delegation from Germany under Walther Rathenau.

Among the Italians, however, Mussolini had an imposing reputation.   The press conferences which the diplomats of this country held were marked by Mussolini's violent outbursts of oratory, which would divide the assembly into hostile camps, the majority shouting the disturber into silence.

Notable among Italy's journalistic representatives was Pietro Nenni, Mussolini's successor as editor of the *Avanti*.   The two had not only worked together but, it will be remembered, during the anti-Tripoli war demonstration in Forli, had spent nights in the same prison, jointly cursing the government which had placed them there.

They were friends, they could talk with extreme frankness, and this is their conversation during a walk on the seashore, as Nenni records it :

MUSSOLINI : Civil war has become a tragic menace. I do not fear the responsibility.   The kindliness of the State forces the formation of a party to smash the Bolshevik menace, re-establish authority, save the victory.

NENNI :   The class of which you have become

the instrument, the right of the working-men to organize themselves for the defence of their social interests and for the conquest of power, is now called Bolshevism. The police personifies authority, and, as for victory, it is conceived only as a form for the survival of the military spirit over the civil spirit.

MUSSOLINI : I know everything about the sentiments of the class about which you speak. I am not their instrument. At a given hour, I have not hesitated to proclaim that one must escape from the bloody circle of violence.

NENNI : Your individualism always strays. I do not care what you have become. I am certain that lacking a sentiment of justice, everything that you do will be marked with the red iron of arbitrariness. The peace which you offer from time to time to my friends is for them a renunciation of their ideal. At that price the bourgeoisie is always ready to act. Moreover, you forget many things.

MUSSOLINI : What ?

NENNI : You forget the dead ; you forget that you were the chief of the Socialist Party ; you forget perhaps the working-men fallen under the clubs and the stilettos of the Black Shirts.

MUSSOLINI : There must be no sentimentalism in life. I know that the dead hang heavily. I frequently think about my past with a profound melancholy. But there are more than a few dozen deaths in a civil war. There were hundreds of thousands killed in the war. We must also defend them.

NENNI : The proletariat against whom you now direct your offensive, defends the dead by fighting against war and against militarism. Frequently they are mistaken in details, but they never mistake their ideal.

MUSSOLINI : Your friends must understand. I am as ready for war as for peace.

NENNI : You have lost the possibility of choosing.

MUSSOLINI : In that case, it will be war.

NENNI : For the past two years it has been war.

This dialogue occurred just eight months before the guerilla warfare, which Fascism had been waging throughout

Italy, was transformed into a civil war by Mussolini at the national congress which the party held in Naples in October.

"All armed prophets have conquered, and the unarmed have been destroyed," Mussolini had read and underlined in his Machiavelli. He had no intention of marching on Rome with the few bayonets of his own illegal Fascisti. He was not so foolish.

To take over the Italian government required not only the leadership of the Fascist squadristi, but the violation of the oath of fidelity to the crown on the part of many generals in the regular army, because it was quite evident that a regiment or two with their usual rifles, a few hand grenades, and machine guns, not to mention some gas bombs or perhaps one battery of three-inch guns firing shrapnel, could, in five minutes, have made the "march on Rome" what the cautious Mussolini, safe in Milan, feared that it would be, a bloody fiasco. But not a regular soldier moved.

The ambitious Duke of Aosta, cousin of King Emmanuel III., was another important part of the Fascist plot. He was a man of great ambition who believed himself the most capable member of the House of Savoy to rule the country. He had great influence with the army. It was one of his followers, General Vaccari, who succeeded General Badoglio as chief of staff, after the latter, who under Giolitti's régime had armed the Fascisti, had resigned. It was Badoglio who had from time to time made the declaration that the Fascisti were not to be feared by the King, because he would destroy their pretensions with one regiment in a few hours.

While the Fascisti were holding their congress in Naples on October 24th, a secret conference was being held in Florence, where Black Shirt leaders, chiefs of the regular army, representatives of the nationalists and the imperialists in parliament, and a representative of the Duke of Aosta, decided that the time had come to take over the Facta government. Even at this late date the man chosen as representative of the "New Italy" was not Mussolini, but the man of heroics, Gabriele d'Annunzio. But the poet refused. The second choice was not Mussolini, but General Peppino Garibaldi, who had led an Italian legion on the French front from the first days of the war. Garibaldi refused. Then it was that Mussolini was chosen, and that the Duke of Aosta's intervention with the army was promised on the basis of his receiving the regency.

The Duke went to Spoleto and put new oil into his motor car, filled up the gasoline-tank, and waited the word to ride into Rome.

Mussolini on the 24th made his big speech to the congress at Naples. It was a thundering speech. The time had come. The country had had enough. It must be saved despite itself. But from what ? From Bolshevism ? From Communism ? There is no mention of these terrible forces. Mussolini had thundered against them in 1920. Now Jove was sending his thunderbolts against—Democracy.

Under that vague term the following forces were joined : the several liberal parties, including the Catholics, Socialists, and Republicans (but not the Communists who had split from the Socialists and drifted weakly away) ; the labour unions with some 2,000,000 members ; and the co-operatives who, despite Fascist fire and sword, were remarkably flourishing in city and country.

The nation in 1922 had recovered from the economic and political chaos of 1920. When, some time later, the distinguished journalist, Hiram Kelly Motherwell, had charts and graphs prepared of the standard of living, exports and imports, rate of exchange, wages, unemployment, etc., from figures officially supplied by the Fascist government, these showed without exception that every line going up or down, all favourable to Italy, had the crucial favourable angle sometime between the end of 1921 and the first months of 1922.

Even the war-time national budget, which had caused deficits of scores of billions of lire in the first post-bellum years, was now about to balance. In fact, the deficit which the liberal premiers cut down to about half-a billion was to be replaced, thanks to the programme of economy outlined, by a flattering surplus.

So much for facts and figures. But the effects of these changes were as far-reaching. If, as figures prove, the standard of living of the Italian masses had gone up, if wages had gone up, if the co-operatives were flourishing, it was evident that some one had to pay for all these magnificent national achievements. These wages had been won by the series of strikes which had so disgusted American tourists and bankers ; but they disgusted even more the Italian employers who were forced by this demonstration of power and solidarity among the working-men to disgorge some of their war profits. Wages increased and the chambers of commerce, the association of metal factory owners, the national industrial associations, the industrial banks, and the employers' organizations which were sorely hit in their financial plexus, and whose thousands of newspapers could no longer raise the shout of " Bolshevism," because this red herring was now a dead herring, turned in their last extremity to the use of violence, in order to alter an economic situation.

The co-operatives were destroying private profits. Therefore the co-operatives must be destroyed. The labour unions were becoming arrogant. Therefore the unions must go. The liberal-socialistic régime in Rome was nothing but a school of gossips. . . .

It was to the financial interest of the big business men of the north to encourage the squadristi to plunder and destroy the co-operatives, the labour unions, the Socialist, and the Catholic institutions. But for the condottiere of the squadrist, Mussolini, it was the weak bombastic parliamentary system which became the objective of attack.

Italy was recovering. In a little while, perhaps only a few months hence, it would be too late to act. In August, armed Fascist bands indulged in a general campaign of terror in the large cities, and the labour unions, demanding that the government should use armed force to smash Fascism, called a general strike. This labour union strike, which had not one glint of red in its spectrum, was a miserable failure. Times were so much better, progress was so rapid, that few heeded the call to protest.

It was then that opportunity, which had knocked at Mussolini's door with the noise of cannon in 1914, and practically smashed in his door in 1919, again visited him. That same Will to Power, of which he spoke daily, that same " star of destiny " which he said guided him always, informed him, that, unless he made his bid immediately, the situation would be for ever changed and locked against him.

" I take a solemn oath," roared Mussolini, " that either the government of the country must be given peacefully to the Fascisti, or we will take it by force."

Again, as at Reggio Emilia and in the Socialist congress of Milan, the violent enthusiasm of the speaker communicated itself to the mass.

" A Roma ! A Roma ! " the Black Shirts shouted hysterically.

And again Mussolini became the master.

He had, as is well known, no intention of marching on Rome in October 1922. He did not know at first, as did d'Annunzio and later Garibaldi, that the military forces were conspiring for a *coup d'état* and needed a leader. Although the Naples congress was intended by him to be a test of his power, it surprised him by its readiness to risk a civil war.

On the 19th of the month he had written to his good friend De Santo, Italian, Fascist, and Rome correspondent of the *Chicago Tribune*—in fact, the predecessor of the present writer—the following letter :

CARO DE SANTO,—

I thank you for your many kindnesses in presenting the Fascist cause to America. I regret deeply that the American ambassador, Signor Washburn Child, does not seem very sympathetic to Fascismo, and I would esteem it greatly if you would take me and introduce me to him.

I am going to Naples in a few days. I do not think that anything of consequence will occur there, and on my way back to Milan I will stop in Rome, and hope you will make the appointment for me.

Cordially,

MUSSOLINI.

But instead of stopping in Rome to see the American Ambassador, Richard Washburn Child, Mussolini went from the Naples congress directly to Milan to lead his " revolution."

The secret of this section was a series of telegrams from Florence, where the military heads who planned the overthrow had made Mussolini their third choice. Among the generals who had betrayed their oath to the King and the Royal constitution were De Bono, Fara, Magiotto, Zamboni, and Tiby. And when they had been informed from Naples that Mussolini had accepted the leadership, they sent him the following telegram :

VENITE. LA PAPPA È PRONTA. LE MENSE SONO IMBANDITE. NON AVRETE CHE A SEDERVI A TAVOLA.
(Come. The food is ready. The dinner is served. You have only to seat yourself at the table.)

Thus revolution began.

On the 26th the Fascisti had sent an ultimatum to the government demanding the premiership for their party. Facta, the Prime Minister, replied by handing his resignation to the King. On the 27th Mussolini went back to his newspaper office in Milan, and the Fascist squadristi got their orders to move.

Under the command of many generals, they " marched " on Rome in three columns. From Umbria, Romagna, and Tuscany the Black Shirts came to Foligno, where General Fara took command and led them to Monterotondo, north of Rome. The men from d'Annunzio's Abruzzi assembled at Tivoli, under Bottai. Genoa, Milan, Bologna, and western seaboard cities and towns, north and south, sent delegations to meet at Santa Marinella, and, as their open trucks went slowly along the dusty roads, the Fascist civilians praised the adventure as friendly, while opponents said simply that it was child's play.

But when the concentration began the city of Rome was alarmed, and the garrison was put to work, stringing war-time barbed wire around some of the gates. On the morning of the 28th the general staff officers received reports that there were no more than 8000 Fascists in the neighbourhood of Rome, scattered, ill-clad, ill-fed and list-less.   Premier Facta, who could have sent a few machine-guns against them, or who could merely have surrounded them and starved them into jail or dissolution, did what was typically in the character of the parliament of that day and in himself—he did nothing but run around excitedly, talking, gesturing.

The King had returned from Pisa on the evening of the 27th.   Angry with the cabinet and particularly with the weakness of Facta, he threatened, " Before I'll give in to them I'll take my wife and children, and leave."   However, the King agreed to declare martial law.   Facta drew up the proclamation.   Certain of the King's promise, he informed the prefects everywhere to take the necessary measures to crush Fascism.

Meanwhile the Fascisti who were not " marching," were " storming " the public buildings of doubtful cities, occupying and holding the railroad stations, post offices, telegraph offices, armouries, all upon the invitation of the authorities.

Facta arrived early on the morning of the 28th with the degree of martial law.   The King weakened.   It might cause revolutionary bloodshed.   Facta, who had a con-summate will to surrender, was caught in the emotions of the King, and did not insist.   But when Facta tried to spread the emotional contagion to the cabinet, it stood firm, and at a few minutes after ten that morning the official news agency announced to the papers that the King had declared martial law.

With this *fait accompli*, Facta ran back to the King, who now firmly refused to sign.   While Facta had been trembling, the King had been acting.   He had received the head of the Nationalist Party, Federzoni, Admiral Thaon de Revel, and other imperialists, who made two declarations, one of which was untrue, and the other doubtful : they told the King that the Duke of Aosta was among the Fascisti outside the walls of Rome, and that he had 80,000 men ready to seize the crown, and that the army had refused to

fight against the Fascisti. The King was frightened. He
believed. He surrendered.

At noon the decree of martial law was declared null.
The King telegraphed to Mussolini in Milan to come and
form a government.

With shouts of joy men who had been scared put on
black shirts and, jumping into railroad trains, refused to
buy tickets, but shouted " To Rome ! To Rome ! " so that
by October 31 about 20,000 were assembled outside the
walls of the Eternal City.

But where was our hero all this time ? He was at the
head of the revolution. While the Black Shirts were riding
in crowded railroad coaches, much to the indignation of
American tourists, and commandeering trucks and even
peasant carts, Mussolini spent anxious moments waiting
for reports from headquarters, which the generals had established in Perugia.

One of the generals, Mussolini relates proudly, then
appeared in Milan with the news that the " offensive " was
proceeding excellently, and that there would be no opposition from the Royal army, or in fact from any of the forces
of law and order. " We know from very faithful and un-
forgettable friends," he repeated, " that the army, unless
exceptional circumstances arose, will maintain itself on the
ground of an amiable neutrality." There was no other
organized armed force in Italy. The liberals and the
radicals had no weapons.

But the leaders knew that there must be bloodshed to
have a revolution. Somehow or other there must be a
blood bath. Mussolini had asked first for the proletariat,
now for the Fascisti, if the thing were to be done properly,
successfully, and impressively. But not one report that
came in of all the street-cars occupied and all the railroad
coaches filled with " marching " Black Shirts, spoke of
anybody getting killed.

Well, if there was going to be no revolution in the open
countryside, perhaps there would be one in Rome or Milan.

" To the barricades ! On to the barricades ! " shouted
the future Duce, but there being nobody making an attack,

and no barricades anywhere to defend, he proposed building them around the *Popolo* office in Milan.

Soon the whole staff, including the women, were busy. Boxes, wood, the little carts which had been used for distributing the paper, trash of every description, were piled into the street, the silent unrevolutionary street, and the barricades arose as in once glorious Paris.

" I put on the Black Shirt.   I barricaded the *Popolo d'Italia*.   In the livid and grey morning, Milan wore a new and fantastic appearance.   Pauses and sudden silences gave one the sensation of great hours that come and go in the course of history.   Frowning battalions of royal guards scouted the city, and the monotonous rhythm of their feet sounded ominous echoes in the almost deserted streets."

Almost deserted.   The police kept away.   The enemy kept far away.   Only the Fascisti were busy running about, building up, moving around, shouting instructions, warnings, greetings, getting their guns ready, peering about for the trace or smell of an enemy.   The barricades were beehives and bedlam, but on the other side there was nothing but sunshine and dead quiet, dead sunshine and pale quiet.   Mussolini had protected his offices " with everything needful for defence."   He knew that " if the government authorities desired to give a proof of their strength, they would have directed their first violent assault at the *Popolo d'Italia*."   One morning he looked out, and saw machine-guns pointed at him.

" I had my rifle charged and went down to defend the doors.   The neighbours had barricaded entrances and windows, and were begging for protection.   During the firing, bullets whistled around my ears," reports Mussolini.

The bullets that whistled so melodramatically behind the heroic ears of " the Duce who precedes " came from behind.   All the confusion, all the hurly-burly of a revolution, was behind the barricades.   All the shooting was there, too.   The entire personnel of the newspaper, including the editors, among them Signora Sarfatti, the devoted, the hero-worshipping one, were behind the barricades making a noise of revolution.   It was midday on October 28 when the first firing was heard, when Mussolini, according to the eye-witness lady editor, seized his rifle and rushed down to the barricade : " At that moment he ran the greatest risk of his life. One of the young men who followed behind him, seeing him mount the barricade, levelled his rifle in the direction of the enemy and fired, the bullet grazing the head of the Chief and whistling through his hair just above his ear."

A frightened Mussolini did not at first know whether the bullet which " whistled around my ears " came from the enemy, or from one of his ardent followers. That shooting, the most memorable of the Fascist revolution, which almost caused the death of its leader-in-chief, resulted in a terrific uproar behind the barricade. With savage anger the staff of the *Popolo* threw itself upon the unfortunate Fascist, who had fired with good intention and bad aim. It was bent on a lynching. For a minute it did look as if there was to be some blood in this revolution, after all, as if there was actually to be blood upon a revolutionary barricade.

But Mussolini himself said, No.

He stepped down from the barricade, rubbing his head. He mixed in the fray, shouting down the would-be lynchers, extricating his zealous followers, and pacifying the others. There was no more shooting.

At midday on the 29th the telephone rang, and Mussolini was offered the place of Prime Minister of Italy. He had conquered.

The last attempt to keep him from his goal of power was made by some politicians. Just after the horrible episode on the barricades, the royal guard had made a peaceful arrangement, a truce, which provided for the removal of the machine-guns. " With that sort of armistice began for me the day of October 28." That night the politicians proposed a truce and armistice with the government itself. Salandra, a nationalist, one time premier, would take the job again, and conduct Italian policies more to the liking of the Fascisti. Mussolini replied :

" War is declared. We will carry it to the bitter end.

The struggle is blazing all over Italy. Youth is in arms. I am rated as a leader who precedes, and not as one who follows. I will not humiliate with arbitration this page of the resurrection of Italian youth. I tell you it is the last chapter. It will fulfil the traditions of our country. It cannot die in compromise."

Then came the telephone call. Guido Barella, of the *Secolo,* and also correspondent for my newspaper in Milan, thus vividly describes the scene in the office that afternoon. Mussolini still had the receiver to his ear. About him were grouped the staff of the paper.

" I will go to Rome," he replied without a tremor in his voice, " when the charge to form a Ministry is official." He hung up.

He stood still a second, his expression serene, his eyes far away. Then :

" My Ministry . . . ! " a dry hard sound like a sob was in his voice. " My Ministry will be thus . . . " ; half closing his eyes contemplatively, he added :

" If they will not accept my proposition, and allow me to put in the men I consider suitable for office, then I will have a Ministry that is entirely Fascist, from the president to the last office boy."

That evening he was still at his post in the newspaper office, a grey raincoat over his black shirt and uniform, a soft grey hat, as usual, down over his eyes.

More telephoning, more excitement, and we are within a few hours before his departure for Rome, in answer to a confirmatory telegram received from the King's aide-de-camp :

His Majesty King Victor Emmanuel begs you to come to Rome at once. He wishes to offer you the task of forming a new ministry.   GENERAL CITTADINI.

(Such was the lamentable state of communications of the execrable Facta régime that the urgent message from the King had taken hours to reach Mussolini, who had not trusted the telephone, and who had remained torn between doubt and hope and wonder.)

Notified by telegrams and telephone messages, the legionaries cheered and shouted :

" To Rome ! To Rome ! "

Time seemed to pass with uncanny swiftness. Of a sudden Mussolini was running down the stairs, and had disappeared in a waiting car.

Thousands of people had gathered in and about the station, as he slowly passed through the throng, alone, in his grey raincoat, hands deep in his pockets, his hat down over his eyes ; the shouting and applause increased until it was a mad delirium.

He was pale, paler than usual.

Flowers were showered upon him as, tranquil and serene, he slowly advanced through the dense crowd to the platform and the train.

He arrived at the steps of the special car reserved for him. The presidential train was on its way to Rome. The son of the blacksmith had become the Duce, and he was going forth to his unending fight.

Just before he left for the station, Mussolini turned over the barricaded *Popolo* to his brother Arnaldo. He then " asked the assistance of God." Still earlier in the day he had gone to the Fascist main barracks, where he had met his faithful friend and henchman, Cesare Rossi, and told him the " boys " could now go ahead, and burn down his old enemy newspaper, the *Avanti*. " I was in a terrible state of nervous tension. Night after night I had been kept awake, giving orders, following the compact columns of the Fascisti, restricting the battle to the knightly practices of Fascism."

As the train took him to Rome and power, the *Avanti* went up in flames, the first knightly act of victorious Fascism.

The Duke of Aosta was kept waiting at Spoleto. He had been used as a pawn, and now he was forgotten.

The Vatican had remained neutral but fearful. It knew that the young atheist of Lausanne was coming into power and anything might happen to the Church—bloodshed, fire, annihilation. The Pope sent emissaries to General De

Vecchi, member of the quadrumvirate, and to Dino Grandi, one of the politicians who had become a power in the north. De Vecchi and Grandi sent back word that the Catholic Church had nothing to fear, that, on the other hand, Mussolini had realized the necessity of having the co-operation of the Vatican in order to establish a successful régime in a country almost wholly Catholic. Mussolini gave orders to respect the Church and its property.

The Fascisti piled out of their trucks, street-cars, and trains and occupied Monterotondo, not far from Rome. Mussolini speaks of 100,000, but other reports say there were but 8000 of them. Both may be right. Only a few Black Shirts came to Monterotondo, yet, when the triumphal parade was reviewed by Mussolini several days later, their number had swelled to many tens of thousands.

Mussolini, some time afterwards, in one of his speeches, when he had worked himself up into a fury, mentioned " three thousand dead " as the cost of the glorious victory. But James Murphy, of the British diplomatic service, and Carlton Beals, the author, who were both in Rome reporting, say there were no dead. Murphy speaks of one boy who succumbed to fatigue as the full casualty list. It is most likely that Mussolini was thinking of the Fascist claims that they had lost several thousand members in all the years of street fighting from the time of the first organization until the glorious March on Rome.

As his train approached the Eternal City, Mussolini got out his black shirt and put it on. The fog lay thin and cold over the land, and the thin notes of a military cornet announced the arrival of *il duce che precede* (the leader who precedes) at Civita Vecchia. Thousands sang Giovinezza as the engine groaned its last.

" Where is he ? " shouted the frenzied multitude.

Pale, " his large eyes reflecting a soul on fire," he stood in the last car, " silently surveying the mob." In the raising of his hand for silence, " there was a feeling of history."

" The Naples Congress," he said, " has its logical conclusion in the irresistible march on Rome. Friends, his

9

Majesty the King has called me to Rome to form a government. I will form it. But I demand calm, order, discipline. It is necessary that nothing corrupts my victory.

" Princes, Triaires, Fascists ! Our movement is victorious. We have conquered without firing a shot, because Fascism has been more than ever stirring to the depths the strict and generous interpreter of the national conscience.

" Italy is in your hands, and we swear to place it on the road of its ancient glory.

" Viva Fascismo ! Viva l'Italia ! "

The crowd : " For Benito Mussolini. Eya, eya, eya. Alala ! "

Fascists, officers, regular soldiers, station hands, women and children cheered.

Mussolini got off the train, motored to the Quirinal in his black shirt, was introduced " without formalities " to the King. " I beg your Majesty to forgive me for appearing in your presence in uniform." he said, after kissing the royal hand. " I have just come from a bloodless battle which had to be fought." The King smiled. The next day some twenty thousand Fascisti who had arrived by train, truck, and horse-carriage, and the many thousands who had arrived after the " capture," were reviewed by Premier Mussolini and King Victor Emmanual together.

The photographs of this event to this very day are labelled " Mussolini leading the March on Rome." But like the Duke of Crillon at Arques, the Duce of Fascismo had not been there.

There was no revolution. No blood was shed. It was a military conspiracy to which the generals and the government were party and of which the industrialists in the north were the financial backers. Nevertheless, it was a great victory for the student of Machiavelli. " I was triumphant in Rome," he wrote triumphantly.

CHAPTER XII

THE VICTOR IN SEARCH OF A PROGRAMME

THE first Fascist dictatorship was established without the loss of a drop of blood. It was a sort of palace revolution, a conspiracy within the army—whole regiments wore the black shirts under their uniforms—at first a mere change in premiership brought about through armed intimidation instead of a plebiscite at the polls.

But a frightened Europe pounded on Mussolini's door, demanding whether he intended to suppress the labour unions ; whether he would respect Italy's obligations to the Allies ; if his policy was peace or war ; and if he would pay the debts to the United States.

Much to every one's surprise, Premier Mussolini announced the formation of the conventional parliamentary coalition government. Immediately the world breathed regularly again. Then, being a professional journalist and knowing that the press made and unmade all the political beds in Europe, the Premier, whose first act had been to proclaim a censorship, issued the following statement : " When conditions are settled I will restore liberty of the press, but the press must prove itself worthy of Liberty. Liberty is not only a right, it is a duty."

To the Allies he said : " France is dissatisfied with the peace and she is right. It is a bad peace. The war was not pushed to its natural conclusion. We should have finished it, you at Berlin, we at Vienna and Budapest. It is necessary to take the enemy by the throat. You have little chance of getting what is owned you. You were deceived. Germany has the will not to pay. She is dangerous."

To the masses he said : " The Fascist movement which

117

began as a bourgeois one, which has now become syndicalist, but of a national syndicalism, takes into account the interests of working-men and those of employers and producers. Please emphasize we are not anti-proletariat."

To the American journalists he gave a special session in the Hotel Savoia : " Nothing but good can be said about the United States. One always speaks well of his creditor— and we all owe the United States money."

The great day of the new parliament came. In his hand Mussolini held the sceptre of semi-legal power. As all the trains out of Rome carried the Black Shirt army, which had not fired a shot in its victory nor enjoyed the delirium of a revolution, back to its homes, the new Prime Minister stood at the head of a government in just the same relationship as his predecessors, the " cowards," " traitors," " incompetents," and " gossips " whom he had denounced. The cabinet was a coalition, continuing many democratic and liberal elements and policies. There was no dictatorship, only a faint rattling of the sword.

" Gentlemen," said the new Premier on his first day in parliament, " that which I have done to-day in this room is a formal act of deference towards you for which I do not ask any testimony or particular recognition.

" A revolution has its rights. I am here to defend and to strengthen to the highest degree the revolution of the Black Shirts by introducing profoundly, like a force of evolution, progress, and equilibrium in the history of the nation. [Applause, Right.]

" I could abuse my victory, but I refuse to. I am imposing limits. With my three hundred thousand young men, armed in every way, resolved to do anything, and so to speak mystically ready to carry out my orders, I could chastise all those who have defamed and attempted to throw Fascism into the mud.

" I could make of this hall, low and grey, a bivouac of corpses. . . ."

Applause, interrupted from the Right benches, where sat all the new parliamentarians who had won their seats by knife and gun. Murmurs of discontent from the Centre.

Protests shouted from the Left. " Long live parliament. Long live parliament," cried Modigliani to the cheers of his followers. The speaker's face grew darker.

" I could close this parliament and establish a government composed exclusively of Fascists. I could do it, but I have not willed it ; at least not for the present moment."

The Right benches remained silent, but the tumult on the Centre and Left increased.

" My adversaries have remained in their hiding-places ; some have tranquilly come out and obtained free circulation, profiting thereby already by spitting their venom and by attempting their ambushes.

" I have established a coalition government, not with the intention of obtaining a majority in parliament, which to-day I can very well dispense with [Applause, extreme Right], but to unite—to aid this suffering nation—all shades and parties who would save the nation.

" Before arriving here we were asked what was our programme. Alas ! it is not programmes which are lacking in Italy ; it is men and the will to apply the programmes. All the problems of life in Italy, all, I say, have already been solved on paper, but the will to translate them into facts is missing. The government, to-day, represents this will, firm and resolute."

But within a few days the old parliamentary game began. Having come into power without a programme—the ragged ends of several old and frequently changed programmes having proved inadequate—and unable to produce anything new except such words as " discipline " and " work " and " patriotism," the new Premier found himself the object of attack by all the Opposition and the neutrals. The great newspapers kept asking him for a programme, and the humorous weeklies made him ridiculous. A dog doctor had a big sign painted over his clinic with an English bull in the centre, a growling likeness of Mussolini, who, as a punster later put it, " hounded " the veterinary out of town. The *Becco Giallo*, or Yellow Beak, Rome's leading comic sheet, added fifty thousand to its circulation with

a series of articles on a modern, humourless, impotent, bellicose, weak, threatening, vascillating, furious, unvictorious
Napoleon. In Turin a journalist, Gobetti, launched irony
and sarcasm upon the theatrical conqueror. The entire
independent as well as the liberal and opposition press,
still untouched by draconic suppression, joined in exposing
the falsity of claims, the failure of action, the lack of definite
aims, the foolishness and fatuity and frustration of the new
régime and its blundering leader.

Fascism had come into power. It was powerless. So
long as legality remained, it was still possible to overthrow
the government by a vote ; if the Black Shirt militia were
to be mobilized again, it was possible that the second time
it would be met by armed force, now that its régime was
proving the same weak and ineffectual debating society
as its predecessors, and losing the confidence of neutral
leaders and the vast mass which had hoped for a miracle
in a few months. The lira, moreover, had continued to fall,
and the economic situation, which for three years of liberal
governments had grown better daily despite the enormous
payment of war debts amounting upwards to 25,000,000,000
lire in one year, now became worse, approached desperation.
Perhaps a second " march within Rome " would be a
failure.

From all sides came criticism, and criticism was one thing
this journalist, who above all others should have realized
and appreciated and valued, refused to hear. He knew the
power of the press and feared it. Criticism can crush
empires. He decided to smash it. Then there was a
stream of irony from the speakers of the Opposition and
from the comic press. This Mussolini could not understand
and therefore could not forgive. He began planning
revenge. In 1923 he organized the Cheka.

The chief enemy, of course, was his old party, the
Socialists. " Skilful and astute in every political art, they
protracted without end all the annoyances they could
devise. It was a game played with the deliberate aim to
destroy and tear down. In this subtle work of exasperation
Matteotti, the deputy, distinguished himself above all

others—he reached a degree of absurdity beyond that attained by any other Socialist."

What Matteotti did was to settle upon Mussolini like a gadfly, a gadfly armed with two stings, irony and humour. The wounds left were incurable because they required, in the blood of the dictator, a prophylactic, a lymph, an antitoxin which he did not possess.   Unable to heal himself he found he must destroy his adversary.

Day after day Matteotti would hurl at Mussolini the planks of the Fascist programme of 1919, the written and signed pledges of 1920, and conclude with, " Well, what are you going to do about it ? "   " You have written that ' the Italian revolution of 1920 [the seizure of the factories by the proletariat] is a phase of the Fascist revolution begun by Fascists in May 1915,' " Matteotti would say, holding aloft the *Popolo d'Italia* of September 28, 1920.   " Do you deny it now ? " and Mussolini would frown and double his fist, and keep silent because he could not answer.

" I see by your own admission that ' Bolshevism is dead,' " Matteotti would say, " and now you declare that the chief object of your party is to fight Bolshevism—you would not whip a corpse, would you ? " and Mussolini would not answer except by a threat and one of his favourite words, " coward " or " scoundrel " or " traitor."

" If, as you said, Italy saved herself when the Socialist Party expelled, in 1920, all the Communists and other violent enemies, how do you intend to save her again ; how do you explain the civil war which the Fascists have inaugurated, their destructions, their burnings, their assassinations ?   How do you explain it ?

" How do you explain that Fascism, playing the adultcress, has passed from the bed of the working-class to the bed of the capitalist class, betraying each in turn, at its whim, at its fantasy ?

" You have declared publicly and in writing that ' Fascism will never throw itself at the foot of the King, because the King has no identity with the idea of Father-and,' and you were the first to throw yourself at the foot of the King, you who had announced a Republic. How do you explain it ?

" You have proclaimed the moral right of the regicide, you have denounced financiers as brigands, you have fought the army, you have attacked the clergy, you have denied that God exists, and to-day you are the chief defender of these persons and ideas. How do you explain yourself ? "

Mussolini refused to reply publicly. But as he left for Lausanne to attend the Allied annual peacemaking congress, he gave Cesari Rossi, the one person to whom the word " friend " might be applied with any considerable correctness, the order to increase the Black Shirt militia to 500,000, a strength superior to the regular army of the King, and to organize within it a powerful secret political police which he called the " Ceca," and whose counterpart was then known in Russia as the Cheka, and now as the Ogpu.

Much to the amusement of those diplomats who knew the secret, was the tardy act of the Swiss government, which some seventeen years before had expelled an undesirable Italian emigrant, placed his name on the consular black list maintained at frontier towns, and who now was forced to expurge it and change all the police records of the new Premier of Italy, about to enter its peaceful borders.

" What is your foreign programme ? " asked Lord Curzon.

" My foreign policy is ' Nothing for nothing.' "

" Indeed," replied Curzon in his cold British Foreign Office way, " very interesting ! Very interesting ! And what has Italy to offer Great Britain ? "

Silence.

From that day on, for many years, Mussolini trailed Curzon like a good little boy and Britain had a lot to say in Fascist diplomacy.

Returning to Rome, he found parliament protesting, playing the old game of talk, and the Italian press, about 80 per cent. non-Fascist, exposing the assaults and violences the Black Shirts, now victoriously ruling, were committing in all parts of the country against Socialists, Liberals, Labourites, and Catholics alike.

All these Opposition parties, their leaders, and the press, united in shouting one question to the new Premier, " What is your programme ? " Never was a nation more puzzled over the supposed policies of a new régime. Fascism, the Opposition said, repeating Matteotti's words, had passed from bed to bed, like an adulteress, stopping a few months with the Communists, a little while with the Republicans, a long time with the syndicalists ; it had been liberal and anti-liberal ; it had proclaimed itself anti-Catholic and apparently had made a treaty with the Vatican ; it had supported the monarchists and the reactionaries, and had at last again proclaimed itself in favour of the proletariat. What was its programme ? What did it intend to do ?

On the eve of the 1919 elections Mussolini had written for campaign purposes the first programme of the Fascio di Combattimenti, helping himself liberally to the ideas of Karl Marx, as the following parallel will show :

Communist Manifesto of 1848	*Mussolini's Fascist Programme of* 1919
Abolition of property in land and application of all rent of land to public purposes.	Extraordinary tax on capital, progressive, causing partial expropriation of all riches.
A heavy progressive or graduated income tax.	Seizure of all property of the religious associations.
Abolition of all right of inheritance.	Seizure up to 85 per cent. of the war profits.
Confiscation of property of emigrants and rebels.	Formation of technical councils for industry, labour communications. . . .
Centralization of the means of communications and transport in the hands of the State.	Proletarian organizations to manage public services.
Extension of factories and the instruments of production in the hands of the State.	Realization of the rights of the railroad workers. (" The railroads for the railroad workers.")
Equal obligation of all to work.	Participation of the workingmen in the management of industry.

And if this original Fascist programme was not Karl Marxian enough, its author elaborated it in the fall of 1919, adding :

The creation of an Italian national assembly to be part of an International Assembly of All Peoples (*i.e.*, the equivalent of the Communist Internationale).

Freedom of thought, conscience, religion, association, press, propaganda, individual and collective agitation.

Creation of a national financial institution (*vide* Karl Marx, point 5, the national bank).

Confiscation of unproductive revenues.

All landed estates given to the peasants.

These two radical-Communistic programmes explain the possibility of Mussolini's negotiations with Buozzi, the head of the labour unions at the time Mussolini planned to make himself theirs and not the condottiere of the industrial associations of the North. It was Comrade Angelica who first opened the books of Karl Marx for the future Duce and taught him the ten points of the Communist Manifesto of 1848 ; it was Mussolini who remembered and rewrote them in 1919 ; and to-day in Italy it costs five years of a man's life to reprint the two programmes given above.

On the 10th of November of the same year of the revised programme Mussolini wrote " We are preparing not against the working-class, but in its favour.

" We are so little kindly towards the bourgeoisie that we have placed at the head of our programme the expropriation of riches, the confiscation of super profits of the war, a heavy levy on capital. *We will accept no dictatorship.*"

On the following day, " We are for liberty and against all tyranny."

And two days later, " The most sacred thing in the world —Liberty !

" In Italy there is no one who would be governed by any one who arises in the name of the Messiah, or a Tsar, or God the Father. We want liberty for all. We demand that the Universal Will govern us, and not the will of any group, or of any man."

Marching to victory, the Fascisti sang their now famous " Giovinezza,"

> " Youth, Youth, thou lovely thing,
> Time of springtime's blossoming.
> Fascismo brings the promise
> Of Liberty to the People."

But amidst the shouts of Liberty there were also mingled the sounds of the slogan inherited from d'Annunzio of Fiume, " Me ne frego (I don't give a damn)." Not a damn for anything but power.

" They ask us what is our programme," exclaimed Mussolini in a speech a month before the " march " ; " our programme is very simple. We want to govern Italy."

More specifically, on the 4th of October he wrote in his *Popolo* : " The imbeciles, Jesuits and Democrats, incessantly demand a programme of us. The Democrats of *il Mondo*, do they desire to know our programme ? To break the bones of the Democrats of *il Mondo*. And the sooner the better."

It was not until March 1923 that the new Prime Minister delivered himself of the famous blast against liberalism and liberty, and announced the first idea of the present Fascism programme. He wrote :

" Liberalism is not the last word ; it does not represent any final and decisive formula in the art of government. . . . To-day the most striking of post-war experiences, those that are taking place before our eyes, are marked by the defeat of liberalism. Events in Russia and in Italy demonstrate the possibility of governing altogether outside the ideology of liberalism and in a manner opposed to it. Communism and Fascism have nothing to do with liberalism.

" . . . The truth, apparent to every one whose eyes are not blinded by dogmatism, is that men are perhaps weary of Liberty. They have had a surfeit of it. Liberty is no longer the virgin, chaste and severe, fought for by the generations at the beginning of the last century. For the intrepid youths who present themselves at this new dawn of history, there are other words that move them more deeply, such as Order, Hierarchy, Discipline.

" In Italy that poor liberalism which fights and sighs for wider liberty is sadly behind the time. . . . Fascism, which was not afraid to call itself reactionary . . . does not hesitate to-day to call itself Illiberal and Anti-liberal. Fascism will not fall a victim to any childish whims.

" Know then, once for all, that Fascism recognizes no idols, adores no fetishes ; it has already passed over the more or less decayed body of the Goddess of Liberty, and is prepared, if necessary, to do so again."

Order, Discipline, Hierarchy ! The three words were taken up everywhere as summarizing the new regime.

" Hierarchy," he wrote a little later, " must culminate in a pinpoint," meaning, of course, without any intention to belittle, no other than himself, the Duce.

Of the original 1919 programme, which consists of seventeen points, only one or two have been remembered. The rest were immediately forgotten. Thus the Commission for Inquiry into the Expenses of the War (similar to the Congressional investigation in Washington into war profits) which the liberals had created, and which would have recommended a confiscation of those profits which Mussolini demanded, was immediately dissolved by Decree 487. Moreover, Mussolini threatened to punish severely any one who dared publish any information of the previous results obtained by the commission, which had already forced the return of several hundred million lire to the Italian treasury.

" Another *volte face*," cried the Duce's enemies ; " he is now the *condottiere* of the war profiteers."

There was no expropriation of the war profiteers, no expropriation of riches, no seizure of the property of the Catholic Church or other radical fulfilments of the programme ; there was no proletarian participation in industry, no abolition of the Senate, no proclamation of free speech and press, no division of land among the peasants. Yet the chief official biographer, Signora Sarfatti, writes that " in less than two years these demands (quoting the 1919 programme, but omitting the final third) had been translated into action by the Fascist government."

Chivalry alone prevents comment.

From Rome the unimpeachable authority, William Bolitho, wrote : " The whole baggage of Fascist theory, its nationalism, its royalism, its gospel of violence, its anti-parliamentarism, and its denunciations of the liberty of the press, its hierarchy and its history of the Pelasgian stock [the forerunner of the Hitlerian Aryan myth], are not clauses in a social theory, but a sophisticated word-spinning around the incidents of an energetic and unscrupulous man's march to power."

But powerful as Mussolini was, he was still not so strong as those who made his career possible ; he could not yet throw his financial backers overboard, nor could he defy the dangerous element which both had used—the army.

What thoughts were clashing in that egotistical mind in those days, what conflicts in his emotions, we can only guess ; but we know that all those plans for justice for the common people, the distribution of land to the enserfed peasantry, the expropriation of the universally hated war profiteers, and all the Communistic plans out of Karl Marx, were in the early days of Fascism no mere word-spinning, no sham demagogic banners to attract the masses. In his own muddled way Mussolini had made a compromise between Karl Marx and his own Ego, between humanitarianism learned out of a book and the inborn Will to Power, a compromise which made explanation and programme announcement difficult if not impossible. He temporized.

Much less difficult was the answer he made years afterwards when an interviewer asked him, " What is the chief problem of Fascism to-day ? "

" Its duration," he replied.

CHAPTER XIII

Personal Vendetta

EVEN before he took his first dictatorial steps, the coalition Premier dispersed his enemies. It was good political tactics, and it also provided the outlet for that powerful spirit of vendetta which had ruled his life from childhood.

He had been taught to trust nobody, and he trusts nobody to-day. " If the Eternal Father were to say to me ' I am your friend,' I would put up my fists against Him," one of his closest associates sympathetically quotes the Duce as saying, and again : " If my own father were to come back to the world I would not place my faith in him." It is the confession of a man who has gone through life friendless and alone. Mussolini never forgives, never forgets.

In 1923 he began his personal vendetta.

It will be remembered that the first to befriend young Benito in Switzerland was the Socialist Serrati—Giacinto Menotti Serrati, a native of Oneglia in Italy, an ardent syndicalist and, like Mussolini, an extremist of the Left wing at a time when Communism was merely a theory.

So closely allied were the two that Serrati made Mussolini welcome at his home. There the latter was treated as a child by the mother of the former. Signora Serrati not only gave him that motherly sympathy which the young man so intensely needed, but she fed him and washed his clothes.

All went well until one day Serrati's sister and her husband arrived for a visit. Then an unfortunate drunken event occurred. After a violent scene, Comrade Benito was asked to leave the house. They did not forgive Mussolini, and he never forgave Serrati.

The latter had drifted easily into extreme Socialism, had at one time been an envoy to Moscow, and at all times true to his radical upbringing. Mussolini had become the arch enemy of his own past and of every man connected with it. Some time after his arrival in Milan the new Cheka spies brought word that there was a radical conspiracy against the régime, and that among the leaders was his old friend Serrati. Serrati was arrested. But the trial for treason and " inciting class hatred " failed, and Serrati was freed. Mussolini greeted the news with fury. Turning to Cesare Rossi,[1] official of both the press bureau and the Cheka, he was reported as having said :

" The next time an affair like this comes along I will send a patrol of national militia to San Vittore to await the liberated prisoner. The judicial authorities may liberate him, but I will shoot him. Each man to his functions." But instead of shooting Serrati, Mussolini set his police agents on him, so that his old benefactor spent his remaining Italian years in misery.

The Mussolini-Nitti vendetta began in 1919, when d'Annunzio occupied Fiume and the first conspiracy to seize Rome was being organized. With Mussolini, the Futurist revolutionary poet Marinetti and several others were arrested on Nitti's warrants, which charged them with " armed plotting against the security of the nation."

Mussolini never forgave Nitti for the one night he spent in jail.

In the autumn of 1923 the Cheka informed Mussolini that Nitti had returned to Rome, and that Opposition deputies and journalists from New York and Manchester were callers at his house. Rossi, head of the Cheka, was consulted. According to him, Mussolini remarked :

" It looks as if the Rome Fascio does not exist, but remains inert regarding men of the Opposition ; otherwise it would make the presence of Nitti impossible in the capital."

Rossi admits he called upon Polverelli and Foschi, directors of the Rome unit, and told them the wishes of

[1] *Vide* Rossi memoranda.

the Duce. The three then decided to call out some university men and others of the squadristi to visit Nitti and sing " Giovinezza " under his windows.

But the small group soon attracted several hundred more Fascisti, and once the mob spirit prevailed it was determined to murder Nitti. The house was entered. But Nitti happened to be hidden in an upper chamber. Everything in the villa was destroyed, including the former Premier's archives and the manuscript of a book on which he was working.

Nitti fled to France. But Mussolini's vendetta did not end at the frontier lines. For several years not a month went by without spies and agents of the Cheka coming to Nitti to attempt involving him in an anti-Fascist plot. The purpose was to prove to the French government that the former Premier was conspiring while in asylum ; it was hoped that France would expel him.

How one of the latest Cheka plots turned out was told me one day by Vincenzo Nitti, son of the Premier.

" Among the spies who came to our house," said he, " were several persons we knew well in Rome and whom we trusted. One of them proposed to us that we finance a revolution. Another brought us complete plans for large-scale bomb manufacture ; if father would supply the funds and give his approval, he would make enough infernal machines to blow up the Fascisti, etc.

" But the best case is that of Signora B——, who arrived with clippings from the Rome newspapers saying she had been expelled from Italy because she was too anti-Fascist. She was a well-known actress, a young and beautiful and talented woman, and a friend of Mussolini's. I suspected at once that she was his agent.

" However, she and I became quite good friends. It was only when I noticed that she had a habit of taking papers—from coat pockets, too—that I became certain she was a Chekist. So I began planting all sorts of letters and documents, all of which she stole. In this way I was able to send directly to Signor Mussolini all communications I could not otherwise have made.

"But all the time I knew Signora B—— she pestered me about our underground press system. As you may know, we published here in Paris the *Becco Giallo*, the old satirical paper which Mussolini never could abide ; we used to photograph it from the big sheets and print the miniature plates on India paper, so that we could send thousands in a small package.

"Well, one day, at a café, I pretended I was very drunk, and the dear lady took advantage of that to ask me again to tell her in deepest confidence how we smuggled the propaganda into Italy. I told her we had two ways : whenever one saw a priest with an extraordinarily large stomach, crossing the frontier, you might be sure that under that black cassock there were several thousand copies of our publication. But our best way was in sardine-tins. In fact, the next day, when she confronted me with my 'confession' and I could not deny it, I had a working-man bring me a sample sardine-tin with a cover, and in it I placed ten copies of the *Becco Giallo*. I showed this to the Signora.

"What happened ? First of all, every fat priest crossing the frontier was hit across the stomach with the club of a Fascist militiaman, and, believe me, that did not further relations with the Vatican. But afterwards there was a diplomatic incident you may have read about. It seems that several thousands of cans of sardines were opened at the frontier. And every can contained sardines, and all were spoiled, and the French and Italian governments got to making nasty remarks to each other about this wastage.

"Then Signora B—— arrived one day and told me she had been severely admonished by Mussolini and was going away to Buenos Aires. 'You've betrayed ME,' were the last words of this spy. And away she sailed to ply her spying trade in the Argentine Italian colony. Of course I cabled our friends to beware. But new Cheka agents arrived weekly, trying to provoke my father and myself into doing something illegal, so that Mussolini could report it to the French Foreign Office and thereby revenge himself on our family."

10

Vengeance against his old newspaper and old colleagues
on the *Avanti* was carried out through many years. Mussolini's last word to Mme. Balabanoff and others of the staff
were words of faith in Socialism and in its journalistic
organ ; he would never forget them, the theory was part
of his blood, he could never betray them, never write
against them, always love them.

But the *Avanti*, restored to anti-militarist editors,
turned against Mussolini, calling him every vile name from
traitor to " hired assassin of the bourgeoisie," the latter
phrase being attributed to the woman who had picked him
out of a dark corner and made him a great man. After a
short campaign of vilification the *Avanti* decided upon
another course : it would ignore him completely, and a
rule was posted that his name should never be mentioned
in the columns.

This rule was kept until November 18, 1919, when the
Fascisti were completely whipped at the general elections
and their political death, as well as that of its leader,
generally (but prematurely) conceded. Said the *Avanti* :

" A corpse in an advanced state of putrefaction was
dragged out of the Naviglio yesterday. It was identified as
that of Benito Mussolini."

This was meant to be an obituary.

Ironic as was this incident, its sequel was tragic. For
Mussolini never forgives and never forgets. He cannot
survive irony. Writing of his parliamentary defeat of
1919 he said later :

" The *Avanti* wrote on that occasion a short notice about
me. ' A dead body has been fished up from the Naviglio.'
It was said in this note that in the night in the modest
Naviglio canal which cuts Milan in two, a dead body had
been picked up. According to the document they said it
had been identified as the dead body of Benito Mussolini—
his political corpse. They did not say that its eyes were
gazing ahead."

What Mussolini never forgot was the mock funeral
which the Socialists and the *Avanti* crowd held that day.
" The procession passed under the windows of my house

. . . I have not forgotten the episode, but I always see it. . . ."

The crowds had gathered in the streets. The Socialist victory had been impressive. Placards were printed with just these words : " Turati 180,000 ; Mussolini 4000," and given away, to be waved under the eyes of the landowners and the factory-owners and the gentlemen looking out of big offices and big club windows. Francesco Zanardi, known as the mayor of the poor folk, came out to salute the masses with a wave of his arms. Speeches were not necessary. There was no hatred, because the election had proved there was no enemy worth hating.

The funeral notice of the *Avanti* thrilled the crowd. Some one proposed a funeral procession, and soon a hack was found, a wooden box, coffin-like, placed on it, black drapings and funereal flowers. A man climbed on the shoulders of another and was carried ahead of the coffin, imitating a priest, singing a ribald litany, concluding always with his " Requiem æternam," to which the mob joyously responded " Amen, Amen." Psalms were parodied amidst laughter and applause. Numerous candles were lighted and relighted, and a sort of carmagnole atmosphere filled the city as vast crowds mocking Mussolini paraded before his house, calling, " Come on out to see your own funeral ! " and, " At last we honour you ! "

(It was two days later that the Fascisti threw a bomb at another Socialist march, and that the government, searching the Arditi clubrooms, found a lot of war material, all of which resulted in Nitti's order for many arrests, including Mussolini's.)

He always saw that ribald funeral. It rankled in his mind, it came back to him the moment he received the telegram from General Cittadini confirming the telephone call to Rome to take over the government. The first thing Mussolini did was to fulfil his vendetta. Rossi describes what happened that day : " The new president of the council, the honourable Mussolini, in this wise began his mission for the restoration of national discipline in October 1922 :

" Meeting me at eleven o'clock in the morning at a
school situated on the bastions of Piazza Nuova and
employed in those days as a barracks by the Fascist
mobilization, he gave to several of his brigades news and
an order. The news was that he had received a royal
telegram charging him to form a new Ministry ; the order
was ' to proceed during the day with the scientific destruction of the buildings of the *Avanti* and the *Giustizia*,
on the San Gregorio road.' "

The two newspapers were scientifically destroyed by
bands led by Negrini and Forni, the latter a Deputy of the
national parliament. The destruction was total. The men
of the Black Shirts, armed with guns, clubs, and fire,
smashed everything, tore up the books, broke the furniture,
and becoming frightened that the picture they left behind
them would be used against them, poured gasoline over
everything and set the buildings on fire. One old man
found in hiding was murdered.

Neither the militia nor the police, who were informed
that the building was being pillaged, made any effort
to stop the squadristi, and the firemen received an
order not to intervene until the vandalism was complete
and there was danger of the fire spreading to other
houses.

To the destruction of the *Avanti*, Mussolini's assistant
editor, Signora Sarfatti, points with pride ; she recalls the
racketeers marching four abreast, carrying a blood-stained
helmet, charred pieces of wood of the building, other
souvenirs of vandalism. " We had begun our offensive,"
Mrs. Sarfatti bursts out rapturously.

Mussolini himself defends it : " As an answer to the
anti-Fascist provocation I ordered another general mobilization of the Fascisti. . . . The Fascisti technicians were to
be brought together to continue the work in the public
services. The squadristi were to disperse subversive
organizations. The Fascisti of Milan assaulted the *Avanti*,
which was considered the lair of our opponents. They
burned the offices."

Another newspaper which Mussolini hated for its fairness, its honesty, and its liberalism was the *Corriere della Sera*. It stood in Italy as the leading honest newspaper, much as the *Manchester Guardian* in England, the *Frankfurter Zeitung* in pre-Hitler Germany, and the late lamented *New York World*. One day Mussolini denounced it :

" The *Corriere della Sera*," said the *Popolo*, " should be treated as a Jesuit and as a scoundrel, and above all, as a coward."

The same evening at eleven o'clock a bomb was thrown at the *Corriere*. Similarly, when the Fascist Minister Giuriati delivered a violent speech in Milan, attacking opposition newspapers, the Fascio again invaded and devastated the offices of the socialist *Giustizia*.

Mussolini first expressed his hatred for the *Corriere* on the day he founded his Fascisti, when, he admits, only fifty-four persons signed " our programme which was necessary to lay the foundations of a new civilization." The meeting passed almost unnoticed. The *Corriere*, however, did in fact mention it ; but " that great liberal newspaper dedicated to this news about twenty lines in its columns ! " The exclamation mark, Mussolini's, is the expression of his chagrin and disgust.

It turned into fury when the *Corriere* accepted Woodrow Wilson's proposal for arbitration on the Fiume boundaries. Treason ! shouted d'Annunzio's consul in Milan.

In 1923 the *Corriere* joined with Don Sturzo and all liberal elements in supporting the proportional-representation law and opposing the Fascist proposal which gave this minority party two-thirds of the Chamber of Deputies. As Fascism could not hope for a majority and yet desired to appear legal, such opposition was extremely dangerous to it. Finally, in 1924, the *Corriere* published the documents implicating Mussolini in political assassination ; and, since the Duce could not suppress his enemy legally, as he had no ground for libel and feared the popular reaction if he used violence, as in the case of the *Avanti* or the *Giustizia*, he smashed the great free liberal newspaper through an intrigue among the intimidated stockholders. When the

Corriere passed into Fascist hands the London *Times* said that Mussolini had made Italy suspected and incomprehensible ; the disappearance of the independent *Corriere della Sera*, it added editorally, was " a serious loss to European civilization."

CHAPTER XIV

The Assassination of Matteotti

BUT how was it possible for Fascism to rule a nation which was strongly anti-Fascist? Five political parties representing a majority of the people, the best part of the press, including all the great newspapers, the labour unions with their millions of adherents, the best minds, including Croce and Ferrero, in fact, all Italy except the associations of industrialists, the bankers, their commercial allies and their Black Shirt militia, opposed the new régime whose military conspiracy they had been unable to frustrate.

The only road from the dilemma was the suppression of the press and the elimination of the Opposition political parties. It was the road Moscow took after the attempted assassination of Lenin in 1918. But Mussolini, although envious of the Russian success, was still afraid to emulate its methods.

Meanwhile he was being attacked by internal enemies. The financial backers were demanding payment on their investment.

One day in the Chamber of Deputies, the now acknowledged speaker of the five Opposition parties, Matteotti, informed the nation that the Fascist State was paying its debts to big business in many ways; it had secretly used public funds to refloat the Ansaldo enterprise, which was near bankruptcy; it had purchased 18,000 shares of the Mineral Oil Refinery of Fiume; it had rescued the Banca di Roma, and it had permitted the heavy industry Consortium to draw upon the banks of issue for credits, in addition to obtaining secret subventions. Moreover, the Fascist régime was engaged in a deal by which the Sinclair Oil Company of America would obtain a monopoly in Italy;

although the American corporation was acting legitimately, several of the highest members of Mussolini's staff were attempting to make millions in graft out of this enterprise.

Matteotti's second point of attack was the corruption of academic liberty in the universities.

His third was an exposure of the violence by which the Fascist victory at the April 6th elections had been achieved.

With a hint of these scandals which he intended to expose by documents in subsequent speeches, Matteotti on the 30th of May 1924, began his campaign against the régime, while Italy listened breathlessly and with secret satisfaction.

" In the last election," said Matteotti, " the government, having declared that it intended to remain in power no matter what the result, nevertheless implemented this declaration by employing its armed militia. . . ."

Mussolini interrupted. " Enough. Stick to the question."

MATTEOTTI : The honourable president perhaps did not hear me. I am speaking of the elections. There exists an armed militia whose fundamental purpose is to sustain a certain chief of government, well known to you, a certain duce of Fascism, and not, as with the army, the head of a state. Now while the law says that the militia must abstain from all political functions, we saw throughout Italy that this militia . . .

FARINACCI : You must have seen the Balilla (the Fascist boy scouts).

MATTEOTTI : In truth, Honourable Farinacci, it was the Balilla which in many disricts did the voting.

The orator then began the list of violences. As each shout of " liar " and " falsifier " and " prove it " arose from the Fascist benches, Matteotti brought out the sworn statements, the Fascist newspapers, the Fascist orders for violence. Mussolini squirmed and scowled.

MATTEOTTI : And at Genoa, when the Honourable Gonzales [a member of parliament] came to address a meeting, the hall was invaded by Fascisti who blackjacked . . . "

Voice from Fascist benches : " Liar."

MATTEOTTI : Well, then I will correct myself. If the Honourable Gonzales spent eight days in hospital it means that he had wounded himself, that he had not been blackjacked. The Honourable Gonzales is a disciple of Saint Francis—perhaps he flagellated himself . . . .

MUSSOLINI : Honourable colleagues, I deplore what is happening. Honourable Matteotti, be brief ; conclude !

MATTEOTTI : I will limit my statement to a nude and crude exposition of facts. . . ." He cited case after case in which members of parliament as well as other speakers had been assaulted by Fascist racketeers. As each new name was added the tumult increased.

MUSSOLINI : Conclude. Honourable Matteotti, do not provoke scenes !

MATTEOTTI : I protest. If you cannot see that it is the others who are stopping me, who are making scenes . . .

MUSSOLINI : Well, you've finished ! Let the Honourable Rossi speak.

MATTEOTTI : What's the idea ? It is your duty to protect my right to speak. I am merely reciting a list of facts. I have the right to be respected.

MUSSOLINI : Let the Honourable Casertano speak.

MATTEOTTI : I protest.

MUSSOLINI : Well, then, speak, but prudently . . . .

MATTEOTTI : I do not desire to speak prudently nor imprudently, only parliamentarily.

MUSSOLINI (with a gesture of disdain) : Well, speak !

MATTEOTTI : The Honourable Piccinini was assassinated in his home for having accepted nomination against the Fascist list. . . .

The list of murders and assaults were continued.

There followed a description of election-day terror—assaults, stuffed ballot-boxes, forcible prevention, threats of death to every elector not a Fascist.

" And so," continued Matteotti with smiling sarcasm, " only a small minority of the Italian people was allowed to vote, and these citizens can hardly be suspected of being Socialists."

In a previous speech Mussolini had listed many political crimes and acts of violence. He repeated the Fascist propaganda claim that Fascist crime was always in self-defence against the criminal provocation of the Socialists. Matteotti took up the crimes one by one ; in every case he quoted Mussolini's own newspaper or the impartial *Corriere della Sera*, the findings of the courts, and the police records ; in every case Matteotti proved from Fascist or neutral sources that the aggressors were always the police or the Fascist squadristi.

Mussolini could not conceal his hatred or his raging anger. Matteotti, like a young apostle, spoke " with inexhaustible energy, indomitable tenacity, with inspired fervour, obstinate, implacable, accomplishing his sacred mission at all costs."

When the Deputies walked out of the Chamber that evening and all the liberal elements clustered around Matteotti, congratulating him, he said, laughingly : " And now, my colleagues, you may prepare my funeral oration for the Chamber."

It is a fact that it was that very day that the Fascist Cheka discussed the case. On the morning of the 1st of June appeared a front page editorial in the *Popolo d'Italia*, unsigned but written by Mussolini,[1] demanding physical violence against Matteotti. The epithets and threats in the Chamber were not enough, said the editorial ; what was needed was a more tangible acknowledgment.

But the first speech of Matteotti's concerning the fraudulent election and the facts known throughout the country of the two forthcoming speeches were having a tremendous political reaction. Mussolini felt it necessary to defend himself, and did so with amazing Machiavellianism. Suppose it were established, he said, that a million and a half votes cast for the Fascist list were fraudulent, the Fascist Party would still remain in power as the rightful representative of the nation.

" You of the Opposition," he continued, " complain that you were restrained from holding free election

[1] The original biography was kept by Fasciolo, the Duce's secretary.

meetings. What of it? Such meetings are of no use, anyway."

But the damning climax came a few days later. Mussolini lost his head completely. On the 6th of that crucial June, with Matteotti scheduled to make his most dangerous revelations of Fascist violence and financial corruption on the 10th, when the atmosphere throughout Italy had become evidently hostile, and the other Opposition leaders continued the Matteotti policy of irony and iron facts, Mussolini became almost hysterical with hatred. When one member drew a parallel between Fascism and Bolshevism, Mussolini shouted :

" In Russia they are great masters. We have only to imitate what is being done in Russia."

Uproar followed. Approval. Disapproval. Shouts. Waving of fists, the Right and Left benches threatening blows.

" They are magnificent masters," Mussolini repeated. " And we are wrong not to imitate them in full, or you would not now be here—you would be in jail."

Uproar. Applause. " We've just come from there," shouted a Communist.

" You would have a bullet through your spine," roared Mussolini. Another interruption. " We have the courage. We will prove it." Applause from the Fascisti. " We are always in time," continued Mussolini, " and it will be done sooner than you think."

That same evening a journalist named Carlo Silvestri met Cesare Rossi, co-director of the Cheka. Rossi, so Silvestri later and at the risk of his life testified under oath, said to him :

" With people like Matteotti the only thing to do is let the revolver speak. . . .

" If they knew what passes through Mussolini's head at times they would lie low.

" Mussolini is fully determined to carry out his threats. Any one who knows him must know that every now and then Mussolini needs bloodshed—and counsels of moderation will not always prevail."

A boy of twelve, to whom Matteotti had been pointed out frequently as a " great man " since he was a member of parliament, and an old woman dozing in her doorway but suspicious over the actions of five men and their automobile, were the two accidental witnesses who betrayed the murderers, and almost caused the downfall of Fascism. The woman had noted the number of the automobile.

" Porca Madonna ! Bastava avessero pisciato sulla targa," Mussolini exclaimed to his secretary, Fasciolo, when he heard about this old woman.

The boy testified :

" I was playing with my companions. Near us was a motor-car which had stopped just by Via Antonio Scialoja. Five men got out and began walking up and down, up and down. Then I saw Signor Matteotti come out. One of the men went forward and, when near him, gave him a violent push, making him fall to the ground. Signor Matteotti cried out. Then the other four men came up and one of them struck him a hard blow in the face. Then they took him by his head and feet and carried him into the car which came by us. So we were able to see that Signor Matteotti was struggling. We saw nothing more afterwards, as they rode away."

Of the five men in the car the ringleader was Amerigo Dumini, Rossi's colleague in the Cheka, and a " household friend " of Mussolini. He was American born, his father having emigrated from Italy and settled in St. Louis, where he married an American woman, Jessie Williams. Returning to Italy, Amerigo followed the calling for which he had been trained in American slums ; he was a common gangster. In Italy he was first heard of as coming and going in Mussolini's office in Milan, and in Mussolini's home. After he had committed his first murder, and the Milan Fascisti under Mussolini's guidance had saved him from punishment, Mussolini began to use him for various purposes. Several times a week Dumini called to receive the " suggestions " of Mussolini and Rossi.

Like a bad man in the bad days of the American Wild West, Dumini made notches on his revolver for each mortal crime. Just before the Matteotti assassination he got into the habit of introducing himself boastfully as " Amerigo Dumini—Eleven murders." Confident that he would be freed, he boasted of the death of Matteotti.

Kidnapped, beaten, stabbed, mutilated, burned, parts of the body of Mussolini's great political enemy were buried, disinterred, left for the foxes and pariah dogs to worry, then buried again. There is no evidence of the report that part of the body had been sent to Mussolini as proof of death ; but there are confessions that bloodstained garments, the passport, and other identity papers of the murdered man were sent to him. With blood on their hands and jubilation in their voices, high officials of the Fascist Cheka came immediately to Mussolini's office to tell him that the enemy was dead.

Parliament had waited, some members angrily, some anxiously, for Matteotti to deliver the last and most dangerous of his accusations ; he had already proved that the election was a fraud ; now he was to prove that most of the Fascist mandates were obtained by fraud or violence, were invalid ; that the Fascist Party, in fact, had no right to occupy the majority benches in the Chamber. Such an exposure at a time when the nation was pretty tired of Fascist pretensions and Fascist violence, and the failure of the régime to redeem its radical promises, could have brought on a new election, with the probable defeat of Fascism.

As the hours passed and Matteotti did not appear it was rumoured that he had been killed. In fact, there were such whispers hours before the murder had been completed. Because that was the mood and circumstance of the nation in those days : when a prominent liberal somehow failed to keep an appointment, to arrive for dinner in time, to show up in his office at his usual hour, it was taken for granted that he must have fallen in with some of Mussolini's glorified squadristi, been beaten up, forced to take castor oil, or murdered. Therefore the Left benches whispered tragedy.

The next day the whispers became loud. They penetrated the inner circle. Turning to faithful Rossi on their way back from Montecitorio, Mussolini said with that heavy sarcasm which his admirers call a sense of humour : " The Socialists are disturbed because they cannot find Matteotti —he must have gone to a brothel ! "

On the morning of the 12th, Rossi not only informed Mussolini that Matteotti had been assassinated, but that " the murder can only have been the work of people belonging to the Fascist Party Cheka." Later in the day Filippelli rushed in frantically with the same news : Matteotti was dead, the Dumini gang had killed him and buried him.

That afternoon Signora Matteotti came to parliament seeking news from her husband's friends. Mussolini sent a messenger asking her to the Foreign Office.[1]

When the widow arrived in the magnificent hall of the Palazzo Chigi, Mussolini sprang to his feet and stood at attention, as before a high officer. The effect of this gesture was to cause Madame Matteotti's collapse in tears.

" Signora, I should like to restore your husband alive to you. You may be assured that the government will do its utmost duty. We know nothing for certain, but there is still some hope."

The murderers had confessed. The hired assassins had come with their proofs, the blood-stained clothes ; the body had been hacked to pieces, burned, buried ; the chief of police had been informed, and he had told Mussolini. But, there was still hope !

The widow of Matteotti was led to the door by the Duce himself. He bowed her out. Returning to his desk, he immediately sent for Rossi.

" There is nothing to be done," he said ; " the boys have made too many mistakes. I am powerless. De Bono is good for nothing. All under suspicion must be patient. I must have my hands free to make the counter-attack. The hour of revenge will come."

At 7.30 that evening, Mussolini, addressing the Chamber, concluded : " I hope that the Honourable Matteotti will shortly be able to resume his place in parliament."

[1] Rossi's memorandum, Salvemini's translation.

That night Dumini was arrested.

The next morning there was panic in Italy.

Mussolini ordered his militia to mobilize. In Rome itself only half its strength responded ; in Milan, the birth-place of Fascism, the Duce's own bailiwick, only a quarter responded ; and no one answered the call to the black colours in the industrial city of Turin.

On that day and the following days the pictures of the most photographed man in the world were torn from the walls of Italy, or smeared with the words, " Assassin " or " Morte a Mussolini." From the liberal printing-presses came a flood of pictures of Matteotti which were pasted over that of the Duce with " Viva Matteotti " in red paint. The black shirt and the black cap disappeared from the streets, the leaders of Fascism were in tremulous hiding, and a cry for freedom and liberty arose throughout the land.

Cardinal Maffi of Pisa, the most brilliant mind, the most liberal thinker in the Catholic Church, telegraphed to Mussolini : " As a priest, I weep ; as an Italian, I am ashamed."

The King considered calling upon the loyal army, proclaiming martial law, abolishing the illegal Fascist militia, restoring democratic government. But he was afraid. The Opposition parties had only to take one decisive action. But for four days they talked and talked, because they foresaw the killing of two or three hundred men in the rioting which must ensue before Fascism was abolished. Despite the fact they had already lost four thousand men, killed in fighting with the Black Shirts, they decided not to shed more blood, but to hope for peaceful evolution without action.

During those four days Fascism was a living corpse. But there was no one willing to kick it into oblivion.

On the day of the panic Mussolini addressed the Chamber. That brave man of twenty feminine biographies, that soldier-hero who loved to taunt the Austrian army by perching himself on the parapet of the front-line trenches, that demigod of power who never knew fear, the implacable, the pitiless Mussolini, arose ; but his body slumped ; he spoke, but his words trembled, his gestures were pale, ineffectual. He was a whipped man.

" If there is any one in this hall who, more than any person, should be heart-broken, even exasperated," he said, in a voice no one recognised as Mussolini's, " I am that person. None but one of my enemies who would during the long nights consider such a diabolical action could have committed the crime which to-day strikes with horror and makes us cry out in indignation. . . .

" The situation, gentlemen, is extremely delicate . . . one must deplore, one must condemn, one must push on with the inquest for the search of all the guilty and all those responsible, and we are here to repeat that all this will be done, tranquilly, inexorably. . . .

" The law will be executed. The police will deliver the guilty to the judicial authorities. . . . One must be calm and refuse to amplify this terrible and stupid incident into a question of general politics and of the policy of the government. . . .

" Justice will be done, must be done, because the crime is a crime which is anti-Fascist and anti-nation. It is more than horrible, it is of a bestial humanity. One must not hesitate before such an act to separate crime from politics."

Justice, of course, was never done. Dumini, it is true, was in prison, but Dumini was a household friend and could be relied upon to keep his mouth shut. That very day agents went to the other four murderers and gave them money to flee the country. And years later Mussolini was able to comment in his autobiography :

" One day Matteotti disappeared from Rome. Immediately it was whispered about that a political crime had been committed. The Socialists were looking for a martyr who might be of use for purposes of oratory, and at once, before anything definite could possibly be known, they accused Fascism. By my orders we began a most painstaking and complete investigation. The government was determined to act with the greatest energy, not only for the sake of justice, but also to stop, from the very first moment, the spread of any kind of calumny. I charged the prefect and police chief of Rome, the Secretary of the Interior, Finzi, and the chief of the press office, Cesare Rossi, with the task of clearing up the mystery. Unstinted activity on the part of the police for the discovery of the guilty persons was ordered. Very soon it was possible to identify the guilty. They were of high station. They came from the Fascist group, but they were completely outside our responsible elements.

" . . . It seemed hardly possible that only a few days after the opening of the twenty-sixth legislature a group of men of position could carry through an enterprise which, begun as a jest, was to end in a tragedy. I always have had harsh and severe words for what happened. . . . "

To this same Cesare Rossi, Mussolini's right-hand man, his most intimate friend from his Socialist days and the writer of eulogistic prefaces to innumerable biographies of Mussolini in the days of Fascist triumph, all the acts of violence of the two years of Mussolini's rule were not jests, they were the bloody realities of successful government. Now on the 14th of June he saw himself made the sacrificial goat of the hierarchy. He went into hiding. But before he did so he wrote a confession, which he intrusted to his friend Virgili, saying it was to be published only if Mussolini betrayed him, and he sent a similar threat to Mussolini.

The Rossi " memoriale " lists criminal acts Rossi charges against the dictator, in addition to complicity in the Matteotti murder. Rossi concludes :

" All this happened according to the direct will or complicity of the Duce. I allude to the clubbing of Deputy Amendola, the order given De Bono, commanding general of the Fascist militia and director of the police, by Mussolini, unknown to me and executed by Candelori, console of the militia ; the beating of Deputy Misuri carried out by Balbo, generalissimo of the militia, at the suggestion of Mussolini ; the aggression upon Forni, a candidate in the April elections, for which the order was given me personally by Mussolini, and carried out in agreement with Giunta, secretary-general of the Fascist Party ; the attack on the villa of ex-Premier Nitti ; the

II

recent demonstrations against the Opposition parties ordered by Mussolini to be undertaken by Foschi, secretary of the party for the province of Rome : the proposal advanced by Mussolini to the Quadrunvirato, the central assembly of the party, in order that the Honourable Ravazolo, a Fascist Deputy, should be given a well-earned lesson in consequence of his insubordination ; the destruction of the Catholic clubs in Brianza, ordered by Mussolini, carried out by the Fascist Deputy Maggi, and then complacently repeated to me. I add that daily Commandatore Fasciolo, Mussolini's secretary, had the order, at the suggestion of Mussolini, to forward to the Fascist locals the names of subscribers of the *Voce Republicana*, *Avanti*, *Giustizia*, *Unita*, *Italia Liberia*, et cetera, so that the subscribers might be dosed with castor oil and clubbed."

In a second memorandum Rossi lists thirty-seven murder and clubbing orders or suggestions from Mussolini. Number 13 : " Mussolini expressed his regret that we did not succeed in beating up Matteotti on his way home from a convention." Number 32 : " Mussolini ordered the founding of the Cheka." Number 36 : " Mussolini's ambiguous relationship to the assassination of Matteotti."

" I, Cesare Rossi," he concludes, " who by his order have been left in the lurch, accused, vilified, and made out to be a liar, have no longer any duty to remain faithful to Mussolini or to conceal the truth.

" I have also lost all faith in the régime and the Fascist Party which accepts and approves not only these acts of violence, but also all terrible crimes. Mussolini, the government and the party, in June made a political crime out of a tragic crime ; it is due to the blind egotism of the Duce, the perfidy of General de Bono, the apathy of the party, and the panicky anxiety of the masses.

" I publish this memorandum to protect my honour. I feel also that I am taking a wise and necessary step in the service of my fatherland. With a firm hand and a clear conscience, I sign, CESARE ROSSI."

But clear as that conscience may be, this same Rossi, as head of the Cheka, stands accused by all parties in Italy,

Fascists, anti-Fascists, Catholics, and Republicans, for many of the crimes he himself lists, including that against Matteotti.

Other leaders of Fascism were going into hiding, fleeing the country, or protecting themselves against Mussolini by writing out confessions to be entrusted to friends or journalists. Filippo Filippelli, director of the Fascist Rome organ, *Corriere Italiano*, in his memorandum given to the journalist Naldi, and attested by him later before a magistrate, accuses not only Mussolini and the assassin Dumini, but also Rossi; he speaks of the agreement for the murder by these three leading gentlemen, and details their complicity. Filippelli relates the events of the Wednesday, June 11, when, alarmed by the news of the disappearance of Matteotti and the rumours that the Cheka had acted, he went to Rossi, who, he testifies, made the following statements:

" That Dumini had told him that he had used the car which in all good faith I had lent him;

" That the matter was serious;

" That Mussolini knew everything;

" That Marinelli and he (Rossi) had given the orders after previously agreeing with Mussolini;

" That the thing must be hushed up, otherwise Mussolini himself would be smashed."

The Filippelli memorandum continues:

" I thought it expedient to inform De Bono, Finzi, Marinelli, and others. From Finzi and others I learned that:

" The victim of Dumini's outrage was Matteotti;

" That the order to suppress him had been given by the Cheka of the National Fascist Party, of which the executioners were Dumini and others well known to Mussolini, who knew also of this special mission:

" That they had had an interview with Mussolini that day [June 11th] and that they had handed to Mussolini the papers and the passport of Matteotti as proof of his disappearance."

Filippelli fled. Mussolini sent his secretary, Fasciolo, to

Rossi, to make terms with him and to ask him to leave Rome. Finzi, seized with the same panic which had driven Rossi and Filippelli to write confessions, made a testament which he gave to his friend, Schiff-Giorgini, and the journalist Silvestri. Finzi's brother told Guglielmo Emmanuel, Rome correspondent of the *Corriere della Sera*, the Hearst International News Service, and the *New York American*, the contents of the confession.

The search for scapegoats continued ; the panic continued, and still the Opposition talked and refused to ask the King to outlaw the outlaw party. Mussolini had Filippelli dragged out of hiding and taken to prison ; he ordered General de Bono to resign as chief of police, and he himself made one of the grandiose gestures of his careers : he gave up one of the many portfolios he, as dictator, had accumulated for himself ; he resigned as Home Secretary, and as a sop to the monarchy and the Vatican, both unfriendly now, he named Federzoni, head of the old Nationalist Party, Royalist, and Catholic, in his place. Throughout Italy members of the Fascist Cheka were placed in jail. Rossi was finally arrested.

Humbly, very humbly, Mussolini began to make amends. To the Chamber he said on the 24th : " The crime against the person of the Honourable Matteotti has wounded and moved profoundly Italian public opinion, which is loudly calling for justice.

" The voice has been and will be heard.

" . . . Out of this crime, which has had profound repercussions on the national conscience, there may be born a period of concord and peace among the Italian people."

On the 26th of June Mussolini abandoned the dictatorship !

With tears in his eyes.

He had in his pocket the letter from Rossi calling him a doomed man—the letter smuggled out of jail, saying, " If during the coming days you fail to furnish me with proof of solidarity, not so much for the past and for my position as your collaborator and executor of our sometime illegal orders, but of your solidarity for essentially governmental reasons, I shall put into effect what I told you. I deem it superfluous to warn you that if the revolting cynicism which you have displayed up to now, complicated by the fear which has seized you just at the time when you should dominate a situation created exclusively by you, should impel you to order free violence, while I am in jail or in the unfortunate case of my arrest, you will be an equally doomed man, and with you will be destroyed the régime . . ."

With tears in his eyes the " doomed man " addressed the leaders of Fascism in the magnificent gold and brocaded Palazzo Venezia.

" There is no longer any question that Matteotti was assassinated," said Mussolini ; " it is no longer a question whether six or fifteen or twenty or thirty individuals are in prison, it is no longer a question whether the Ministry is to remain or to be transformed, if the party is to be cleaned : one sees now clearly the goal of the Opposition. It is the régime itself. They propose to annul all that it signifies, from the point of view of morals and politics. I declare to you I do not propose to see annihilated a state of things which we have created with grand efforts, with much pain, with, indeed, much bloodshed. . . .

" I admit that the militia should be promptly included in the armed forces of the State.

" And because I have been reproached for not having let it take the oath of allegiance to the King, I undertake to have that formality executed now.

" What will be my programme ?

" What I have said before, I repeat. I propose to have the Chamber, parliament, function. I repeat : it is my intention in the future not to issue decrees, because if the government makes its own laws, then the Chamber has nothing to do.

" We will enter the path of absolute legality, and repress illegality ; clean up the party. . . . I am disposed to follow a policy of conciliation, and to forget the past, to forget all the battles of the past."

The abolition of the illegal militia, the one element upon which Fascism rested, forcing itself upon a mass now no longer willing to give it a chance or to accept it at any price, would have meant the collapse of dictatorship. To " enter the path of legality " would have meant the collapse of the dictatorship. The moment the five Opposition parties could be assured of a legal election they would have obtained a legal majority, reducing Fascism to a third or fourth party. The abolition of rule by decrees would have meant the end of dictatorship. All this Mussolini promised the day he was a doomed man and had tears in his eyes.

This abnegation of dictatorship was due to the reaction of the press. After two years of Fascism the total number of readers of the party papers was 400,000, while the anti-Fascists with their great and popular journals and their support by the great majority of Italians had at least 4,000,000 readers.

Scared by the press, Mussolini had, in accordance with its demands, resigned one office, and rid himself of members of the Quadrumvirate, the Pentarchy, the men who made him and his party. Among the founders of Fascism who were driven out were General De Bono, Under-Secretary of the Interior Finzi, Chief of the Press Bureau Rossi, administrative Secretary of the Fascist Party Marinelli, Editor of the Fascist Organ Filippelli, Chief Assassin Dumini, and " six or fifteen or twenty or thirty individuals," all in prison.

The press almost brought about a revolution. It did in fact inflame the mass mind to the point of rebelling. A word from the King or an order from Amendola, the new leader of the five Opposition parties, would have ended by small violence the dictatorship Mussolini himself had declared to be abandoned. But no word or order ever came.

The morning after the Premier's confession of a return to legality the Opposition parties met at Montecitorio, and unanimously voted a motion. They talked a lot, and what they did was to sign a paper. The document is important, because it is the indictment not only by Matteotti's party, but also by the Republican Party, the Catholic Party, and two other non-liberal or non-radical parties, of Mussolini as the responsible accomplice of the assassination.

The resolutions called international attention to the existence of the Fascist Cheka, "grafted on the very organisation of the government and by the confidants of the Chief of Government [Mussolini] "; it placed the blame for the assassinations upon the President of the Council [Mussolini] ; and it concluded by announcing the abstention of the Opposition parties from parliamentary participation.

In America not a line appeared about the Matteotti case, because the newspapers were filled to overflowing with news of another murder, that committed in Chicago by two young, neurotic millionaires, named Loeb and Leopold. But in England, Premier MacDonald attended a meeting of the Labour Party, at which a resolution was passed condemning the assassination and sending the sympathy of British Labour to the Socialist Party of Italy.

Pope Pius was terribly shocked. Finzi, whose complicity was generally admitted, had married a niece of Cardinal Vannutelli, dean of the Sacred College and one of the closest associates of the Pope. Cardinal Gasparri made visits to both the mother and widow of Matteotti, expressing his sympathy and horror.

From New York Luigi Barzini, editor of the *Corriere d'America*, cabled Mussolini, advising him to purge the Fascist Party, drive out the Black Hand, see that justice was done and that Fascist prestige was restored.

Italy's leading intellectual, the philosopher Croce, passed the following verdict upon the régime : " The Fascist movement is incapable of setting up a new type of State despite the ostentatious utterances of its supporters ; therefore Fascism in my judgment could not and should not be anything more than a bridge to lead to the restoration of a more strictly liberal régime in the frame of a stronger State. . . . Because Fascism cannot create a new constitutional and judicial organisation as a substitute for that of Liberalism, it finds itself forced to move along by the same violent means as accompanied its birth, and so it perpetuates what should have been occasional and transitory. In this series of violent actions we cannot exactly see at what point we are to stop."

Weeks passed. The five Opposition parties became known as the Aventine. They met. They talked. Their one great gesture was to withdraw from parliament ; after which they did nothing. They were socialists and reformists who did not believe in direct action, in arms, in violence, legal or illegal.

Not so Farinacci. " Farinacci the Sadist," as he was frequently called, was unaffected by bloodshed or murder or revolutionary hysteria. He sneered at weakness. He despised the Socialist pacifists and he jeered at Mussolini for acting as timidly as they did. The Duce became the meek follower of his assistant ; the desperate, sick man acccepted doctor Farinacci's violent remedy, and between July 29 and September 30, 1924, he instructed the Cheka and the squadron leaders in metropolitan centres to revive the 1922 terror. Sixteen anti-Fascists were murdered, 36 seriously wounded, 172 assaulted ; 46 homes and clubs of Socialists, Catholics, and Labour organisations were destroyed.[1]

Most important of all was the decree abolishing freedom of the press. (Freedom here is underlined to distinguish it from a later decree abolishing the opposition press ; the first placed it in the hands of censors, the latter ended its existence.) Newspapers were burned, presses smashed, buildings destroyed.

As the voices of opposition were stilled in fire and blood, the hero-conqueror found his own. He forgot his promise of justice, he forgot the " return to legality," he issued nothing but decrees, and the militia which he had sworn to disband he used for the purpose of destroying his political enemies. And when the time came for him to write his autobiography for the *Saturday Evening Post* he forgot even the fact that Matteotti had been murdered.

" The course of Italian public life from June to December 1924," he wrote, " offered a spectacle absolutely un-

[1] The complete documentation for these figures, which apply to North Italy only, has been published by Bolitho.

paralleled in the political struggle in any country. It was a mark of shame and infamy which would dishonour any political group. The press, the meetings, the subversive and anti-Fascist parties of every sort, the false intellectuals, the defeated candidates, the soft-brained cowards, the rabble, the parasites, threw themselves like ravens on the corpse [of Matteotti]. The arrest of the guilty was not enough. The discovery of the corpse and the sworn statement of surgeons that death had not been due to crime, but had been produced by a trauma, was not enough. . . .

" I did not have a moment of doubt or discouragement . . . the swelled frogs waited for their triumph . . . this base and pernicious crew. . . . The contemptible game lasted six months. . . .

" I held the Fascist Party firmly in my hand during this period," comments the later-day Napoleon. " I curbed the impulse of some Fascists who wanted violent reprisals, with a clear order : ' Hands in your pockets ! I am the only one who must have his hands free.' In Florence and Bologna, however, there occurred episodes of extreme violence. I understood then that it was time to speak and act."

The speech came on the 3rd of January, 1925, when the situation had so completely reversed itself that Mussolini at last was able to accept and to glorify the assassination of his chief rival.

" On June 10," said Mussolini, addressing the Black Shirts, " there was sequestered in Rome the Honourable Matteotti, who during a ride succumbed.

" This event was singularly enveloped in a certain mystery for the purpose of shocking public opinion. The Fascist revolution had been very gentle. . . . Just the same, the Honourable Matteotti, who during the war had affirmed the most dangerous principles of defeatism, after having always and everywhere offended Fascism, pronounced in the Chamber a terrible and vicious attack upon the regimé.

" Sentimentalism in Latin countries is very dangerous. . . .

" The sequestration of Matteotti, with its consequences, belongs morally, politically, historically to Fascism. It is useless and stupid to search for the guilty at the moment when the fact arrives. This, only this, can be the language of revolution."

When the Fascist Deputy Cesare Misuri stepped out of the party traces to declare that "Mussolini had fallen among bad companions," and named Rossi, Luigi Freddi, Finzi, Francesco Giunta (to which list the press added De Bono and Marinelli, four of these six being under charge of complicity in the assassination), Mussolini took cognizance and for once—that is, for a while at least—stood by his colleagues. "The men denounced as 'the bad counsellors of the good tyrant,' " he said, "are five or six men who reported to me in person every morning. I herewith made distinct avowal that I look upon them as my closest collaborators and fellow burden-bearers, who share with me the salt bread of direct responsibility for the acts of the Fascist administration. I declare in your presence that I owe them the deepest sentiments of gratitude and affection."

These early days of 1925 ended the crisis. When the Rossi memorandum was published and there was a last wave of antagonism, Mussolini replied by threatening to mobilize the Fascist militia. This time it was too late for the King to mobilize the army; it would have meant civil war, and Amendola and the other leaders again talked about a general strike, which could well have been called were it not for the fear that Mussolini would use the militia against the working-men. It became apparent that the psychological moment, that of June, could never be revived. From January 1925 on, Fascism grew stronger than ever and its course seemed certain so long as economic pressure (which vies with violence in shaping history) did not militate against it.

The atmosphere was now clear for the Matteotti trial.

CHAPTER XV

Blood and Irony

ALTHOUGH the Duce himself said, " it was worse than a crime, it was a blunder," the assassination of Matteotti was in fact a necessary step in the consolidation of power. With Matteotti alive Mussolini could not be certain of success. The man who sentenced the leader of the Opposition to death obeyed literally the rules for guidance of princely power as written and expounded many years ago.

The Machiavellian Prince was bitter in his victory. Above all else it was being spoiled by the wit, the humour, the irony of that other young man who, although born bourgeois and grown wealthy, stood up as a leader of the proletariat and jested over the story of the Socialist blacksmith's son who had become the champion of the steamship lines and automobile manufacturers of Milan and Turin and the tourist-promotion society of Rome.

" Remember, Razumof," says one of Conrad's characters in *Under Western Eyes*, " that women, children, and revolutionists hate irony, which is the negation of all saving instincts, of all devotion, of all action."

Matteotti the revolutionist loved irony ; Mussolini the revolutionist had neither irony nor humour. Matteotti smiled ; Mussolini frowned. Matteotti was irony's gadfly, nipping the dictator, bringing up deeply felt hatred and rage in his black glowing eyes.

He was two years younger than Mussolini. His well-to-do family sent him to Rovigo to be educated, then to the University of Bologna, where he obtained a doctorate in jurisprudence. His interest in Socialism at first was academic. Unlike Mussolini, he suffered from no inferiority

complex, no minority complex, no "suppression" by
family or circumstance.

He was careful, precise, logical; he had an ordered
mind and was not swayed easily by emotions. His brother,
a physician and Socialist, and he discussed liberal ideas as
philosophy, not as a course of action.

In 1914 Matteotti, like Mussolini, spoke for absolute
neutrality. It was the duty of the proletariat, of all independent minds, of all persons having ideals, to oppose
this war, any war. For several months these two men in
far-removed centres preached the same thought. But
Matteotti never sold out—for wealth or power or a seat in
congress or a newspaper. He was arrested in June 1916,
for a speech denouncing war. After his acquittal he was
drafted and remained in the army three years. Most of
that time, however, he was interned in a British camp on
account of his pacifist views. In 1919 and again in 1921 he
was elected to the Chamber of Deputies, where he became
an expert in finance and economics.

He had a fiery face, like Mussolini's, but a cold mind.
His appearance was cold, but flashing; he had a sensitive
nature which his passionate eyes betrayed. Father of three,
an affectionate husband, he loved to forget the life of politics
he had chosen for himself out of an ideal of human liberty,
and to stay at home playing with his children.

"Every time I saw Matteotti," says his friend, Giovanni
Zibordi, "his face and figure full of energy, his movement
agile, I would think of an 'espada,' a Spanish matador,
one with every part of his body alert and his muscles of
iron, his nerves taut and his heart unmoved, who plays
with a fine blade, conquering the huge and blinded fury of
the bull. . . . Such was Matteotti in the parliamentary
arena, alive, prepared, vigilant, a fencer, direct and valiant,
always armed with documents and with facts, with reason
and with opportune blows and adequate replies.

"Irritating? Yes. He had a thin sharp voice which
was not checked by sweet inflections, but a manner of
speaking in a flow of irony, of logical irony—an audacious
fighter."

Matteotti stood in the way of Fascist progress. His words, his pen, his activity were a daily reproach to tyranny. He had no fear of the Fascisti ; the Fascisti were afraid of him. They could not answer him. They assassinated him.

Mussolini had no moral or intellectual arms to equal Matteotti's. And he simply could not live under irony. So he nodded yes to the Fascist Cheka plan of assassination.

But even after death, tragic irony played its part. The trial of Dumini and the other four confessed assassins became a trial of the dead.

It was held in March of 1926, almost two years after the murder, at a time when Fascism had so entrenched itself that nothing could shake it ; it controlled the army as well as the militia now, had suppressed all the newspapers and corrupted the entire judiciary. Judge Giuseppe Danza presided. Chieti was chosen because it was an out-of-the-way village where the secret service could control the journalists and the proceedings easily. Co-accused with Dumini were : Albino Volpi, Amleto Poveromo, August Malacria, and Giuseppe Viola, all members of the service and all present in the automobile during the murder. Malacria had served a prison term for swindling. Poveromo had been sentenced once for robbery. Viola had a record of bankruptcy and of desertion.

Roberto Farinacci, secretary-general of the Fascist Party, was appointed by Mussolini to defend the murderers. If there was one man in Italy who more than Mussolini himself was an advocate of violence in the achievement of power, that man was Farinacci, the so-called " left " or extreme hand of the Duce. The trial began with Farinacci's attack upon Matteotti. In opposing Fascism, said Farinacci, Matteotti had proven himself plainly a traitor to his country, and therefore his death was justifiable. After this declaration the trial became a tragic farce.

One murderer testified that because Matteotti refused to sit quietly in the car it became necessary to subdue him. " I knelt on his chest," he testified, " but he kept on resisting. So I pressed my knees into his chest until the arteries broke and the blood came out of his mouth."

Dumini, the American gangster, was the star witness, despite his numerous contradictions.

" When we had Matteotti in the car," he testified, " he made us all very sore by the way he thrashed about, and as we did not want to attract any attention and had determined to take him far away in the campagna, I hit him several times with the butt of my revolver.

" He then was quiet for a while, but soon started again to struggle, and when he threw the weight of his body against me while I was at the wheel, I crushed in his skull with my *manganello* [blackjack].

" Then when we saw that he was dead we did not know what to do next, for I had not really at first intended to kill him. We drove about for many hours and it was getting dark. Then we decided to cut up the body and burn it, and this we did in a lonesome byway near the Grotto Rossa [about twelve miles out of Rome]. What remained of the body we buried in different spots, and I don't remember now where that was done."

The day following this admission the humorist Dumini changed his mind.

" We were riding along peaceably," he testified, " when suddenly Matteotti developed tuberculosis and died of a hæmorrhage."

But this was a little too much for even a Fascist judge.

" Then how do you account for the thirty-six stab wounds ? " asked the court.

" Who said stab wounds ? " demanded Dumini.

" Doctors—experts," replied the judge.

" Oh ! " replied Dumini. " I thought in these modern days that ' experts ' were no longer allowed to testify."

Testimony was offered that Dumini, some months previous, had been smuggled out of prison by Fascist agents, given a bag filled with 1000-lire notes, and packed off to France. He had been recognized at the station of Termini and rearrested. A letter was found on him which again implicated Mussolini. This letter from his sister Blanche read :

" Vaselli [Dumini's lawyer] says all will be well, but it

will take time on account of the judges, who are Freemasons, who wage war on the government and the party. They are trying to get rid of them as they did of one before. It takes time, but all will be well.

" What have you arranged for communicating with Vaselli ?

" Why have you told so much to Vaselli ? Why have you come to this extreme with the Duce ? Do you want Rosati for the defence ? If you do, communicate by letter. Vaselli told us he let Mussolini know he had been betrayed. De Bono is already out. Which papers were they which concerned De Bono ? It is not true what Cesarino [pet name for Cesare Rossi] said. Vaselli told mother he will make arrangements for your future with Mussolini. Do you agree ? Is it true that you are taking the whole responsibility ? Do not speak too much, and remain where you are. Mother says the arrangements will be made as quickly as possible, and a large sum will be deposited for you when you come out. Be calm. We are all interceding for you, but it is a terrible moment ; nevertheless we will succeed. Kisses.--BLANCHE."

This letter, together with the testament of Finzi and the confessions of Rossi, were not allowed in evidence.

But it is interesting to note that Dumini, the humourist, shortly afterwards walked about the streets of Rome, and when occasions came or he could make them, smilingly introduced himself : " Dumini, *twelve* murders." In fact, he talked too much. Bragging in the cafés of the capital of how easily he got off at Chieti and how Mussolini had stood by him so nobly, he became the object of Fascist concern. One day his demands for hush-money reached their limit, for he addressed to Mussolini a legal summons,[1] in which *inter alia* it was declared :

1. that he, Dumini, received 60,000 lire from the Directorate of the Fascist Party, and

2. that the expense of the trial, 32,754 lire, was to be paid by the Fascist Party, in addition.

[1] Registered in the courts of Rome, Bureau of Private Orders, No. 5555, Vol. 356.

Dumini was arrested, tried, sentenced to a year in jail one day in September 1926, and from that time on he has stayed in jail, in silence.

Albino Volpi, an associate of Dumini, and likewise a member of the Fascist Cheka, testified :

" While we were beating and stabbing Matteotti he appeared heroic. He continued to the end to cry, ' Assassins!' ' Savages !' ' Cowards'! But he never had a weak moment, and he never asked for mercy. And while we were stabbing him he kept repeating : ' Kill me, but the idea which is in me you can never kill.'

" Probably if he had been humble for a moment, and if he had asked to be saved, and if he had confessed the error of his ideas, we perhaps would not have accomplished our work. But no. Just to the end, so long as he had breath, he cried out, ' My idea will not die,' and ' My children will be proud of their father,' and ' The working-men will bless my corpse.'

" He died saying, ' Long live Socialism ! ' "

This is the chef d'œuvre of Fascist crime which the Duce was afterwards to call " a practical joke on Matteotti—he should not have resisted his jesters."

Viola and Malacria were acquitted. Dumini, Volpi, and Poveromo were found guilty of *unintentional* homicide, sentenced to five years' imprisonment, and freed almost immediately afterwards by Mussolini's amnesty for *political* offenders which had been issued in 1925. Rossi and Mussolini had reached an agreement whereby the former was to keep quiet ; he was accordingly allowed to escape from prison, and from his refuge in France he turned against his chief, and issued another confession and accusation, this second memorandum concluding with the words :

" All the moral responsibilities of the circle from which came the Matteotti crime are on Mussolini."

But the vendetta of Mussolini followed Rossi unrelentingly year after year, to France and Germany and Switzerland. Agents came with guns and knives, and plots and secrets whispered in his ears. Rossi withstood all these. Then, in 1930, a charming lady appeared in Paris and Rossi was smitten. The lady proposed a honeymoon in lovely Switzerland, and Rossi went. He went too far. One day the lovely lady proposed an excursion to the Italian frontier, and although Rossi became a little suspicious, he took great care never to come within a hundred yards of the border. But the lady made a signal, and several Fascist police ran across the frontier into Switzerland, seized Rossi, and carried him off to jail. The lovely lady laughed.

Just before his trial the representative of Mussolini came to Rossi and told him that the death penalty had been ordered ; if Rossi wanted to save his life he must withdraw all his confessions, especially the document commonly known as " The Thirty-seven accusations against Mussolini," and must swear never to accuse the Duce of the Matteotti murder again. To save his life Rossi withdrew everything, promised everything, and began a sentence of thirty years in prison for " libelling " Mussolini.

Marinelli and Filippelli appeared before the Court of Appeals in Rome, where on the 1st of December 1925, the charges were dismissed, because it was found that the accused had ordered the kidnapping, not the assassination, of Matteotti. General de Bono was acquitted of complicity at a trial before the Senate in July 1925. The reason given was " lack of sufficient evidence."

It was at this time that the campaign for the suppression of the liberal press and the intimidation of foreign correspondents reached its height in Italy. No dictatorship, Black or White, has ever been able to survive the publication of truthful reports of its actions or its ideas. Yet Fascism was hesitating before adopting the open honest terrorism of Bolshevik Russia. It was still professing liberty. It used intimidation. Detectives followed every American journalist. The concierge of the house where the *New York World* correspondent lived was forced to report daily, while around the office of Emmanuel, the representative of the Hearst Service, numerous spies were stationed. All the Italian journalists who acted as assistants in the American offices were ordered to report to Grandi's bureau. But

12

special favours were shown to all members of the Cortesi family, who, representing the Associated Press of America, the *Daily Mail*, the *New York Times*, and several other important publications, have done Fascist propaganda a greater service than all the paid agents. Without a single exception, every journalist who was not a voluntary or subsidized propagandist denounced the trial of Chieti. Even friends of Fascism did so. But no one resident in Italy dared do so in the press. During the trial John Clayton, then representing the *Chicago Tribune*, wrote privately :

" We are bound by the worst censorship ever imposed. We must not write anything that might reflect on the Fascisti. *We are confined to an apology for political assassination.* It broke my heart not to be able to report the Matteotti case as it should be done, but *it would have meant arrest and expulsion from Italy.*"

The truth about the Matteotti trial was almost completely suppressed by the régime. But because he believed it to be a most unusual and cruel miscarriage of justice, Bolitho, unable to withstand the dictate of his conscience, fled from Italy when the hearings were half over, and, from the first free town, in France, wrote for the *Manchester Guardian* and the *New York World* a series of despatches which startled public opinion.

A few liberals in America protested. In England Professor Gilbert Murray wrote that the tragedy at Chieti was " a mock trial in order to give absolution and public thanks to the murderers. No element of fraud was lacking ; . . . the Matteotti trial will probably remain for some generations a classic model of the perfect perversion of justice."

As Bolitho, in order to escape arrest on his return to Italy, had used a pseudonym which the Fascist Cheka had been unable to identify, the head of the press bureau in the Foreign Office called in all the Anglo-American journalists for cross-examination. He even threatened those in whose papers Bolitho's syndicated articles had been used. But to the credit of those who knew the secret it must be said that none betrayed him. With two exceptions, in fact, the Anglo-

American press corps in Rome rejoiced over Bolitho's successful publication of the facts they themselves had been unable to send. The exceptions were the Italians who represent American and British journals and news agencies.

In defence of Mussolini, Luigi Villari, his chief apologist in London, has written that " the trial was conducted with absolute fairness and in an atmosphere free from pressure or outside influences . . . not a scrap of real evidence had emerged incriminating the government or the leaders of the Fascist Party, and all the fantastic structure erected by the Opposition has crumbled."

Professor Salvemini, of course, produced the documents incriminating the government, the leaders of the party, the Duce himself. The reply of Signor Villari is one of the supreme achievements of the Fascist mentality. The prosecution, he wrote, " committed Dumini and his companions for unpremeditated murder, which is *not* the same as manslaughter. By rejecting the charge of premeditation the alleged complicity in the murder of political personages is evidently knocked on the head."

This is typical of the apologia delivered in foreign countries a year after Mussolini, powerful, and restored in confidence, accepted " the full responsibility " for the assassination.

The cynical (and not unwelcome to the Duce) viewpoint was that of Mr. Bernard Shaw. Comparing Mussolini with Napoleon, he said they differed in that the former had no military victories ; they were alike in one respect—for the murder of Matteotti, Napoleon had the murder of the Duke of Enghien on his conscience.

Contrasted with the Shavian cynicism is the naïveté of the lady biographers. According to Mme Bordeux : " To accuse Mussolini openly of the murder of a member of his own parliament was next to impossible. . . . No, Mussolini was never openly accused of more than of having instigated the murder of Matteotti. . . . Matteotti's murder was premeditated and carried out by his own personal enemies in his own party."

Stranger still are the references to Matteotti in the long biography by Mussolini's Egeria. Whereas the Duce himself devotes thousands of words to denouncing his opponent and defending himself, Sarfatti, in 352 pages of joy bells and hosannas of Fascism, slides over the thin ice of the greatest crisis in its history with two sidesteps. On page 181 we read : " And after the assassination of Matteotti, Mussolini's first utterance in an address to the Grand Council of the Fascists was one of vehement impatience with the storm which then broke out, because it prevented him from applying himself to the task of ' ordinary administration '—the only task which he regarded as vital and essential, that of giving the people what they really wanted and were asking for, bridges, water, roads." And on page 275 : " He was really very much taken up by his dramatic schemes. A short time after the sinister Matteotti affair, which caused him such terrible suffering that for a while his life seemed completely wrecked, I met him going out one day looking more cheerful. He showed me a manuscript packet, which he told me was his new play, with which he had succeeded in distracting his mind when in need of relaxation from his worries and his troubles. It was a play based on the life of the campagna ; and this man, tired, exhausted, worn out by his bitter experiences, had found refreshment in recalling the incidents of his childhood." There are no other references to the assassination, the trial, or the vast results from the crisis.

In the judgment of Louis Roya, a French writer who prefaces his opinion by praising Mussolini as a patriot and friend of Latin civilization, the responsibility of the assassination " can be inferred from imponderable facts, from an ensemble of troubling circumstances, such as the letter to Dumini from his family, and finally and above all (this is the thesis of Rossi *contre* the Duce) from the orders for violence given by Mussolini. Seen from that viewpoint, the culpability of Mussolini is irrefutable in the eyes of the universal moral conscience. And, a thing most impressive, all Italians who have fled from Italy to escape the Fascist tyranny, unite in recognizing that the first and the highest responsibility rests on Mussolini : that, too, is the opinion of the international proletariat.

" There can be no doubt about it that when the day comes in which Fascism falls, the Matteotti trial, the real trial, will begin again : and the principal accused will be— Mussolini."

CHAPTER XVI

The Sons of Brutus

GIOVANNI AMENDOLA inherited the leadership of the five Opposition parties commonly known as the Aventine.

If Matteotti had been the Brutus of the Fascist régime, Amendola was the son of Brutus. He was one of the leading intellectuals of Italy, a savant, one of the ideal university men who had given up a cloistered career for politics and journalism, and yet had found time for serious and learned creative work. He was brilliant, and like Matteotti he frequently employed irony in his unanswerable attacks on Fascism and illegal violence.

Shortly after the assassination of Matteotti many men said that Amendola would be the next to die. In fact, the first threat against his life had been made by Mussolini a year earlier when he wrote : [1]

"The Deputy Amendola demands why we do not suppress the national militia at a time when Fascism has general approval ?

"To this gentleman, who again promenades in the streets of Rome without annoyances, we reply that the militia has not been instituted against the people, but, on the contrary, against a minority of scoundrels, very vicious, without credit, scoundrels who have always betrayed Italy.

"This Amendola who craves liberty, just as if all the pits of Italy were full of corpses, and all the lamp-posts decorated with anti-nationalist carcasses, has, up to now, enjoyed too much liberty.

"Fascism has been too generous to him, as it has been to other delinquents whose names are Nitti, Albertini, Don Sturzo, Treves, Modigliani, Serrati, Turati, and others.

[1] *Popolo d'Italia*, August 24, 1923.

[Every man mentioned, except Albertini, has either been beaten up, arrested, or forced into exile, since then.]

" Ah, if Fascism, instead of being so good and so naïve, had done away with all these scoundrels who infest the nation ! Fascism to-day is paying for its faults, for having made a revolution with the blood of its soldiers instead of the blood of its adversaries.

" But, for this reason, to repair this first omission, the militia must remain at its post ; the militia would do well to give a lesson to the scoundrels who have not already been nailed to lamp-posts."

The militia and also the Fascist university students and the squadristi gave Amendola, " this Amendola who craves liberty," not one but several lessons.   This is the records of the assaults :

December 26, 1923, in a crowded street in Rome.
March, 1924, in Naples, during a political speech.
May 30, 1924, on leaving the House of Parliament.
April 6, 1925, in Rome, after a speech on liberty.
July 20, 1925, at Montecatini, in Tuscany.

The first attack occurred in the Via Francesco Crispi while hundreds were passing. Many noticed that an automobile filled with militiamen was slowly following Amendola, and they knew that an assault was planned. The militiamen finally stopped the car a few feet ahead of the Deputy, leaped out, drove the passers-by away, and beat Amendola with their clubs, leaving him with his head covered with blood, apparently dying on the sidewalk. Adjutant-Major Vico Perroni of the 112th Legion of Fascist militia, later testified under oath that the order to attack Amendola came from General De Bono, who was head both of the militia and of the Rome police. He asked whether the order came direct from the Duce. " I was impressed with the mention of Amendola's name," reads his signed confession, " so I personally made sure that His Excellency Signor Mussolini required this to be done. Discussions followed with His Excellency General De Bono, who was particular in directing that Signor Amendola was merely to be clubbed." De

Bono had declared the matter in order because he had received the command from Mussolini himself. Rossi also confirms this.

The high court of justice which tried De Bono for complicity in this and other cases, was the Fascist Senate ; in its findings, it stated that it was true that the two carabinieri posted to safeguard Amendola were mysteriously recalled the day of the attack, that many persons saw the militiamen preparing the attack, that the attackers fled to the militia barracks at Magnanapoli, and that the chauffeur, Zaccagnini, spoke to Colonel Candelori about De Bono as the official who had sanctioned the crime. But the court found insufficient evidence. This ground, in Italy, however, is in itself an accusation ; for the law states that persons so freed must never hold government office. But as this was a pre-Fascist law, merely a constitutional law, Mussolini defied public opinion by appointing De Bono governor of Tripoli on the night of the verdict.

The young Fascist squadristi gathered outside the offices of Amendola's newspaper, *Il Mondo*, and sang :

> " *Amendola, Amendola, devi morire*
> *E col pugnale che abbiamo affilato.*
> *Amendola, Amendola, devi morire.*"

> [" Amendola, Amendola, you must die
> By the stilleto which we have sharpened.
> Amendola, Amendola, you must die."]

When this Opposition leader planned to speak in the province of Caserta, the Fascist Deputy Greco obtained an advance copy of the speech and took the text to Rossi, who took it to Mussolini. The Duce then told Greco that the Amendola demonstration must be stopped at any price. It was.

Ten days later, on leaving the Chamber, Amendola and his friends were again attacked by Fascist militia. As Amendola carried an umbrella that day, he defended himself, while the militia, although outnumbering the liberal Deputies, five to one, ran away. The next afternoon the Fascist Deputies offered a resolution asking that parliamentary immunity be suspended, so that Amendola could be arrested for assaulting a Fascist militia chief !

One can well believe that Amendola with an umbrella was the equal of five. He was an enormous man, about six feet high, huge but not fat, muscular and vivacious. I never spoke to him. Although I interviewed all the leaders of the Fascist government in 1925, I particularly refrained from trafficking with the Opposition, knowing that the Foreign Office would look upon such action as treason. As it was, my telegrams regarding Amendola resulted in Mussolini's protests to our ambassador, Mr. Fletcher, who in Mexico had shaken his fist when Carranza imprisoned an American journalist, but who, in Italy, preferred to act " diplomatically."

What I reported was the circumstances of the attempted assassination of July 20, 1925, when Amendola, already a sick man, left secretly at midnight for Montecatini for a rest cure. When Amendola arrived at the Hotel Pace there were one thousand armed Fascists waiting to kill him. Some of them had travelled twenty miles. All of them, as I learned and cabled, had received an *alerte* from the Rome Cheka headquarters which was in the same building as the militia offices, and orders had been given to the squadristi of several towns.

At first the hotel proprietor refused to surrender his guest ; the Fascists then stormed the building, invading the rooms of Italians and foreigners, smashing down resisting doors, threatening with death all who stood in their way. Amendola, however, had fled in his car. An official offered him protection, but when they had ridden several miles, betrayed the chief. Several automobiles filled with Fascisti arrived and twenty men clubbed Amendola, leaving him for dead in his car. This is what I had reported. Amendola suffered agony until April 7, 1926, when he died of his wounds in southern France.

To his deathbed he called his friend Campolonghi and said :

" The Fascisti have abolished parliament, and so I have lost my liberty of speech. They have abolished the liberty

of the press, and so I can no longer write. They have
assassinated me, and so I have lost the liberty to live. All
this is nothing. The evil is that they will end by assassinating Italy."

The death certificate shows Amendola died of clotting of
the blood in his lungs, the result of clubbing. As a racketeer's
crime it was perfect : they do not want to kill outright like
their Chicago brethren !

Mussolini's *Popolo d'Italia* congratulated the squadristi.

In the case of Gobetti, the complicity of the chief
Fascist condottiere is more clearly proved.

Gobetti was only twenty-five. In Turin he published a
periodical called *The Liberal Revolution*, satirizing Mussolini,
irritating Mussolini again. But there was not a word in
Gobetti's irony which, if read in court, would sound
libellous or insulting, and the Duce could find absolutely
no ground for suppressing the paper. Gobetti was ambushed and severely beaten. But he recovered and continued his satire. In January 1924, Mussolini sent the
following telegram to the prefect of police of Turin : [1]

Prefect Turin, I am told that Gobetti went to Paris recently,
but actually is in Sicily. Please inform me precisely. See to
it again that life is made difficult for this stupid opponent of the
Fascist government.   MUSSOLINI.

Gobetti's office was pillaged, his possessions requisitioned,
his correspondence stolen, his paper suppressed ; and
finally the prefect issued an order denying him the right to
exercise the profession of journalist, his one means of
making a living. The Fascists again beat up their victim
and he fled to France, where, like Amendola, he died of
lung trouble.

Further evidence is given by Guido Narbone, former
vice-secretary of the Turin Fascists, who writes proudly
that when he and other leaders of Torinese Fascism were
received by Mussolini at the Palazzo Chigi, the Duce said :
" You must act Fascistically and with the maximum

[1] The original, in Mussolini's handwriting, was saved by his secretary
and afterwards published.

energy. You know Professor Gobetti in Turin ? He needs a severe Fascist lesson. You are charged to give it to him."

Still another victim of Mussolini's lack of a sense of humour was Alberto Giannini, who edited the *Becco Giallo* in Rome for many years. So long as the press was free, it was impossible to stop the humorous papers, so the *Becco* held out until a general order abolished every publication but those belonging to the régime. From France, however, the new edition, with added bitterness to its satire and humour, was smuggled into Italy. The Fascist Cheka then revenged itself on the Giannini family. Said the editor to the present writer in 1931 :

" I am in my fourth year of exile. My house was entered twice by Fascisti ; what they did not destroy they stole. They stole stocks and bonds worth many thousands, in fact my entire life savings, and when Mussolini suppressed my newspaper and sentenced me to five years of ' enforced domicile,' I was penniless.

" A former officer of an Alpine battery, I had little difficulty in crossing the Alps and finding refuge in France. My aged mother, my wife, and three children, remained behind. It is against them that Mussolini takes his vengeance. For fear that they may try to escape, he has them followed and watched day and night. My wife fell ill. In the hospital, during the long months of her illness, two police agents stood at her bedside until she died ; I am told that they expected that in her last agony she would reveal some information useful to Fascismo.

" My children remained in Rome. One would think that Mussolini had had enough revenge. But no. Fascist agents follow even the smallest of my children to school and back, sit near them when they go to lunch, stand by them when they play with other children, never letting them escape their eye when they go for a walk.

" Meanwhile Mussolini sends me emissaries to persuade me to give up my activity as a journalist in opposition to his régime, which is one of violence, and which has made of my family imprisoned hostages. Cruelty against my family will be continued until I cease to work. These are the

ferocious and barbaric methods of Fascism, and its worthy
Duce."

Criticism, humour, irony—Mussolini could not withstand these forces, especially when they were employed by
men of intelligence and power. The politicians, the scholars,
the writers, and the journalists who attacked Mussolini
with words were in turn " eliminated from circulation " or,
in American slang, " put on the spot " by the student of
Machiavelli.

Among the few left who dared use their voices were one
or two of the great heroes of the war, and most notable
among them was the same Raffaele Rossetti who, to aid
d'Annunzio, had brought to Mussolini's office the enormous
fund with which the nation had rewarded him.

But Rossetti, Italy's greatest war hero, was made a
pacifist by his experiences in the war. He was opposed to
all bloodshed. And as he watched Fascism consolidate its
power by that means he became an anti-Fascist. The story
of Mussolini's wrath is told in Part XII of Rossi's memorandum :

" In the spring of 1923 a Fascist ceremony took place
at which, I think at Rapallo, certainly in the eastern
Riviera, General De Vecchi was present. Among the
onlookers was Signor Rossetti, one of the men who were
awarded the gold medal for bravery during the war. He
was a bitter opponent of Fascism. Although not provoked,
he thought it good to arouse the anger of the majority of
the crowd by calling out, ' Long live free Italy ' and ' Down
with Fascism.' The next day Mussolini complained of the
long-suffering of the Fascists of the region and expressed
his astonishment that General De Vecchi had allowed such
provocation to pass without prompt punishment. He
remarked : ' Signor Rossetti, gold medal or no gold medal,
was there to give provocation. Therefore, without further
ado he should have been struck down on the spot.' "

Inasmuch as the Fascisti had failed to strike down
Rossetti, Mussolini ordered them to arrest the hero, and
this was done. Rossetti, however, managed to escape from
Genoa in a rowboat ; he was wrecked in the Mediterranean,

but dragged, more dead than alive, on to the beach at Nice, and to-day he is setting type in a Paris publication devoted to attacking the Fascist regimé.

The physical and moral incapability of the Fascisti to tolerate criticism is called by Rossi " the fundamental fault " of the party in power ; " this mentality is the key to the political tragedy of the Italian nation." In the view of H. G. Wells " the deadliest thing about Fascism is its systematic and ingenious and complete destruction of all criticism and critical opposition. It is leaving no alternative government in the land. It is destroying all hopes of recovery. The King may some day be disinterred, the Vatican may become audible again, the Populist Party of Catholic Socialism hangs on ; but it is hard to imagine any of these three vestiges of the earlier state of affairs recovering enough vitality to reconstruct anew the shattered and exhausted Italy. Fascism is holding up the whole apparatus of thought and education in Italy, killing or driving out of the country every capable thinker, clearing out the last nests of independent expression in the universities. Meanwhile, its militant gestures alarm and estrange every foreign power with which it is in contact."

Men of goodwill, like Mr. Wells, may deplore the course of the régime and counsel the Duce to adopt other methods. But he remains under the influence of the cynic of Realpolitik, the philosopher of dictatorship, Machiavelli, who wrote : " He who creates a tyranny and does not kill Brutus, and he who creates a Free State and does not kill the sons of Brutus, will endure but a short time."

This is the guide-book to power which Mussolini read and underlined in his youth. It explains his present success.

CHAPTER XVII

PURGE OF THE FREEMASONS

AFTER the personal vendetta had passed its crisis, after Brutus and the sons of Brutus had been " eliminated from circulation," to use the brilliant euphemism of the Duce, there still remained, in addition to the impotent Opposition parties, whose slogan for ever was " No violence is ever justifiable," one formidable element of danger to the consolidation of the Fascist régime. This was Freemasonry.

In 1925 all the journalists resident in Rome, and notably the American, British, Scandinavian, and others who came from Protestant nations, were collectively and individually lectured by the Fascist diplomats concerning a decree Mussolini had prepared, which would abolish secret organizations. We realized it was an attack on Masonry, and the Foreign Office admitted it. But in this instance, we were informed, the Duce was for once doing something consistent with his past. Had he not attacked Freemasonry in 1914, when he was a Socialist, declaring that membership of both organizations was incompatible ? To-day it was the same with Fascism. When we asked why this was so, the answer was, " Because Masonry is a common enemy." When we protested that, so far as we knew, Masonry did not interfere with a man's politics, the spokesman for Mussolini explained further :

" You Americans and British," said he to the group of which I was a member, " do not realize that your Masonry and ours are as different as the tropics and the poles. Your Freemasons are all of the Scottish Rite ; ours are all of the Grand Orient. While it may be true that these two organizations have some features in common, fundamentally they are different. Your Masonry is decent ; it keeps out of politics, out of dirty intrigue ; ours is nothing but an intriguing organization, undermining the army and the State ; yours does not fight the Catholic Church, ours exists mainly for that purpose. Our Masonry is the secret enemy of the government ; it is a plot against the government. Mussolini shows his consistency in always attacking Masonry, that is, Grand Orient Freemasonry."

However, in 1925, I gathered from the Vatican that Mussolini's decree, which did not name the Masons specifically, but abolished all secret organizations, had troubled the Pope. The Catholic Church, I was told, was opposed to the new law. The Pope realized that the law, as promulgated in its ambiguous manner, could just as easily be used for the destruction of the Order of Jesuits.

Of Mussolini's rare consistency in attitude towards the Masons, the explanation is now quite simple. The Order, since its foundation, has always been a refuge for men who believed in individual and political liberty ; it has always opposed dictatorship in any form, whether Bolshevist or Fascist ; it has always favoured a constitutional government ; and ever since the day Garibaldi impressed it with his great personal seal, it has remained the standard-bearer of freedom. That is why the most rabid of radicals, the Benito Mussolini of 1914, sought to destroy it, and why the most reactionary of dictators, the Benito Mussolini of 1925, finally did so.

The Duke of Middlesex established the first lodge in Italy in 1773. Under warrant of the Grand Lodge of England he came to Florence, and soon after the foundation there was considerable papal opposition. In 1862 the Grand Orient of Italy was organized, and, upon reorganization some eleven years later, it began to be a power. That there was antagonism between Italian Masonry and the Vatican is only too true. A writer in the *Masonic News*, an American publication, states that " owing to religious and political conditions in Italy it was almost impossible for the Grand Orient to remain outside of politics." The reason was simple : " On the one side was the Roman Catholic Church, always seeking to destroy it ; on the other side was a government, suspicious of secret societies, which in Europe nearly always have a revolutionary purpose, and liable at any time to fall under the control of the Vatican."

Garibaldi and Mazzini, founders of the New Italy, were both Grand Masters. The former addressed a letter to a general assembly in Naples, June 17, 1867, saying :

" Masonry being the oldest bulwark of liberty and justice and therefore the true antagonist of the papacy, which is the antitheses of progress and civilization, I implore all my brothers of all the Italian lodges to assist the poor Romans, oppressed by the immoral domination of the harsh enemy of Italy and Humanity." And, of course, it was Garibaldi who uttered the exclamation : " The Vatican is a dagger in the heart of Italy."

But if the Freemasons were anti-clerical, the extreme radicals, of whom Mussolini, then the apostle of atheism, was the leader, were not only anti-papal but Antichrist.

When Fascism, under the same atheist, later began its punitive expeditions against its radical enemies, it found at first an unexpected support in Freemasonry ; and for many years, despite the suppression of facts by the Fascisti, there was a brotherly understanding between the two organizations. From the time the first Fasci was formed, until after the march on Rome, Masonic lodges co-operated, went so far as to organize Fascist locals and to join the employers in subsidizing Mussolini. Professor Salvemini states that the amount of money they gave the Duce and his generals to assist in the capture of Rome was 3,500,000 lire, or £35,000. Signor Domizio Torrigiani, then Grand Master, published in November 1922, a few days after Mussolini became Prime Minister, a declaration of confidence in the new government and in Fascist principles. It was not until the new party had been in power for almost a year, and when the necessity of a rapprochment with the Vatican began to impose itself for purely opportunistic reasons, that the estrangement occurred.

Then events moved quickly—from the passage of laws to actual massacre.

First of all the decree which abolished the freedom of

the press, the *sine qua non* of all Fascist repression, was of particular importance because many great liberal papers were owned, edited, and supported by Freemasons. The journalist Mussolini realized that so long as he could not muzzle them he could not destroy them, and the decree which followed the Matteotti assassination, silencing all opposition, silenced the Masons also. In 1925 the branch of the Grand Orient in Florence, the spiritual headquarters of the Order, realizing that Mussolini had begun his plans for a treaty with the Vatican, and that the press muzzle was directed against it as well as the five political parties, began a violent campaign in the press. The Fascisti replied by seizing the Florence press club. Newspapers were suppressed, some were bought, editors were beaten up and all precautions taken to hold the massacre with as little publicity and opposition as possible. Freemason judges, magistrates, officials, were forced to resign, and in some instances bankers were replaced by enemies of Masonry.

Then the whispering began. In the cafés of Florence the Fascisti sat around and whispered about coming trouble, while in other cafés the Masons gathered to discuss the sinister whispers. At first they would not believe that any real danger to their lives was imminent ; there would be the usual Fascist excesses, the burning of newspapers, the destruction of clubs, the clubbing of leaders ; perhaps a few knife wounds and some revolver shots were probable, but a massacre, never.

Then the atmosphere changed. " We must do all the good we can to our friends and must inflict all the harm possible on our enemies," said Mussolini. " Now, as Masonry has fought us, as it has given us trouble, as it has attempted to split and divide us, and as it has in certain cities succeeded in creating dissensions more than usually idiotic because of their underground origins, for all these reasons, even if there were no others, we are within our plain and sacrosanct right to defend ourselves and to pro-ceed to the attack, because, as you are teaching me, the best defence consists in attack."

These veiled words were followed with a notice to the

13

press from the Fascist Directory. It is generally understood
to have been written by Mussolini himself, but this has
never been affirmed or denied. As it appeared in the
Battaglia Fascisti it read :

"The Fascist Council assumes complete responsibility
for the holy actions of retaliation and violence, performed
by the Fascisti, even the slightest, and commands that
every Fascist should endeavour to identify those unworthy
Italians affiliated with Masonry so as to be able to know
better what are the most useful means in order to accomplish a radical, a decisive punitive action.

"The fight against Masonry continues with great
intensity. The enemy is more ready, more prepared than
before. The fight against Masonry is a fight to a finish
and there is only one possible programme :

"Masonry must be destroyed and Masons should have
no right to citizenship in Italy. To reach this end all means
are good, from the club to the gun, from the breaking of
windows to the purifying fire. In a word, no avenue of
escape should be left open to Masonry. . . . The Masons
must be ostracized. Each and every one of their acts or
movements must be stopped. Their very life must be made
impossible."

The phrase "to render life difficult," to "make life
impossible" for an enemy, and "to remove from circulation," were well understood. The followers needed no
explanation.

The massacre of the Freemasons of Florence began on
the 26th of September and lasted until the 4th of October
1925. There were 300 victims, 137 dead. The order came
from Rome. The massacre was not the usual wild debauch
of bloodshed which characterized other Fascist "reprisals,"
but a highly organized, carefully planned military attack,
with its objective in lives and property. "I have the name
of every man in Italy inscribed on the rolls of Masonry,"
Mussolini had said, and the chief of the Florence Black
Shirts had a list of the persons marked for death. Eighteen
men were systematically murdered.

The Fascist squads, dressed in their uniforms, carrying

banners and singing the "Song of Youth," went rioting
in the streets (it is strange that the thousands of our tourists
who sing the praises of law and order and of the trains
running to time, these thousands who fled from Florence
that week, never said a word about the affair) ; the Fascisti
looted shops, cracked safes, stopped innocent persons and
felled them with their blackjacks.

Thirteen lawyers and notaries had their offices destroyed.
All were Masons. One clinic was destroyed. The apart-
ments of the Socialist Deputies Targetti and Baldesi were
looted and burned. The Fascisti entered the home of one
Becciolini, and during the riot he killed one of them. They
returned in force, lynched him, dragged his body into the
public square, and exposed it there as a warning. Cafés
were looted, wine and spirits flowed in the streets, eager
Fascist youth drank itself drunk and staggered. Houses
were set on fire. In the week of rioting were heard the cries :

" Viva Mussolini ! Viva Dumini ! (My name is Dumini,
twelve assassinations !) "

One of the most savage incidents was the assassination
of the Socialist Deputy Gaetano Pilati, war hero and cripple.
Pilati's widow tells the tragic story :

" The assassination of my husband had been decided a
long time in advance. I learned later from the café-keeper,
Pietro Serpieri, who lives opposite us, that during the month
of September 1925, my husband had been followed con-
stantly by a young man, thin, tall, blond, called Senesi.
This man was able to place information about the location
of our bedroom.

" The night of October 3rd a Fascist named Lupporini
was killed when he entered, with a gun in his hand and
followed by another militiaman, into the home of an old
Freemason for the purpose of killing him. The Fascists,
after having killed Becciolini, the presumed murderer of
their fallen companion, organized more reprisals. Anti-
Fascists were tracked down, their studies and their shops
were sacked, their homes burned.

" It was almost midnight when several inhabitants of
my quarter saw a black automobile, lights out, stop about

500 metres from our house. A dozen persons descended. One, drawing his revolver, stayed to guard the chauffeur. The other went along the Africo, obliging all whom they met to run. In the street Fratelli Dandolo, where our house was, many were at their windows, watching the burning of the furniture of the Honourable Baldesi, which had been thrown into the street. The Fascists fired several shots in the air, summoning all to withdraw. This did not stop any one, the lights being out, from following events in the street and in our house, by looking through the shutters.

"That evening my husband returned late after paying his workmen, and after dining, retired, being very weary. We slept soundly, and neither heard nor perceived what happened in the street.

"Suddenly we were awakened by a great noise. I lighted the room. Before us was a man, small, sinister, with a hat over his eyes. He brandished two revolvers. A second person, who had also entered our room, approached my husband and in a menacing voice said, ' Dress and follow me to Fascist headquarters.'

"' I will follow you,' replied my husband, and seated on the bed began to put on his trousers on the one leg he had left after the war.

"' Come quickly,' said the Fascist. ' Are you really Pilati ? '

"' Yes.'

"Hardly had he said that word when the two bandits discharged their revolvers at him.

"After receiving the first shot in his left shoulder, my husband rolled from the bed to the door, either because he wanted to leave the bed so as not to expose me to more shots, or to block the door to our son's room.

"Maddened by terror, I screamed.

"At the open window suddenly appeared the sinister figure of a third bandit.

"I heard another shot, and the man who had already spoken cried, ' Quick, quick, let us depart.'

"He had hardly gone when my husband, groaning

painfully, said to me : ' Look, look, how many wounds. Give me a bandage.'

" Another tenant saw the bandits flee. One of them, while the chauffeur was blowing his horn for all to return, proposed to them : ' Let's go have a drink on me. I was the one who killed him, you know.'

" My husband was taken on a stretcher to the hospital of Santa Maria Nuova. To the porter who asked what had happened to him he replied :

" ' The Austrians have mutilated me ; the Italians have murdered me.'

" After three days of agony he breathed his last . . . The funeral, by order of the police, was held secretly.

" In March 1926, during the hearing, I was confronted with Ermini, who was defended by the attorney Meschiari. I, however, was unable to find an attorney to take up the case. I recognized, without hesitation, one of the assassins.

" When the day came for the trial I was the victim of all sorts of pressure and threats for the purpose of making me deny the identity of Ermini. I was offered much money, which I refused with indignation.

" I asked for passports for myself and my son. I was told I would get them if I would give up going to the trial. Every one was canvassed to conquer my resistance, the Attorney Pacchi, the Colonel Lanari, the Deputy Delcroix, the prefect.

" Finally the attorney who had charge of my interests was summoned by the prefecture and by the Fascio to abandon me.

" I had to resign myself to do without assistance.

" The trial began in Chieti at the end of April. I was exhausted, sick, I was in bed. But the fear of betraying my dead husband by my absence gave me a new strength.

" At the trial I was veritably attacked by the lawyers. But I remained firm and confirmed my identification of Ermini.

" The assassins were acquitted. At Florence they posted police at my house. The assassins returned to my quarter, amusing themselves by coming under the windows and insulting me."

The listing of Masonic leaders and their destruction was partly the work of the head of the Florentine Fascio, Lupporini, who, as fate would have it, was accidently shot in a scuffle. It was the death of Lupporini which supplied the immediate reason for holding the massacre in September.

On Sunday, October 4th, so many British, American, and other foreign citizens had been clubbed and robbed that the terrified tourists fled to the consulates for refuge. The American, British, and Swiss consuls raised their flags, as if for a holiday or for a war ; the frightened nationals poured into the diplomatic buildings, and the consuls telegraphed their protests directly to Mussolini. It was the next day that Farinacci sent word to Florence, "Cease hostilities."

More than a week of rioting and murder and hardly a word in the foreign press about a state of revolution in one of the most beautiful and popular tourist centres of Europe. For Fascist censorship it was a great success. The cables were stopped in the post-offices, telegrams to Paris held up, letters opened, the foreign journalists held almost incommunicado. Then the Fascist press bureau began issuing statements which the venal Stefani agency, the Italian journalists representing the American papers, and some leading but betrayed American and British reporters, accepted as true and sent out. In these Fascist reports it was stated that the Masons and the Socialists had attacked a Fascist without warning and killed him, that the mob demanded vengeance and acted without authority. The government then pacified the city.

It was more than a week after the massacre before the honest journalists saw that the official reports were not true, but then it was too late to send out sensational news ; the matter was now historical—and therefore dead. The *Ligue des Droits de l'Homme* later sent its protest :

" The savage onslaught on Masonry then organized at Mussolini's instigation was nothing more than a move to use these artifically provoked sanguinary upheavals as a plea for indefinitely putting off the date of the Matteotti trial : because Mussolini knew that at the public hearing of the evidence in court it would not be possible for him to prevent the disclosure of his own personal responsibility for the atrocious crime."

But that was not news, either.

A correspondent was invited to ask Mussolini questions about the massacre of the Freemasons. " Could your Excellency explain the reason for the Fascist war on Masonry ? " His Excellency could :

" I am very glad you asked that question, because there is a lot of misunderstanding in Anglo-Saxon countries over this question. We must once and for all make clear the great difference between English and American Masonry and the political Masonry of Italy. . . . Italian Masons have nothing in common with English Masons except the name. . . . The work of Masonry on behalf of our independence has been much exaggerated.

" The sect must be absolutely abolished because its influence is deleterious to discipline in the army, to the impartiality of the courts, and tends to subvert that order which should obtain in all public offices. Masonry has overturned all regulations. . . .

" Fortunately, Fascism has struck Italian Masonry such a blow that it will be difficult for it to regain its legs again for some time. . . . The grave attempt on my life on the anniversary of our glorious victory, and the plot to throw the whole nation into disorder, show what a sinister influence the Masonic sect—which undoubtedly inspired the criminal attempt on my life—has on the minds even of Italians, who, because of their social position and past military experience, ought to be better able to understand the folly and shame of this latest exploit."

This " latest exploit " to which Mussolini refers is the Zaniboni plot, which will be told in due time. William Bird, the noted journalist from Paris, where he was free of censorship, quoted one of Mussolini's admirers as informing him that " either Mussolini is rapidly going mad or else the worst elements among his entourage have so completely dominated him that he is no longer free to act according to his own judgment. This so-called plot is too obviously trumped up to deceive anybody. It was intended simply as a pretext for dissolving the United Socialist Party and for closing the Masonic lodges."

The other point emphasized by Mussolini in his interview, the difference between the Scottish Rite and the Grand Orient types of Masonry is hardly supported by what happened to the Scottish lodge at the time the Fascists were killing the Masons of Florence. Of those, John Bond, of the Fellowship Forum, wrote :

" In Rome the Masons of the Scottish Rite had their offices in the great palace right opposite the church of the Jesuits. . . . While a meeting of the lodge was in progress, Mussolinian thugs armed with cudgels broke down the doors, beat the members of the lodge, and then set fire to the premises. . . . No mention was made in the Roman newspapers.

" Commendatore Raoul Palermi, the Grand Master of the Scottish Rite, well-known to leading Masons all over the world, a scholar and a gentleman in the truest sense of the word, had to give up his home in Rome, as several attempts had been made to break in and set it on fire. He had been spared in the general massacre because he enjoyed the esteem of men who were close to the King. . . . He was ' advised ' by the prefect of the Roman police to leave Rome . . . and went to a little town near Palermo. . . . One morning he was found unconscious in his writing-room, stabbed. The police gave out a statement to his friends (no news of the fact was permitted to appear in the press) that the wounds seemed to have been self-inflicted. Happily they were not fatal."

It is an obvious fact that the Scottish Rite was suppressed in Italy, and it is another obvious fact that Fascist propaganda has not only ignored this, but perverted the news for the press. Mussolini frequently has come to his own defence with vast vague attacks. Thus on one occasion he links Masonry with Bolshevism when he speaks of " Italy's imps, the red dabblers, our organization of so-called Freemasons." Again he resorts to his habitual characteristic methods of using foul language ; thus he cautions us not to forget that " this shady institution with its secret nature has always had in Italy a character typical of the briber and the blackmailer . . . the Masons of Italy have always represented a distortion, not only in political life, but in spiritual concepts. . . . Its secret character throughout the twentieth century, its mysterious meetings, abhorrent to our beautiful communities with their sunlight and their love of truth, gave to the sect the character of corruption, a crooked concept of life, without programme, without soul, without moral value. . . . For my direct, methodical, consistent course of policy the hate of the Masonic sect persecutes me even now. . . . This is a war without quarter, a war of which I am a veteran. . . . I have always had against me our Masonry. But that organization, which in other times was very powerful, has been beaten by me. Against me it did not and cannot win. Italians won this battle for me. They found the cure for this leprosy. . . . I obeyed the positive command of my conscience, and not any opportunism. My attitude had nothing in common with the anti-Masonic spirit of the Jesuits."

And finally he speaks of the " corrupting, sinister, tortuous power as that of international Masonry of a political type, as distinguished from the Masonry known in the Anglo-Saxon countries."

According to an American Masonic investigation, the Fascisti destroyed 1000 lodges and clubs, pillaging most of them, throwing the emblems into the street or auctioning them off with a ribald ceremony, and burning what they could not dispose of otherwise.

The Grand Master of the Grand Orient Domizio Torrigiani was deported to the isle of Ponza ; General Luigi Capello, the erstwhile commander of the Italian Second Army, was sentenced to thirty years' imprisonment and became convict No. 3246 ; General Roberto Bencivenga, former chief of the general staff of General Cadorna, was also deported to Ponza.

Whether Masonry was guilty of anti-Fascist activities

cannot be answered definitely. One fact is certain : from the time the Masons of Italy ceased to give money and moral support to Fascism, from the time they saw Fascism assume all authority and realized that Mussolini was waging war against the lodges and their leaders, they began to draw to themselves all those who hoped for another risorgimento. Garibaldi had once called Masonry his bulwark of liberty ; perhaps some new leader, some new Matteotti or Amendola, would join with Masonry and under the banner of the Aventine Opposition rally all elements for another battle of restoration of personal and public rights. So Masons thought in 1925. In destroying Masonry, therefore, Mussolini destroyed the one great secret habitat of a possible future enemy, an enemy which might prove dangerous to his soaring will to maintain himself throughout his lifetime in full and absolute power.

CHAPTER XVIII

MUSSOLINI CONQUERS THE MAFIA

AMONG the minor forces dangerous to the progress of Fascism was the Mafia, the secret terroristic organization which was particularly active in Sicily and the southern provinces. This menace Mussolini met and in his typical way conquered. It is one of the achievements most loudly and universally acclaimed in the press.

Mussolini found that in reality there were two big secret terror organizations called indiscriminately the Mafia. The one protected the countryside, the other the city ; the one levied tribute on farmers, the other on urban merchants, and among themselves they fought. Every one was a victim. If a peasant wanted to take a bullock-load of vegetables into Naples or Palermo he had to pay a small percentage to some gangster who would assure him " safety" on the trip both ways and his money. Likewise city merchants were mulcted. Sicily saw the origin of all the beer and movie and pants-pressing rackets of Chicago, and it happened generations ago.

Mussolini soon realized that the urban Mafia was far superior to the rural Mafia. S. S. McClure, one of Mussolini's best apologists in America, believed that Sicily was " under a tyranny of the worst and most powerful criminal oligarchy that ever existed," making the American urban system of murder, robbery, blackmail, kidnapping, and other forms of violence " mild " in comparison. In the province of Palermo there were 1750 murders in one year : Chicago would have to have 7000 murders a year in place of 300 to equal it.

These thousands of Mafiosi, who for half a century had become a great power in the American underworld, who had established the Black Hand system in the Italian colonies in New York, Chicago, and other large centres, and who were later to take the leadership in bootlegging and racketeering, were now doomed to remain in Italy.

To meet the situation Mussolini appointed the Honourable De Carnezza, governor of Sicily, and sent Cesare Mori to Palermo as prefect.

Some forty years ago Mori, an artillery officer, entered the police department as a delegato, the lowest rank, and began his new career in Trapani, which, with Palermo, shared the reputation of being the centre of Mafia activities. His chief work was rounding up the cattle-maimers whose specialty was hamstringing the live stock of landowners who refused to pay their " contributions." It was racketeering in its purest Chicago form.

So successful was Mori that he gained advancement and medals for courage, military, and civil valour. When Nitti was made Prime Minister he gave Mori the highest rank, quæstor in Rome.

In 1923, when Mussolini had been in power for almost a year, the leading urban business men of Sicily came to Rome with the request that Mori be sent back to command the forces against the Mafia. Naturally enough, these prominent gentlemen who had contributed liberally to the Fascist cause wanted their business protected by the new government, instead of the bandits who were preaching " the pernicious doctrine that the police and the law were the enemies of the common people," and who were extremely active in levying a tax on the wealthy city merchants.

Mori, who did not play politics, went to work as a soldier ; but Carnezza, who was a Fascist politician, carried out orders from Rome.

Mussolini, adding a new twist to the axiom, *divesa et umpera*, ordered that a distinction be made between the city and the rural bandits ; the former, which was the larger section, was armed and given moral encouragement, while the latter division was proscribed. Under these circumstances country banditry soon disappeared.

Mussolini then incorporated the urban branch of the Mafia into the Black Shirt militia. According to Don

Sturzo it was the Honourable De Carnezza who, in addition to all their other weapons, added the Fascist manganello to the Mafia equipment, and Bolitho, after an investigation two years later, found that " De Carnezza took into his service the celebrated Mafia and the hardly less redoubtable ' squadra del baltico ' for whom he found much employment in the elections."

The addition of this criminal element to the armed forces of the new state made itself felt. According to Gilbert Murray, " many parts of Italy have long been accustomed to the rule of private extra-legal societies like the Camorra, the Mafia, and the Black Hand. The Fascist Society is only a Camorra on a grand scale."

To-day there is no longer a vegetable-racket in Sicily. The peasants come in peace, the merchants haggle in peace, and quiet reigns. Because the Mafiosi, the Black-handers, have been transferred throughout the kingdom, doing their work on a national scale, levying taxation upon men and industries, administering castor oil to small offenders, shooting working-men who attempt to flee into Switzerland or France, clubbing critics of the government and generally engaging in the old racket.

Their work is to get the money from the little men and to keep the little men in the Fascist line. For big-time work there are more important persons, the podestas, the minor dictators of cities and provinces. Thus the street-repaving job in Rome in the Holy Year 1925 was found recently to have entailed a graft of $70,000 for the Black Camorra, while other municipal improvements so highly praised by Holy Year pilgrims netted another big sum. In Milan racketeering reached unprecedented heights. In many cities and rural districts Fascist Party racketeers levy tribute on their original backers, the big banks and industries. Following is a sample instance, a communiqué sent by the *ras* of the province of Pesaro Urbino to the wealthy :

" I have audited recently the amount of subventions given the Fascio by the proprietors in this province.

" It is useless for me to declare that I do not know how to employ so much money flowing into our treasury.

"Certain gentlemen, proprietors of many millions, have offered us sums which, in proportion to the capital which Fascism has saved for them, amounts to almost nothing. On this account, considering that by the systems we have employed up to now we have taken in practically nothing, I warn the proprietors of the province of Pesaro Urbino that I will impose upon them taxes in proportion to their capital and in such fashion that I soon will be able to systematize definitely the finances of our province."

So it is that to-day, when a black shirt is buttoned over a leading Fascist bosom, the fingers frequently are those of an old Black Hand. When an automobile side-swiped another somewhere in New York or Chicago in the old bad days, when a stream of sub-machine gun bullets "rubbed out" a gangster, the finger on the trigger very likely was that of an old Mafiosi of Sicily who had been able to get away in time. And when a man is put on the spot, whether in Italy or America, it is frequently by the same common methods, because the same type of men from the same native towns are employed. Fascism, instead of eradicating the Black Hand, Camorra, and Mafia systems, found a new use for its clever members.

Instead of terrorizing, extorting money, or killing for the purpose of private gain, the "totalitarian" Mafiosi are trained to employ their talents "for national and patriotic purposes." They are dispersed throughout the country, and some have important positions in the new secret-service organization which the new régime found necessary to its existence.

CHAPTER XIX

CHEKA—SPELLED CECA OR OVRA

POWER rests on fear as well as the consent of the governed. The corner policeman still plays a part in our lives. We, the fortunate, who are governed by a President, a Congress, or a parliament whom we elect, and who are not dictated to by a man in absolute power, frequently may protest against actions by the forces of law and order as terroristic, but we cannot, even when we go touring in foreign lands, completely realize the state of fear that exists under a political system which employs terror as an instrument.

Even in time of war, when an enemy occupies a country, the very necessary mass terrorism which frees the rulers from the alternative of appointing one policeman for every inhabitant, is mild in comparison to the dictatorial system.

Terrorism is the finest and cheapest weapon of the modern tyrant. But if he wishes to avoid the ignominious fate of a weakling, of a Primo de Rivera for example, the tyrant of our day must be ruthless, unsentimental, unswerving. He must have little regard for human life. He must be implacable, and he must remain fixed on the idea of survival.

To meet that problem Mussolini found that the methods of his predecessors were useless. After he had dispersed all the organized elements of opposition, from the political parties to the comparatively unimportant Mafia in the south, he realized that he had to employ the same terroristic organizations as the rulers of Russia forced upon Lenin in 1918, when leniency with enemies of the régime resulted in growing discontent and the attempted assassination of the head of the government.

Mussolini already had his bodyguard, his little group of

men who carried out the secret orders. He now began to
build a powerful organization. At the same time he made
public and press statements denying its existence, and one
day had the courage to repeat them to the Chamber of
Deputies.

" Gentlemen," he said, " I am the one who brings forth
in this hall the accusations against myself.

" It has been said that I have founded a ' Cheka.'

" Where ? When ? In what way ? Nobody is able to
say. Russia has executed without trial from 150,000 to
160,000 people, as shown by statistics almost official.
There has been a Cheka in Russia which has exercised
terror systematically over all the middle classes, and over
the individual members of those classes, a Cheka which
claimed to be the red sword of revolution. *But an Italian
Cheka has never had a shadow of existence.*

" Nobody has ever denied that I am possessed of these
three qualities : a discreet intelligence, a lot of courage,
and an utter contempt for the lure of money.

" If I had founded a Cheka, I would have done it by
following the lines of reasoning that I have always used in
defending the one kind of violence that can never be eliminated from history.

" I have always said—and those who have always
followed me in these five years of hard struggle can now
remember it—that violence, to be useful in settling anything, must be surgical, intelligent, and chivalrous. Now,
all the exploits of any so-called Cheka have always been
unintelligent, passionate, and stupid.

" Can you really think that I could order—on the day
following the anniversary of Christ's birth, when all saintly
spirits are hovering near—can you think that I could order
an assault at ten o'clock in the morning ? . . . Please do
not think me such an idiot."

Yet despite his calling on all saintly spirits that Christmas day, despite his disavowal of violence, a Cheka which,
it is true, still had no name or definite organization, was
already flourishing in Italy in the Year One, Era Fascisti.
The Saint-Just of the Italian terror system was that same

Rossi who was so prominent in the Matteotti case. He himself was a great admirer of Djerdzinsky of Russia, and commonly among themselves, Mussolini, Rossi, Dumini, and the others referred to their little group as the " Ceca," which in Italian is pronounced Cheka.

Following the threatened uprising in 1924 it was nationalized. According to its chief, " Several days before the Matteotti tragedy, in the face of the acts, gestures of indiscipline, and nonchalance of Fascist Deputies, such as Rocca and Ravazzola, Mussolini before me and others of the National Directorate expressed his astonishment that the party police, the famous ' Ceca,' had given no sign of life. On that occasion he is reported as having said in absolute tranquillity : ' Action against these parliamentary gentlemen cannot be taken by any legal arm ; we deplore, we expel, we demand the resignations, but they do not care a darn. . . . There is nothing to do but beat them without mercy. This Ceca, does it function or not ? '

" The mother-idea of this Ceca was Mussolini's alone. . . . The necessity of an organ for defence and for vengeance was explained by Mussolini as follows : ' The régime does not yet dispose of legal means for beating its enemies. Laws which exist represent the liberal spirit against which Fascism has arisen. To fill in this gap all governments in a state of transition have need of illegal powers to put their adversaries in place.'

" If, as a result, in the activity of the Cheka there were committed acts which were arbitrary and inopportune, this does not diminish the responsibility of its author, Mussolini. To attribute them solely to Rossi and Marinelli is the height of audacity and puerility."

Several years ago, when the Cheka was still a mystery, Paolo Valera made the declaration that this organization was a part of the Ministry of the Interior, and " appears to be a society of criminals and assassins. Its chief . . . is said to be Cesare Rossi, head of the press bureau of the Ministry. . . . Its agents are ,famous for their crimes." Prezzolini, one of the rare intellectuals who have spoken

14

in favour of the régime, admits that " the Matteotti and preceding crimes compel the admission that there existed a veritable criminal association preparing and executing the attacks and destruction inspired by Cesare Rossi."

So long as the censorship flourished and foreign correspondents were afraid to write anything which might offend Mussolini or were covetous of his goodwill, the Cheka was never mentioned. But on July 13, 1925, came the supreme test for honest journalists. It was on that day that of the 140 members of parliament who had seceded more than 100 signed an indictment against the Cheka. The signatories were not only Socialists, who were mourning their secretary-general and leader, but also representatives of the Catholic, Republican, Democratic, and Liberal Parties. This document read :

" In conclusion, the inquiry conducted by the High Court has brought out evidence more than sufficient to show that, under the auspices of the Head of the Government (Mussolini), men in confidence, sharing the functions if not the real and proper responsibilities of government, organized crimes to punish Deputies for their opposition to the régime ; and that for the preparation of these crimes there was a special collective organization (Cheka), of which several members are known."

Journalists who cabled the above became *personæ non gratæ* with the Fascist government and were expelled.

On the 29th of May, 1923, Misuri, a member of parliament, who had quitted the Fascist Party and therefore earned the undying hatred of its leader, made a speech full of criticism to which the Duce replied by a public threat of punishment. Almost immediately Misuri was attacked by Cheka men and beaten up. In a statement to the press [1] Misuri charged Mussolini with giving orders for the assault to several gangsters. There was no contradiction of this statement, no libel suit.

" The Misuri incident," reported James Murphy, " is

[1] *Il Popolo*, Rome, December 25, 1924.

a definite landmark, and probably marks the first official operation of the Cheka in its official functioning as a normal organ of the government."

The complete exposure of the Cheka as a murder organization and also as a racket was made before the Senate of Rome by Dr. Donati, editor of the Catholic newspaper *Il Popolo*, during the trial of General De Bono. The evidence states in part :

" The criminal association—or the Cheka, as it is more commonly called—bound together under a pact of mutual common action in crime the highest leaders of Fascism (Rossi, Marinelli, and so forth), the professional assassins (Dumini, and so forth), and the non-official coadjutors (*Corrierre Italiano*, Filippelli, and so forth). It had its headquarters in a government building, the Viminal, where Senator De Bono also had his dual head-quarters, as Director-General of Police and Chief of the Militia.

" The Cheka, which had already existed in embryonic form, was endowed with a regular constitution of its own at a meeting held in the private residence of the Premier, in the Via Rasella. Among those present was General De Bono, who had already been appointed Director-General of Police and First Commander-General of the Militia. There is explicit mention of this meeting in the affidavit drawn up by Finzi, which was submitted to three gentlemen who can give evidence as to its contents. These are Signor Schiff Giorgini, Commendatore Guglielmo Emmanuel, head of the Roman office of the *Corriere della Sera*, and the journalist Carlo Silvestri. This is also borne out by the evidence which these gentlemen have already given before the Crown Prosecutor, and confirmed by Finzi himself in a recent conversation which he had with Silvestri. Therefore the Cheka represented a constitutional organ of the Fascist Party and the Fascist Government.

" As we shall see, the Cheka was entrusted with a two-fold task : (1) to spy attentively on all movements of political parties and persons opposed to Fascism, also on lukewarm friends and open dissenters ; (2) to suppress the

more dangerous adversaries by violence in style,[1] under an
astute system of protection which ensured the impunity
of the assassins and their paymasters.

" The executive of the Cheka is identical with the General
Command of the militia. The General Command recruited
the hired gangsters, furnished the material and financial
means, arranged the plans, gathered information, provided
—through the office of the Premier's press agency (Cesare
Rossi)—for the ' working up ' of public opinion, and made
arrangements with the police authorities to guarantee the
impunity of the direct culprits.

" The Cheka was regarded as an instrument necessary
for the government of the country, according to the literal
expression used by Finzi in his affidavit. To this Cheka
organization we are to attribute the well-known acts of
violence committed against the Deputies Mazzolani, Misuri,
Buffoni, Amendola, Forni, Bergamini, Nitti, and the
journalist Giannini ; also the murder of Father Giovanni
Minzoni at Argenta, the murder of the labourer Antonio
Piccinnini, Socialist candidate in Reggio Emilia, and the
murder of Matteotti."

While the Fascist Senate refused to indict General
De Bono for alleged complicity in the murder of Matteotti,
" for lack of sufficient evidence," it did not deny Donati's
charges that there was a Cheka functioning in Italy,
and even referred to it as " the committee which has been
organized against the enemies of Fascism." In corroboration of Donati's charges there were General Balbo's letter
about the Minzoni murder, the confessions of Rossi and

[1] " Bastonatura in stile " (bastinadoing in style) is the technical phrase
used in the orders sent out from the headquarters of the National militia.
It stands for a distinct type of cudgelling, and those who are entrusted
with the task have been specially trained in the barracks, where they
have a dummy figure on which they practise. The weapon used is a
specially made bludgeon, which is rather heavy towards the end and is
somewhat flexible. Most of the blows are inflicted on the lower part of
the face, for the purpose of breaking the jawbone and thus laying up the
victim for months. Care is taken not to fracture the skull, lest death may
ensue. This is of great importance when such men as Amendola are to
be punished, for the murder of another Deputy would bring ruin on
Fascism.

Filippelli, and other sworn statements, most of which the Senate declined to read. Threatened with immediate death, the Catholic editor fled to France the day the Senatorial report was issued.

In January 1927, the French government discovered how vast and international the Fascist Cheka had become, when Ricciotti Garibaldi, one of the grandsons of the founder of Italian liberty, who seemingly was active in France in the struggle for restoration of freedom in his native land, was arrested by the police of Nice.

At the trial, in November, testimony was given that there was a conspiracy in southern France to organize two armies, one of Spaniards, the other of Italians, and march against the dictators. Garibaldi had involved Colonel Francesco Macia, the ardent Catalonian patriot (and after the Spanish revolution, governor of Catalonia), in gun-running to Spain, and had furnished the information to Mussolini directly, so that the Italian dictator could retail it to his Spanish colleague De Rivera and thus further their secret treaty of co-operation and good-will. Moreover, Garibaldi had conspired with gunmen in Paris, with leading Freemasons and republicans, and with labour leaders and patriots who saw in him the possible liberator of Italy. So cleverly did he do his work that even Fascist agents were fooled. Thus Luigi Villari at the time wrote that the " neo-Garibaldian movement was being prepared under the leadership of Ricciotti Garibaldi, Junior . . . with the support of Italian and French Freemasonry. The aim was actually to attempt an armed invasion of Italy. . . ."

Villari indignantly reports meetings between the Paris Freemasons, Garibaldi, and Torrigiani, head of the Grand Orient of Italy, and connects them all with the conspiracy of Tito Zaniboni to assassinate Mussolini. The fact is that Garibaldi was sent to Mussolini to do several jobs as an agent provocateur, but his main purpose in going to France was twofold : to earn 2,000,000 lire for stealing the documents signed by Mussolini [1] from Signor Fasciolo, one-time

[1] Gobetti telegram, etc., and letters relative to the American oil deal of 1924.

secretary to the Duce, and to earn another 2,000,000 if he
succeeded in putting Fasciolo " out of circulation." He
succeeded in neither of these things, but he did earn
645,000 lire for what he did accomplish.

On November 6th it was reported that " Garibaldi
confessed to being an agent provocateur, a stool pigeon in
the pay of Mussolini. Mussolini's government is exposed
as deliberately fomenting plots ; as sending its secret agents
to France to play the spy and traitor ; as paying 100,000
francs in a single sum for a mean piece of work done on
French territory in violation of the French laws." [1]

The official criminal-court record at the Paris trial shows
Garibaldi confessing that he had intrigued with a man
named Scevoli to go on a mission to Rome ; having obtained
Scevoli's passport, Garibaldi sent it to Lapolla, chief of the
Fascist police, who used it for secret trips between Garibaldi
and Mussolini.

Of the 645,000 lire received, Garibaldi confessed,
400,000 came from Federzoni. Papers and letters from
Federzoni and from Gino Lucetti, one of the would-be
assassins of Mussolini, were introduced and read. At the
close of the first day's hearings there was more than a
suspicion that Garibaldi might have been involved in a plot
to assassinate the Duce for the benefit of dissenting Fascist
leaders, of whom the most notable in 1926 was Federzoni,
the nationalist and royalist.

The second day's hearings, which coincided with reports
from Rome of 100 dead and 1000 wounded in the three-day
riots which the Fascists carried out as reprisals for the
Zamboni shooting, Ricciotti was confronted by Sante
Garibaldi.

" There is not one among us who would not have gone
blindly to death at the bidding of this man, because of the
name he bears," said Sante Garibaldi, pointing at Ricciotti ;
and then addressing the latter : " If you have the lightest
sense of honour left, there is but one thing remaining for
you to do. What are you waiting for ? Why don't you
beat out your brains against a wall ? "

[1] *New York World*, November 6, 1926.

"I am a victim of fatality," muttered Ricciotti. He had come to court wearing his monocle and his Legion of Honour ribbon ; he had tried for a few minutes to deny and to brave it out, but now he was almost in tears ; "It was Mussolini who led me into a trap," he concluded.

"Traitor," shouted Sante Garibaldi : "you have dragged the name of our family, glory, and honour into the mire."

"I am a victim of an awful fatality," mumbled Ricciotti, "I have taken money, it is true, but I have not betrayed the cause of liberty." He fell on his knees, clasped the hand of his young brother to his lips, and asked forgiveness.

Macia and Garibaldi were found guilty. Mussolini apologized to France.

Altogether there were nineteen conspirators on trial. Maître Torres defended Colonel Macia.

"It is true. I admit," said the Catalonian patriot to the court. "It was my duty as a patriot. When I am free I will begin again." He confessed that the Catalonian arms were shipped as "brooms" to sweep out Catalonia ; bayonets were marked "toothpicks," and rifles "flutes."

Garibaldi, Macia, and sixteen others were given short terms in prison for possessing firearms ; as the seventeen men came up for sentence, each in turn dramatically walked past Garibaldi, pointed at the chest full of hero medals, and uttered the word "Traitor."

The trial also brought out the following facts :

That there existed in Europe and America a large organization of spies and agents provocateurs in the pay of Fascism.

That acts of violence committed in Paris, New York, Buenos Aires, and other big Italian centres against Fascists are frequently instigated by Fascist agents themselves for the purpose of furnishing pretexts for prosecutions and protests from the Italian government.

That Italian state functionaries did not hesitate to "sequester" persons, steal documents in foreign countries, and instigate attempts at assassination.

That all such actions were developed with the assistance

of the Italian embassies. Ricciotti, for example, received his money and instructions in the diplomatic mail-bag to France.

All the foregoing is legal testimony ; the French government has acted upon it, the Italian government has made amends. Yet in Mussolini's autobiography there is only this reference : " The manœuvre of the former Premiers definitely failed and became ridiculous, just as did other artificial structures attempted about that time. One was a movement inspired by Benelli, under the name of the Italian League, to create a secession from Fascism, and another an underhand manœuvre by some short-weight grandchildren of Garibaldi." Apparently the employee was not worthy of his hire !

It is of course possible for the head of a government, the founder of a secret police, to remain ignorant of its ramifications, its plottings, and its assassinations. Perhaps Mussolini never knew that the " short-weight grandchildren of Garibaldi " were employees of his own Cheka.

That the consulates abroad were filled with Fascist squadrist leaders or former racketeers is generally admitted. Some of these young men now occupying diplomatic positions have never been anything but leaders of the " reprisal " gangs which terrorized small towns, administered castor oil, burned, looted, beat up the adversaries pointed out to them by Fascist political leaders. Street fights, political assassinations, and espionage trials have proved that everywhere the Italian embassies and consulates are centres of Fascist intrigue, just as the Bolshevik embassies, consulates, and trade commission headquarters have frequently harboured Cheka agents and the political spy system.

Several high Fascist officials were some time ago recalled from Brazil to explain numerous " incidents." There had been demonstrations against the embassy and consulates in which not only anti-Fascisti, but native Brazilians, had taken part as a retaliation for Fascist racketeering. In San Paulo the police had to rescue the Fascist consul from an infuriated mob. In Buenos Aires a Fascist consul tried by force to shanghai an anti-Fascist engineer who was visiting an Italian warship ; the result was a fist fight and a public scandal ; another consul to Brazil was accused of plotting the murder of a rich man in order to marry the widow ; in Argentine a Fascist consul was arrested for dealing in obscene post cards. Almost all the consuls were members of the former squadristi.

In a more recent international scandal, in Brussels, it was testified in court that the Fascist agent Menapace, who planted the dynamite, revolver, and incriminating papers in the home and pockets of the anti-Fascist journalist Cianca, was an employee of the Italian embassy. Menapace was exposed by the liberal paper *Le Soir*, but the embassy succeeded in helping him to escape the country. Some time later the pro-Fascist newspaper of Switzerland, *Suisse*, demanded the withdrawl of the Italian consul at St. Gall and of eight Fascist spies, so flagrant had become the racketeering in that canton. The Swiss government easily expelled the eight gangsters, but had to negotiate with the Italian ambassador because the Fascist consul claimed diplomatic immunity.

After officially denying for four years the existence of a Ceca, or Cheka, Mussolini by virtue of Article 8 of the law of November 25, 1926, " legalized " the organization, by establishing exceptional tribunals " for the defence of the State," a euphemism which the French used during the Commune, and the Soviets in 1918. The law provided that it was to remain in force until December 6, 1931, Mussolini expressing the hope that within five years he would extirpate all opposition. Meanwhile a new penal code was written, which became operative on July 1, 1931. But the Fascist Party, realizing that its strength of a little more than 1,500,000 was not enough to intimidate the majority, held a special session of the Grand Council on March 6, 1931, which decided that " political crimes, as comprehended by the new penal code, must be submitted to the special tribunal for the defence of the State, whose functions are prolonged until 1936." The special tribunal is the O.V.R.A., Organizzazione Vigilanza Repressione Antifascismo ; it is the terroristic arm of Fascism and Musso-

lini's personal vengeance ; it is the old bastard child of
Fascism, the Ceca, grown up and legitimatized by its
brilliant father.

To-day the work of the O.V.R.A. is international ; it
employs thousands if not several hundred thousand agents ;
in fact, Bolitho believed that every tenth man in Italy is
at least a part-time worker of the organization.

Ever since its emergence from secrecy, the activities of
the Cheka have received notice in the official press, usually
a few lines like the following :

" The special section O.V.R.A. of the department of
public safety, a part of the Ministry of the Interior, has
discovered a clandestine organization. . . ."

" The O.V.R.A. has likewise identified a Communist
organization in Emilia and has made arrests, denouncing the
chiefs to the special tribunal.

" The O.V.R.A. has discovered in Rome an anti-Fascist
group developing criminal activity by the clandestine
distribution of defamatory literature.   The chiefs have been
arrested :   Mario Vinciguerra, Renzo Rendi, and Madame
De Bosis, a widow."

Thus, many years after Mussolini had officially denied
that in the Ministry of Interior, the Viminale, he had under
him a branch of government commonly called Cheka, it
was officially announced that the O.V.R.A. of the Viminale
Palace, where Mussolini still presides, was functioning
excellently.

It was the third of these announcements that interested
America, because Signora De Bosis was born Lillian Vernon,
of Springfield, Missouri.   Her father was dean of a college
in upper New York State, and her son, Dr. Lauro De Bosis,
professor at Columbia, was head of the National Alliance
which the O.V.R.A., through an agent provocateur, had
succeeded in crushing.   This Alliance had three objectives :
to tell the news which the press suppressed, to form a union
of the constitutional parties, and to prepare the " men of
order " to take over the government when Fascism collapsed
and a Bolshevik reaction followed.   The Alliance sent out
circulars written by Lauro De Bosis ;   Vinciguerra and

Rendi were sentenced to fifteen years' imprisonment on the charge that they mailed the circulars. Both are journalists, the former once on the liberal *Mondo*, the latter an occasional literary correspondent of the *New York Evening Post* and *New York Times*.

Another plot netted twenty-four intellectuals. The O.V.R.A.'s agent was Carlo Del Re. From the time of Rossi and Dumini, Mussolini has always had some important, usually quite intelligent, man in his Cheka who carried out personal orders and pursued personal enemies. In 1925 it was Quaglia, in 1926 it was Ricciotti Garibaldi, in 1928 Di Gaeta, in 1929 Menapace, and in 1930 Del Re.

This agent was sent by the O.V.R.A. to visit prominent leaders abroad who were Mussolini's enemies. In October 1929, for example, Del Re came to Brussels to interest Count Sforza in a little dynamiting. He began by asking the former Minister of Foreign Affairs if ideas were enough and whether violence was not better; he, Del Re, had some nice chemical plans for bombs and believed it would be a fine gesture to throw one at the Pope, or at least blow up Saint Peter's, as a sign to the world that there was anti-Fascist activity. Count Sforza asked Del Re to leave the house, so the agent went after smaller game.

Returning to Milan, Del Re trafficked with numerous professional men; one of them, the chemist Umberto Ceva, member of the old Republican party, liberal and democrat, he tried to interest in his bomb schemes. Ceva answered he would not care to play the game of violence. Del Re, however, on leaving the house, placed a piece of paper with the design for a bomb, on Ceva's table, and it was found in the place indicated to them, by the O.V.R.A. agents and militia who made the arrest the next morning.

On being given the third degree in prison, Ceva, believing Del Re an honest if too violent anti-Fascist, refused to admit the origin of the paper with the bomb design. He committed suicide rather than betray the betrayer Del Re. A few days later the press officially announced Del Re was the agent of the O.V.R.A. Ceva's suicide was kept secret by the Fascist government until a protest from groups of British intellectuals asking for a fair trial was sent to Mussolini.

Another of Del Re's victims was Mussolini's personal enemy, Ferruccio Parri, who with Carlo Rosselli aided Filippo Turati, for many years head of the anti-Fascist movement in France, to escape from Italy. Parri, a major on the general staff during the war, liberal-democrat-republican, was sentenced to a year in prison, then to "forced domicile," then to the island of Ponza, then to Lipari, and finally, having expiated not only his original crime, but every charge the O.V.R.A. could bring, he returned to Milan. Here Del Re attempted to get his consent for a dynamite plot, and despite Parri's being declared not guilty by the Special Tribunal, he was in 1931 sent to an African colony for five years.

Another personal enemy of Mussolini's, Camillo Berneri, professor of philosophy, was the victim of the O.V.R.A. agent Menapace, who placed a false passport and a quantity of an explosive called cheddite in Berneri's pockets, then informed the Brussels police. As this occurred at the time the Italian Crown Prince was shot at in Belgium, Berneri was arrested, deported, then arrested in France and in Luxembourg and in France again. The professor to this day doesn't know what all the political intrigue is about.

An American journalist of many years' residence in Rome, one who is forced by circumstances to send glowing reports *via* the daily cables, and one of the many who has smuggled true reports to the present writer, thus sums up the situation :

" The Fascist system has given modern Italy the atmosphere in which the Medici and the Borgias would find themselves perfectly at home. After years of Fascist rule and consolidation, the Italian people are still deprived of all liberties. They accept this as a measure of force majeure, silently, but they suffer from a sense of slavery to an oligarchy which does not represent the best elements in Italian life. The right to keep silent is practically the only one left.

" The opposition is watched, tracked down like wild

beasts. No one can find out how many unfortunates are imprisoned in the unhealthy isles or in the prisons of the mainland. The special tribunals have condemned wholesale large groups. One tribunal in one year condemned 400 persons to 2000 years' imprisonment. . . . All these events are carefully concealed so that no indignation may be aroused abroad. . . . The Duce admits 100,000 professional policemen. There are even more in plain clothes. . . . Amateur spies are daily denouncing persons they suspect according to the best traditions of a reign of terror. Petty and private tyranny takes the most exasperating and minor forms. . . . All this is never felt nor suspected by the visiting tourists. . . .

"All this is accepted supinely and in silence by the Italian people, who are waiting for something to happen which will deliver them from a denomination and a fate which they do not think they deserve, and from a system which is entirely alien to their civilization and beliefs. . . . It would require too much space to recall the incidents revealing the miasma of oppression and repression under which Italians live. . . . The special revolutionary tribunal functions with harshness and ferocity. . . . Families of persons sent to *confino* (island exile) and of those who are *fuorusciti* or exiles, are subject to reprisals and held almost as hostages. . . . The secret police and system of national espionage penetrate every corner of Italian life. Persons are careful in talking to any one. Every one, accordingly, lives in an atmosphere of submission, without open expression.

"General Capello, the hero of Gorizia and friend of the King, is in confino. No one except Mussolini knows how many Italians are there. The estimate is as high as 200,000, but Mussolini put it at 1500, and the truth is somewhere between these two extremes. With hundreds of persons being sentenced monthly to the islands, the figure is certainly not Mussolini's. Hundreds are in the Mediterranean Siberia without trial.

"The régime has gained little hold on the majority of the upper and educated classes. . . . The surveillance of

Benedetto Croce and Professor Ferrero is on longer kept
secret. Fascism's hold to-day is sustained by the military
dominance of the Black Shirts and the secret police."

No one knows how many persons have been killed by
the Fascisti. Labriola, former Minister of Labour, announced
that from the time Mussolini took service under the employers' associations in 1920, until he entered Rome in 1922,
his squadristi murdered 4100 non-Fascists, of which murders
full case records exist. There are also lists of thousands of
victims in the ensuing years of Fascist rule. Mussolini's
one reply has been that the Bolsheviki in Russia killed more.

Mussolini defends not only violence as his means to
power and means of maintenance in power, but terrorism
as well. " In the creation of a new State," he says, " which
is authoritarian but not absolutist, hierarchal, and organic
—namely, open to the people in all its classes, categories,
and interests—lies the revolutionary originality of Fascism,
and a teaching, perhaps, for the whole modern world,
oscillating between the authority of the State and that of
the individual, between the State and the anti-State.
Like all other revolutions, the Fascist revolution has had a
dramatic development, but this in itself would not suffice to
distinguish it. The reign of terror is not a revolution : it is
only a necessary instrument in a determined phase of
revolution."

This phase of the Fascist revolution has now officially
been extended for almost ten years.

CHAPTER XX

THE FATE OF HEROES

IN the march of the Fascist Party from a weak, opportunistic, compromising minority to absolute dictatorship, it was necessary to employ methods tested in medieval times, proved invaluable by the Germans when they held enemy Belgium, and more recently used with abundant success in Russia. Sentimentalists and idealists alone raised horrified hands at the taking of hostages and the shooting of high officials. But realists and militarists know only too well that it was impossible for Ludendorff in 1914, and Lenin in 1918, to withstand the plotters and the snipers unless they used terrorism.

In Italy Mussolini was ably assisted by his generals. Of the original Quadrumvirate, the Generals De Bono, De Vecchi, Italo Balbo, and Michele Bianchi, who more or less led the march on Rome, all but one shared in the work of establishing the necessary Black Terror; and Bianchi died too soon to enjoy its fruits.

Many of the original minor heroes of Fascism have already been mentioned: Dumini, Rossi, Marinelli, Filippelli, Finzi, Volpi. Of the major heroes, the most impressive is Italo Balbo. At the age of twenty-five he was repaid for his devotion to the Duce by being put in command of the Black Shirt militia and given the title of *ras*, or sub-dictator, of the province of Ferrara. Here in the town of Argenta he found the leading anti-Fascist to be the veteran priest, Minzoni, who remained a follower of Don Sturzo, and who preached the old Catholic Party ideas of social reform. On August 23, 1923, the militia organized a " punitive expedition " to Argenta, where they burned and destroyed Catholic institutions and murdered the priest.   More than a year later public opinion forced the government to stage a public trial of the murderers.

During the hearing, in November, the following document was published in the Opposition press.   It relates to a trial of several men accused of anti-Fascist activities, but as no evidence, real or falsified, was produced, the Fascist judges were forced to free them.   Whereupon Balbo wrote :

TO THE COMMANDING GENERAL,—

As far as the men acquitted December 2 are concerned, it will be necessary to explain to them that a change of air and establishment in another province is necessary.   If they insist on remaining and consequently causing moral discomfort, it will be necessary to beat them—not too much, but as is customary—until they decide to leave.

Show only this part of my letter to the prefect and say to him in my name that I have sufficient evidence to justify my demand that the ruffians should leave the city and province. The *questura* will do well to persecute them at least weekly and let the prefect notify the King's procuratore that for a possible beating, which must be *in style*, a trial is not desired.   Read this part of the letter to the *consiglio federale*.   If I write this from Rome it is certain that I know of what I speak.   Basta.

ITALO BALBO.

On the occasion of a luncheon given Marshal Balbo by the Lord Mayor of London in December 1930, the latter read a long series of telegrams of congratulations, among them the following :

Unable to participate at your luncheon in the flesh, I am present in spirit.   DOM MINZONI.

There was a fine burst of British applause, but Balbo went as white as Macbeth on first seeing Banquo's ghost.

After his flight to America Balbo was honoured with an invitation to the White House, and thousands of columns of biography greeted the hero on arrival. But almost immediately upon returning to Rome to

THE FATE OF HEROES

receive the congratulations of a proud nation, Balbo was surprised to find every newspaper publishing an official history of his conquest of the Atlantic, a history which gave credit to Mussolini for organizing and directing the entire adventure. This surprise was turned into chagrin a little later when Balbo was sent to Africa as governor of Libya. Again the world understood that there was room for only one Caesar in Rome.

Quadrumvir De Vecchi alone has escaped the Duce's jealous wrath. Shortly after the "capture" of Rome, at a time when the Opposition were ridiculing the event which the victors called a "revolution," the Fascisti realized that a "blood bath"—to use the exact phrase which Mussolini once made—was necessary to consolidate the victory. On December 17, 1922, occurred the Massacre of Turin. On that day and the next several hundred anti-Fascists were beaten and at least a score murdered. Several more succumbed later. When, on the first day of the massacre, the Fascist headquarters in Turin was informed by journalists that only fourteen of the men listed for execution had been found dead, the reply was given that "The Po will deliver up the remaining bodies." On January 1, 1923, Under-Secretary of State De Vecchi said in a public speech :

" Yes, the reaction of a few days ago was necessary ; and though I was not there, I accept responsibility for all that happened."

In Part XXV of his confession Rossi states that " I must in good faith declare that in this case no orders were sent from Rome. The responsibility lay entirely with the Turin group of Fascists. The judicial authorities and the police were in collusion."

The extent of the massacre having surpassed all in Fascist history, it caused a tremendous reaction throughout Italy. In Mussolini's cabinet, at the time, there were still several liberals who opposed violence and demanded that the guilty be punished. A commission of inquiry was sent. Gasti, its chief, took testimony which led Mussolini to recall Gasti and dissolve the commission. The Grand

Fascist Council met ; instead of expelling those responsible as the nation had expected, it sent them out of the country —as colonial premiers or ambassadors.

Farinacci of Cremona, a railroad worker who became the chief exponent of terrorism, surpassing Mussolini himself, devoted his home-town newspaper to advocating reprisals, punitive expeditions, " making life unbearable " for his opponents.   One day his supporters rounded up the small Socialist delegation and chased them ; the latter found refuge in a barn of a peasant.   Petroneschi was felled with one blow and left for dead.   In this way he escaped death ; but his colleague, Bolderi, president of the workers' co-operative of Cremona, was clubbed to death.   The chief murderer was a boy of sixteen.   Although Mussolini later deplored the crime, Farinacci declared in an interview with the press of all factions that he accepted " on behalf of Fascism responsibility for the murder of Bolderi."

Farinacci conducted the trial of the corpse of Matteotti at Chieti, but immediately afterwards, instead of being rewarded by Mussolini, was permitted to resign his high offices.   He accepted a provincial secretaryship.

Many of the " punitive expeditions " which Mussolini boasts of in his autobiography were led by Dumini ; they included the attack on the villa of ex-Premier Nitti, where the building was burned after being ransacked.   The assaults on the Deputies Misuri, Forni, and Amendola were also organized by Dumini.

He had a personal reason for assassinating Matteotti also.   The Opposition leader had promised that when he had finished exposing the 1924 election frauds in which he claimed that 1,500,000 false ballots had been counted by the Fascisti (enough to lose them their majority in parliament if there was a true recount), he would take up the subject of the commercial corruption of Fascist officials, predicting he would tell who was to get the graft if the (American) Sinclair Oil Company concession went through, and how a " household friend " of the Duce's was getting rich through betraying Italy by smuggling arms to her arch enemy, Jugoslavia.   The smuggler was Dumini.

Various evidence has been given regarding this record-breaking racketeer. Colonel Sacco, a director of the secret police—he was forced to resign later for revealing this—said that just an hour before the kidnapping of Matteotti, Dumini said boastfully : " We are about to make a fat expedition ; it will be *punitive* and *it is I who will lead it.*" Signor Giurin, a vice-president of the provincial deputation of Milan, pictures Dumini as fatalistically saddened when he declared, " I now have twelve murders on my conscience, but they were done under orders, and I am chained and in the power of those for whom I am working. Now there is nothing I can do but continue in this work. If I refuse there is nothing left for me but to be crushed, denounced, taken as a galley slave."

Prezzolini, a defender of Mussolini, says it is difficult to understand how the Duce could not only tolerate but actually accept with pleasure the friendship of such men as Finzi, Rossi, and even Dumini, " who have dealt a serious blow to both his own prestige and to that of Fascism. . . . He allowed the most intellectually and morally worthless people to group themselves against him. . . . On the day he formed an exclusive Fascist Ministry began his conflict with Fascism. His most serious troubles, his most insuperable obstacles, his severest threats, have always come from Fascism."

But here again there is a counter-picture. The Fascist press not only at one time lionized Dumini, but one paper wanted to erect a monument to him. Said the *Popolo Valtellinese* of Sondrio : " It appears to us that Dumini and his co-accused are deserving of a monument, because if they are themselves really the murderers of Matteotti they have delivered the nation from a furious caluminator of the fatherland, a saboteur of the World War, in other words, a traitor."

Another hero, " a Fascist from the first hour," on the Duce's roll of honour, is Dino Grandi, who for many years was described in the popular press as being probably the heir to Mussolini's toga. Grandi began his political career as head of the Bologna squadristi ; later, he headed the

local Cheka branch, and in 1926, when there was a plot
in the Fascist ranks to upset Mussolini, it was he who saved
his chief.

Belloni was sent to the penal islands. Filippelli, who
had escaped punishment in the Matteotti business, met with
a similar fate. He was caught in a municipal swindle.
As long as the gangsters, the former members of the Mafia,
the high officials of the party, and the members of Mussolini's household cabinet limited their activities to enemies
of the régime they usually escaped all penalties. When,
however, they became financial embarrassments instead of
political assets, the Duce never hesitated to treat them as
common criminals.

The fate of heroes pursues the newer men as well as
Fascists of the first hour. In 1932 the Stefani agency
issued a simple announcement : " It is reported from Turin
that Signor Augusto Turati, the former secretary-general
of the Fascist Party and a former director of the *Stampa*,
has been interned in a sanatorium." That was all. It was
the epitaph on the political grave of the most powerful man
in Italy next to the Duce. Three years earlier Turati had
renamed Mont Blanc " Monte Mussolini," despite French
protests that the peak lay within the French frontiers. The
only plausible explanation of the break between Mussolini
and Turati is the enmity of Farinacci for the latter, which
translated itself in published charges of immorality. The
" sanatorium " officially announced as Turati's present
residence is generally understood to be an asylum.

In August 1934, Leandro Arpinati, who since the downfall of Turati was known as " Mussolini's right hand," was
removed as Under-Secretary of the Interior, and sentenced
to five years in the penal islands. Twenty of Arpinati's
Bolognese friends were also dismissed from the party on
the charge of " connivance." No explanation has ever
been given.

There is the famous fable of the ruler who sent a messenger to a colleague asking him how to deal with ambitious
men within the kingdom. The second ruler, unwilling to
commit himself to writing, took the messenger walking

in the garden, and during the conversation knocked off the heads of all the taller flowers. So it has been in Fascist Italy. Whatever head has risen above the crowd has invariably fallen. Federzoni, Farinacci, Grandi, Balbo, Turati, and Arpinati each in turn became a power second only to the Duce, and each in turn was struck down.

Arpinati is the only leader within Fascism to whom a suspicion of having plotted against Mussolini is attached. However, there have been many plots inside and without the party against the existence of the régime and the life of the Duce.

CHAPTER XXI

" ' Live Dangerously ' is My Motto "

AT the Lausanne conference the journalists fought for the first interview with the new dictator. Lincoln Steffens found him with his large eyes sharply scrutinizing everybody and a revolver ready. He asked a pertinent question.

" I was looking for the fellow that is out to shoot me," replied Mussolini.

" Why that, what for ? "

" To shoot him first."

" What makes you think you'll be shot ? "

" History," replied Mussolini.

" History ?—Yes, that's right. History says dictators are apt to be shot. . . ."

" Ah," continued Mussolini, " if a dictator knows history, the dictator can look out and—shoot first."

In the early days of 1923 a report circulated in Rome that one of the guards of the Chigi Palace, the then dictatorial headquarters, fired on the Premier. There is the record of the arrest of a guard, no record of a trial, and the fact that the censorship suppressed all cablegrams on the subject.

That same year, Mussolini returning from an excursion in the country, chose to drive his car, placing his chauffeur in his accustomed seat. As the automobile passed the Colosseum and was slowed in traffic an unidentified assassin fired from a window of a neighbouring house. The chauffeur was killed.

In September 1924 Mussolini returned to Rome alone from the Badia San Salvador, but the entire entourage, which he was supposed to lead, followed in the evening. It was fired on.

No mention of these three attempts on the life of the Duce appeared in the world press, but on the 4th of November 1925 occurred an incident which had tremendous repercussions. It was Armistice Day in Italy, the national celebration of victory and honour for the Unknown Soldier. In the afternoon the foreign journalists were informed by the press department that a certain Signor Zaniboni had been caught with a rifle in his hand standing at a window facing the palace, ready to assassinate the Duce. For once foreign correspondents were told they could go as far as they liked without fear of censorship.

Mussolini himself, after referring to Zaniboni as " a vulgar Socialist," the recipient of " two cheques for 150,000 francs each from Czechoslovak Socialists to lead an anti-Fascist struggle," and " a drug addict," complains that Zaniboni " chose the sacred day of the commemoration of victory. He ambushed himself in the Hotel Dragoni, just in front of the Palazzo Chigi, from the balcony of which I usually review the processions which pass on the way to the altar of the Unknown Soldier to offer their flowers, their vows, and their homage. Having an Austrian rifle with fine sights, the fellow could not miss his aim. . . . He was discovered. He had been followed for a long time. A few days before, General Capello had generously given him money and advice. Masonry had made of him its ensign. But by simultaneous action, Zaniboni, General Capello, and various less important personages in the plot were arrested one hour before they planned the attempt."

The journalists,[1] however, did not cable the sensational news as Mussolini himself wrote it. They were too well aware that the underlined sentences belied the truth of the information officially given them. They could not afford to repeat the statement of the supreme journalist of Italy.

Months later an investigation showed that Zaniboni was a Freemason, one who had suffered injury and desired revenge. But he had had no violent intentions until one day he met a man named Quaglia who expressed sympathy and suggested

[1] In November, Bolitho wrote, " Zaniboni would have been unable to see him, much less shoot him. . . ."

a plan for assassination. For months Quaglia urged
Zaniboni on, alternately postponed the date, and finally
hired the room in the Hotel Dragoni and supplied the gun.

The reason for the postponement was simply this :
Quaglia was a Fascist agent, and the greatest showman in
the world wanted the attempted assassination staged on
the most patriotic of national holidays, so that the sympathy
of the world could be stirred more easily, and the political
actions he had planned more easily put into practice.

However, to make sure that no accident would occur,
the Fascist secret service arrested Zaniboni in his room
an hour before Mussolini was scheduled to appear on his
balcony for the great oration of the day.

And still another precaution was taken. The would-be
assassin's room, which faced Mussolini's office, was just
across the street from the Palazzo Colonna, in which,
incidentally, was situated the office of the present writer.
These three buildings and the open square of the Piazza
Colonna complete the scene, Mussolini, as seen frequently
by the present writer, had to appear on his balcony
facing the square in order to speak to the multitude, whereas the Dragoni faced the other wall of the
Chigi. It would therefore have been impossible for an
assassin to see Mussolini unless he had, in addition to his
Austrian rifle and its fine sights, a new invention which
made it possible to fire around a corner.

These stone-wall facts explain why the American
reporters of the Zaniboni affair usually referred to it as an
" alleged " attempt at assassination.

At his trial Zaniboni testified that Carlo Quaglia had
for eight months talked to him about the matter, had
lived in his house, had reported almost daily to the police,
had arranged everything, and had in fact offered to do the
shooting himself. " I swear by my child, the dearest thing
I possess," he said, " that you, Quaglia, told me you would
like to have the honour of shooting Mussolini."

The Honourable Violet Gibson, sister of Baron Ash-
bourne, shot Mussolini in the nose just as he emerged
from the Congress of Surgeons on April 6, 1926. Mussolini

went back to the congress, and a piece of sticking-plaster was put across his nostrils. He then stood for the photographers.

The would-be assassin in this case was a recent convert to Catholicism. It was testified by the sister superior at the convent where Miss Gibson lived that the Englishwoman was subject to hysteria. There was also evidence that she was incensed over Mussolini's professed atheism and the treatment given several priests and Catholic institutions by the Fascist squadristi. "A supernatural force entrusted me with a lofty mission," she said.

The Roman mob smashed the windows of the Soviet Embassy in reprisal. The Milan mob smashed and burned the offices of the *Avanti* and the *Unita*.

Mussolini ordered an end to violence. "I do not want reprisals," he shouted. "It is my Will."

To the jubilant crowd the dictator said :

"The episode which provoked your magnificent demonstration, whose sincerity I appreciated, has now faded from my memory. If I do think of it, it is with a feeling of annoyance, of boredom, as with foolish things.

"I do not want exaggerations. Mussolini has that in his composition which loves to participate in risk, and although I understand a certain anxiety, I declare I have not the least intention to hide or lose touch with the Fascist masses and the Italian people. . . . In no case, under no circumstances, will Fascism soften its programme. At this moment everything is prepared. Let it be known at home and abroad, because Fascism will continue to rule the destinies of the Italian people with an iron hand."

To an American journalist the Duce said : " The bullets pass, Mussolini remains."

It was the first time he used the third-person-royal.

Almost immediately afterwards he sailed for Africa at the head of the Italian war fleet. " We are of the Mediterranean and our destiny has been and always will be on the sea," he said to the accompanying journalists. The words " Our destiny lies on the sea " appeared in thousands of red, white, and green sheets on all the kiosks and walls of the country. Landing in Tripoli, the conqueror exclaimed, " Rome carried the beacon lamp of strength to the shores of the African sea. No one can stop our inexorable Will."

In Rome, on September 11, as Mussolini was motoring to the Chigi Palace, a youth named Gino Lucetti threw a bomb which hit the car, bounced back, and exploded, injuring eight persons. It so happened that this, the third violent attempt of the year, came at a time relations with France were strained and the annual charge that France harboured anti-Fascist emigrés was made in the daily press. To the 50,000 Fascisti frantically gathered in the Colonna square Mussolini thundered : " This must end. It would be well for responsible governments to take note of this, because otherwise their friendship for the Italian people may be fatally compromised.

" Tell the Americans and the Italians of America that neither pistols, bombs, nor other instruments of death can make me desist from my course. This is the third attempt against me in the brief space of several months, but like the others this one has not disturbed me in the slightest.

" I consider myself a soldier who has specific orders and is ready to confront any risk."

To Percy Winner of the Rome bureau of the Associated Press, who brought him a fifty-pound bundle of American clippings on the Lucetti affair, the Duce said :

" My star protects me as Italy is protected. I shall die a natural death. As I live now there is adventure."

At the same time he asked the death penalty for assassinations and would-be assassins. The King of Italy reminded the Premier that his father, King Humbert, had been assassinated, and that there had been a popular clamour for the death penalty for regicide, to which he, the present King, had refused to listen.

While press and politicians debated the question, still another attempt at assassination occurred.

On October 13, 1926, a triumphant procession of automobiles headed by the Duce was thrown into disorder by a
revolver shot. The bullet hit Mussolini's chest but glanced
off. Bolitho's report that the Premier was wearing a
bullet-proof vest was thereby confirmed.

In the next car were high officials of the Fascist Party.
Signor Arconobaldo Buonaccorsi slit the throat of the boy
accused of the shooting. Signor Italo Balbo fired his
revolver twice into the writhing body on the ground. The
other notables, amidst terrifying shouts and common
frenzy, shot, stabbed, kicked, and rushed at the body
in such a fury that two of them were so badly injured they
were taken to the hospital. This fact even the Fascist
press recorded. And, by a mistake of the censor, the report
was also passed that the would-be assassin wore a black
shirt. The Associated Press sent to America a completely
false report that a Communist plot had been discovered.
To this great American news agency the Duce said a little
later : " To discredit Fascism certain journalists give proof
of an inventive power which would well be used to write a
movie scenario. They have not as yet invented—it would
be the height of absurdity and ridiculousness—that I
purposely invent the attacks on my life, one after
another."

To the United Press the Duce said : " I don't know
what it is that protects me from assassins. Certainly it is
a mystic something."

To his townsfolk he declared, " Nothing will happen to
me before my task is done."

But in a public address to the inhabitants of Milan, the
reinstated administrative secretary of the Fascist Party,
Signor Marinelli, who had been sent to jail for the murder
of Matteotti and amnestied almost immediately, said
that " the first words of the Duce yesterday after the
attempted assassination were these : ' Italy and the
whole world must know that the criminal has been
lynched.' "

The body was identified as that of Anteo Zamboni,
fifteen years old, a Fascist belonging to the Balilla. Inas-

much as Mussolini himself had said to his companions that the man who had fired at him " was a man of medium height, in a light suit, who had stepped a pace in front of the protective cordon," and the policeman who had spoiled a second shot by tearing the revolver from the man's hand confirmed Mussolini as to the grey suit, it was quite obvious that the wrong man had been lynched. The Cheka thereupon proceeded to make a case of it by arresting the entire Zamboni family.

As it was impossible to contradict Mussolini, the public prosecutor then declared that apparently two men had fired simultaneously, but the Duce, his four companions, and the policeman had noted only one of them—the one who got away. As for Zamboni, the prosecutor admitted he was a mere boy, " never interested in politics, and his association with the young members of the Balilla would certainly not lead him to think of our Duce as a tyrant." Therefore, it was argued, he had accomplices, and the man in grey must have been Anteo's brother, Ludovico. " The proved innocence of Ludovico would destroy the very basis of the charge," continued the prosecutor, and on the following day Ludovico proved so satisfactorily that he was innocent that the court acquitted him. There was now nothing left for the Fascist prosecutor but to accuse the father and aunt of the two boys—the mother went insane before they could arrest her. It was therefore testified that in 1907 [sic] the aunt had carried a red flag in a funeral procession, and that the father had never been legally married in a church, nor had he had his children baptized. The august court thereupon sentenced the father and aunt of the two loyal, enthusiastic Fascist boys to thirty years' imprisonment for inciting to assassination, and the press was instructed to drop the matter.

On the 9th the Fascist Assembly passed the Duce's law making it a capital crime to attempt to kill Mussolini. The King, who was opposed to this act, could not do anything about it. In that exciting week the Fascisti invaded the home of the philosopher Croce in Naples and that of

Roberto Bracco, the dramatist, in Caligari. They also broke into the French consulate in Vingtimilia and the offices of *Nuovo Mondo* in New York.

In the two years which followed the passage of the law reinstating capital punishment there were no publicly announced plots against the Duce, although bombs were exploded in various parts of Rome now and then. In June 1928 the Fascist press made the claim that a bomb which went off in Milan was timed to kill the visiting King. According to Bolitho many enemies of Fascism were arrested, but the authors of the crime were never caught nor were any names ever published. Arnaldo Mussolini used his newspaper to accuse the " intellectuals " generally. Bolitho expressed the opinion the whole affair was a little Fascist scheme to make it appear that the Fascisti had saved the life of the King ; to bind the King closer to the party ; and at the same time to arrest and imprison the intellectual enemies of the régime.

In November 1930 there were mass arrests of the former liberal and Conservative leaders for an alleged conspiracy with certain military chiefs, royalists, to over-throw the régime. In Trieste, numerous Yugoslavs were imprisoned. The authorities of this former Austrian city announced that one Yugoslav prisoner, on trial for " terrorism," had given the court a written confession of a plot to kill the Premier. Accordingly, four Yugoslav boys were sentenced by General Cristini, head of the military Cheka, to be shot. Throughout Yugoslavia there were mass demonstrations against Mussolini, based on a report that the King of Italy's desire to pardon the youths was negatived by Mussolini.

In 1931 Michele Schirru, a naturalized American citizen who had been a banana-dealer in the Bronx, New York, was found guilty of planning Mussolini's death. There was no evidence that the bombs which Schirru was accused of owning were intended for that purpose, but Schirru promptly was shot. In 1932 Angelo Shardellotto, who, according to the Fascist press, confessed he had come to Rome to avenge Schirru, was killed by a firing-squad. At the same time one

Domenico Bovone, accused of being the director of the
plot, was also put to death, although the co-accused, his
mistress, Margharita Blaha, was sentenced to prison and later
reprieved. Bovone, according to the Italian newspapers,
was not an anti-Fascist, but merely an employee of Mussolini's enemies in Paris, who had offered $50,000 for the
death of the Duce and $5000 for the death of the Crown
Prince. The obvious contradiction—the Crown Prince
being notorious for his emnity to Fascism—was not noted
in the general press. A Swiss newspaper answering its
Italian colleagues who accused France of harbouring and
encouraging would-be assassins, said that " what is important is the confirmation that the life of the Duce of the
Black Shirts is continually in danger. That is the fate of
all tyrants. Zaniboni, Lucetti, Zamboni, Schirru, Shardellotto . . . the series of unfortunate terrorists grows longer.
But it is oppression which creates the atmosphere of
attempted assassinations ; it is the injustice, atrocities,
and cruelties of the Fascist régime which they seek to
avenge. . . . Perhaps Shardellotto wanted to avenge
Schirru. And to-morrow Shardellotto may in turn find an
avenger. The executioner shall find justice ; it is the destiny
of régimes based on violence."

In March 1934 Leonardo Bucciglioni, Renato Cianca,
Claudio Cianca, and Pasquale Capasso were accused of
firing a bomb in St Peter's and, as a Fascist corollary,
plotting the life of the Duce. They were not executed.
The press was told this was the best proof of the stability
of the Fascist régime.

In Italy to-day it is said, generally, that Mussolini has
escaped sixteen attempts on his life. Although the more
important were probably more theatrical than real, it
cannot be denied that he has lived dangerously. Ever since
he had read Nietzsche in Switzerland he had proclaimed
the phrase " Live Dangerously " as his motto. And in
another way his own words have come home to him—
with a vengeance. It was he who said that assassination was
the common risk of the professional ruler.

But in the time between his Swiss exile and his supreme

rule he had learned his Machiavelli well. He had become not only the philosopher of violence, but the brilliant exponent of the political uses to which press-made national hysteria may be put when violence in turn was directed against him.

CHAPTER XXII

THE SILENT REVOLUTION

WHETHER planned or fortuitous, each of the many attempts on the life of the Duce was with Machiavellian opportunism exploited by him in enforcing a Fascist programme on a people whose majority was still frankly anti-Fascist.

If one takes the dates of the passage of the most drastic laws, the so-called " Mussolinian reforms," which completely repealed every individual and collective liberty which Italy had enjoyed since the days of Garibaldi, he will find that they coincide with the days of excitement following an attempted assassination, when the emotions of the masses were deeply stirred, when the calm, calculating leaders could more easily enforce stern decrees. That several of these moments were artificially planned is a conviction shared by most of the foreign correspondents in Rome and not a few diplomats.

" All my adversaries," said Mussolini on one of these exciting occasions, " from the most hateful ones to the most intelligent, from the slyest to the most fanatical, thought that the only way of destroying Fascism was to destroy its Duce. . . .

" A policy of force was absolutely necessary. . . .

" I launched the laws for the defence of the régime. . . .

" I abolished the subversive press whose only function was to inflame the minds of men."

The Fascist " revolution " does not date from the bloodless march on Rome of 1922 ; it stems from the murder of Matteotti in 1924, and really dates from the time Mussolini, no longer trembling with fear, could make " sequestration " one of the victories of Fascism. It dates from the era when he could say, truthfully or otherwise :

" In all that time I credit myself with the fact that I never lost my calm nor my sense of balance and justice. Because of the serene judgment that I endeavour to summon to guide my every act, I ordered the guilty to be arrested. I wanted justice to follow its unwavering course. Now I have fulfilled my task and my duty as a just man. . . ."

At the very moment when that change in the mentality of the trembling leader came about, the real Fascist revolution began. It was to lead to hierarchy, an attempt at a " corporate " state, the " totalitarian " idea, and finally " Italianity " as an international cause, newer, and therefore superior to Pan-Slavism, Pan-Islamism, and Pan-Germanism.

To achieve " totalitarian " Fascism, it was necessary to destroy the entire edifice of liberty begun by Garibaldi and built up by many liberal leaders in half a century. Press, parliament, the Freemasons, and the Liberals all represented the Garibaldian State. To achieve the Fascist State, Mussolini determined to crush them all. Only by this means could he make sure that he would never have to face another Matteotti crisis.

The Fascist revolution's first act was the abolition of the free press.

Of the score of decrees by which the dictatorship established itself, this is the only one issued in 1924, the year of Matteotti's assassination. The others followed, most of them in 1925. But it is important to note how strong Mussolini, " an old newspaper man himself," considered the power of the press, because the edict of July 1924 had been prepared by him and signed by the King in 1923 for just such an occasion : a national mutiny against the ruling party. The decree provides for " warnings "—*i.e.* suppression, " if any newspaper or periodical by false or misleading news causes any interference in the diplomatic action of the government in its foreign relations, or hurts the credit of the nation at home or abroad, causing undue alarm among the people, or in any way disturbs the public peace. . . . If the newspaper or periodical, by editorial articles, notes, titles, illustrations, or other insertions

16

incites to crime or to class hatred, or to disobedience of the laws of the established order or upsets the discipline of those engaged in public service, or favours the interests of foreign states, groups, or persons as opposed to Italian interests, or insults the nation, the King, the royal family, the Summo Pontifex, religion, the institutions, or the authority of the State or of other friendly powers.

" Newspapers or other periodicals published in violation of the preceding provisions shall be suppressed. . . ."

(This decree was supplemented on December 31, 1925, by a new censorship law, which suppressed all independent publications and forced all journalists into a police docket register. It contained ten points of which the last was :

" Prefects of police are empowered to seize editions of newspapers which attack the government press, or which injure the national cause at home or abroad, or which alarm the people without justification." Any reference to Mussolini and Matteotti was under this decree termed an injury to the nation and resulted in the suppression of the paper.)

Under the press law, the first dictate of absolutism, Mussolini acted slowly but inexorably. Any criticism of himself or Fascism was announced an act of treason, the newspaper confiscated, and frequently, on orders from the Cheka, the editors beaten and the printing-plant destroyed. No other violent decrees were issued until the press had been so completely subjugated that all danger of it causing a serious reaction had passed. Then came laws in quick succession.

At the end of November 1925 (the Zaniboni affair) Decree 2029 abolished the right of public association. Freemasonry in Italy was destroyed.

Actually the law requires all associations, organisms, or institutes functioning in the kingdom or the colonies " to communicate to the authorities of public security their constitutions, their interior regulations, the complete lists of their membership, their social functions, and all other information relative to their organization, their activity, everything that may be required by the aforementioned authorities, for reasons of public order or security."

The police and government are given the fullest power of intervention so that they can dispose of the life and functions of all associations. In addition, Article 3 of the municipal and provincial code was interpreted as giving the prefects the right to limit and almost to suppress the right of individual citizens to join associations.

The abolition of parliament came next. Again there was no clean direct action, but the first of a series of decrees, each a little stronger, until the present state of parliamentary zero was reached. The first decree, Christmas Eve 1925, made the Chamber of Deputies merely consultative ; it could discuss and ratify, but nothing more. The head of the government (Mussolini) was given the right to initiate laws, the parliament could initiate nothing but could suggest and present only ideas approved by the Duce ; the Premier was responsible only to the King, and could no longer be criticized or checked or overruled by the Chamber.

The liberty of teaching and the liberty of the magistracy were abolished the same evening. The decree, No. 2300, declares that " all functionaries, employees, agents of all orders and grades, civil and military, those who are in the administration of the state upon which they depend, who by any manifestation, in and out of service, do not give complete guaranty for the accomplishment of their duties faithfully, or who place themselves *in a situation incompatible with the political directives of the government,*" may be removed.

This law was used almost exclusively to force university teachers to be friendly to Fascism and to force the magistrates of Italy to free Fascists accused of violence and punish anti-Fascists, guilty or not guilty.

Naturally, free speech was next suppressed. The rights of the individual having already been circumscribed in every way, it was hardly necessary to pass a new decree, so one day on conferring more power on the Duce it was announced that any one criticizing the head of the government was punishable with six to thirty months in prison and a fine of three hundred to three thousand lire. Nor is any one under this law allowed to criticize the *policies* or the purposes of Mussolini or his government. It is under this law that from two thousand to six thousand men, mostly intellectuals, were sent to the terror islands in certain years.

Two decrees stripped King Victor Emmanuel III. of all his powers. One took the command of the army and navy away from him ; this was a mere formality, as the King could not use them in the old days without the approval of parliament and Premier, but now the soldiers and sailors of the nation were placed at the disposal of the dictator. The King was denied the right to change Prime Ministers. The second law placed, above parliament and the crown, the Grand Fascist Council as the highest ruling body, a veritable " Comité de Salut Public " of the old French Terror.

Universal suffrage was abolished. It is one of the ironies of history that shortly before this decree was passed Mussolini, after listening for hours to a debate on the question of enfranchising women, banged the table, said, " Basta," enough talk, and ordered parliament to vote as he directed, in favour of the law. The Marchesa Piccolo-mini, one of the Duce's first women converts, and an ardent suffragist, was in the balcony, beaming upon her hero, who turned his limpid, passionate eyes upon her and passed her law for her. Shortly afterwards, universal suffrage for men and women was suppressed. Later, by order of the Grand Council, on February 20, 1928, it was decreed that in the future the Fascisti would announce a list of candidates, and every one, men and women, would have a right to vote " Yes " or " No," but only for these candidates, and woe to the man who dared vote " No."

In turn the law courts were Fascistized. Article 71 of the Statutes, guaranteeing freedom in the courts, was abolished, and the clause " there must never be created either special tribunals or extraordinary commissions " was erased, when Decree 2008 of November 25, 1926 (following the Lucetti and Zamboni affairs), was put into force. A special tribunal " for the defence of the state," a tribunal composed of a majority of Fascist militia, came into being.

It denied the last of the human liberties (including habeas corpus), and functioned arbitrarily, sending thousands of persons to the islands, to prison on the mainland, and to confino, or enforced domicile, under police surveillance. The militia tribunal is commonly known as the Fascist Inquisition.

The inviolability of private homes was abolished. Local police authorities, as well as the national militia, were empowered to invade any one's domicile at will, search and seize, while all the janitors of Italy were registered and made espionage agents of the régime.

The inviolability of private correspondence was abolished. It is very interesting to note that whereas the Bolsheviki cut letters open and deliver them marked " censored " and bearing rubber stamps and seals, the more modern Fascisti employ numerous agents in the main post offices to steam letters open and to seal them as carefully as possible in an effort to hide the fact that there is a censorship and to fool as many customers as possible. The present writer not only has many such envelopes, but has proof from three journalistic colleagues still in Rome that letters to all persons on the " list of suspects," which includes several American and British newspaper men, are steamed open and secretly resealed. The government reserves the right to confiscate outgoing and incoming letters, and frequently does so.

The right freely to chose and exercise a business or a profession was abolished. This was done by a series of legislative and ministerial measures dating from the law of April 3, 1926, to the publication of the Labour Charter on April 21, 1927. The order of the *questore* (chief of police) of Alexandria illustrates this law. When the time came for the new lawyers and students to be registered at the bar, those suspected of not being Fascisti received a legal document to sign. This document reads :

" I, the undersigned, Lawyer . . . . , who until now have remained outside the Fascist Party and régime on account of my sectarianism or my views, believe it my duty to-day to declare :

" 1. I disown my past, in as far as it concerns open or secret dissension with the action or régime of the Fascist Party.

" 2. That on my own volition I have deemed it necessary to renounce this apostasy as reparation for conduct politically damnable.

" 3. That from now, with sincerity and conviction, I will give my adhesion to everything which the party and régime do in carrying out their powers.

" 4. That I recognize that Fascism has saved the country and is deserving of that recognition by all Italians.

" 5. That from now on I will exercise my profession and develop all my activity, not only without any factious spirit, but with the purpose of collaborating to make of Fascism the sacred religion of every Italian.

" In confirming the authenticity of this declaration I sign it and authorize the Fascist Party to make what use of it it desires."

Free movement was abolished. Two classes were caught by this law, the peasants who frequently moved from province to province, seeking better working conditions, and the victims of the régime who sought freedom in Switzerland and France. The workers, by this law, came under a sort of serfdom, being required to stay in certain localities and work for wages imposed upon them, and under unbearable conditions. As for those seeking liberty, they were chased, fired upon, and in many instances killed by the frontier guards.

Liberty of conscience and religion were curtailed by the laws which favoured the Catholic Church as a State Church.

The right of an Italian-born subject to choose another nationality was denied. Before the war only two semi-civilized countries, Russia and Rumania, had such laws ; at present Italy is the only country which cannot admit that a man may change his nationality. The Italian law, moreover, provides for the confiscation of property of those abroad who criticize Fascism or change their nationality, and although the law does not provide for this, the families of emigrants are frequently held as hostages, subjected to terrorism or blackmail.

Article 30 of the Statutes, containing the consecration and traditional guarantee that no unjust taxation shall be levied unless passed by the Chambers and sanctioned by the King, was abolished.

Finally, on February 4, 1926, all municipal liberty was suppressed.

On more than one occasion one of these decrees was passed a day or two after one of the attempts on Mussolini's life ; on more than one occasion the publication of a decree led to a violent reaction by the public and a massacre. Accused of violence, Mussolini in his speech on May 26, 1926, assumed all responsibility.

" It is I," he said, " who have dictated the measures taken : the repeal and revision of all passports for foreign countries ; the order to shoot without warning any one trying to cross the frontier secretly ; the suppression of all anti-Fascist publications, daily and periodical ; the dissolution of all groups, associations, and organizations which are anti-Fascist or suspected of anti-Fascism ; the deportation (to the islands) of those who are anti-Fascists or conduct any anti-revolutionary activity ; the creation of a special police force ; the creation of secret bureaux of investigation and a special tribunal.

" All the opposition newspapers have been suppressed, all the anti-Fascist parties have been dissolved. The special police already gives signal service. The political bureaux of secret investigations have been created. The Special Tribunal has been created, it functions in a remarkable fashion."

The democratic state was destroyed. The monarchial constitution was broken. The individual was robbed of all liberty.

Violence, which from the day of Fascism's coming into power, in 1922 and throughout 1923 and 1924, had remained actual but illegal, was made legal in 1925.

In 1925 Fascism and the nation became one.

The revolution, which failed to occur in 1922, came about through the passage of decrees in 1925 and 1926.   Quietly.

Fascist absolutism was built over the body of Matteotti.

Mussolini's revenge for the Matteotti uprising was complete.

PART III

MUSSOLINI VICTORIOUS

CHAPTER XXIII

MUSSOLINI *VERSUS* THE POPE

THE history of the Catholic Church is divided into three parts : the Church Persecuted, the Church Militant, and the Church Triumphant. The first refers to the early days, the second includes the centuries of successful establishment and our own times ; the third refers to heaven. But with Fascism, as with Communism, the three eras are more condensed, and the third stage, Triumphant, refers to the present.

Mussolini Victorious asked the people of Italy to endorse his régime in the plebescite of March 1929 ; for this event the Fascist Party published its list of achievements, which may be summarized as follows :

Bolshevism and social disorder have been abolished.

Industry and commerce have been revived.

The trains run on time ; magnificent automobile roads have been built ; the marshes have been drained.

Employment has increased.

Wages and the cost of living have been balanced.

Order, Discipline, Hierarchy (the Fascist slogan) have been made actual.

The budget has been balanced ; despite the abolition of many taxes the nation's finances have been placed in a state of prosperity.

Agriculture is flourishing.

The army, navy, and air force have been enlarged and restored to high efficiency.

The prestige of the nation has been restored. Italy is now respected and feared abroad.

It is the purpose of the concluding portion of this book to discuss these and later claims of Fascism achievements. At various times Mussolini has called the creation of the Corporate State, the stabilization of the lira, the increased grain or child production the victory he prized most. But future historians, who are able to take the long view, will most probably place the settlement of the Roman Question first under the name of the Duce.

And if this truly happens they will have a magnificently ironic caption for their chapter ; they could call it " The Atheist who liberated the Pope."

We have already witnessed the struggle between Mussolini and his chief political opponent of 1922, Don Sturzo, the Catholic leader ; we have seen the youthful Benito defying God to send a thunderbolt against him, and we have heard him saying bitter things about the popes, the priests, Christianity, and all religions. We know he was born an atheist. In fact, in the province where he was born the majority of the poor and oppressed were Socialists and the majority of Socialists were atheists ; all the rebels against the social system were enemies of the Church ; Socialism was a sufficient religion for them, and they hated equally the rich, the employers, the monarchist politicians, also the priests and the established Church, whom they considered the protectors of all the economic forces against which they fought.

The early struggle between the deeply religious mother and the agnostic father for little Benito's soul ended in easy victory for Papa Alessandro. It was not necessary for him to use his belt or the whip, as he did for other corrective purposes. Had he done so it is likely that the child would have fled to the consoling dogmas of the Church which his mother represented. Atheism, however, was in the air, Benito was nourished on it, it became part of his being, and it remained there. In vain did the mother drag the child to church where the smell of incense in the vitiated air sickened him ; in vain did she send him to the

Salesian friars ; because their moral and physical beatings served only to increase the boy's disdain for religion, and make him swear a revenge against the priests, their Church, and their God.

The Swiss episodes are not the only proof of this vendetta. At the time of the execution of Francisco Ferrer in Spain there was an outbreak of anti-clericalism in Italy also, and in Forli Mussolini led the mob which stormed the central square of the town and destroyed the column surmounted by the Virgin Mary. In the trenches one day the corporal read one of the King's exhortations to the troops which concluded with a call for divine providence to aid the noble Allied war. Mussolini sneered. " We shall conquer without God," said he.

After the war, addressing a convention of veterans one day, he said : " I love a pagan and warlike people, a people which refuses its allegiance to revealed dogma and which is not fooled by miracles." At about the same time he wrote : " There is only one possible revision for the Law of Guarantees [the act that made the Pope the ' Prisoner of the Vatican '], and that is its abolition, followed by a stern invitation to His Holiness to leave Rome, to re-enter Avignon, or, in conformity with the taste shown by the Vatican during the war, to go to the Boches." [1]

Mussolini seemed to have a grudge against the popes. He never forgave Benedict XV. for calling the war a " useless massacre " ; as recently as 1928, in his autobiography, he attacks the memory of Europe's first pacifist, calling his effort to make peace in 1917 " ambiguous conduct," adding that the " Catholic Church had ever been a stranger to wars when she did not herself provoke them." He insulted Pius XI. on more than one occasion. In April 1924 there was a savage attack by the Fascisti upon the Catholic institutions of the district of Brianza which had voted for the Catholic ticket. The Pope sent 500,000 lire to restore the buildings, and addressed a bitter message against Fascist violence. Mussolini replied by dubbing Pius XI. " Papa Brianzolo."

[1] *Popolo d'Italia*, November 18, 1919.

But now we must look at the seeming contradictions in the behaviour of the Duce towards the Pope. The sending of emissaries to the Vatican in preparation for the march on Rome was not a sudden impulse ; it was the penultimate action in a well-thought-out plan. Even before that was done, in June, Mussolini had written that " Fascism has nothing to gain by exiling God from the sky and religion from the earth," and immediately upon taking office the Duce, in the conventional manner of all statesmen and politicians, called upon God to direct his endeavours. Such expressions shocked those atheist Fascist followers who had understood from the original programme that among the first actions on gaining power would be a concerted and continual attack on the Catholic Church and the Vatican. But they soon learned of Mussolini's change of programme, if not change of heart.

The first climax in the relationship between Mussolini and the Vatican followed the Matteotti affair, when the populace turned against Fascism, and the Fascisti took off their black shirts and removed the lictor's emblem from their buttonholes, and pretended they had never trafficked with the party which stood accused before the world as one of bloodshed and assassination. Mussolini turned toward the King, whom he had more than once intimidated by a plan to replace him, and toward the Church, which he had spared on entering Rome. The Duce's agents called upon Monsignor Pizzardo, the confidant of the Pope, and immediately afterwards there was a campaign against the Socialists and the Populari launched in certain newspapers. This was the only moral support Mussolini had at the time. But it was important. It helped him to emerge from his pose of remorse, his cringing attitude, and to assume his old rôle of superman. It was then he announced that he was certain the Matteotti affair had something to do with Freemasonry, which was seeking to ruin his authority, and that he would soon settle that matter too.

The whole history of the negotiations with the Vatican is a record of threats, provocations, and promises. One morning Mussolini would write in his *Popolo* that the

Fascisti would tear down the cross from St. Peter's and replace it by the lictor's axe if the Pope interfered with his régime, and the next day there would be an emissary waiting on a papal representative. In the spring of 1925 Mussolini applauded the production of Pirandello's *Sagra della Nava* in the subsidized art theatre, while the Catholic press denounced the Duce, Pirandello, and the theatre for producing one of the most subtle and dramatic attacks on the Catholic faith. Then in turn Mussolini would forbid the American Methodists to build the church they had planned on a hill overlooking the Vatican, or he would propose a bill for outlawing Masonry.

In July 1925, and again in August and December, Fascist violence against Catholics was especially intense in Florence and Pisa. Cardinal Maffi, the leading intellectual of the Church, who had received the second largest number of votes on several ballots at the conclave which elected Pius XI. Pope, assumed the leadership of Catholics *versus* Fascists. And because there was a censorship of the press, Cardinal Maffi issued his anathema of Fascism in the form of a pastoral letter, which called the Duce and his followers the " Race of Cain," and concluded with these words :

" It is said of murderers that they boast of the number of their victories. But the word is merely on the lips, presented rather than pronounced, in a moment of confusion and excitement. Other words come in the night, and ring with a different sound, causing fears to arise that are uncontrollable and sometimes even insane. O Cain ! O Judah ! O, all ye who shed the blood of your brothers, you lie when you speak of security ; for we know you have it not. Nor could you have it. Do we not see you turn pale and look furtively around, as if seeking some way of escape, at a chance sound that may strike the ear, at a chance light that may strike the eye, even at the murmur of the wind, at the chirping of the birds ? . . .

" War had and has its poison-gas, its liquids of destruction ; but bear this well in mind : No acid, sulphuric or nitric or prussic, and no sublimate is so corrosive as one drop of blood criminally shed. There is no chemical basis that will

resist or neutralize it. There are no forces to control it.
Armies will not hold it in check. It flows on. It corrodes.
It destroys. Woe to the hand that sheds blood. Woe
to the feet that trample on the corpse. O, Dynasty of
Cain, carry on. But listen to this : where men fail, God is
to the rescue—God, who gives no quarter to the culprits
but incessantly pursues them, crying out judgment over
them: Accursed! Accursed! Accursed in time. Accursed!
in eternity ! "

Following the publication of this pastoral letter,
Cardinal Maffi called upon other Catholic leaders to join
with him in united and continuous action against Fascism.
Mussolini then apologized to the Pope, and Federzoni,
strong nationalist and devout Catholic, again made over-
tures of friendship to the Vatican.

The objective of the Fascisti was the destruction of the
power of the Azione Cattolica, the association of elders,
and the Catholic Boy Scouts, which enrolled children.
Fascism, claiming to be the true leader of youth, in 1926
established the opera Nationale Balilla for the political
and military education of the young of Italy. " The organization," explained the Hon. R. Ricci, " requires that its
pupils at the time they come of age, shall be capable of
suitably entering the higher schools of the army, the navy,
and aviation. It will try, above all, to develop the sentiment
of absolute devotion to the country in peace-time as in time
of war. This preparation of young people for military
life has properly scandalized faint spirits in certain so-called
democratic countries.

" Peace and war are two phases in the life of the people,
equally necessary to their development, to their greatness
and their growth. Fascism only wants to realize in Italy
what modern states have realized among themselves since
the beginning of the ages, the ability to defend themselves
with arms, at all times and against whoever threatened
their existence and their prestige."

Militarism and nationalism, the ideals of the Balilla,
were the exact opposites of the ideals of the Catholic
organizations. On January 9, 1927, Mussolini rushed

through a royal decree abolishing all existing Catholic Boy Scout organizations in localities of less that 20,000 people. The Pope, in a letter to Cardinal Gasparri, replied by abolishing the entire organization, explaining that he did so because he had to yield to force, and that the Scouts still remained " the apple of my eye."

The world at that time, however, had only a suspicion that serious negotiations were under way for the settlement of the Roman question. Behind the acts of violence and reprisals there were diplomatic advances. Actually on the 8th of August 1926—as the Marquis Francesco Pacelli, brother of Eugenio Cardinal Pacelli and later general counsellor of the Vatican State, revealed—Domenico Barone began the decisive negotiations with representatives of the Pope. By the autumn of that year there had been considerable progress. Mussolini had asked and received a complete statement of the Vatican's terms for peace. Signor Pacelli, in transmitting them, informed the Duce that there were two questions on which he could cede nothing : the sovereignty of the Pope in a recreated papal state, and the recognition of religious marriage on a par with the civil rite.

In 1927 Mussolini, who had already known that the Pope disapproved of the plan for the Corporate State, announced the Labour Charter. The Pope again showed his displeasure. The official *Osservatore Romano* said it was " contrary to the Christian conception of the State and individual liberty." By order of the Duce's press department, this and similar declarations by the Pope and his official organ were not reprinted in Italy.

Early in 1929 the rumour of a treaty was confirmed. And then arose the question : Why is Mussolini making peace with the Pope ? Why is the atheist so anxious to please the head of the Catholic Church, and why is he making concessions which were not even demanded of previous Prime Ministers, from Cavour to Nitti ?

The reasons were many. First, and most important, Mussolini, who had studied his Machiavelli and followed many of his precepts, had been convinced, in the course of years, that the dictum which he had questioned was, after all, the most logical in Italy : one must rule with the aid of the Church. Seven years of conflict had convinced him of this fact. But perhaps more important still was the politico-economic situation in which Mussolini found himself during the two years of negotiations. In 1926 it was already apparent that a crisis was imminent : unemployment was increasing, exports were down, emigrant remittances had taken an alarming drop, the officially announced balanced budget was, in fact, not near equilibrium, and dissatisfaction was spreading.

By 1928, despite the flotation of billions of lire in loans in the United States, the crisis was on. Wage cuts and increased taxation failed to effect a cure. And now the bankers and the large industrialists, the subsidizers and owners of the Fascist party, as well as the general public, were aroused against Fascism. While the front of the edifice still glittered with decorations and looked imposing, the foundations were sinking into economic mud.

Mussolini was hard pressed. There was even a possibility that at this point he would actually revert to his original programme, the plan for a socialized co-operative State evolved by him nine years earlier out of Karl Marx, and give the world the semi-Communist régime which was obviously his original intention. He did, in fact, begin taking over certain industries—those which were in insoluble financial difficulties — and making the State participate in production and distribution. But again he changed his mind.

Something was needed to restore his prestige, at home and abroad—some newer, greater gesture which would unify the masses again, rally them in his vanguard against the threatening desertion of the business leaders. Politics and economics and Machiavellian opportunism dictated the move ; it is a practical masculine world, and only feminine naïveté, as exhibited by female biographers, make Mussolini, like Saul of Tarsus, see the great light on the road to Damascus and become a repentant Paul. His was not a gesture of a repentant. It was a politico-economic move.

On February 7, 1929, Cardinal Gasparri, Secretary of State of the Holy See, announced to the diplomats accredited to the Vatican that the temporal power of the Pope had been restored, the Pontiff released from his prison,[1] a new State created.

Behind the present accord stands the figure of Father Tacchi-Venturi, who for years had guided Mussolini in his relations to the Holy See. It was this powerful Jesuit who had planned to have Mussolini make a public confession of faith during the anniversary celebration of St. Francis of Assisi ; but there was too much ribald hilarity over the atheist-politician's proposed action to make it profitable. However, the Duce's children—those he so gallantly calls his " first series "—having grown up, and noble marriages being proposed, Mussolini permitted himself to be married in the Catholic Church,[2] thereby legalizing their birth, had his " second series " baptized, thereby saving their souls, and allowed himself to be photographed in dark-eyed prayer before the statue of St. Peter in the Cathedral, thereby reaping another harvest of publicity.

Explaining this treaty to the Senate on May 13, Mussolini began with Cavour's formula, " a free Church within a free State," adding that the new situation created " a sovereign State within the Kingdom of Italy ; the Catholic Church with a certain pre-eminence loyally and voluntarily recognized ; free admission of other religions." To a Senator who proposed " a free and sovereign Church, a free and sovereign State," Mussolini said :

" This formula might create the belief that there are two co-existing sovereignties, but they do not co-exist. One counts as the Vatican City, and one counts as the Kingdom of Italy, which is the Italian State. It must be understood that between the Italian State and the Vatican City there is a distance which can be measured in thousands of miles,

---

[1] On November 1, 1870, the Vatican had announced that " His Holiness declares that he is in a state of imprisonment and that he will not partake with Belial."

[2] This is the now generally accepted report, but no official document of marriage to Rachele Guidi has ever been found by investigators.

17

even if it requires only five minutes to go and visit this State and ten minutes to walk around its confines.

"There are, then, two sovereignties, perfectly distinct and well differentiated : perfectly and reciprocally recognized. But within the State the Church is not sovereign and is not even free. It is not sovereign and is not free because in its institutions and its men it is subject to the general laws of the State, and is even subject to the special clauses of the Concordat."

On Christianity the Duce said, sarcastically : " This religion was born in Palestine but became Catholic in Rome. If it had been confined to Palestine it would in all probability never have been more than one of the numerous sects which flourished in that overheated environment, like that of the Essenes or the Therapeutæ. The chances are that it would have perished and left no trace."

After giving flat denials to several of the Pope's statements, Mussolini exclaimed :

"We have buried the temporal power of the popes, not resuscitated it."

"Any other régime than ours," he continued, "may believe it useful to renounce the education of the young generations. In this field I am intractable. Education must be ours. Our children must be educated in our religious faith, but we must round out this education ; and we need to give our youths a sense of virility and the power of conquest."

The Pope read Mussolini's speech on May 14 at eleven in the morning, an hour and a half before the first pilgrimage was to visit him. To the professors and pupils of the College of Mondragone he made the famous reply in which he referred to Mussolini as the devil.

The Pope began by attacking the Fascist Spartan educational principle that children belong to the State. " The State should interest itself in education," said the Pope, " but the State is not made to absorb and annihilate the family, which would be absurd and against nature, for the family comes before society and before the State. The State should perfect the activities of the family in full correspondence with the desires of the father and mother, and it should especially respect the divine right of the Church in education.

" We cannot admit that in its educational activities the State shall try to raise up conquerors or encourage conquests. What one State does in this line all the other States can do. What would happen if all the States educated their people for conquest ? Does such education contribute to general world pacification ?

" We can never agree with anything which restricts or denies the right which nature and God gave the Church and the family in the field of education. On this point we are not merely intractable, but we are uncompromising just as we would be forced to be uncompromising if asked : ' How much does two plus two make ? ' Two plus two makes four and it is not our fault if it does not make five or six or fifty. When it is a question of saving a few souls and impeding the accomplishment of greater damage to souls we feel courage to treat with the devil in person. And it was exactly with the purpose of preventing greater evil that we negotiated with the devil some time ago, when the fate of our dear Catholic Scouts was decided."

Although the Pope's reply was suppressed in the Fascist press, some weeks later Mussolini published his speech, retaining all its violent language, misquotations, and insults to the Pontiff. The Pope addressed a letter to Cardinal Gasparri, published June 5, calling the Duce's words " heretical, and worse than heretical."

Two years after the signing of the peace treaty the Fascisti were again breaking into Catholic clubs and using violence against members ; the Pope was reported to be making plans for leaving Italy, and Mussolini's newspapers were again using language such as this : " If the Duce orders us to shoot all the priests, we shall not hesitate an instant. . . ." [1] In 1931 Mussolini regretted his surrender to the Vatican.

The two years of peace had not been two years of harmony. The Church continued to insist on its right to rule

[1] *Gazetta Fascista*, quoted by the French writer, Emmanuel Bourcier.

the family and raise the children of Italy ; the régime continued to enforce the decrees making the State the supreme power over the individual and especially over youth. A brilliant paragrapher has summed up a situation which it might have taken books to expound : " As we understand the controversary between Church and State in Italy," said Howard Brubaker, " the whole question is who gets the custody of the child." As both the Pope and Mussolini rest the future of their régimes on the education of the coming generations, the conflict was bound to occur, and is bound to occur again and again.

The Concordat was based on ambiguity. The two parties had agreed to collaborate on the following points : nomination of priests, status of the religious Orders, recognition of religious marriage, dogmatic religious instruction in the primary and secondary schools, etc. But the grave problems were not definitely settled ; the question of the education of youth, the question of the attributes of the Church, and the question of the State control of the individual remained unanswered.

On these questions Fascism has its own moral theses, which are completely independent of the Church: the State is absolute, it absorbs the family, the individual, the new-born babe, the future citizen. As against this stood the thesis of the Church: the family is the original unit, independent and fundamental, where the child is to be raised ; the individual is an atom in the mass, but sacred to society, possessing inviolable rights which the State cannot curtail or restrain.

The theses are opposed ; the treaty, however, could perhaps have been maintained had there been unbounded goodwill and no political intentions on the Fascist side, because compromises are always possible when politics are concerned, but much more difficult when religious and moral issues are disputed. Here the incompatibility was profound, and fundamental, ancient Christian doctrine clashed with new Fascist doctrine, and a retreat by one force became inevitable.

Meanwhile Catholic institutions had been making unparalleled progress. Not only were the youth organizations strengthened, but the Azione Cattolica showed from twenty-five to fifty per cent. membership increases in a short time. According to the Fascisti the old leaders of the Popolari and their followers were swamping the Catholic organizations for the purpose of using them as political centres.

The Fascist organ, *Lavoro Fascista*, accused the Catholic League of debating " explicit proposals for supplanting Fascism " ; on May 26, 1931, it accused Monsignor Pizzardo, diplomat and chaplain-general, of declaring that ". Catholic Action must be strong enough to seize power." " It is time to resort to extreme measures," concluded the official organ.

A fortnight of violence throughout Italy, and especially in Rome, followed. Fascists attacked priests, plundered the Catholic clubs, the Jesuit house of the Civiltá Cattolica, and invaded the palace of the Chancellery, which is protected by extra-territoriality. In the Piazza Colonna, near the Foreign Office, they burned copies of a book, *The Pope*. One Group found an oil-painting of the Pontiff in a Catholic club, and marched with it through the streets, finally trampling it with cries of " Traitor." A bomb was thrown into the Catholic headquarters at Imola.

The Pope replied, on June 29, 1931, with his encyclical *Non abbiamo bisogno*. Because of the strict Fascist censorship the Pope himself was forced to smuggle out his encyclical. He called in two notable dignitaries, Monsignor F. J. Spellman, who is now assistant to Cardinal O'Connell, archbishop of Boston, and Monsignor Vanneufville, a canon of the Lateran and member of the higher council of the Propaganda Fide, also the correspondent of the Catholic organ, *La Croix*, in Paris ; and published the encyclical in France.

" They have tried to strike to death all that was and will be always dearest to the heart of Our Father and Pastor of Souls," wrote the Pope in his encyclical, recounting numerous " brutalities and beatings, blows and bloodshed— and all this lamentable accompaniment of disrespect and violence accomplished with such intervention by members

of the [Fascist] party in uniform, with such condescension
from the authorities and from the forces of public safety,
that it is necessary to believe that these decisions came
from above." The Pope then denies the official versions
sent from Rome, " genuine slander spread by the party
press," and by the Radio d'Italia. Finally the Pope
denounces as ridiculous the statement that the Azione had
become a " nest " for the Popolari. Of the directors of
250 diocesan organizations, 4000 sections of Catholic men's
clubs, and 5000 groups of Catholic male youth, only four
men were connected with the old Popolari, " and, we must
add, that in the four cases in question, there are those who
are sympathizers with the régime and the party, which they
look upon favourably."

" And here We find Ourselves," continues Pius XI.,
" confronted by a mass of authentic affirmations and no
less authentic facts which reveal beyond the slightest
possibility of doubt the resolve (already in great measure
actually put into effect) to monopolize completely the
young, from their tenderest years up to manhood and
womanhood, for the exclusive advantage of a party and
of a régime based on an ideology which clearly resolves
itself into a true, a real pagan worship of the State—the
Statolatry—which is no less in conflict with the natural
rights of the family than it is in contradiction with the
supernatural rights of the Church.

" We have seen, in fact, in action a species of religion
which rebels against the directions of the higher religious
authorities, and imposes or encourages the non-observance
of these directions . . . a religious sentiment that goes to
extremes, and permits others to indulge in insulting words
and actions against the person of the Father and of all the
faithful, even to crying out ' Down with the Pope, and death
to him ! ' This is a real teaching of parricide. It is a
semblance of religion which cannot in any way be reconciled
with the Catholic doctrine and practice. . . .

" A conception of the State which makes the young
generations belong entirely to it, without any exception,
from the tenderest years up to adult life, cannot be reconciled

by a Catholic with the Catholic doctrine, and cannot either be reconciled with the natural right of the family. . . .

" You ask Us, Venerable Brethren, in view of what has taken place, what is to be thought about the formula of an oath [1] which even little boys and girls are obliged to take about executing without discussion orders from an authority which, as we have seen and experienced, can give orders against all truth and justice, and in disregard of the rights of the Church and its souls, which are already by their very nature sacred and inviolable, and to have them swear to serve with all their strength, even to the shedding of blood. The cause of a revolution that snatches the youth from the Church and from Jesus Christ, and educates its own young forces to hate, to deeds of violence, and to irreverence, not excluding the person of the Pope himself, as the latest facts have very evidently demonstrated . . . such an oath as it stands is unlawful."

This encyclical, suppressed for several days by the Italian press, made a great sensation and won world-wide sympathy for the Pope, from Protestants as well as Catholics.

On July 9 Mussolini ordered the Fascisti to abandon the Azione Cattolica. The Pope declared Catholicism and Fascism incompatible ; Mussolini declared Fascism and Catholicism incompatible. Both are right. After two years endeavour to render unto the Duce the things which are the Duce's and unto God the things that are God's, the real crisis had come, and both sides realized that there would be no friendship between two opposing ideologies.

On September 3 the Vatican and the Chigi Palace announced a compromise agreement which made the Azione Cattolica strictly diocesan, dependent on the bishops, aloof from politics, foreign to trade unions. It was regarded as a codicil to the Lateran Pacts. The Fascist government restored compatibility between party and Catholic institutions. On the third anniversary of the Vatican treaty,

---

[1] " I swear to obey the orders of the Duce without questioning them, and to serve the cause of the Fascist Revolution with all my force, and if necessary with my blood."

Mussolini, accompanied by his ambassador, Count Cesar-
Marie de Vecchi di Val Cismon, the same gentleman who
voluntarily assumed responsibility for the massacre of
Turin, and during the Matteotti uprising proposed " three
minutes of shooting to destroy the Opposition," paid a
grand ceremonial visit to the Vatican. The Borghi and
neighbouring quarters were put in a state of siege, and
several thousand persons were obliged to spend their time
in jail until the 13th of February. Mussolini was closeted
with the Pope from 10.45 to 11.15, one of the longest
interviews ever given a visitor.

Did Mussolini kiss the Pope's slipper ? European diplomatic circles and the whole Catholic world were greatly
intrigued by this visit. *Le Peuple* of Brussels, which claims
editorially to have obtained the description from one " in
close touch with ' the eye of the Vatican,' " thus describes
the historic occasion :

" A painful silence reigned. . . . Finally Mussolini
precipitated himself at the feet of the Pope, and kissed the
slipper humbly, at the same time giving himself great blows
on the chest. With infinite bountifulness the Successor to
Saint Peter raised his visitor and said to him :

" Repent, repent, my son ! All is not yet lost for
you ! '

" A few minutes later the Pope asked Mussolini what
time it was. Mussolini went pale. He quickly caught the
significance. He said :

" ' I have only a Swiss watch, but it is not the one I
placed on the table at the time the police of His Majesty
the King of Italy, Victor Emmanuel, did me the honour of
tracking me down as my men now track down those who
now think as I then did. The cheap nickel watch which I
placed on the table in addressing an ultimatum to God was
pawned by me when I was outlawed. In this connection I
have to confess that I have failed to reimburse those comrades who aided me out of their pocket-books in those
regrettable times.

" But to-day I no longer deny God by according Him
five minutes in which to strike me dead as proof that He

exists. I now know why I was not struck by lightning : the Church needed me.' "

Interviewing the Duce some time later, Emil Ludwig asked him whether or not he kissed the Pope's slipper. Mussolini replied :

" In general I do as the Romans do. That is to say, I accept the custom of the country where I am being entertained. At the Vatican I was left to follow my own bent."

Has Mussolini been converted ? In the Fascist Catechism he had written : " Fascism is not atheistic, but an army of believers. Religion alone makes possible the realization of great human ideals. Science . . . cannot explain all the phenomena of life ; there remains always a closed wall on which one word alone should be written : ' God.' " To an American woman admirer he was even more outspoken. " I feel God deeply," he said, lifting his eyes. " While God protects me no human force can stop me. I live dangerously and God protects me." But to the astute Ludwig, whose interviews Mussolini himself corrected and officially stamped, he admitted frankly that he is still a free-thinker. This paragraph, it is not strange to say, was deleted from the second Italian edition.

With considerable irony a Catholic newspaper headlined Mussolini's visit to the Vatican, " Caesar and Peter have shaken hands." It had in mind Mussolini's favourite poet, Carducci, who wrote :

> *Quando porge la mano Cesare a Piero*
> *da quella stretta sangue umano stilla ;*
> *quando il bacio si dan Chiesa ed Impero,*
> *un astro di martirio in ciel sfavilla.*

> [When Cæsar shakes hands with Peter, human blood flows ;
> when the Church and the Empire embrace, the star of a
> martyr is lit in the heavens.]

The press of Italy considered the new accord a Fascist victory. It declared that although the encylical was extremely violent, although the Pope denounced the " Totalitarian " idea of Fascism, the Vatican has come round to the thesis of the régime. Although it need not be admitted that the Catholic Action has been engaged in politics, it is certain that in the future it is pledged never to do so. By the new arrangement, not only must members restrict themselves to religious and spiritual works, but they cannot engage in social action, cannot in any way rival Fascist action, and the youth movement loses all its character which was antagonistic to the Fascist or militarist youth movement.

It marks the end of the plan of a vast Catholic party with a Christian as opposed to a Fascist programme.

If the Vatican, through Father Tacchi-Venturi, has obtained assurances that the Totalitarian plan will be changed, that the religious teaching of youth will be liberalized, that the incompatibility of Christianity and Fascism will be solved, these facts are secret. That a tacit understanding of this nature exists has been admitted by *La Croix*, the official French Catholic publication.

Officially, it must be said, the settlement of the Roman question has been a magnificent example of political opportunism. The old axiom, *Religio instrumentum regni*, has taken on new life in Italy. " Fascism," in the opinion of the editorial writer of *The Times*, " respects pietism, bigotry, and superstition so far as they serve to keep the peasants, particularly in the south, in ignorance and submission, but it does not allow, for instance, the Church to take any part in the education of youth (hence the abolition of the Catholic Boy Scouts), or to take care of the moral and social welfare of the faithful (hence the persecution of the Demo-Christians). The crucifix is in the schools, but several priests are in the prisons."

In the first large engagement, 1929, Mussolini had won a Pyrrhic victory ; in the pitched battle of 1931 Mussolini triumphed. According to non-Fascists it was a triumph of desperation made necessary by the growth of the movement within Catholicism against the political régime. It is quite true, as Fascists contend, that all the liberal, democratic, and intelligent minority in Italy, driven under cover, had taken refuge in the Azione Cattolica, the only institution in the country where there was a trace of freedom left.

And now the Catholic Action had been emasculated as a political body.

On Mussolini's proud chest to-day appears, surrounded by decorations of a military character, the Order of the Holy Sepulchre. Good Catholics ask : Can this cross over his heart cover the years of Fascist violence ? The assassination of Matteotti, the bombs sent to Cardinal Ferrari with Fascist compliments, the murder of the heroic priest of Argenta, the attacks on the Catholic Scouts, the destruction of Catholic clubs and co-operatives, the dissolution of the Catholic Party, and finally the emasculation of the Azione Cattolica ? Good Catholics shake their heads doubtfully.

The Pope, like the King—it is no secret in Rome—remains anti-Fascist. He knows that his adversary is acting a part. He knows also that a dictatorship can disappear as suddenly as it is born and that the Church goes marching on. He watches all the reverences, the kneelings, and the professions of faith of the neophyte as that of an atheist of yesterday and probably of to-morrow. The Pope's own verdict on Fascism is very simple : " Nothing built on violence ever endures," he said. The Totalitarian or Corporative State, in the opinion of Pius XI., remains " unchristian." The Pope has not changed his mind.

For the time being the victory is Caesar's. But the Kingdom of the Pale Galilean and the Hierarchy of the heretic of Predappio cannot exist for ever, cannot morally function, side by side, one within the other. The eventual triumph lies in the future.

CHAPTER XXIV

DIPLOMACY : CORFU TO ETHIOPIA

IN diplomacy, the waging of wars and the directing of their occasional interruptions — Peace — Mussolini's course has been rather helter-skelter : in fact, in this field more than any other he has shown himself a zigzag Caesar.

The record can be divided into three important sections. First there was the flamboyant period, with the attack on Greece, defiance of the League of Nations, loud fulminations in praise of violence, demagogy in international affairs, on a par almost with internal affairs, imperialistic gestures without corollary actions, all in all the manifestations of the same youthful spirit which was first in evidence on the Socialist soap-boxes of three countries. The Duce became an international figure at the age of thirty-nine.

But years of contact, as a journalist and as a colleague, with Lloyd George, Curzon, Chamberlain, Simon, Poincaré, Barthou, Stresemann, and other professional diplomats of the conventional school, and the fatality of compromises, softened Mussolini in his second phase. He learned quickly and adapted himself to circumstances with the unequalled ability which he had demonstrated throughout his career. This, then, became the period of the great Anglo-Saxon flirtation, when the Duce dropped his threats against Britain, whom he never forgave for being the possessor of Gibraltar, Malta, and Cyprus, and became in turn the chastened follower of Downing Street diplomacy, at the same time espousing the cause of the German people and of Germany's allies, the Revisionist nations.

The third, or present, stage of Mussolinism contains many elements of the first : instead of Greece the enemy is Ethiopia, and the army and navy are again on the road to conquest ; and again the League of Nations, which

Mussolini at one time dominated through the brilliance of his representative, Dino Grandi, is the object of scorn ; imperialism again rules his mind, and there is more evidence to-day that growing desperation of a broken home economy demands foreign recompenses.

The first test of Mussolini's diplomacy followed an incident on the Greek-Albanian border. An Italian general named Tellini and his staff of four were ambushed on August 24, 1923, and assassinated by Albanian bandits in the forest near Janina. Without a moment's hesitation, in which he might have learned on whose soil the murders occurred and the nationality of the murderers, Mussolini, who had yet to wage his first war, sent an ultimatum to Greece. He demanded (1) an official apology ; (2) a formal memorial service for the dead ; (3) honours for the Italian flag ; (4) an inquiry into the affair within five days ; (5) capital punishment for the murderers ; (6) an indemnity of 50,000,000 lire within five days ; (7) military honours for the Italian victims, and (8) a reply within twenty-four hours.

Greece accepted five of these points immediately and asked for a compromise on the others, notably the size of the indemnity, which Greece could not deliver at once. On the advice of the Council of Ambassadors which was held in Paris on the 30th, Greece agreed to hold the suggested conference.

That same day, however, Mussolini mobilized his fleet with remarkable speed and efficiency. The battleships sailed proudly out of the harbours of Italy, and the nation re-captured the hot transcendental feeling of patriotism. At three in the afternoon of the 31st an Italian officer visited the prefect of Corfu to inform him of the imminent capture of the island. The prefect replied that the old fort was not occupied militarily, but was used by refugees. (A later Italian statement claimed that the officer did not understand this statement). The prefect said he had no troops, that he had no means of fighting, and that his only course could be passive resistance.

The ultimatum having been delivered, the Italian navy began its bombardment at five o'clock. Shell after shell crashed down on the police barracks and the fort. There was no reply. For an hour the bombardment continued, and at six the victorious Fascisti landed and stormed the silent fort. From its wreckage came the screams of wounded and the groans of the dying. Of the hundred victims, according to Colonel Bowe of the American Near East Relief, there were twenty dead, of whom sixteen were infants, the wards of American charity. Greece appealed to the League of Nations ; the American Red Cross buried the dead ; in Rome Fascism celebrated its first military victory.

An astonished and indignant world accused Mussolini of a " brutal assault " upon a peaceful and innocent nation. Outside of Italy press and public united in sympathy for Greece. Mussolini sent special cables to many newspapers. In one of them he explained his actions in this way :

" I ordered the Italian navy to occupy Corfu because I know the Greeks, and was aware that if I did not take a pledge for their payment of reparation I would get nothing out of them. I have now taken a pledge, and I will retain it until there has been a complete and literal fulfilment of the conditions of my ultimatum to them. If the Greeks fulfil these and pay up, I will withdraw from Corfu, but they had better pay soon, for next week the price will be higher. These naval operations are expensive. Battleships won't steam on songs. If for any reason Greece does not pay, I will remain in Corfu indefinitely. It was Venetian territory for four centuries, anyway. I have no intention of occupying more Greek territory, or of inflicting other penalties, unless, of course, the Greeks are foolish enough to attack Italian subjects or property. In that case I shall be forced to take immediate military action.

" Italian public opinion does not like the League of Nations, for a very good reason. We respect its aims, but I completely deny its authority to intervene in a matter affecting Italian honour. The present affair does not come under the League Covenant, as there is no danger of war." [1]

But the League thought otherwise. Lord Robert Cecil,

[1] *New York Herald.*

on September 1, informed it there was no doubt whatever of its competency to deal with the conflict nor of its duty to do so, and Branting of Sweden demanded action against Italy. The Marquis della Torretta stated to Lord Curzon that the League had no business in the Corfu affair ; Lord Curzon replied that the whole weight of British prestige was behind the League, and the press began speaking of an international boycott and of joint naval action against Italy.

But bravely Mussolini stuck to his guns : " In case the Council of the League of Nations shall declare itself competent," he said in an official statement dated the 4th, three days after the Council had already done so, " the question whether to remain or resign from the League of Nations will arise in Italy. I have already voted for the second solution."

That week, not for the first and not for the last time, the tension at Geneva reached a breaking-point, and the collapse of Woodrow Wilson's foundation seemed imminent. But, as occurred again when Japan withdrew, and when Germany withdrew, and when Italy again threatened to walk out in the summer of 1935, over the Ethiopian crisis, the directors of the society of peace capitulated before the man of war. As in all diplomacy, a " formula " to save faces had to be found, and in this instance it was decided that, although the League was not to insist on its competency, the Council of Ambassadors in Paris, consisting of much the same set of diplomats, should make the decision. This decision, naturally enough, was on the side of force and possession : the evacuation of Corfu was purchased by Greek fulfilment of the ultimatum, the 50,000,000 lire in cash having been provided, according to report, by Sir Basil Zaharoff.

From their point of view, military, political, or patriotic, the victory was Mussolini's. His and Italy's prestige soared high. Europe sat up and took notice of a new man who would probably have a lot to say in its international affairs in the future. The official report of the mission, headed by a British, a French, and a Japanese colonel, after a month's investigation, found that Greece was entirely innocent of the Janina affair.

There was, however, one important diplomatic aftermath. " The first anniversary of the occupation of Corfu," writes V. Demetrio in *La Politica estera di Mussolini*,[1] and neither the Italian nor the British Foreign Office had denied it, " was celebrated by Great Britain, not by Fascist Italy.

" It was exactly twelve months after the ephemeral occupation by the Italians that the British admiralty organized large manœuvres in the Ionian Sea, and it was on this occasion that the British government obtained from the Greek government permission to land heavy artillery in Corfu for the purpose of participating in a mock war.

" A similar permission had never before been asked for nor granted.

" That was Great Britain's reply to Mussolini.

" Unfortunately, on this account, Italy was obliged to watch without the power to resist the making of a wicked precedent, on whose account the Mediterranean equilibrium has been disturbed without adequate reason."

But the Greek adventure, with its sixteen dead children and its indemnity of 50,000,000 lire (the expedition cost 288,000,000, a fact almost successfully hidden in the budget), and its salute for the Italian flag, while not the great military success anticipated, still did lead to something for Mussolini. In Livorno, on September 30, 1926, Mussolini and Sir Austen Chamberlain held a Machiavellian conference, from which came reports that the Italian Premier had promised support for an expedition against Turkish Anatolia, where territory could be seized for both nations, or that, should the adventure be cancelled, Mussolini would be given a free hand in seizing Albania, provided, however, that he supported the British in intimidating the Turks, who were claiming Mosul and preparing a descent upon Bagdad.

Whatever arrangements were made between the two

[1] Milan, 1925 (before the suppression of the free press), p. 27.

great statesmen is their own affair, and the records, if they exist, remain archive secrets. Historically, however, what happened was that after this famous meeting at Livorno, Chamberlain without a blow drove the Turks from the Iraq frontier, and Mussolini without a blow began the complete economic, military, and political penetration of Albania.

The first important nation to adopt Mussolini's brand of Fascism was Spain, as the latest is Germany. The universal Fascism of which Mussolini speaks also embraces Austria, Hungary, Poland, Bulgaria, Yugoslavia, and Esthonia. In the Far East the government of Chiang Kai-Shek may be termed completely Fascist, while that of Japan is the nearest to Fascism of all reactionary governments.

In addition, Fascist parties have grown extremely powerful in Ireland, Finland, Rumania, and Spain ; Fascist elements of considerable if varying strength have appeared in Portugal, Holland, France, and Greece, and there have been beginnings in England, Switzerland, Czechoslovakia, Sweden, Cuba, and—although leaders and members deny and express abhorrence of the name—in the United States.

In Spain, Germany, Austria, Bulgaria, Greece, Hungary, and Rumania, Mussolini has played a not unimportant part. In September 1923, General Miguel Primo de Rivera established a Fascist dictatorship with the approval of the king and the aid of the artillery officers, and in November he came to Rome for a consultation. Mussolini laid down the principle of Discipline, Order, and Hierarchy ; Primo agreed ; together they made a secret military pact against France [1] and a commercial pact against the United States—they agreed to exploit South America together, and undermine the influence of Yankee traders—and like two commercial travellers, they divided the market for spaghetti, oranges, wine, artificial silk, olive oil, and other products. Commenting on the success of his visit, Director Primo uttered these exalted words :

[1] The contents of which were published by the Spanish diplomat, Santiago Alba, after his exile to France.

18

" On Mussolinism has been formed a creed, a doctrine of redemption, which is drawing to it an army of recruits throughout the world."

In 1926, following Mussolini's example of 1924, Primo held a plebiscite to endorse his dictatorship, and, like his preceptor, he ordered that no opposition votes should be cast. In announcing the resultant great popular victory, the Spanish dictator declared : " I believe with Mussolini that the principle of liberty is pretty as a principle, but is no longer effective as a rule of conduct for a nation, and must be replaced by the principle of authority.

" Public opinion must be strictly controlled.

" The masses must not direct the government, but the government the masses.

" The parliamentary system has had its day . . . it is no longer indispensable ; it is harmful.

" My system will last, not for my personal convenience, but for the good of the country.

" Mussolini's actions showed me what I had to do to save my country. Mussolini is a torch which affords light to nations."

Two years later de Rivera supplemented his views : " There are few who can deny," he said, " that from a material point of view dictatorships in Europe have, on the whole, proved profitable.

" I condemn noisy and sterile assemblies. It is true that when nations and their parliaments reach a high degree of culture they escape the peril. Mussolini has declared that a democratic parliamentary régime is a luxury for rich nations. He is perfectly correct. In rich countries and highly civilized ones, parliament has its uses.

" As for Italy, every one is aware that chronic strikes have ceased, that the lira has been stabilized, that the provinces of the south are making progress, and that regions formerly unhealthful are now being developed.

" As for my own country, dare any one deny that the dictatorship has made considerable material progress, which is manifest in every branch of our economic life ? "

The answer to this question was given by the republican

government which followed the resignation of de Rivera on January 28, 1930, and the collapse of his successor, General Berenguer, on April 12, 1931. In 1928 it was announced that the economic system of dictatorial Spain had broken down but it was saved by a loan of 25,000,000 pesetas from J. P. Morgan & Co. In 1931 the complete collapse was so imminent that the dictatorship was negotiating with the banking houses of Morgan, Chase, National City, Bank of New York, Kuhn Loeb, Guaranty Trust, Dillon Read, and Lee Higginson for $38,000,000, and with the Banque de Paris et des Pays Bas for an additional $22,000,000.

Tremendous financial scandals were brought to light, proving that the business men and militarists behind Primo had made millions of dollars in profits, while the dictatorship had falsified the budget for years ; instead of the officially announced balances there had been expenditures of 4,000,000,000 pesetas and a deficit of a quarter of a billion. The treasury had only 68,000,000 pesetas on hand instead of the officially announced 320,000,000. The Duke of Tetuan blamed the dictatorship for the flight of capital, the loss of confidence, the financial crisis, dishonest elections, the suppression of liberty, unparalleled waste, and the general distrust of the people of Spain.

Niceto Alcala Zamora, emerging from the prison where the dictatorship had placed him, assumed the Presidency, and one of his first actions was to send a cablegram to Italian anti-Fascists to make Spain their home, and look upon the republic as their friend. Francesco Macia, once imprisoned in France as a result of the plot by the Fascist agent Ricciotti Garibaldi, was proclaimed President of the Catalonian Republic. The military treaty between de Rivera and Mussolini was denounced.

Thus, if only temporarily, ended the first of the important Fascist dictatorships modelled upon that of Italy.

In February 1925, the Grand Council of the Fascist Party under the presidency of its Duce discussed a " Preliminary examination of the possibility of a universal understanding between the Fascist and similar movements." There was little repercussion in the world press. But, within the next decade, as Fascism made headway in many parts of Europe, journalists questioned the Duce.

" Fascism is purely Italian," the originator replied to one ; " Fascism is not an article for export," he said to a German ; and " America has no need for Fascism," he remarked to an American. Then in the spring of 1930 he wrote, signed, and sold an article recounting seven years of the achievements of Fascismo, in which he said :

" Fascism is a typically Italian product, as Bolshevism is a typically Russian product. Neither one nor the other can be transplanted and live outside its country of origin." [1]

However, in his tour of northern Italy in May, Mussolini, when not rattling the sword, and defying France and Yugoslavia, extended an invitation to other nations to follow his successful methods. " Europe, tormented, uneasy, and disheartened," he said in Milan, " will not find its salvation except through the coming of Fascism."

(On September 14, 1930, Reichstag elections were held in Germany, giving the Fascists—the still little known National Socialist Party of Adolf Hitler—a considerable victory.)

Celebrating the eighth anniversary of the taking of Rome, il Duce made one of the most important explanations of Fascist diplomacy of his career. He explained the spring tour of oratory which had offended a large part of the peace-seeking world ; extolled Italy as the champion of the Revisionist bloc which sought to amend or destroy the peace treaties upon which the Status Quo nations led by France insisted, and announced the universality of Fascism. He said :

" By the year 1950 Italy will be the only country of young people in Europe, while the rest of Europe will be wrinkled and decrepit. People will come from over the frontier to see the phenomenon of this blooming spring of the Italian people. . . .

" Only toward the East can our pacific expansion occur. . . .

" Their phrase [referring to the German press] the

---

[1] *New York World*, March 2, 1930, magazine section, p. 1.

' Fascismo is not an article for export ' is not mine. It is too banal. It was adopted for the readers of newspapers, who, in order to understand anything, need to have it translated into terms of commercial jargon. In any case it must now be amended.

" To-day I affirm that the idea, doctrine, and spirit of Fascismo are universal. It is Italian in its particular institutions, but it is universal in spirit ; nor could it be otherwise, for spirit is universal by its very nature.

" It is therefore possible to foresee a Fascist Europe which will model its institutions on the Fascist doctrine and practice, a Europe which will solve in the Fascist way the problems of the modern State of the twentieth century."

Then, in 1932, Mussolini and Ludwig engaged in the series of interviews already mentioned. Ludwig, mindful of the German press report that Mussolini had said : " Fascism is not an article for export," and had later said it was not his phrase, since it was so banal, asked :

" Can Fascism be exported to Germany ? "

" To no country," replied Mussolini. " It is an Italian growth. . . ."

Thus ended many years of preaching the gospel of Fascism as an indigenous miracle. Up to the end of 1930 Mussolini had had only one important follower, Primo de Rivera of Spain. But in 1933 one of the really great nations of the world was apparently ready to accept the dictatorial, militaristic, big-business State which he had created. The pragmatic politician, therefore, felt he was at liberty not only to deny his signed statement on the impossibility of Fascism to live if transplanted in foreign soil, but to ridicule those who had published the manuscript he himself had sold them.

" Fascism," he announced after Hitler came into power, " is a religion ; the twentieth century will be known in history as the century of Fascism " ; and celebrating the anniversary of the founding of the party, he said to the Grand Council on March 18, 1934 : " Since 1929 . . . Fascism has become universal. . . . One need only look about to see that the principles of the past century are dead.

We admit unreservedly that they had their period of fecundity and grandeur ! But that is over.

" Those who would check the course of history, those who would arrest its movement or stem its tide, have been overwhelmed. The political forces of the last century— Democracy, Socialism, Liberalism, Freemasonry—are spent. . . . The trend is towards new forms of civilization, both in politics and in economics. The State is resuming its right and its prestige as the sole and supreme interpreter of the needs of society."

During the years of mere protestations of friendship and of declarations of the indigenousness or universality of Fascism, Mussolini had more than platonic relations with Fascist minorities in many countries of Europe. He went one better than the Bolsheviki. Whereas the Third Internationale had been accused by almost every nation in the world of spending sums that would total many times more billions than the world possessed on propaganda work abroad, the Fascisti engaged in the more practical and paying business of smuggling arms to the Fascist parties in Europe.

Thanks to the social consciousness of several Austrian railroad working-men, Italy was caught black-handed in January 1928 in a plot to send twenty-two freight-cars loaded with munitions to Rumania, and five car loads of machine-guns, marked for delivery in Poland, but really intended for side-tracking into Hungary. This became known as the St. Gothard affair.

The League of Nations intervened and reported. The Italian diplomats attempted to have the report suppressed, and so it might have been but for the astuteness of American journalists. Not only was the 1928 case reported in full, but evidence was obtained from the archives of the League that Italy had been engaged in smuggling arms to Fascist parties from 1922 onwards. In 1925 the main shipments were to Hungary, Bulgaria, and Adolf Hitler in Bavaria. The sender of the arms was revealed as the Commercio Universale di Ferramenta Ordigni, which Geneva reported to be a blind behind which were hidden the factories under control of the Fascist government, and whose stock was held by Fascist generals.

It was found that in December 1925, eleven freight-cars passed through Bolzano, in the Southern Tyrol, for Rosenheim, the military headquarters of the Hitler-Ludendorff movement. The addressee was Marx & Co., a commercial house in Rosenheim, the sender Frumenti, a well-known Fascist vice-duce in Bolzano ; the contents were small arms, machine-guns, and ammunition. Upon seizure by the Austrian border authorities, the Fascist Frumenti came to the customs-house, paid a fine of 27,000 lire for false customs declaration, and the next day sent Fascist militiamen to Rosenheim to investigate the report that Italian railroad workers had given away the secret.

The League of Nations in the St. Gothard affair warned Hungary to preserve the evidence intact, but the Hungarians sold the 2000 machine guns—a number enough to equip fifty regiments—for junk. Mussolini, while not attempting to deny Fascist complicity, issued an order to the press to attack the League for interfering with business, and to describe " certain nations " who were afraid of the arming of " defenceless Hungary," as " cowards."

Smuggling continued. Occasionally there was a scandal. Then in January 1933 came the Hirtenberg affair. Italy, Hungary, and Austrian Fascists were caught in a conspiracy to violate the Trianon and St. Germain treaties by the smuggling of 50,000 rifles and 200 machine-guns to Fascist elements, notably to Prince Stahremberg, who with M. Mandl operated the arms factories at Steyr and Hirtenberg. Prince Stahremberg commanded the Austrian Fascists in 1933, with the blessing of Monsignor Seipel, the ex-chancellor who had planned to make himself dictator.

Again Socialist workmen exposed the plot, and the Allies, more concerned with Austria than with the shipments to Bulgarians, Hungarians, and Hitlerites, sent an " ultimatum " to Dollfuss, which, despite a request for secrecy, was published by the Fascist press bureau. Dollfuss, having to choose between a £8,000,000 loan from the Allies and the support of Stahremberg, was forced to return the shipment. The guns, accordingly, were returned to Italy. At this moment Berthold Koenig, the head of the Socialist Railway Workers' Union of Austria, according to information given by him in the Austrian parliament, was offered 150,000 shillings for his association, if the workmen would permit the shipment to take a wrong switch at a point indicated, so that the guns would be delivered at Sopron, in Hungary, where, the arms having been removed, the cases would be sealed officially and sent to Italy.

Upon the exposure of the plot by Julius Deutsch, the Socialist leader in parliament, Dollfuss was forced to dismiss Dr. Egon Seefahlner, the director of the state railroads. But he did not pursue the case further. Koenig testified that Seefahlner, although the author of the bribe offer, had conspired with the Hungarian government for the delivery of the guns and with the Fascist government in furthering this scheme and arranging to accept the empty cases in silence. At this moment Sir John Simon acted. Britain brought such pressure upon Austria that Stahremberg could not retain the guns, and in July the British Foreign Minister announced their safe return to Italy.

In France this scandal was followed by another, involving the delivery of Italian war planes to Hungary in contravention of the peace treaty : Eighteen Fiat pursuit, thirty two-seaters, and twelve Caproni bombers, besides twenty tons of gas and twelve tons of serial bombs.[1] In Prague Dr. Benes informed parliament that " only one or two out of a hundred contraband lots had been caught " ; he demanded in the name of the Little Entente that the League take action to prevent Fascist smuggling operations in the future.

At this point Mussolini broke his unusual silence. On his instructions to the press there followed a series of articles showing that France, Czechoslovakia, and Britain were shipping about a hundred times as much arms as Italy. There was one point, however, the Fascist press was instructed to overlook : the Allied arms were being shipped to Allies, which was legal, whereas the Fascist arms were

Journal Officiel, March 10, 1933.

being shipped either to ex-enemy countries in violation of the peace treaties, or to extra-legal organizations, in defiance of law and ethics.

In all Mussolini's intrigues in Germany, Austria, the Balkans, and Africa, his proposed union of dictatorships, his alternate defiance and attempted leadership of the League of Nations, the penetration of Albania and the various enterprises in Tangiers, Tunis, and Ethiopia, the visits to Cyrenica and Tripolitana, and the final declaration of the universality of Fascism, there runs the thread of a dream : the old Roman dream. Charlemagne was the first of the long series of imitation Caesars who attempted to conquer and rule the old empire, and the refugee Wilhelm in Doorn is not the last to nurse that dream. The son of the Forli blacksmith sitting under the bust of Julius cannot escape it.

World empire through Pan-Fascismo seemed a possibility for a little while in 1930, but that dream was torn by shell-fire in the battle of Vienna, when the impossibility of co-operating with Hitler was made evident. But before that event and even now there has persisted the idea of a Holy Roman Empire, to be divided equally with the Pope, which would embrace the Catholic countries from Italy to the Danube and include the Rhineland, Hungary, Croatia, a part of Yugoslavia, and Bavaria. And a third idea of a similar nature was presented to the world in Mussolini's 1932 " Cry of Alarm," published universally, in which he suggested himself as a leader of a coalition of all the European nations in a holy crusade against Russia, who, in the face of universal depression, was announcing the successful completion of the first Five-Year-Plan in four years.

In one form or another, therefore, the Caesarean idea remains. Either as the commander-in-chief of the Revisionist nations against the Status Quo nations, or as the leader of Europe against the common enemy, the Red Menace, or as the founder of a new African empire, or as the directing head of a Danube confederation or a Catholic bloc, Mussolini's mind can find the right place for himself.

When Briand proposed his United States of Europe the loudest advocates of nationalism were not opposed to it ; on the contrary, the Fascist viewpoint, as shown by one of the semi-official publications, was one of approval—under conditions. If Europe united as one super-nation, " it would be necessary," declared the Roman voice, " to present a new and formidable political idea, a code of life, which could assure the collaboration not only of languages and nationalities, but also of classes, and provoke a rapid development of equilibrium and economics, and envisage at the same time a wise valorization of all creative possibilities. It will therefore be a Fascist idea, because only Fascist Italy has been able to realize that which might serve as a model. In organizing the United States of Europe it will be necessary to name a president, a chief, and a man must be chosen, the most genial, the most celebrated, the strongest and the most respected on the Continent. Evidently it will be Benito Mussolini, because he combines all these qualities."

The future may bring Mussolini some realization of the hope of world empire ; the past can be summed up as follows : Corfu was a failure, but the penetration of Albania a good success ; the intrigue with the Bavarian Nazis was at first a success, but is now, at least temporarily, a failure ; the secret co-operation with the dictator of Spain was a complete failure ; the rôle of patron saint of discontent is no longer applicable, because Germany, chief of the Revisionist nations, has, without Mussolini's aid, destroyed rather than revised the Versailles Treaty ; and yet vicariously that success, whether pleasant or not for the Allies and for the world, must go to Mussolini.

He has made Italy an imperialist nation. Whereas that other Caesar of our time said that " Germany, like the spirit of Imperial Rome, must expand and impose itself," the Duce exposed his principle objective in a declaration to a German editor when he said : " We are obliged to fight on our soil, too small for our overpopulation, for the smallest grain of nutritive substance. Despite scientific effort, Italy cannot nourish its people. *We must expand or ex-*

plode.[1] I do not feel myself authorized to believe in the humanitarian idealism of the pacifists."

For the explosion itself Mussolini then named the year 1935. And it is rational to expect an explosion. The admitted overpopulation is a danger to the peace of the world, intensified by both the encouragement of the birthrate and the refusal of the colonial nations to cede rich land to Italy. And more important than all else is the necessity of imperialism to explode because its economic structure makes explosion, rather than peaceful methods, the one way out of its own dilemmas.

[1] To Theodore Wolff, editor of the *Berliner Tageblatt*, January 30, 1930. The Associated Press, whose Rome correspondent was then an Italian, cabled a similar interview with the italicized phrase as " We must expand or suffocate."

CHAPTER XXV

THE CORPORATE STATE : PEOPLE UNDER FASCISM

ALTHOUGH in turn the Battle of the Lira, the Battle of the Grain, the Battle of the Babies, and many other triumphs have been announced by Mussolini as the outstanding event of his reign, the Duce is also the author of the statement that his greatest gift to civilization and the harassed modern world, the accomplishment for which he will be remembered for ever, is the Corporate State.

" There is one battle which I intend to win—the battle for the economic restoration of Italy," he declared in July 1926 ; " I am now giving my earnest attention to the restoration of the balance of trade and the stabilization of the lira." That same day the following decrees were also issued :

Abolition of the eight-hour day.
Abolition of the right to strike.
Limitation of newspapers to six pages ; crime news must be diminished.
Luxury hotels, cabarets, and the building of luxurious homes prohibited. Abolition of luxury imports.
Potato-raising must replace spaghetti-making.
A ten-o'clock curfew for tea, coffee, and alcohol.

This was part of a programme of " prosperity by edict " ; in the press of the United States and the free nations of Europe labour leaders declared that " Labour's greatest gains in a century of struggle have been wiped out." Almost immediately afterwards Mussolini announced the completed Corporate State.

" For the first time in the history of the world a constructive revolution like ours realizes peacefully, in the field

270

of production and work, the incorporation of all the economic and intellectual forces of the nation to direct them to-day to a common purpose. . . ."

Simultaneously with the establishment of the Corporate State came a series of loans in America and the intensification of the propaganda, begun the year before, when the $100,000,000 Morgan loan was floated, that Fascism was the antithesis of Bolshevism, that Mussolini had saved not only Italy, but perhaps all of Europe, from the Red Menace ; that the Corporate State was the answer to the universal Utopian urge which elsewhere, notably in Russia, was making itself known in a manner quite unacceptable to the organized profit-making system.

This new phenomenon, therefore, must be judged from three important points : whether it actually spells " salvation " from Communism ; whether it actually functions ; whether the people under the Corporate State have gone forward or backward.

To begin with, it must be said that, despite the best American public-relations counsel employed by the international bankers, despite the newspapers and magazines which voluntarily surrendered to the Fascist propaganda machine, it is a historic fact that the whole Mussolini-Bolshevik story was a pure myth which dates from the time of the foreign loans ; and the most important historian who first admitted that the Bolshevism of 1920 (the worst year, the time of the occupation of factories) had disappeared long before the victory of Fascism, wrote in 1921 :

" The Italy of 1921 is fundamentally different from that of 1919. This has been said and demonstrated several times. Fascism must not have the air of monopolizing for itself the credit for such a profound national change. It is enough to count Fascism among the most powerful and disciplined forces which have operated in that direction. After having thus limited our merit, there is no man or party who can attack us.

" To say that the Bolshevik danger still exists in Italy is equivalent to trying to exchange, for reasons of self-interest, Fear against Truth. Bolshevism is conquered.

" More than that, it has been disowned by the leaders and by the people."

This editorial is signed by Benito Mussolini.[1]

This same statesman who in 1925 and 1926 informed American journalists that Fascism arose to destroy Bolshevism is the same Mussolini who advocated not only the confiscation of wealth, but the lynching of the patriotic body of war profiteers, the confiscation of land and industries, and, in short, played the part of the devil's or Lenin's advocate in Italy.   But in December 1920, three months after the factory seizures, he had also written in his *Popolo* :

" It is honest to admit that for the past three months, or precisely after the referendum on the occupation of the factories, and after the return of the mission to Russia [Serratti and others had brought back unfavourable reports on Bolshevism] the pyschology of the working-masses has moderated.   The famous wave of disgust and weakness seems conquered. . . . It is indisputable that the Italian working-class continues to offer the spectacle of laborious activity and discipline ; one cannot refuse them a participation more or less vast in the government of the nation."

If Mussolini's statement that Bolshevism had ceased to menace Italy after 1920 needs corroboration, he had had it from modern historians like H. G. Wells and Professor Salvemini.   If Liberal and anti-Fascist historians are not enough, we have the testimony of Professor Aulard of the Sorbonne, who states that long before the march on Rome " Bolshevism had been conquered, annihilated in Italy by the efforts of the sane democratic elements."   Sanford Griffith reported in the conservative *Wall Street Journal* that " it is a distortion of fact to picture Italian business conditions as in a state of chaos, and the country as on the brink of Red terror, when Mussolini and his Fascisti came into power."   And Fascism's defender, Prezzolini, wrote that " Fascismo can hardly be called the destroyer of Italian Bolshevism, because when Mussolini's movement assumed the violent forms which gave it such a spectacular history, Bolshevism was already on the decline as a result of dis-

[1] Vide *Popolo d'Italia*, July 2, 1921.

couraging reports brought back by emissaries from Russia.
. . . In more than one sense it (Fascismo) is the heir to
Italian Bolshevism."

But popular opinion—and the bankers—needed a Saint
George, and therefore refused to accept Saint George's own
admission that there was no Bolshevik dragon for him to
kill in 1922. Popular opinion, therefore, finds consolation
in those American economists, *littérateurs*, and philosophers
of the daily press and weeklies which boast readers by the
million. One of these writers [1] states that " Ruin impended. Mussolini took the short and unconstitutional cut
which is the dictatorial way. He smashed precedents, turned
red terror into white fear, and brought order and—what
was even more important—economic revival out of the
dust and din of class war and political bicker. In the last
analysis, Fascism is not only a political force of historic
moment, but it has been the impetus of an impressive commercial renaissance as well." This same political economist
precedes this statement with an unqualified declaration
that " the traditional parliamentary systems of Europe are
failures," and a suggestion that France should join the
dictatorships. It is true that the same writer in 1930 ate
all his praise of dictatorships, but he remained the agent
of the Italian Bolshevik myth. He wrote :

" Sovietization, with its attendant social and fiscal
dislocation impended. The workers had seized the factories
in all the important productive centres. Chaos loomed.
In the darkest hour a strong man rose up and saved the
day. The stern will of Mussolini, reinforced by the cohort
of Black Shirts, imposed a régime that made for historic
rehabilitation. Dictatorship achieved its best."

Another writer, a more flowery one,[2] believes that
" everybody who has looked into the Fascist movement in
Italy is agreed that it was a greatly needed movement and
that it saved the nation from descending into a chaotic
whirlpool of Communism and financial disaster that would
have made Niagara's whirlpool look like a placid puddle
of rain - water in comparison." This is incidentally the

[1] Mr. Isaac Marcosson. [2] Mr. Kenneth L. Roberts.

same historian who glorifies Cesare Rossi as " the hero "
who defends the castor-oil treatment, and who tells
Americans that " in spite of his [Mussolini's] many changes,
there has never been a word uttered against his absolute
sincerity and honesty," and that " Mussolini's dictatorship
is a good dictatorship."

This version of the Bolshevik myth accepted by such
eminent gentlemen as Isaac Marcosson, Sir Percival Phillips,
Kenneth L. Roberts, Lord Rothermere, Luigi Villari, Lord
Beaverbrook, Otto H. Khan, Thomas Lamont, and Judge
Gary of the United States Steel Corporation, eventually
was noticed by the superman himself. The clever journalist
realized that the world of big business was honouring him
for something which he had denied, and he was opportunist
enough to seize the tribute. From the time of the American
loans onward he has been declaring himself the original
Bolshevik-fighter of Europe.

" Adversaries of Fascism," he said in an oration in 1927,
" have for a long time past been attempting to deny the
revolutionary character of the events which took place
towards the end of October 1922, bringing the following
argument in support of their allegations. First, that there
was no real resistance, and therefore no conflicts, leading
to bloodshed ; secondly, that all the anti-Fascist parties
withdrew, leaving the road open, because—so add these
commentators of evil faith—the Bolshevist danger had
already disappeared since 1920, when the occupation of the
factories ended in a bubble of soap. . . . In the face of
these untrue assertions aimed at diminishing the generous
and bloody effort of the Black Shirts we must never tire
in our work of affirming and riveting the facts which led
to the Fascist revolution." The Duce concluded by naming
his facts : The Bolshevik danger existed ; the march on
Rome was a bloody battle ; etc. Forgotten were the signed
editorials of another day, forgotten the statement to the
King, forgotten everything which the opportunist mind
wills to forget.

And so we find Mussolini in 1931 publishing his " Cry
of Alarm," in which the world is warned that, unless

economic remedies are found for the economic collapse, "Bolshevism will break through the Vistula "; again he made his bid as the leader of the united nations against Russia, and again he recommended in interviews that Europe adopt his Totalitarian idea in order to prevent the Communist idea from spreading.

What, then, is this new Corporate State, this substitute for Bolshevism which Mussolini has invented and recommends? It is, to begin with, philosophically based on Hegel; from this thinker who also influenced Karl Marx is drawn the first article of the Labour Charter which defines the new Italian nation as "an organism having aims, life, and means of action superior to those of the single or grouped individuals who compose it."

But after Hegel there came d'Annunzio, who in his *Carta della Regenza Italiana del Carnaro*, in his nineteenth article, created ten corporations which were to include all the people of Fiume and its dependencies, as follows: salaried workers of industry, agriculture, commerce, and transportation, etc. ; members of technical and administrative bodies, of industrial or rural firms ; commercial workers who are not labourers ; employers ; public employees ; intellectual flower of the people, studious youth, teachers, sculptors, painters, architects, musicians, etc. ; free professions ; co-operative societies of production, labour, and consumption ; seamen. . . .

Of one category, the tenth, the poet wrote, it "has neither art, number, nor vocabulary. Its fullness is awaited like that of the Tenth Muse. It is reserved for the mysterious forces of the people in travail and in ascension. It is almost a votive offering to the unknown genius, to the appearance of the newest Man, to the ideal transfigurations of works and days, to the complete liberation of the spirit above burdensome anxiety and bloody sweat. . . ."

D'Annunzio put into noble strophes the ideas of his Prime Minister, De Ambris; Mussolini recooked d'Annunzio's poetry and combined it with the "philosophy "of nationalist-syndicalism of Alfredo Rocco ; he was aided in this by Edmondo Rossoni, a former member of the American

19

Industrial Workers of the World, whose habitat had been Brooklyn, New York, and who proposed the syndicalization of workers in vertical unions, embracing all parts of an industry. All these gentlemen helped themselves from the writings of Georges Sorel, the French syndicalist.

The most important document of the new State is the Labour Charter, whose first eight articles were written by Mussolini. These provide that :

> Labour, intellectual, technical, manual, is a social duty.
> Syndicates are organized and controlled by the State.
> Collective labour contracts are established.
> Labour courts are established ; the State intervenes and settles controversies.
> Each corporation constitutes the organization of one field of production, nationally.
> Private initiative is encouraged.
> Wages are paid " as best suited to the needs of employees and the undertaking."

The Labour Charter is a statement of aims, not a series of laws. It does emphasize the Totalitarian State idea, that the State is everything, the individual nothing. Although the working-man is called a " partner " in industry, he has no voice in it. Although lock-outs are barred equally with strikes, and although the corporations which consist of employers and employees are entitled to elect the political directors of the Corporate State, it has surprised no one to find that in the hundreds of thousands of cases of labour unrest there are few instances in which the arbitration boards have had to deal with lock-outs, whilst politically the corporations are in the control of either the employers or the Fascist Party.

The best summary of the corporate idea was made by Giuseppe Bottai, who represented it in the Fascist cabinet :

" The Corporate State idea, which Fascism has conceived and enforced, is an absolutely modern idea. The corporations of the Middle Ages were closed institutions ;

Italian corporativism, on the contrary, is founded essentially on the idea of syndicates, organizations to which access is in principle freely open to all those who ply the same trade. Italian corporativism preserves the syndical structure likewise in the workers' syndicates as well as the employers' confederations, the two parallel organizations being united in a higher state which is the corporation.

" The directing idea is to integrate the syndical forces within the State, to utilize them. We do not deny the existence of the war of the classes ; we do not suppress it ; we simply enforce regulations by means of collective contracts of which 9000 have been made, of which 300 to 400 apply to the whole of Italy, the rest being of provincial character.

" The corporations penetrate all branches of public life. They are represented in the Chamber of Deputies by the Deputies, employers, and employees, and equally in the Grand Council of the party. Furthermore, there exists a central committee of corporations.

" The influence of the corporations has produced in Italian industry a concentration whose happy results have been felt in its rationalization." [1]

When the Labour Charter was published, Rocco called it the Bill of Rights of Labour, but Rossoni, whilst admitting it did guarantee minimum rights for the employee, said the employers would take advantage of its vague terms. Rossoni was asked to resign. Labriola and Buozzi, the exiled labour-leaders, said it was simply a charter of slavery. But in February 1929 Mussolini asked Buozzi, who had been head of the Italian Federation of Labour, to return from France to head the labour syndicates. In his refusal Buozzi said that the Duce's proposal showed that seven years of Fascism had not reconciled labour to the movement ; that the workmen still trusted the old leaders ; that he had once before refused to sell them out or to compromise his ideals and would not now do so.

The first practical step in the formation of the Corporate State was the prohibition of strikes under penalty of fines

[1] *Prager Presse*, January 1933.

and imprisonment. In confirmation of Buozzi's views came the confession, at the Congress of Fascist Syndicates, June 30, 1929, that labour was not getting a new deal. Arnaldo Fioretti and the Hon. Begnotti, Fascist syndicate leaders, according to the official publication *Lavora Fascista*, told the congress that working-men were not fairly treated by employers, that the new labour contracts were not respected by the captains of industry, that the working-men had lost faith in the Fascist syndicates, and that the Corporate State cannot be said to exist until the hostility and reprisals of employers against workmen had been removed and unjust dismissals stopped. No newspaper in Italy printed these official statements.

In May 1930, Mussolini announced that the National Council of Corporations had been inaugurated, " to crown the Corporative State." He called it an economic revolution : not only was peace between capital and labour enforced, but prices would be regulated, and the quality of production as well. The syndicates were announced as complete : six employers' federations in industry, agriculture, commerce, land transport, sea and air transport, and banking ; and six corresponding employees' confederations. In addition there was a federation for all intellectual workers.

" We have thus created a united Italian State," said Mussolini. " Since the fall of the Roman Empire, Italy has never been a unified State. It is the State alone that makes the nation self-conscious."

In the national council there were fifty-two of Mussolini's picked men and thirteen representatives of the corporations.

In 1932 Fascist official figures showed that 4,181,848 Italians out of some seven or eight million working-men had become members of the syndicates. What is remarkable about this figure is that it is comparatively small, because employment in Italy, as in Russia, is extremely difficult, if not impossible, for those who do not join the State organization. But more remarkable is the figure of 995,828 employers who have joined, out of a possible 3,707,893 who come under that classification.

In 1933, despite the fact that the Rome correspondent of the *New York Times* and the majority of correspondents of the other important newspapers resident in Rome had been announcing from two to seven times, in the course of seven years, that the Corporate State was functioning, Mr. John Strachey made the statement that " No corporations exist except on paper." He was immediately attacked by unbelieving critics and reviewers. Mr. Strachey's declaration seemed stupid in the face of unanimous reports in the daily press.

Shortly afterwards there appeared the first complete volume dealing with the problem. It was written by a Fascist with the co-operation of the officials of the Ministry of Corporations. On page 110 of this study [1] in a chapter entitled " The Corporations in their actual working " [*sic*] the author states : " Only a single corporation, viz., that of the stage, has so far been established in Italy."

However, the only important thing for us to consider is whether, functioning or not functioning as a Corporative State, the Fascist system of planned economy, the substitute for the planned economy of Bolshevism, has or has not achieved anything up to date. It is Mussolini who said that the State's ultimate goal is " the well-being of the Italian people " ; it must be judged " and measured directly by the masses as instruments through which these masses may improve their standard of living. Some day the worker, the tiller of the soil, will say to himself and to others : ' If to-day I am better off practically, I owe it to the institutions which the Fascist revolution has created.' "

In just this manner let the following facts pass judgment :

In 1926, when the few untrammelled journalists reported that there was already a crisis in Fascist economics and that the publicly announced balanced budgets were mere jugglery, official figures showed that wages were below 1921 and that the cost of living had gone up 30 per cent. In 1927, with the stabilization of the lira, Mussolini found a much more serious economic crisis. He therefore

[1] *The Italian Corporate State*, by Fausto Pitigliani, London, P. S. King & Son.

announced a reduction in rentals, reductions in the price of manufactured goods, and a wage cut throughout the nation of between 5 and 20 per cent. He promised that the cuts ordered in the high cost of living would more than offset the reductions in salary. At that time the general price index was 670 ; wages stood at 585 ; in real wages the workman was 13 per cent. worse off than before the war.

That Fascism had proved a failure so far as the working population of Italy is concerned long before the world crisis of 1929–35 was openly admitted in the 1932 report of the Secretary of State for Corporations, who wrote :

" Between June 1927 and December 1928 the wages of industrial workers have gone down by about 20 per cent., and a further reduction of 10 per cent. was made in 1929 ; during 1930 there has been a general reduction, varying for the different categories of workers from 18 to 25 per cent. Many other adjustments [sic] have been realized in 1931."

But that is not all. The decree of December 1, 1930, cut the salaries of those earning more than £600 a year by 35 per cent. and those below £400 by 12 per cent., and wages of 300 lire (£3 : 2 : 9) to 1000 lire (£10 : 9 : 6) a month 8 per cent., and those above 1000 lire 10 per cent. This cut affected 1,000,000 labourers in the industrial centres of the north—Milan, Turin, and Genoa. The government announced that it " hoped " to reduce prices of commodities accordingly.

Then, on April 1, 1931, Mussolini in another of his great public orations informed Italy that it need fear no more wage reductions. He admitted frankly that " we have reached a limit in wage cutting ; there is danger lest the antidote should become a poison. . . . Italy was the first to apply what has now been adopted by almost the whole of Europe. . . . Speaking generally, certain symptoms of recovery may be seen, but . . . we are still waiting for the factors of recovery—in the first place *moral* factors— to enter into play simultaneously and collectively."

By 1932, however, an official of the Fascist syndicates [1] figured that the wages of glass-workers had declined by

[1] *Living Age*, May 1934.

between 30 and 40 per cent. ; signalmen's earnings were down 40 per cent. ; silk-workers, 38 per cent. ; bricklayers, 30 per cent. ; miners, 30 per cent. ; while the cost of living had declined by 20 per cent.

In 1933, moreover, despite the Duce's poison-warning, every Italian salary and wage was ordered to be reduced by an average of 10 per cent., and Mussolini announced a similar reduction in rents, food, manufactured goods, etc.

And again, on April 14, 1934, " the urgent necessity of lightening the national budget, which shows an annual deficit of between 3,000,000,000 and 4,000,000,000 lire "— the admission is made by Mr. Cortesi of the *Times* himself— " caused the Cabinet Council . . . to apply a general reduction to the salaries of State employees, effective April 16." Twenty per cent. was deducted from the income of high-salaried officials such as Cabinet members ; 6 per cent., the minimum, was the tax on those making more than 500 lire a month ; others were exempt. When it is considered that one man in five works for the government, the size of this, the sixth reduction since 1927, will appear evident. The Fascist apologist, Cortesi, claims that the 1934 cut brings wages down to the pre-Fascist era, and says : " The general lowering of the cost of living which will ultimately result in the lowering of production costs in industry and agriculture is deemed necessary by economists. . . ." The facts, however, are that real wages are far below the pre-Fascist era ; that living costs have never paralleled the decline in wages ; that the buying power of the Italian people has decreased rather than increased, and that while the philo-Fascist journalists continue to find explanations and publish excuses in the *New York Times*, the official figures of the League of Nations and the statements of Mussolini himself, and other lesser enthusiasts for Fascism than the *Times* correspondent, have admitted the economic degeneration of the Italian people.

To complete the chronicle, it was announced by Mussolini on December 11, 1934, that a nation-wide and simultaneous reduction in salaries and the cost of living was being worked out which affected every person in the kingdom, directly and indirectly, the cut being similar to that of October, 1930, and similarly carrying with it a reduction in cost of rent, light, heat, food, and transport of between 10 and 12 per cent.

But, instead of mentioning the obvious collapse of the Fascist economy, the American press heralded each of these seven events with an appropriate excuse furnished by the Fascist propaganda department. The headlines, for example, said that the 1927 cut was due to the success of the stabilization on a gold basis. In 1933 Mr. Cortesi of the *Times* supplied a story which was headed, " Italy cuts wages to aid recovery " ; the first 1934 reduction was linked with one in Russia, and the joint headline read, " Russia and Italy slash pay-rolls in Economy Wave " ; the second 1934 cut was reported by the *Times* as " Italy to slash wages and cost of living to meet competition of non-gold nations."

Before presenting the documentary proofs of failure of Fascist economics, it may be interesting, perhaps, to give another sample of pro-Fascist journalism, typical of some magazines as contrasted with the newspapers. Whereas the daily press is supposed to deal with facts, the monthly journals devote themselves largely to opinion and inter-pretation. Here, then, are some extracts from the work of Howard R. Marraro,[1] of the Italian department of Columbia University :

" In a world whose troubles are at bottom mainly economic, nations are rightly judged according to their success or failure in terms of genuine human welfare. What then has Fascism done to bring about a happier state of affairs in Italy ? . . .

" The Italian to-day is much better fed than he was. . . .

" . . . the standards of living of the Italian people have improved from 1913 to the present. This improvement is particularly marked during the twelve years of the Fascist régime, and it has not been interrupted by the world economic crisis. . . .

" Thanks to the labour legislation of the Fascist régime,

[1] *Current History*, May 1935.

there has been no important strike or lock-out in Italy since
1926. . . . Of the 153 strikes which have come before the
courts, a considerable number were due to the uncertainties
prevailing in the early days as to the interpretation of the
act. . . .

" . . . the economic and social achievements of Fascism
are truly impressive . . . a more prosperous and happy
nation."

So much for opinion and interpretation. The facts are
that under Fascism, from 1923 to 1932, the cost of living
was reduced 5 per cent. and wages reduced 40 to 50 per
cent. ; if this is not a fact, then the League of Nations has
been badly fooled. These statements are from the *Bulletin
mensuel de statistique*, Geneva, February 1933, page 74.
Fascist official figures show a reduction in the cost of living
of only 10 per cent. as compared with 1914.[1] In other words,
six wage cuts averaging 40 to 50 per cent. and a cut in
living costs of 5 or 10 per cent. The Fascist *Corriere della
Sera* (July 27, 1932) admitted that in four years the wage
cuts totalled 50 per cent. The official *Lavoro Fascista*
(November 29, 1931) admitted that in some provinces
wages had been reduced from 45 to 60 per cent. in 1931.

The International Labour Office of the League of Nations
made the following report on real wages, in July 1930 :

United States	190	Poland		61
Canada	155	Austria		48
Great Britain	100	Jugoslavia		45
Holland	82	Spain		40
Germany	73	Italy		39

The *International Labour Review*, March 1932, gives the
daily farm labour wage in 1923 as 12·88 lire ; 1926, 14·24
lire ; 1931, 10·49 lire. Real wages for agricultural workers
stood at 107 in 1923, 89 in 1926, and 87 in 1931.

An examination of Fascist official figures shows that the
average wage in 1928 was two lire an hour ; that it fell to
one and three-fourths lire in 1932, and one and a half, or
eight cents an hour, in 1933. In other words, labour is
worse paid in Italy than in any country in Europe.

[1] *Bolletino dei prezzi*, January 12, 1933, p. 44.

Before Fascism arrived it is true that Italy was not among the first of the thirty or more nations which reported to the League ; but neither was it the very last. It reached that position in a steady retrogression from 1926 onwards. Moreover, the Labour Office, in its statistics on social welfare of workmen throughout the world, also lists Italy last among the important nations of Europe, because it spends less per man and because it has not yet (1932) organized a decent system of insurance against unemployment.

If the foregoing facts require an objective interpretation, here is one made by Constantine E. McGuire with the co-operation of the Institute of Economics : [1]

Rents are nearly four times higher than before the war.[2]

The low wages earned by employees and often by professional men frequently render it impossible for them to bring up their offspring according to the pre-war standard.

The deduction may fairly be made that the standard of living of students living in university dormitories has distinctly fallen.

The universities and higher institutions of learning are relatively deserted.

One may gather . . . that those who are students to-day are likely to have in the life of to-morrow an efficiency below that of those who were students before the war.

It is evident that a condition of this sort can hardly continue without the progressive decay of the Italian national organism. At this very moment that organism is in a pathological condition. . . . By a pathological condition we mean precisely one which cannot continue without bringing about the breakdown of the organism itself.[3]

When the problem of the high cost of living continues on and on and for a greater or lesser fraction of the population without any other fraction thereof being able to realize exceptional profits—which is precisely the state of affairs existing in Italy for some time—the conviction that living

[1] *Italy's International Economic Position* (1927).
[2] *Id.*, p. 545.   [3] *Id.*, p. 547.

is costly really signifies that at least for some categories of the population the national income is insufficient to maintain the standard of living which they have accustomed themselves to observe.[1]

So low is the standard of living of the Italian workmen that it could not be lower without impairing his productive powers. The wage level . . . in Italy . . . is the same as in Austria, over whose population the world is in the habit of weeping ; and Italy's wage level is actually lower than that of Spain or that of Poland.[2]

The facts are that the standard of living of Italy has fallen dangerously under Fascism ; the question is whether or not it has fallen below the subsistence level.

In 1932 Professor Bottazzi, a physiologist and a member of the Fascist National Academy, published an academic study of this subject. It showed conclusively that the masses were not eating enough to satisfy hunger. In 1929 Mussolini had admitted that " there are communes in Sardinia and in South Italy where for months at a time the inhabitants have to live on wild plants,[3] and the Deputy Zingali had reported to parliament that " I have been collaborating in the preparation of the material concerning the American debt. It was my duty to ascertain the standard of life in Italy, and I arrived at this disturbing conclusion : that the food ration per head and per day amounted to only 3100 calories—*i.e.*, to 200 calories less than the physiologists consider necessary for adults. Our ration is probably lower than that of any other European country." [4]

And finally, for the benefit of the Cortesis and Marraros, here is the original language of the *Discorso* of the Duce in the Fascist Chamber of Deputies, December 12, 1930 :

" *Fortunamente il popolo italiano non è ancora ambituato a mangiare molte volte al giorno e, avendo un livello di vita modesto sente di meno la deficienza e la sofferenza.*"
" Fortunately," said Mussolini, " the Italian people are not

[1] *Italy's International Economic Position* (1927).   [2] *Id.*, p. 535.
[3] Discourse, Chamber of Deputies, June 22, 1929.
[4] *Parliamentary Reports, Chamber of Deputies*, December 5, 1929.

yet accustomed to eat several times per day and, having a modest standard of living, feels want and suffering less."

The " modest standard of living " is the lowest standard in Europe, one of the lowest standards in the civilized world ; it was reached during the Fascist régime and it is one of the chief results of the Fascist economic programme. In the United States, in 1935, there was a serious discussion among the physicians attending their annual national convention, whether or not the amounts paid the unemployed and their food ration were sufficient to keep these millions above the subsistence level. Yet under Fascism not the unemployed on the dole, but the entire working nation, has been reduced to just about or below that level.

And at the same time the burden of taxation has increased. In proportion to income, the Italian people pay more taxes than those of any other important country. In 1914 the taxation as percentage of national income was 13 ; in 1925 it had already reached 20 per cent., and in other Fascist years it was even higher. Thus, concludes Mr. McGuire, " Even with much more substantial allowances *per capita* for the minimum of subsistence, it is probable that no other important country would show so great a percentage of income absorbed by taxation. Thus, Italy's appearance of vigour and prosperity [in 1926] cannot cover the fact that from an economic point of view her people are poorer, taken on an average, than they were before the war." [1]

Compared with war-time, rents increased from two to three times according to testimony given to officials by the Home Owners' Association,[2] while the purchasing power of money had fallen to one-fifth or one-sixth. Taxes, on the other hand, had increased fourfold, and various expenses and dues an average of sixfold. From these figures the home-owners concluded that the effective income has been reduced to one-half.

In 1932 a study of official figures revealed that taxation

[1] McGuire, *Italy's International Economic Position*, p. 103.
[2] *Id.*, p. 535.

had almost doubled under Fascism. The amount was 20,000,000,000 lire a year, or 30 per cent. of the national income, as compared with 12,000,000,000 lire or approximately 15 per cent. in pre-dictatorial days.

Bread is taxed 3 farthings a pound, sugar 6½d., salt 1½d., and other necessities of life in proportion. Returning to his ancestral land, Anthony M. Turano was surprised to have a friend say to him, " You are fortunate you can smoke without counting the puffs. Smoking has become the privilege of the upper classes." Mr. Turano investigated. He found [1] that an assistant stone mason earned one and a quarter lire an hour, and the cheapest cigarettes were four lire for twenty ; in other words, a man must work three hours to half a day for his cigarette money. Unemployed who for a time are allowed 3.70 lire a day cannot, therefore, buy a packet of cigarettes with their dole.

To Mussolini's declaration, " I am the first to declare that the pressure of taxation has attained the limit "— quoted by Mr. Marrano—Mr. Turano adds that despite this warning " not to tax the taxpayers to death," it still continues. Bachelor taxes have been increased, but when the desperate bachelor marries he is told he must pay 25 lire a year as family tax ; he is taxed for keeping a hog and he is taxed if he slaughters the hog ; and so it goes on.

The latest available figures on the subject show that the working-men of Italy have to contribute 160,448,000 lire for the maintenance of the embryo corporations. The individual worker pays not only his regular dues, but contributes to the unemployment fund, sick benefit fund, summer resorts fund, winter insurance, federal secretariat, Fascist home fund, and to extraordinary levies, a total of somewhat over 216 lire. The American trades-unionist pays about $30 a year ; the Italian pays less in dollars, but more in real wages, since the American gives up about one week's pay, whereas the Italian is legally forced to surrender almost one month's pay to the corporations.

It is true that there has not been one first-class strike since 1926. In every instance where workmen threatened

[1] *American Mercury*, September 1934.

or began a strike the Fascist militia has suppressed it with violence and bloodshed. And this is, of course, one of the great achievements of Fascism—from the point of view of the chambers of commerce and industrialist associations. The Labour Charter prohibits strikes. The militia see that the charter is enforced. That is about all there is to the struggle between capital and labour in Italy.

And yet in the reports of Fascist officials there is the proud claim that of the 142,000 labour disputes in 1932, 37,000 were settled in the courts, the balance by the syndicates. The claim to settlement is also an admission that disputes exist. But the Italian press has been ordered and the foreign correspondents warned, not to emphasize or mention social unrest, labour troubles, tax revolts. Although the *Manchester Guardian* and *Times* have frequently reported such episodes, there has almost been no mention of them in the American press.

In May 1927 an armed rebellion against the Fascisti was led by Don Galbiati, the parish priest of Inveruno, and there were other uprisings and riots throughout Italy in protest against the wage cut and the increased cost of living. At that time the anti-Fascist press, secretly printed, still had a circulation of 500,000 copies daily. Early in 1931 the weavers of Parabiago and Legnago walked out. Wages had been reduced to half a crown a day. In the American press this was reported as the first strike since the announcement of the Corporate State ; it was, in fact, the first of thousands of strikes which was reported in the foreign press. The Fascist militia soon reduced both the Galbiati uprising and the weavers' strike to silence.

On September 8, 1931, there was a revolt of the peasants of Montenero di Basaccia. The podestá, or vice-duce, of the province had imposed taxes the people could not pay. With cries of " Death to the podestá ! " and " Death to the famine-makers ! " the populace stormed and sacked the mayor's office, tearing up the pictures of Mussolini and destroying the archives. The officials fled. The Fascist militia deserted.

In the afternoon a commissioner of police arrived from

Campobasso with regular police (carabinieri). He informed the populace the Fascist officials had been sacked and a better régime would begin, but that night he began arresting the supposed ringleaders. The peasants sounded the alarm. In a battle with the police the latter fired 200 shots, killing three men, Antonio Lonzi, Antonio Suriani (aged over seventy) and Pasquale d'Aulero, and wounding thirteen others.

That same month there was a bloody demonstration of working-men of Carrara in which the Fascisti killed two and wounded many. On the 27th at Roccacasale in the Abruzzi the angry populace stormed the mayor's palace. At Villa Santa the podestá and the municipal secretary were shot by peasants. At Vereno di Piave, near Treviso, during the Vatican-Fascist conflict over the school régime, the population shouted, " Our hour has come ! " barricaded the provincial route, and attempted to surround the Fascist barracks.

On January 8, 1933, the *Chicago Tribune* reported that the militia and carabinieri were sent to the villages of Monte San Giacomo and Sassano to quell disturbances which followed attempts by the authorities to collect taxes. On April 19, 1934, the Associated Press carried a fifty-word report of " a violent outbreak in protest against provincial taxes in which one person was killed and fifteen wounded," at Pratola, in Central Italy. " Mountaineers chased the collector to the railroad station, cut the telephone and telegraph lines, and damaged public buildings before they were quelled by Fascist militia."

The plebiscite of 1934, according to Robert Briffault,[1] was an indispensible preliminary " to putting into force the drastic reductions of wages and other measures imposing misery and starvation, rendered necessary by the economic bankruptcy of the Fascist State. It was attended by a terrorism not excelled at the time of the ' March on Rome.' The balloting was open, and the most violent intimidation was exercised by the State forces. Nevertheless, in Turin the negative votes were estimated at between 12,000 and

[1] *Forum*, October 1934.

15,000, and those who abstained from voting numbered 40,000. Similar reports were forthcoming from Milan. In Venice the ' plebiscite ' led to violent riots, which the militia were unable to control before several of the ' Dopolavoro ' houses had been wrecked.

" Open opposition to Fascism, despite all measures of terrorism, has been assuming ever larger proportions in recent months. Practically the whole of Sicily and Calabria is now manifesting openly its anti-Fascist spirit. At Bistari, Mussolini was burnt in effigy. At Catanzaro, a procession was stopped by masses of rioters shouting anti-Fascist slogans. At Udine, in February, large demonstrations, including women and children, paraded, crying ' Down with Fascism.' Anti-Fascist riots have taken place in Licorno. Everything indicates that the opposition to Fascism, which is in reality almost universal among the working-classes, is daily becoming bolder." So it is apparent that there is unrest and occasional revolt.

It was said by the late William Bolitho that the Duce's agricultural programme in 1928 was making serfs out of the Italian farm labourers. More recently, Professor W. Y. Elliott of Harvard summed up the situation as follows : " Fascism has succeeded in depriving the labourer of the weapon of free association and the right to strike, and has reduced him, at least for the time being, to a condition of State-controlled serfdom " ; and in October 1934 the secretary of the British Trades Union Congress, Walter M. Citrine, when urging the American Federation of Labour to declare war on Fascism, declared :

" The record of Fascism is one of repression, brutality, and terrorism. Personal liberty has been destroyed, trade-unionism has been crushed, and the status of the citizen has been reduced to that of a serf.

" Far from being saved by Fascism, Italy has been brought to the verge of economic bankruptcy. Since 1922 wages have been reduced 40 to 50 per cent. and are now the lowest in western Europe. Even Mussolini admits that the living standards of Italian workers can be reduced no further. American money is helping Mussolini to maintain his power.

" Fascism's record in the constructive sphere is one of failure and futility. It has contributed more than any other factor to the feeling of insecurity which has brought the possibility of widespread war to the forefront."

In 1934 the National Joint Council,representing the Trades Union Congress, the Labour Party, and the Parliamentary Labour Party of Great Britain, issued " British Labour's Call to the People," an official declaration of war on Fascism, Italian as well as German. On October 13th of the same year the American Federation of Labour declared a boycott of goods made in dictatorial countries, including Italy. In February 1935, following an investigation of Italian agents' activities against the trade unions, President Green of the A. F. of L. publicly condemned Italian Fascism.

Of course the fact that free labour throughout the world is anti-Fascist—seeing in Italian, German, and other forms of Fascism a return to mediæval serfdom—can be interpreted conversely, that Fascism would be highly welcomed by the employers of labour. And so it was, in fact, by Judge Gary of the United States Steel Corporation. And that leading philosopher and economist of big-business, Mr. Marcosson, glorifying the Corporate State, wrote in 1930 that " under the Fascist trade-union law strikes have been outlawed and compulsory arbitration is enforced. No Mussolini measure was so fraught with constructive possibilities."

In Britain, America, France, and other free countries labour is becoming the chief antagonist to the Fascist movement. After all, it is Labour which is hardest hit. One man's Corporate " constructive possibilities " is another man's Helot State.

The evidence is therefore overwhelming that Mussolini did not save Italy from Bolshevism ; that the Corporate State, which may or may not be a substitute for Soviet-planned economy, does not function ; that the standard

20

of living of Italy has gone down with six or seven wage cuts ; that under these circumstances " the well-being of the Italian people " has not materialized, but their misery increased ; that, in short, Fascist economy is a failure.

CHAPTER XXVI

Fascism Finance

THE confession that Fascist economy has failed is made by Mussolini himself.

Addressing the Chamber on December 18, 1930, the dictator who had stabilized the lira, announced balanced budgets for many years, proclaimed the economic viability of Fascism, and invited other nations to adopt the Corporative instead of the Communist idea of economic planning, informed Italy and the world that : " The situation in Italy was satisfactory until the autumn of 1929, when the American market crash exploded suddenly like a bomb. For us poor European provincials it was a great surprise. We remained astonished, like the world at the announcement of the death of Napoleon, because we had been given to understand that America was the country of prosperity, of endless and absolute prosperity, without eclipses. Every one was rich there.

" Every one knows the data of American prosperity— there was one motor-car for every eight inhabitants, one radio set for every four, one telephone for every three. Every one gambled on the stock exchange, and since stocks rose incessantly, every one bought at 20, sold at 100, and pocketed the difference, with which he purchased a motor-car, radio set, and telephone, or made a trip to Europe, paying for it by instalments, and built a house in the country. All this was fantastic, and we on this side of the Atlantic had a sense of envy.

" Suddenly the beautiful scene collapsed and we had a series of black days. Stocks lost 30, 40, and 50 per cent. of their value. The crisis grew deeper.

" Black days followed black days, and prosperity was

replaced by long lines of unemployed waiting for soup and bread in the great American cities.

" From that day we also were again pushed into the high seas, and from that day navigation has become extremely difficult for us."

The best American comment on this great explanation was made by Howard Brubaker : " Mussolini," he said, " has calmed growling Italians with the information that Wall Street is responsible for their lower salaries, their unemployment, their low returns on farm products. About the only crimes not attributed to Wall Street were the earthquakes of last July."

But shifting the blame on America does not shift the main issue, which is simply this : Does Fascism offer the world a new and workable economic system ; is it merely part of the universally (outside Russia) accepted system, and has it succeeded in meeting a crisis successfully ? By ascribing Italy's financial failure to Wall Street's failure Mussolini confesses that his is no new or different or independent system, or, if new and different, that it is not a better one because it, too, has broken down.

In fact, the making of Wall Street the scapegoat is one of the master-strokes of the modern Machiavelli, because Fascist economy broke down long before Wall Street collapsed. It is the purpose of this chapter to discuss the finances of the years 1922 to 1929 and to show, from official Fascist figures, that the crisis of Fascism began in 1925 and reached an alarming condition in 1927 and 1928. Paradoxically, Mussolini was spared the *political* consequences when the rest of the world—outside Russia—also joined in the collapse of 1929. The world was now in the same boat, and growing discontent in Italy was therefore stilled.

The first economic victory which Mussolini reported was the stabilization of the lira. It seems that the whole subject of economics first came to his attention in January 1922, when he as a journalist, preparing to attend the peace conference (at Cannes, on the French Riviera), exchanged some money in Milan. For each one-hundred-lira note he was given a fifty-franc note.

" It was a grave symptom. It was a humiliation. It was a blow to the self-respect of a victorious nation, a vexing weather-vane ; it indicated our progress towards bankruptcy : up leaped the thought that this situation must be cured by the vital strength of Fascism."

This emotion engendered in the patriotic breast was not ephemeral. It took root. It was later to flower in a gold stabilization which was higher than that of France. What is significant is the behaviour of " the man of action," the ideas and the procedure of an economist like Mussolini, whose nationalistic egotism, whose Italian pride is hurt by the financial situation, and who thereupon rules that " Fascism must change all that."

And so, commenting in 1928 on his actions of the past year, Mussolini declares with pride that " in December 1927, at a meeting of the Council of Ministers, I was able to announce to the Italian people that the lira was back on a gold basis, on a ratio which technicians and profound experts in financial questions have judged sound.'

He flatly makes the statement that " to-day we have a balanced budget. Self-ruling units, the provinces and the communes, have balanced their budgets too. Exports and imports and their relationship are carried on in a precise and definite rhythm—that of our stabilized lira."

He has the pleasant unbelievable surprise of a child which for the first time turns an electric light off and on, when he says that he had " solved a complex and difficult problem of national finance, such a problem as sometimes withdraws itself beyond the will and influence of any political man, and becomes subjected to the tyranny and mechanism of more material relations under the influences of various and infinite factors. Only a profound knowledge of the economic life and structure of a people can reach, in such an insidious field, conclusions which will be able to satisfy the majority."

" I felt the pride of a victor," exclaims Mussolini, and well might any man feel the pride of a victor who has not only marched into Rome, but who had smashed the tyranny of economics, laws which rule world finances, and which no other politician or nation has ever been able to conquer.

It was nothing short of a miracle : the sun of economic fatality stood still in the heavens at the command of the prophet, and the American international bond-floaters sang the epic of the great deed as they issued $600,000,000 in loans to Italy.

Six hundred million American dollars is a sum. It was surely worth the employment of public-relations counsel and the aid of the banking-houses in protecting it. Time after time, between 1925 and 1929, the American public dumped the Italian bonds back on the market, and each time the dozen houses which floated them intensified their campaign which created the Mussolini-balanced-budget myth, while they threatened the banking and brokerage firms which represented them with being denied partici-pation in future business if they failed to dispose of the Italian goods.

The Duce, of course, has always been party to the financial myth-making. He declared the stabilization at 19 was approved by " profound experts in financial questions," but it was later proved that Finance Minister Volpi and his good friend, Andrew W. Mellon, had advised against that figure.

It was always the head of the government who struck the note for the orchestra of the press to follow. When the bankers and the press agents and Italians who wrote for the Agencies and American newspapers portrayed the stabili-zation at 19 to the dollar as a victory, when they reported that Bolshevism threatened in 1922, that the budgets were balanced, that the municipalities were out of the " red " literally and figuratively, and that prosperity had crowned the planned economy of Fascism up to 1929, they were but playing variations on the tune which the master musician originated.

This tune, of course, is the only one heard in Italy and America. From his exile in England, however, Count Sforza, the former Minister of Foreign Affairs, has issued a statement calling it " an offence to Italy to give the impression abroad that she wants truth to be wrapped in gentle lies." " To pretend to-day that the present difficult financial situation in Italy is due to the American crisis," he continues, " simply means that the men now in office in Italy do not dare to face their responsibilities, that they slander the brave, thrifty Italian nation by showing her up as a sick person to whom only lies can be administered. . . . The truth is that the specific present Italian crisis has nothing to do with the general world crisis. Indeed, the general world crisis is a crisis of over-capitalization, while that in Italy is one of lack of capital. . . . But there are more direct proofs of my assertion. The Italian crisis began years before the American and general crisis—precisely, between 1924 and 1926."

Count Sforza is one of Mussolini's enemies. But so are the official statistics of the Fascist régime. In 1922 Italy's bankruptcies—commercial failures, since personal bank-ruptcy does not exist under that country's laws—were 3858 ; in 1926, 8580 ; in 1929, 11,106. In 1926 there were 181,000 unemployed in Italy, and in 1928, 439,000 or more. In fact, it is estimated, non-officially, that there were 800,000 unemployed, including those kept inside the factories by Fascist orders, and those working a day or two a week for their food. Imports in 1925 were 26,000,000,000 lire, and exports 18,000,000,000, while in 1928 imports were 22,000,000,000 and exports 14,000,000,000.

The American commercial attaché, H. C. MacLean, reported from Rome on January 16, 1928, that " the out-standing characteristic of Italy's relations with the rest of the world is the large excess of the country's merchandise imports over its merchandise exports, a condition prevailing for many years. To compensate the large adverse trade balance invisible terms (notably remittances from Italians resident abroad and expenditures of foreign tourists in Italy) must be largely depended upon."

The attaché then points out an adverse balance of almost 5,000,000,000 lire for the first ten months of 1927, adding, " Having accepted 5,000,000,000 as Italy's adverse trade balance and 1,500,000,000 as its net outgo on financial transactions, we have a total of 6,500,000,000 lire for which compensation must be found on the credit side of the country's international accounts."

He then shows that "emigrants'" remittances have sharply declined. Whereas in 1926 the withdrawals from postal savings banks were practically compensated by new deposits, during the first ten months of 1927 such withdrawals exceeded deposits by no less than 570,000,000 lire."

On July 9, 1928, the American Commercial Attaché, Mowatt M. Mitchell, cabled that "Italian industrial and business conditions continue unsatisfactory, and are at present still further depressed by the growing seasonal slack."

The continuation of unsatisfactory conditions was confirmed by the January 14, 1929, report of Mr. Mitchell, who radioed : " Foreign trade suffered from the high stabilization point of the lira. Imports increased and exports decreased, resulting in an adverse trade balance of nearly 7,000,000,000 lire as compared with 5,000,000,000 in 1927."

The American attache was of the opinion, however, that the government finances were in good shape, with large cash reserves, but the Italian treasury report [1] showed that the cash reserves had decreased continually until they were half of 1926 : cash reserves, June 30, 1926, 2,841,000,000 ; June, 1928, 1,706,000,000 ; November 30, 1928, 1,389,000,00.

In fact it is Mussolini's first economic triumph, the boasted stabilization of the lira, which marks the intensification of the Fascist economic crisis. It must be remembered that the Italian, as well as the French, money had been guaranteed by the Allies during the war. When the guarantees were removed, both fell ; the lira was 8 to the dollar in the first half of 1919, and reached its just value somewhere above 20 ; its lowest was 23.91 in the second half of 1920, those fatal days of the so-called Bolshevik occupation of the factories, after which it improved generally so long as the democratic government existed. The lira was back to 20.15 just before Fascism in 1922.

[1] Conto del Tesoro, November 30, 1928.

When, then, did the " humiliation," this " progress toward bankruptcy," occur ? Under Fascism the lira dropped consistently, semester after semester, until it reached 30·53 under the miracle-working Duce in August, 1926. These are official figures. (Yet lady biographers of the Duce [1] can state without hesitation that " under the new government the lira ceased its downward trend.")

Mussolini stabilized at 19 plus, and the American commercial attachés immediately reported bad results, although " experts " writing for the million-circulation weeklies applauded. Mr. Marcosson of the *Saturday Evening Post* had to confess in 1930 that " much of the disruption is traceable to the stabilization of the lira at too high a price. Despite the advice of the best banking brains of the country, Mussolini, with a characteristic imperialistic gesture, decreed the figure at 19 to the dollar, which was out of proportion to the exigencies of the situation. All experts agreed that the lira should have been anchored to stability with the French franc . . . at 25 to the dollar. Instead, the will that has dominated every other activity had its way here, with the result that industry, because of the high price of raw materials and of inability to meet competition in the world markets, has been increasingly handicapped."

In 1925 the first reports were sent from Rome that jugglery, trickery, and distorted official figures and statements had marked Fascist finance. The Irish journalist and former diplomatic attaché in Rome, James Murphy, has published in German, French, British, and American magazines numerous articles charging fraud which have never been challenged. He states, for instance, that the Fascisti, to maintain confidence and goodwill abroad, especially among banking interests, have organized a system of propaganda about their economic position, have given to the public " a state budget which has little or no relation to the real financial condition. It is simply a piece of propaganda. I should not make such a statement without being in a position to bring forward proof. Take

[1] Mme Jeanne Bordeux, *Mussolini the Man.*

De Stefani's budget for 1923-24. For that year I find that under one heading alone there was an expenditure of fourteen billion of lire (£140,000,000) not a penny of which is debited in the State budget. The expenditure was officially announced in the official gazetta.[1] It figures in the treasury accounts, *but it is carefully* kept out of the budget that has been published. That sum alone would practically consume the whole income from taxation for the same year. Therefore De Stefani's first budget had really a much heavier deficit than those of his predecessors, even if we confine the deficit to the above expenditure and say nothing of other treasury debts incurred. To keep all such questions dark, the press is muzzled and foreign journalists are watched and persecuted lest they begin to pry into the question of Italy's finances. By such means and by the expenditure of huge sums for propaganda abroad, the Fascists think that they will be able to stave off the day when their real economic and financial position may become known to foreign bankers and foreign industrialists."

Mr. Murphy likewise questions both Mussolini and Thomas Lamont on the subject of balanced budgets by the municipalities. " One of the immediate purposes of the dictatorship obtaining control of the municipalities," he declares, " is the facilitation of Fascism's shady finance. It is well known that a favourite trick practised since Mussolini got control of things is to falsify the State budget by transferring State expenses to the municipal budgets. All the municipal budgets show a deficit ; but this does not appear in public. And there will be no chance of its coming into the light now, when there will be no local supervisors appointed by the people. The system will be understood if we imagine all the municipalities as subordinate corporations grouped under the one parent corporation, which is the State. The balance sheets of the subordinate corporations are being thrown more and more into a state of insolvency in order to make the parent balance sheet look healthy. Yet the parent corporation is solely dependent on the solvency of all the subordinated corporations taken together.

[1] *Gazzetta Ufficiale*, June 27, 1924, p. 16.

" American financiers who have visited Italy have been
too simple-minded to spot this trick. They have also been
too simple-minded to ask for the treasury accounts and
collate them with the budget. And so the Fascist financial
bluff has gone ahead triumphantly. Mussolini wants to
show the unwary Yankee how splendidly everything is
going in Italy, so that he can raise loans in the United
States."

To such general statements must be added the official
figures from the Fascist government's publications. The
debts of the provinces on January 1, 1925, are 954,000,000
and on January 1, 1928, 1,326,000,000, while the debts
of the capital cities of the provinces are as follows :

```
January 1, 1925 .      .      .      . 3,066,000,000
January 1, 1928 .      .      .      . 5,481,000,000

     Increase in debt .      .      . 2,415,000,000
```

which somehow does not agree with Mussolini's statement
that " the provinces and the communes have balanced
their budgets too."

Fascist Italy, say European economists, is the only
country in the world which announces balanced budgets
while showing deficits in the treasury.

Strange things have happened. For instance, Mussolini
with his annual pride announced a credit balance of
2,200,000,000 lire in 1925-26, but the announcement of the
treasury-audits court added that " from this surplus
1,800,000,000 were deducted in order to provide for expenses in connection with the economic reconstruction of
the country for the period of the same fiscal year 1925-26."
Only Fascist finance has provided this minor miracle of
eating one's surplus and having it too.

When Count Volpi and Mussolini quarrelled about this
ultra-modern way of dictating to the economic system, the
former was dismissed and the latter declared that " from
now on the data of the budget will be of crystalline clearness." Immediately afterwards 1,211,000,000 lire were
cancelled among the cash items of the treasury account

published the following month, July 31, 1928. It was declared that it represented a sum " not liable to be spent." Apparently Mussolini was trying to show that Volpi was making a slight error of a little more than a billion. But the next year the treasury account announced that the fiscal year had closed on June 30 with a surplus of 2,352,000,000 lire, while a supplement published a month afterwards showed a slight correction to be necessary, a reduction of 2,845,000,000, with an explanation of " crystalline clearness " : " reduction of the cash fund for operations to be credited to the preceding fiscal year." Next month there was another correction of 83,000,000, so that two months after Mussolini had informed the world, and particularly the American bond-holders, that he had more than two billion credit, there was a deficit of 574,000,000 lire.

In 1930 the budget showed a cash surplus of 2,261,000,000. The supplementary account, published a month later, brought a correction of 1,581,000,000, which reduced the surplus to 680,000,000, and there was no explanation, crystalline or other.

One billion lire of national bonds, due to theVatican under the Lateran treaty, was taken from the " Cassa depositi e prestiti " under agreement to return it in ten years,[1] but the Casa enters in its assets this billion which the treasury owes it, while the nonchalant treasury, which should enter a corresponding liability, enters only the annual instalment of 85,000,000 and the interest on the rest of the principal.

Although the Bank of Italy lists assets of 1,801,000,000 gold which it claims are deposited abroad, as being due to it from the State, in the treasury account no mention is found among the liabilities of this State debt. The treasury explains that it means to return to the Bank of Italy the gold deposited with the Bank of England. Economists, however, declare that while the State debt is real, the gold in London is a security which will be returned " if and when " Italy pays the fifty-eight annuities still due of the sixty-

[1] Decree 851, May 27, 1929.

two (or about 30,000,000,000 lire) under the Volpi settlement.

The Bank of Italy reserve just before stabilization was 12,516,000,000 lire, but in April 1929, only 10,004,000,000, at which figure it fluctuates only slightly, and this loss of about two and a half billion is claimed to be due to the stabilization at 19 instead of at a reasonable, logical, 25.

Although Count Volpi announced that the new silver currency which replaced a billion and a half of small paper notes " have their counter-value in pure metal," the value in silver is about one-sixth legal value.

A search through official Fascist figures reveals that in the year 1928–29 State receipts were 19,447,000,000 lire and payments 22,741,000,000, or a deficit of 3,294,000,000. More recently the régime issued several series of statistics, an explanation of the 1928–29 budget, the finance Minister Mosconi's revelations to the Chamber of Deputies [1] which neutral economists declare " render equally unintelligible the real financial situation in Italy." It is said that the actual state of the budget cannot be determined from all these figures, but the movement of cash reserves (page 33) shows that the treasury revenue for 1928–29 was 23,015,000,000 lire and expenditures 25,960,000,000, making a deficit of 2,945,000,000.

Minister Mosconi then attempted by various statements to reduce this deficit to 575,000,000 lire, claiming that there were important credits abroad, but on page 51 mentions a credit of 6,358,000,000 and a debit of 11,829,000,000 in the budget.

On page 73 the Minister speaks of the extreme gravity in the local financial situation, but, having admitted a rotten state of affairs, concludes with an oration : " The government of Benito Mussolini does not dissimulate the difficulties of the present time, but one must not doubt that he has unshakable confidence and a profound force, which continues with a will of iron, with a lively energy, with an obstinate passion, to march towards the future."

[1] *Exposizione finanziaria fatta all Camera dei deputati nella seduta del* 31 *Maggio* 1930–VIII.

The apparent fraud of the official announcements of balanced budgets, the apparent paradox of a tremendous increase in national works expenditures without an increased public debt and increased national income, which was first discovered and reported in 1925 to 1928 by Messrs. Motherwell, Murphy, and Bolitho, has now been completely substantiated and explained by Professor Gaetano Salvemini former professor of history at Florence University and more recently at Harvard. The time for the exposure was extremely appropriate. The United States in 1935 was keenly interested in substitute systems of national economy ; it was watching both the Fascist and Communist governmental planning ; the American government was engaging in public works expenditures totalling many billions, and the national debt was rising proportionally. How then was Mussolini able to produce balanced budgets while great land reclamation projects were going forward successfully, magnificent public buildings were being erected, express auto roads were being completed, new ships for commerce and war were being built, a modern army equipped, the military budget doubled, and a vast list of minor Fascist achievements—all costing millions if not billions—were announced to a despondent and jealous world?

The Fascist mystery and miracle play was not easy to explain. Italy's budget is unlike Anglo-American budgets, which are integral and clear ; the Italian consists of two, one showing revenues and expenditures legally assessed, the other as they actually result. Moreover, Professor Salvemini points out [1] that " one set of official figures for the four years from July 1, 1928, to June 30, 1932, gives yearly deficits of, respectively, 2,576 millions, 507 millions, 288 millions, and 2,300 millions, a total deficit of 5,671 millions.[2] Another set of official figures for the same four years gives, respectively, surpluses of 555 millions and 170 millions, and deficits of 504 millions and 3,876 millions.[3]

[1] *Foreign Affairs*, published by the Council on Foreign Relations, April 1935.
[2] Cf. Rendiconti Generali Consuntivi.
[3] Bolletino Mensile di Statistica, August 1934, p. 746.

The difference between the figures amounts to 2,025 million lire."

Professor Salvemini examines the infallible index to the nation's financial status, the national debt, using the official Fascist statistics, the parliamentary reports, and the annual reports of the finance ministers. And here he discovers the magnificent modern contribution the Duce has made to the national economy: the government, instead of paying for its activities out of current revenue and borrowing from the public as other nations do, has issued promises to pay in instalments, ranging from ten to fifty years. The list of annuities and dates contracted for are: March 29, 1924, 6,546,000,000 lire; end of 1928, 26,219,000,000 lire; December 31, 1930, 65,390,000,000 lire; March 31, 1932, 75,118,000,000 lire; and February 28, 1933, 74,315,000,000 lire.[1]

This vast indebtedness, incurred from 1924 to 1933, which has been hidden from the Italian people and the world, aggregates an increase of more than sixty-seven billion lire, as shown by the parliamentary finance committee reports. In plain words, Fascism has taken up the instalment idea somewhat like the American people who bought their furniture, cars, radios, and electric refrigerators in the boom days, mortgaging their futures at a time salaries were good and prospects grand. "One of the remarkable features of this situation," continues Professor Salvemini, "is the fact that out of the 74,315 million lire of annuities outstanding on February 28, 1933, nearly two-thirds, or 51,243 millions, were for ordinary expenses, and only one-third, or 23,072 millions, for extraordinary expenses."

Inasmuch as the 74,315,000,000 lire is to be paid out in instalments up to 1986–87, Professor Salvemini has taken the present capital value of the debt, which is 35,000,000,000 lire, and added that, instead of a sum more than double, to

---

[1] These figures are from the Conto del Tesoro, *Gazzetta Ufficiale*, March 29, 1924, No. 76; the Parliamentary Report on the Budget of 1927–28, Camera dei Deputati, No. 30A, and the Reports of the Senate Finance Committee for the years 1931–32, 1932–33, and 1933–34.

the national debt, which he has compared with the last
pre-Fascist statistics. Here follows the result :

NATIONAL DEBT OF ITALY.

	June 30, 1922.	June 30, 1932.	June 30, 1934.	Increase or decrease over 1922
Consols . . .	44,576	71,736	9,892	−34,684
Redeemables . .	12,010	18,907	83,055	+71,045
Floating debt . .	28,188	6,657	10,233	−17,955
Miscellaneous . .	5,901	7,554	9,282	+ 3,381
Autonomous authorities	..	1,184	1,184	+ 1,184
Current capital value of State annuities .	2,7000	35,000	35,000	+32,300
Total . .	93,275	141,038	148,646	+55,377

Fascist apologists bring up the fact that the liberal
régime which preceded them had raised the national debt
by thirty-seven billion lire from July 1919, to June 1922,
and, while these statistics are a fact, the national budgets
also show that between 1919 and 1922 the liberal régime
paid out a war debt of fifty-five billion lire ; it paid out
twenty billion in 1921–1922, and left the Fascists to pay
only six billion in the next fiscal year, five billion in 1923–24
and about a billion and a third in future years. In other
words, the pre-Fascist deficit and enormous budget increase
was the result of the World War ; the Fascist deficit is the
result of Fascist economics. It is the equivalent of waging
a war. Only in the latter instance it is a war against the
Italian people.

Naturally enough, the Fascist innovation in hiding the
bankruptcy of its finances has been termed a fraud by leading
economists the world over. Fascist apologists, however,
have tried explanations. The leading business magazine
of the United States, *Fortune*, devoting an entire issue [1] to
the glorification of the Duce and Fascism, had this to say
of the social-economic-financial system :

" Fascist accounts are not faked : they are merely

[1] July 1934.

divided or delayed—on the general principle that solemn
news is accepted more easily if delivered in parts, and that
no news is commonly accepted as good news. Thus the
Fascists delay payments on budgeted expenses up to the
legal limit, and delay the charge-off of those expenses to
the same limit. . . . But these annuities are not reflected
in the regular public-debt statement. We have seen how
forty billions of these annuities help to raise the *regular* debt
statement of ninety-eight billions to the *actual* debt figure
of some one hundred and seventy billions.

" And yet that one hundred and seventy billions fails
to tell the entire story. . . .

" A great question remains : does Fascist finance pay
dividends to the Italian people ? The long-established
poverty of the Italian masses has been emphasized elsewhere. . . . Like the Japanese, the Italians have for
centuries been used to living on next-to-nothing with a
smile. In recent years that next-to-nothing has been
reduced. The average wage of Italian agricultural and
industrial workers has fallen perhaps 25 per cent. in the
last five years. The last published figure is 1.5 lire (four
pence) per hour. The masses are struck at every turn by
the indirect tax policy of the State. Unemployment has
been slowly increasing, with a January official estimate of
1,160,000. The standard of living of Italian labour has been
estimated as the lowest of any country in Europe. An
indication of the effects of Fascist economy of middle-class
levels is provided by the gradual increase of bankruptcies
from 1800 in 1921 to 14,000 in 1933. The conclusion seems
inescapable that if Fascism has paid dividends to the
Italian people, they have been paid in the coinage of
patriotic excitement. . . . Fascism has paid its people no
cash dividends. . . ."

We can now arrive at objective conclusions : Mussolini
announces that the budget for many years was balanced :
Fortune, typical of the apologists for Fascism, states that
the budgets are not " faked " ; Thomas Lamont, on behalf
of finance capital, declares that the budgets were balanced ;
official statistics show that annuities totalling seventy-four

billion lire and having a present capital value of thirty-five
billion have been kept out of the budget and from the
knowledge of the people ; the official Italian national debt
has been announced annually as hovering in the neighbourhood of ninety billion lire, only a fractional increase from
the pre-Fascist figure. It is obvious, therefore, that the
question revolves about a euphemism. If the budget has
not been " faked " it has been " tricked " and " juggled,"
and these are the very words used by Messrs. Motherwell,
Murphy, Bolitho, and the present writer in reporting on
Italy from 1925 to date.

" Since 1925," concludes Salvemini, " the Italian budget
has never been balanced. The Italian national debt in the
last ten years has increased, on the average, by a yearly
amount of over five billion lire, even though the war claims
had been reduced to negligible proportions. . . . The
government is concealing from the public at large the true
composition and size of the national debt."

On July 8, 1935, the ace of Fascist apologists [1] was permitted by the Fascist censorship to report that " The
public debt, which has increased considerably, now stands
at one hundred and five billion lire, against one hundred
and two billion in May 1934, and ninety-seven billion in
1933." Apparently Mussolini at last has decided to show
at least a part of the one hundred and forty-eight billion
lire burden which the Italian people, its children and grandchildren, must pay. It means increased taxation, a still
lower standard of living, and resultant misery and degeneration.

[1] The Rome correspondent of the *New York Times*.

CHAPTER XXVII

A Journalist suppresses the Free Press

IN the chronology of Fascist progress there have already been references to Mussolini's decrees and methods in dealing with the free press of Italy. Here, for once, the dictator has been consistent and logical.

The foundation of all free, democratic, enlightened States is liberty, and the bulwark of liberty is the free press. Such axioms, though platitudes, are nevertheless true, and were as well known to the Duce as they are to us. But whereas we do little or nothing to safeguard the freedom of the press, permitting that phrase to be made into a slogan by certain publishers who want to keep wages down, and their men from organizing their economic and moral freedom, the Duce, who regarded liberty as a " rotten carcass," over which Fascism had to pass, devoted a large part of his time to destroying the first and last bulwark of the Italian people.

It must be admitted, of course, that the press of Italy, as that of practically all continental Europe, with a few notable exceptions in Scandinavia, Switzerland, and Holland, has never been, nor is it to-day, a news press. There are thousands of journals, but almost no newspapers. The journals are expressions of opinion, the policies of special interests which range all the way from the Catholic Church to the munitions-makers. There are the publications of capitalist organizations and parties, Communist, Socialist, and labour organizations and parties, personal organs of bankers, politicians, and other men seeking or holding political, social, and economic power.

In Italy, with the exception of the *Corriere della Sera*

and two or three smaller liberal journals, there were no real newspapers, in the Anglo-American sense ; the task for Mussolini was, therefore, the easier. He had simply to order the suppression of all the organs of the Opposition, of unfriendly bankers, industrialists, politicians, and parties, and encourage the journals of the banks, the industrial associations, and the rich individuals who supported Fascism.

In many respects Mussolini followed the methods of other dictators. Lenin had been editor of the *Iskra* ; Trotsky practised journalism in Siberia, Switzerland, and Second Avenue, New York, while Stalin undermined the Kerensky régime when he edited the Petrograd *Pravda*. Pilsudski was once a Socialist editor of the *Rabotnik* (*The Worker*.) Kemal Pasha also published a paper to further his aims, and Hitler for years raged in his *Voelkische Beobachter*. A large number of leading dictators gained by experience in journalism the knowledge of the power of the press, and all in turn knew enough to abolish opposition newspapers as the first and probably most important act to ensure stability of a dictatorship.

The difference between the radical and reactionary dictatorships is this ; the Bolsheviki have promised Russia a Utopian era of unlimited freedom once the various five-year-plans have been successful, once the nation is economically independent, and once the danger of invasion from Germany and Japan and perhaps from a coalition of European nations, is over. They consider themselves in a state of war with the capitalistic world. In war-time every one agrees to censorship, and suppression of opposition opinion is necessary. In Moscow, therefore, there is a censor functioning publicly.

In Rome, however, Mussolini makes no such admission. Foreign correspondents who seek to send true news out of Italy are either bribed or intimidated, flattered or censored ; if they are honest they make the best of things, trim their sails, smuggle out a little news when possible, indulge in almost daily compromises. Numerous correspondents have been arrested, imprisoned, or expelled. Meanwhile, with perhaps humorous cynicism, Mussolini makes the statement that " the press of Italy is free, freer than the press of any other country, so long as it supports the régime." He denies publicly that he has instituted a censorship, but orders the telegraph office to hold up all doubtful cables, submit them to the Foreign Office, and frequently to " lose them through bureaucratic carelessness." There is no censorship ; the moment a journalist sends news which is factual but which offends the Duce or the régime, he is sent an official warning ; the second time he is deported.

In the journalistic situation in Italy control of the Italian press is the most important feature for two reasons : because it has succeeded in a totalitarian way in making the newspapers the propaganda organs of the régime while completely destroying the possibility of getting true news through to the Italian people ; and because, after all, the newspapers, and the government press bureau which supply them, are the main source of news for the rest of the world.

Mussolini, himself, his official press bureau, the local governors, and the police departments of cities and provinces give instructions to the nation's editors. Here is a verbatim example set down by an editor who has since escaped to Switzerland. The telephone in his sanctum rang, and the following conversation followed :

" To whom am I speaking ? "

" The director of the paper."

" *Bene.* This is the civil governor."

" I am Editor Fulano."

" Very well, Editor Fulano, take note that by order of the Chief of the Government (Mussolini) you are prohibited from mentioning the failure of Bank X. . . ."

" All right."

" Take note that you are prohibited from mentioning the fact that the family of Mussolini is visiting in Rome."

" Very well."

" Note that you are not to mention the aviation disaster of yesterday."

" Of course not."

" By order of the secretary of the party you are not to mention the violence which occurred yesterday in Savona."

" All right."

" And one more thing, refrain from republishing any article from yesterday's *Osservatore Romano*."

And so it goes on day by day.

Another editor kept a record of the important orders of suppression received during four months :

August 5 : It is prohibited to publish any news of the interview Rabindranath Tagore gave the *Neue Frei Press* in Vienna in which he denies that he expressed himself to be an admirer of Fascism, as reported in the Italian press.

August 20 : The President of the Council orders that the press refrain from any discussion of the return to the gold standard, whether favourable or critical.

August 25 : It is prohibited to reproduce the manifesto of a group of intellectuals in London against conscription.

It is prohibited to mention that between Rome and Sant' Ilario an automobile in Mussolini's suite upset a wagon.

August 30 : It is prohibited to publish any information about war materials purchased in Italy by foreign countries.

September 3 : It is prohibited to mention details of the swindle of 200,000 lire by a lawyer attached to the Savings Bank of Milan.

September 4 : No allusion must be made to the incident in the Eden theatre (Fascisti invaded the theatre and prevented the showing of a French revue).

September 12 : It is prohibited to mention incidents which followed the Lucetti *attentat* and especially the hostile demonstration against the French consulate.

September 15 : The prefect recommends the greatest prudence in the publication of foreign articles, especially on the subject of differences between France and Italy.

September 16 : The order is given by the President (Mussolini) that all polemics with the French press cease immediately.

September 21 : It is prohibited to mention the visit to Rome of the Egyptian Minister of Foreign Affairs for the settlement of the Zarabub question.

September 23 : By order of the President (Mussolini) :
1. No mention must be made of the inquest on the death of the Fascist Luporini and the anti-Fascist Becciolini in Florence.
2. It is prohibited to speak of the economic financial and political penetration of Albania.

September 24 : No mention must be made of the voyages of Mussolini.

October 1 : No mention must be made of the Greek book by Jewos on " The Dodecanese Question."

October 9 : No mention must be made of the visit of the King to Trani last Sunday.

October 13 : It is prohibited to publish anything about the thefts committed by Italian soldiers in the hotels of Merano.

November 6 : All discussion of Franco-Italian rapports is prohibited. It is also prohibited to mention the difficulties of the Pordenone Bank.

November 9 : It is prohibited to publish news of the destruction of political clubs following the Zaniboni *attentat*, or the arrest of deputies.

The range of these prohibitions is all the way from the ludicrous and trivial to the influence of international diplomatic relations. But even those which appear of no importance may have a bearing on world reaction to Fascism. Thus Tagore's visit to Rome was exploited by the Fascist press ; naturally, British, American, and other foreign correspondents, some of whom at times like to do the Duce a good turn, sent out columns of praise of Fascism and Mussolini, quoting from local papers. But Tagore was not the author of the statements attributed to him ; a guileless philosopher, he did not know what was happening, and when he found out, it was too late to obtain satisfaction from the Fascist press. In Vienna, however, he explained his horror of Fascism and Mussolini, denounced the Italian press, denied the reports sent to foreign newspapers, and concluded with words which, of course, never found their way into Italy, perhaps not even to London or New York.

" It is absurd," said Tagore, " to imagine that I could
ever support a movement which ruthlessly suppresses
freedom of expression, enforces observances that are against
individual consciences, and walks through a blood-stained
path of violence and stealthy crime." This is Tagore's true
opinion. Yet the Fascist reports of his praise linger in the
public mind. Thus are explained the beauties of the
censorship, the making of international opinion, and the
astuteness of a dictator, himself a journalist, who knows
how to rule the press.

As proof of the assertion that many Fascist editors are
really anti-Fascists at heart is the frequent appearance of
Mussolini's secret orders in the anti-Fascist press. In 1932
an Italian editor brought to Paris the following illuminating
dossier of Mussolini's " Notes and Recommendations " :

" It is necessary that directors and editors-in-chief of
the newspapers attentively review the articles and all that
is eventually to be published, in order to avoid the appearance in the dailies and the reviews of paragraphs or corres-
pondences and articles that are in opposition to the interests
of Italy and the action of the régime.

" During the course of the past few days, there appeared,
for example : in the *Reste del Carlina*, an article on the
fight against flies. In the *Mattino*, an article on the damage
to the harvest of nearly one thousand million, caused by
the rotting of the wheat. In the *Tribuna*, finally an
article entitled : 'Are the Summer Climacteric Cures Really
Useful ? '

" But it will have been enough that the director, or
at least the person in charge of the newspaper, should
consider the things that we are going to enumerate from
the political point of view, to be persuaded that they should
not in any way allow such things to be printed as are in
obvious and evident contradiction with the action of the
régime, in the same way as they are with the interests of
our country. . . .

" The journals are also formally asked to abstain from
all propaganda in favour of spas and thermal resorts of
foreign tourism."

("Note—Recommendation " by Mussolini, July 25) :

" (1) The papers are asked to support the summer cruise which will start on August 28, by the steamer *Giulie-Cesare*.

" (2) The papers are asked to recall the general strike in Italy on July 30 and 31, 1922, the principal references to be the transmission of the powers of the Central Committee of the Workers Alliance to a secret committee, the threats of Filippe Turati, the revolutionary manifesto : in order to prove once more an evident historic truth, namely, that the march on Rome was only a counter-blow to destructive forces."

In a " Note " of July 27, 1932, the papers are asked " to write an article on the return to the land," pointing out how the régime has since 1922 made an eminently rural policy ; " to emphasize the words spoken by Gorguloff during the course of his questioning, and in which he says : ' All my sympathies go to the socialists,' which proves once more that those who attribute the quality of Fascism to Gorguloff lie with impudence."

(Service Order of July 29, 1932) :

" (1) The attention of the newspapers is called to the necessity of applying in the strongest possible fashion the dispositions already given to avoid publication in papers and periodicals of pictures of thin women. The phenomenon of the slim woman has no other significance than the reduction of the birth-rate.

" In Italy, one also owes to it the decrease in the birthrate, which our enemies have not failed to emphasize with apparent pleasure.

" Now it is absolutely necessary to avoid all that gives pleasure to our enemies. To this end, the paper should deplore with a great deal of tact the phenomenon of the decrease in births, by remarking, for example, that it has already been the subject of satisfaction to our enemies."

(Service Order of August 1, 1932) :

" (1) The newspapers are asked to make no mention of the automobile accident which unexpectedly happened to the Minister Di Crellalanza, near Montefiascone.

" (2) They are asked to ' feature ' prominently the dispatch of the Duce for the aqueduct of Monferrate, and to do the same for the message of Sidky Pasha.

" (3) They are asked to single out the noticeable affluence of travellers in the popular trains, by calling attention to the fact that a similar initiative has never been realized by past governments, and that abroad similar facilities for the benefit of the working-classes do not exist to the same extent.

" (4) Concerning the German elections, they are asked to bring out the defeat of the Weimar Coalition and the victory of the Hitlerites.

" August 4 : (1) Play up on the first page that one hundred warships will participate in the naval manœuvres ; the same holds true for thirty submarines.

" (2) Always, apropos of the next naval manœuvre, take into consideration that, although aviation also participates in the manœuvres, the important rôle is held by the navy.

" Let the papers take account of this fact, and see that they do not make the mistake of a Rome paper, which in a headline gave the greatest prominence to the airplane manifestations.

" It is further recalled to the papers, that, given the dispositions in power, it is absolutely forbidden to speak of the eventual trips of the King. This prohibition holds equally for the next naval manœuvre.

" August 6, 1932 : The big naval manœuvres shall be placed in the most prominent place possible and on the front page. Publish the most extensive reports, and each day the photographs of ships and submarines. Furthermore, make a note of the fact that the Italian war navy is equipped according to the most modern technique, and that it has been entirely renovated and modernized by the Will of the Duce during the course of the ten years of his régime."

It must be noted that one of the first powerful groups to be thoroughly Fascisticized by Mussolini was composed of editors, reporters, and publishers. Nevertheless these confidential instructions from the Duce, which are sent with the utmost secrecy to the responsible editors of Italian newspapers, all of which support the régime, are always being betrayed to the outside world. In December 1933, *La Stampa Libera*, an Italian-language paper published in New York, was able to obtain still another of Mussolini's list of do's and don't's, by which he rules journalism :

" August 4, 1933, Anno XI. (Era Fascista). Warning is hereby given to abstain from using the words ' supreme hierarchies,' as the party has only one : Il Duce.

" In announcing the celebration to be performed on the arrival of the Atlantic fliers in Rome, the *Carlino* made use, in yesterday's number, of the word ' apotheosis.' This adjective [*sic*] is too extravagant, because the arrival of the fliers is several days off, and also because up to that date the event must be kept within reasonable bounds.

" August 7, 1933. Little space should be devoted to the preparation for the arrival of the fliers in the Azores ; great prominence, instead, should be given to the reports of their take-off for America.

" With regard to the step taken by France and England in Berlin, too much stress should not be laid upon it.

" Do not advertise the success of the loan in the United States, and do not speak of America's inflation policy.

" Feature the acclamations to Il Duce by the 2800 teachers of the Opera Nazionale Balilla.

" Do not make up the paper in such a way as to have all the reports of accidents and crimes follow one another, for it is not desirable to fill half-pages with catastrophic news.

" Some papers in their outside editions have extravagantly praised prefects and hierarchs on account of certain orders issued by them. Such a mistake should never be repeated, for they are but executors of orders issuing from the centre.

" August 9, 1933. Feature, avoiding all exaggeration, under a two-column headline, the visit paid by Il Duce to camp Sandro Mussolini.

" Reproduce extensively the comments of the foreign press calling attention to the rightness of the course followed by Italy.

" An article study on the depression has appeared in the *Régime*. It is not timely. The papers should rather concern themselves with the signs of recovery. The depression will be examined and studied when it has disappeared.

" August 10, 1933. With regard to the news success of the foreign policy of Il Duce all news appearing in foreign papers on the subject should be reprinted without, however, undue exaggeration in the headlines or in the commentaries. No surprise is to be shown at this recognition by foreigners, as this is not the first time Il Duce has embarked on the right course.

" The *Ambrosiano* had yesterday a headline on the increase of monetary circulation. In this regard it will be advisable to abstain from commenting on the constant increase of the gold reserve in order to avoid drawing to it the attention of foreign financiers. Emphasize the soundness of the lira as a political-social element, but avoid all technical discussion.

" August 17, 1933. Reprint from *The Daily Mail* the article ' Will France Go Fascist ? ' by Huddleston."

With great frequency the Duce, with his old-time insouciance, reverses himself in his dictates to the press. Thus, for instance, in July 1928, he gave an example to the press for the glorification of Nobile, the unfortunate explorer who had been driven by the impatience of the Fascist press to fly over the North Pole on a day which his experts had warned him was meteorologically dangerous. Nobile flew, dropped a gigantic crucifix, the Italian flag, the Fascist insignia, and nevertheless was wrecked. When the Russians saved the Nobile expedition, it was obvious to every nation except that controlled by the Duce's press, that the expedition had been a sad failure and that the only heroism was Bolshevik.

" The greatest polar explorer in the history of the world," said the Fascist press under Mussolini's orders. It was a Fascist achievement of the first rank. Mussolini struck the note ; the whole Italian press responded as a helot orchestra. Meanwhile the press of the rest of the civilized world without instructions or censorship poured criticism, ridicule, and abuse upon this great Fascist triumph. The bitterness of the French press wrecked treaty negotiations, and led to challenges from Roman journalists to duels. The French government made an official protest asking the Duce to stop the flow of billingsgate in the Roman papers. But from the Brenner Pass to Milan, from Milan to Rome, the people met Nobile with rejoicings ordered by Mussolini and with their hymns of praise were mingled the shouts, "Down with the jackal anti-Fascist press of the world."

Three months later Mussolini ordered the newspapers of Italy never to mention the name of Nobile again, and threatened the arrest of those who went to interview him or those who printed his apology or explanation of the North Pole fiasco. (Nobile found refuge in Russia.)

Similarly with a matter of great political importance. We have already seen Mussolini ordering the press to play up Hitlerite victories ; in 1933 the reward was close co-operation between the two Fascist régimes, and in July 1934, when Hitler again went one better than Mussolini, and instead of the Italian slow method of " purgation " resorted to two days and nights of murder and assassination, the Italian press chief again ordered support for his colleague. " The ability to put an end to such a situation is an excellent example of power," said the keynote article in Mussolini's *Popolo d'Italia.* " . . . The right to execute traitors and enemies is not a new discovery. It is the most legitimate revolutionary reality that exists." Courts and trial by jury were all right at times, but there are " exceptional occasions when the individual servant of revolution has the right to administer justice with his trigger finger." The press of the world accused Hitler of murder ; Mussolini alone supported him.

But a few weeks later Nazi terrorism broke loose in Austria. Dollfuss, who had approved the machine-gun killing of hundreds of working-men, was in turn assassinated. He was the ally of Mussolini and his murderers were Hitlerites. Mussolini immediately gave the order to the Fascist press to join the universal chorus of disgust and repudiation of the Hitler régime. Expediency, opportunism, as usual, dictated the dictates of the Duce. The Italian people were, as usual, merely the huge woodwork of the piano upon whose keys, the newspapers, the Hierarch was playing his own international tune.

The chief instrument for the control of public opinion in Italy is the official press bureau, Stefani. In the old liberal days this organization, which ranked with the American Associated Press, England's Reuters and Germany's Wolff, gave its subscribers the news with only a natural nationalist tinge ; it did not resort to perversion, censorship, and falsehood, nor was it ever corrupted by the money of a foreign power, as was proved in the case of certain French sources when the Russian archives were opened.[1]

Fascism has changed all that. That the Stefani issued nothing but Fascist propaganda and pro-Fascist news after 1922 is, of course, true, because it had orders from the régime which it could not disobey. But from 1925 on, Stefani's began to take liberties with the news. Here is an example of how news was changed in the Stefani office :

The Official Stefani Agency :

Lloyd George declared that after the war Socialism in Italy had a disastrous effect on industry. The nation in desperation accepted Fascist succour. " I recall the joy with which the Liberal Party approved the Fascist revolution, its admiration for the Fascist movement, and its powerful chief, the honourable Mussolini . . ." said Lloyd George.

Official Record of Speech :

I recall how the Fascist revolution has caused and is still causing in the ranks of the Conservative Party, admiration and adulation for the Fascist movement and for its powerful chief. Italy, a terrestrial paradise where the snake of anarchy was chased out by cherubim clad in Black Shirts who guarded the garden against a return of the reptile ! That was the picture of a year ago.

You can see for yourself what there is now : Liberty is entirely suppressed. Repression, menace, arson, confiscation, assassination have become the instruments of government. . . . (Lloyd George.)

---

[1] Published in Paris : L'Abominable Vénalité de la Presse.

And here is another example of how the Fascist press rewrites criticism of Mussolini to make it into flattery :

Statement by Bernard Shaw :	*The Same in the Italian Press :*
Mussolini has done for Italy what Napoleon did for France, except that for the Duc d'Enghien [who was murdered by order of Napoleon] you must read Matteotti.	Mussolini, without Napoleon's military prestige, has done for Italy just what Napoleon did for France (from the *Gazzetta del Popolo*, October 12, 1927, page 1, col. 6).

But while it must be admitted that Mussolini has had a complete success with the press at home, his efforts to influence international opinion have not rewarded him as fully. This is due largely to the fact that foreign correspondents from free nations, led by the Anglo-American group, are the real upholders of freedom of the press in Europe. Frequently these journalists, some of whom represent papers friendly to Fascism and other dictatorships, have had opportunities to show Mussolini just where they stand.

A notable example is the Locarno Conference of 1925. When that "peace" congress was drawing to an end Mussolini burst into the scene in his usual sensational manner, with a shouting and bustling entourage, clearing the road for the victor, by a racing motor-car, breaking all traffic laws and endangering himself and pedestrians, and by a racing motor-boat from Stresa to Lake Maggiore to Locarno.

The day after his arrival, Mussolini summoned the world press for a conference in the Palace Hotel where all the delegations were staying. It was hinted by the Fascist attachés that a world-shattering pronunciamento was about to be delivered. It behoved every journalist, and there were between two and four hundred of them at each of the peace conferences, to be present.

But the time was just after the most flagrant suppressions of journalistic liberty in Italy, and the expulsion of British, German, and American newspaper men, all of whom wrote for liberal newspapers. In the lobby of the hotel these facts were discussed. A Frenchman, a German, and an Englishman, George Slocombe, the representative of the

Daily Herald, the mouthpiece of the Labour Party and of Ramsay MacDonald, determined not to be present at the Fascist conference. Within a few minutes the word went the round of the hotel and other press meeting-places, and a spontaneous boycott of Mussolini occurred. Slocombe relates the incident :

" Mussolini descended the stairs of the hotel, swept like Caesar at the head of a Roman legion across the hall into the press-room, followed by Fascist officials and Fascist journalists. In the conference-room there was consternation written large on the faces of the Fascists. Only a handful of correspondents, some of them servile, a few friendly, to hear Mussolini. The others were with me, filling the lounge of the hotel. Even the great news agency men boycotted the conference.

" In the almost empty large conference-room, I was told afterwards, Mussolini asked a Frenchman if all the journalists were there. The Frenchman, embarrassed, replied that he thought there must be some kind of demonstration elsewhere. But Mussolini sensed the boycott. He said, with his usual jeer, snarl, or sneer, or whatever it is :

" ' If they have a protest to make I have a wastepaper basket ready.'

" But he was visibly annoyed. He read abruptly a short statement of his policy, refused to entertain any questions, stalked out. When he appeared at the entrance of the lobby of the hotel, he saw me standing at the other end and walked haughtily towards me—afterwards he gave out that he had approached me in the most friendly manner, since we were old friends from the Cannes conference before the Fascist *coup d'état*, when I met him for the first time. Anyhow, he stalked up to me, followed by his Roman cohort, and when he was within a few inches of me, said :

" ' *Eh! bien, est-ce que le Communisme marche toujours ?* ' (' Well, how is Communism getting along ? '). I do not know why he should have taken me for a Communist unless it was because we had discussed Communism, Socialism, and Sorel's philosophy of violence on the Cannes occasion.

" I stared at him coldly, keeping my hands in my pockets, although he had put out his hand, and said, ' *Je ne saurais vous dire* ' (' I am not able to tell you.')

" ' *Eh ! bien, pourquoi ?* ' he asked.

" ' *Parce que je ne suis pas Communiste* ' (' Because I am not a Communist.')

" ' *Alors*,' he replied, ' *je me trompe* ' (' Well, I've made a mistake ').

" ' *Oui*,' I replied, looking him in the eye, ' *vous vous trompez* ' (' Yes, you made a mistake ').

" Then a Dutch journalist, who was standing at my elbow, made the really devastating remark :

" ' *Ça vous arrive souvent*,' he said. (' That happens often to you.')

" With that Mussolini almost broke a blood vessel. He looked at us speechlessly for a moment, and then said, ' *Peut-être* ' (' Perhaps ') in a theatrical voice, and stalked away, followed by his trembling satellites.

" The Fascist headquarters announced later in the day that I had misunderstood the attitude of the Duce, and that he had meant to be friendly, but there was no mistaking the unfriendly nature of our boycott. I think really he had approached me in order to let me know he had remarked our abstention from attendance at his press conference, but did not intend a little thing like that to affect his superb disdain or to affect our own personal relations or ironic semi-affectionate understanding. However, we never met again, and I have heard since that I am on the Fascist black list."

At this point the reader may ask how it has come to pass that Fascism has enjoyed a tremendous popularity in America and other countries, when it is evident that the foreign journalists in Rome are almost unanimously opposed to the movement and its Fuehrer. There are many answers.

By the Fascist decree of February 20, 1928, Article 1, a roll of professional journalists was created, and no Italian is permitted to practise journalism unless his name appears on the list. " Professional journalists, apprentices, and publicists are minutely controlled. Every applicant for

22

admission to the roll must give ample proof of good moral and political standing, the latter being judged not only by the officials in charge of the roll, but also by the prefects of the provinces. Foreigners may practice the profession of journalism provided they fulfil the same requirements." [1] In other words, every Italian journalist must be a Fascist ; if a foreigner he must be pro-Fascist. " The Agenzia Stefani, a press agency similar to the Associated Press in America and Havas in France, is still intact and furnishes national and international news. . . . By means of this agency it is obviously easy to supply uniform, censored, and official approved political news to all Italian papers. Official announcements and news favourable to Fascism are continually issued by Stefani both at home and abroad." [2] The journalists' syndicate, according to an official of the press bureau, has been made into " an instrument uniquely political, at the orders of the Duce and the Fascist Party."

One distinction must be made : the foreign correspondent, who is forced into almost daily compromises, will suffer merely deportation if he offends the government, whereas the Italian who represents foreign newspapers faces five years' imprisonment on the penal islands, if he writes news unfavourable to Fascism.

Extracts from cables from the " New York Times " regular correspondent, Signor Arnaldo Cortesi :

The people have become accustomed to the idea that war is not only inevitable, but also necessary for a solution of some of Italy's most pressing problems.

Nobody who watched the troops leave the cities for embarkation points *en route* to East Africa could doubt that they were keen and happy to go.

Extract from wireless from " The Times " special correspondent, Anne O'Hare M'Cormick :

. . . Mr. Mussolini has not gone out of his way to make unnecessary enemies. Yet he faces the most difficult time since the killing of Giacomo Matteotti, Socialist deputy, by Fascisti.

In many years this correspondent has not heard such widespread open grumbling, particularly among the

---

[1] Summary of Articles 5, 6, and 7. From *Making Fascists*, by Herbert W. Schneider and Shepherd B. Clough.

[2] *Idem.*

The present Italian public opinion was shown during Mr. Mussolini's recent trip to Sardinia. The population of that proud, warlike island, which supplied the army's best divisions during the world conflict, gave overwhelming approval to the course he has followed. The Sardinians were roused to great patriotic fervour. . . . With public opinion in its present mood, Mr. Mussolini's truculent policy has the support of all Italians. . . .

peasants. The war boom and active building operations keep money circulating in the cities, but privation pinches in the rural districts. The people everywhere are restive under the tightening of political, economic, and financial restrictions.

The Cortesi item is dated July 5, and the M'Cormick item July 2 ; on June 13 Mussolini had ordered the expulsion of the *Chicago Tribune* correspondent, David Darrah, who arrived in Italy to take the present writer's place almost ten years ago. For ten years Mr. Darrah had honestly tried to cable all the news about Italy, stopping short of facts which he knew would lead to his expulsion, and waiting, as most correspondents in Rome wait, for a story important enough to risk that eventually. It came in the Ethiopian crisis.

In the Cortesi cable it will be noted that Sardinia is the happiest of all Italian provinces over the prospects of the bloodshed in Africa. In the Darrah correspondence, for which he was deported, a different story is told. On the Saturday before his expulsion from Italy Darrah had " a story commenting on the situation of a quasi revolt in Sardinia culminating in the sending of the cruiser *Zara* to Cagliari to impress the population with Il Duce's visit, and his distribution of largesse to the suffering Sardinians. He also sent another story pointing out the catastrophic condition to which thirteen years of Fascism had brought the Italian public finances, with an incredible increase in the national debt." [1] Darrah had also cabled that there were mass arrests in Italy, a fact which the *Manchester Guardian* had published weeks earlier, and a report that the

[1] Cable from Paris to *Chicago Daily News*, from Edgar Ansel Mowrer.

King and several high officials were opposed to adventure in Ethiopia.

The foregoing episode is the latest in a thirteen-year series of deadly parallels which have been or might be made between cables from Italian journalists in the service of the foreign press, and the cables of the majority of foreign journalists in Rome.

There are three types of correspondents in Rome : the volunteer unpaid propagandists, the bribed, the mental lackeys, and the Italians ; the majority, fundamentally honest, who are realistic enough to trim sails and make necessary compromises until a situation arises which makes a decision imperative ; and the few who defy the censorship, smuggle news across the frontier, fight the dictatorship, and accept deportation as part of the game.

The commonest form of bribery is the gift of the free use of the Italian cables or wireless up to 5000 words a month. When the present writer took over the *Chicago Tribune* bureau in 1925 he was almost immediately threatened with the loss of this Fascist gift if he failed to support the Duce.

A handshake from Mussolini has been found to work wonders in emotional reaction from leading democrats and self-announced exponents of freedom of the press. There are also many American editors and correspondents who take the Commendatore Cravat as seriously as the ubiquitous French *Légion d'honneur*. And there is, of course, the annual 5,000,000-lire propaganda fund for press propaganda abroad.

All in all, as has been said, Fascism has been a great success in the world press, and credit is due almost entirely to the journalist who is dictator. Thanks to his efforts, the vast majority of newspaper readers throughout the world believe that he led the march on Rome, that he saved Italy from Bolshevism, that he advanced the Budget, that Fascism economy was a success until Wall Street crashed in 1929, and that Fascism is a social philosophy worth serious consideration among desperate nations.

The world may also have been told that freedom of

the press exists in Italy. In January 1927 the Duce said to a congress of journalists : " You express an error if you suppose I have suppressed the liberty of the press." On May 26, 1927, he admitted that " all the journals of the opposition have been suppressed," but in 1930 he wrote and signed and sold an article in which he stated :

" Italian journalism is free because it serves only a Cause and a régime ; it is free because it can, and does, exercise functions of control, criticism, and propulsion within the compass of the laws of the régime. I deny absolutely in the most absolute manner that the Italian press lives in the realm of dullness and uniformity." [1]

When Marmontel, author of *Les Contes Moraux*, was a prisoner in the Bastille, he complained to the governor. The governor replied : " It is true you are not allowed to go out of here, but inside the Bastille you are as free as any man in the world."

[1] *New York World*, March 2, 1930, first page, magazine section.

CHAPTER XXVIII

LET THERE BE CULTURE!

"Without Art there is no civilization.   I believe that Art marks the dawn of every Civilization. . . ." (Mussolini, address, Accademia delle belle Arti, 1926.)

EVENTUALLY the necessity of exhibiting to the world an advance in culture as well as in patriotism and in the train schedule, impressed itself upon the fulminating mind of the dictator.

Himself a novelist, dramatist, essayist, student of philosophy, violinist, and associate of the Futurist artist Marinetti, Mussolini in the years of relative peace which followed the silent revolution felt himself competent to direct the seven great arts and censor the seven lively arts.

In politics he had accepted as his hero Machiavelli's prince, who was a Borgia ; he had proclaimed himself a modern " enlightened tyrant," but in the arts he thought of other tyrants, one of them contemporary with his hero, Lorenzo the Magnificent, the great patron, and another who long before Italy gave birth to the Renaissance ruled over an era of grandeur in Athens.

The age of Pericles and Plato, the golden age of Greece when creative mind reached unequalled fruition, when art and science flourished, when even everyday workers, stone masons who cut the steles for the tombs of the dead, were possessed of a feeling of beauty such as has never been felt by a race or a people before or after, followed, it is true, closely upon victories at sea and on land, Marathon and Salamis.   But Athens then did not become, as Kaiser Wilhelm once hoped or Mussolini now desires his people to become, swollen with military glory, dominating other peoples and spreading culture to all lands considered inferior. All that Athens had after her wars was a feeling of safety and freedom : the enemy no longer threatened her gates and the wolf no longer skulked at the doors of men who felt the creative instinct.

Mussolini, in writing of tyrants, compliments his predecessor, Pericles. The Greek was much of a demagogue and something of a tyrant, the true enlightened tyrant whom Mussolini once called the best of governors and whom he wished to emulate. Pericles had the breadth of mind of a statesman, a prince, and an artist. Under him Athens rallied to rebuild the ravages of war and to make life a finer, nobler thing ; under the modern tyrant all life becomes a struggle for survival, a battle for food and clothing and shelter, and while the tyrant rebuilds the army there is no rebuilding of the human spirit. Pericles emptied the war-chests for remaking and ennobling his city-empire ; Mussolini spent the national wealth upon maintaining himself in power, by creating a private militia, doubling the strength of the army, preparing the nation for war.

Pericles, innately an artist, gathered about him the leaders in sculpture, architecture, philosophy, science, art, and learning, while he who calls himself an enlightened tyrant to-day followed the example by creating a national academy subsidizing its members, and organizing art exhibitions where the painters are given Fascist propaganda themes before they are allowed to put brush to canvas.

In April 1929, when the thirty members of the first Fascist Academy were announced, the great men of Italy were conspicuous by their absence. D'Annunzio, Croce, Ferrero, Papini, Ugo Ojetti, Sem Benelli, and Grazia Deledda had either refused membership or had not been asked to join. Croce the philosopher and Ferrero the historian were not asked because they were living under police surveillance, since they were avowed, although inactive, anti-Fascists, and Signora Deledda, who won the Nobel prize for literature in 1927, had two failings—she was not a Fascist and she was disqualified by her sex. The absence of D'Annunzio was the most remarked. In 1930 he had occasion to explain the mystery. He had replied to Mussolini's invitation with a short note.

" A thoroughbred horse," wrote d'Annunzio, " should not mix with jackasses. This is not an insult, but an eugenic-artistic fact."

Notable members of the Academy are Pirandello, Marinetti, and Guglielmo Marconi. On accepting the presidency, the inventor of the wireless said : " Italy's soul is growing as its body grows. The Arts never were on a higher plane. Intellectual freedom never was so prevalent." (That same month seven professors in almost as many universities were arrested for insisting on academic freedom.)

For the new academicians Mussolini established a new uniform consisting of a three-cornered hat reminiscent of the war of 1812, a coat similar to that worn by officers of the coloured branch of the Knights of Pythias, with frogs, epaulets, and gold braid, and trousers like those worn by the Louisiana Zouaves in the Civil War, but in the colour of the French spahis ; polo boots, a sword, spurs, and side-arms. The Academy was instructed to combat every foreign influence in art, notably American motion-picture films, German architecture, and French literary style. No artistic work was to receive approval unless 100 per cent. Italian in style and inspiration.

The education of youth was entrusted to the only philosopher who has accepted Fascism, Gentile, whose first occupation was the reformation of the entire public school system. The now famous Gentile reform is " based on the principle that the State should aim at a formative rather than a practical education, seeking to educate in the original sense of the word rather than to instruct ; a humanist education would achieve this end." [1]

In practice, the system has not been carried out completely ; it has come into conflict with the Catholic Church, and it has been thoroughly corrupted by the militarization of youth which Mussolini later insisted must be injected into it.

Gentile aimed at humanitarianism ; Mussolini estab-

[1] Prezzolini.

lished rifle practice in the high schools and machine-gun shooting in the universities of Italy. The one aimed at the ennobling of the character of youth, the latter made class hatred an absolute part of the intellectual life of the nation's fountains of learning and enlightenment. Mussolini has had all the text-books rewritten, so that to-day there is an actual perversion of the facts of world history, and he has banned from the public schools and from the universities all those who are not adherents of his party or who refuse to remain at least silent and docile followers of the course of instruction set down for them by the political party of which he is the hierarch.

It would indeed be difficult for the Anglo-American mind, or even the Latin mind in those nations living in a tradition of freedom, to comprehend the situation in Italy. It would require an American citizen, for example, to imagine such a situation : The Democratic Party, let us say, having organized a secret militia and obtained arms through conspiracy with the Secretary of War, marches into Washington and establishes a party dictatorship. Having pacified the country, it proceeds, in due time, to appoint presidents of universities who are judged more by their enthusiasm for the party than on their pedagogical merits, orders every public-school teacher to become a politician or quit, then rewrites the history of the nation, and gives orders regarding painting and science and general culture, all of which, in the future, must have a political party bias.

Under this new régime, then, George Washington and Abraham Lincoln, having been classified as Republicans, are pronounced inferior to, say, James J. Whiffletree, the man who led the " march on Washington," and the Battle of Gettysburg is placed second to that event. Eventually the Whiffletree-Democratic Party announces that it is the element which won the World War. It is so written in the new school-books. Militarism is exalted as the rule of success, and the defeatist words " First in peace " are erased from the remaining statues of Washington, while " First in war " are underlined. Jefferson, the Garibaldi of his time, is erased from history books for having been a

" radical, traitor, and Bolshevik." Under the new régime whatever Whiffletree decrees is art is Art.

This is just what Fascist education has done or aims at doing. Going from the ridiculous to the actual. Here is an instance : The government has published a series of " unique " text-books, one for each grade, which are obligatory in private as well as public schools. In the reader for the fourth form there is given the life of the greatest man who ever lived in Italy, Benito Mussolini, paraphrased like the life of Jesus Christ, from the time of birth in the house of his poor parents in Nazareth-Predappio, until that day when his spirit conquers Rome. In this book the martyrdom of Christian saints is replaced by the history of " Fascist Martyrs," the young men who, although armed with guns and clubs, sometimes met their death in battles with their usually unarmed and outnumbered opponents. " One can hardly believe that human barbarity had reached such depths," comments the text-book. The Fascist militia is exalted in many pages, and children are taught it is their duty " to love at the same time the book and the gun, the two arms of knowledge."

In geography, astronomy, and history, Fascist teachers have to acknowledge that there is a universe, and that a few but less important nations exist ; but practically all the teachings relate to Rome and Italy, to the Caesars who built the past empire and their successor who just as capably rules the present one.

The second greatest event in recent history is the World War, and it was won almost single-handed, too, by the Fascisti. I myself am not a military genius nor a super-patriot, but with some pride I have heard from the lips of two men, Hindenburg and Foch, calculated statements that the 10 or 20 per cent. advantage in troops which America had at the front broke the stalemate which the French and British had succeeded in maintaining, and won the war—it is not only historically but militarily true—but in Italy some millions of children repeat in the Coué fashion, over and over, " At the battle of Vittorio Veneto the Italian nation won the World War ;—at the battle of Vittorio

Veneto the Italian nation won the World War." The Italian nation, as every well-brought-up child ought to know, was the Fascist nation. Mussolini, single-handed, had forced the country into the war. He had reorganized the nation after Caporetto. It is true there were other nations involved, but they were merely allies of Italy.

But in all history the greatest event is the conquest of Rome in 1922. Much more important to world civilization than the war. Because here it was that Mussolini capitalized the war victory and gave the victors, the Fascisti, their reward, the rule of the nation. Their heirs and assigns, the children-readers of this text-book, must drink deep of the fountain of militarism. They must repeat :

" Italy, a hundred years ago divided and enslaved, is to-day one of the greatest powers of the world, presenting an admirable spectacle of discipline, work, and faith. The heroes and the martyrs of the Risorgimento, of the Great War, and the Fascist Revolution have made our country free, united, prosperous, and strong. It is now your turn to grow up healthy in mind and body, to continue the work, so that Italy may once more be a splendid lighthouse of civilization. You must be ready, as were your fathers and grandfathers, if the country calls you, to fly to arms and die serenely, should the safety and greatness for your country exact from you this supreme sacrifice."

In intellectual centres to-day, there is no longer any protest. It is the accepted order. A critical date in the history of Italian cultural degeneration is March 28, 1926, when the universities held their national congress of philosophy in Milan. The subject for discussion the opening day was " Culture and Liberty." Both items scared the mayor of the city. He ordered the dissolution of the congress the very afternoon of the opening day, and the congress closed after voting a protest " against an act of violence which pretends, but in vain, to limit the domain of philosophy and the thoughtful life."

But the university men guessed wrong. It is neither a pretension nor is it in vain ; it is a very real fact that from 1926 to the present day the minor inquisition of the univer-

sities has brought about their complete Fascistization.
To-day no professor may teach in the higher schools unless
approved by the Fascist Party and given a card of legitima-
tion or tessera. He must declare himself an adherent of
Mussolini's. As first assistant to the Duce, Augusto Turati,
had declared that " In my capacity as secretary of the party
I assume the direct organization of the professors, lecturers,
and assistant instructors of Fascist universities, the most
important category of studies efficaciously operating in the
kingdom, with the definite intention of giving them a solid
and harmonic organization according to the principles of
the necessity of Fascism. . . . Outside the universities
in the Fascist federation, the university professors will
bring the precious contribution of their wisdom. . . ."

Every day the Fascist press brings news of how things
go under this " totalitarian " system which is making
Italy a Fascist Utopian cultural state. As for example : [1]

Revocation

The Professor Livio Prati is dismissed from the chair of
psychiatry and neuropathology on account of incompatibility with the general political directives of the Government. (D.M. July 14, 1930.)

Professor Joseph Rensi, who for many years had the
chair of philosophy at the University of Genoa, and who is
considered one of the leading intellects of the kingdom, was
arrested, imprisoned, dismissed, because the post-office
censor found some remarks derogatory to Mussolini in a
letter which Rensi's wife sent him.

In November 1930 the new secretary-general of the
Fascist Party addressed a circular to the university students
of Italy, asking them to spy on their professors and instructors ; it was not only their right, it was their duty to
do so. They could show their fidelity to the party best by
denouncing their teachers if the latter at any time said or
did anything offensive to Fascism. " Your judgment,"
said Giuriati's circular, " towards your professors must be

[1] *Bulletin of the Italian Institute of Bio-Chemistry*, Milan, September
15, 1930, p. 432.

free and dictated by the surest Fascist intransigence ; it must not depend on the kindness or the severity of the professor." Students are asked to be the instruments, " the most vigorous will of the battle of Fascism against the old world of democratico-liberals " with which there could be no relations in common.

And so it goes.

First to see that culture would die under a political party's control of the universities was—Matteotti. He declared there was an internal police system at work in the universities, watching both students and professors, and reporting to the Fascist Cheka on all liberal thought and action. Matteotti said : " With the imposition . . . of a State philosophy in the secondary schools and with the political oath imposed on all teachers, even in the universities, the education system has completely lost its lay quality . . . the teachers' organizations have been rendered valueless . . . the decrees promulgated by the Fascist Minister of Education, profiting by the plenary powers of the government, have thrown the education system of the country into confusion."

Education, that is, pure education, has ceased to exist. In Italy as in Russia it is now class education, in Russia Communist education, in Italy Fascist education, which aims to give a political propaganda bias to everything. It succeeds in history completely, somewhat in geography and philosophy and other branches, in almost everything, in fact, but mathematics. (It is only in Germany, the present great stronghold of anti-Semitism, that the universities and their students have rejected Einstein, not because they understand or fail to understand the theory of relativity, but because they know that after all its exponent is nothing but a " sau Jude.")

In Italy, as in Germany, the chief purpose of the ultra-nationalist movement is military superiority. The schools are merely primary grades for the Fascist militia and the army of the future. Militarism, inculcated in youth, will make easy the militarization of the whole country. Moreover, the first education in army training is distinctly

Fascist, as distinguished from royal, or belonging to the King, and the spirit of the warrior is a party spirit, which the school-teachers are ordered to prepare.

Every morning and every holiday at least 400,000 youths, aged eighteen to twenty, all too young to be called for the obligatory eighteen months' army service—a shorter term, it may be mentioned, than the three-year period which the Duce himself escaped by going to Switzerland when he reached the age of conscription—are lined up on all the army parade-grounds of Italy, which for those days become an armed camp, when officers give the first instructions. Any one failing to attend is severely punished. Fearing a protest from the Pope, the Fascisti announced that " field masses " would be held and the blessing of God called down upon those preparing for future bloodshed.

" The dawn of life," " The hope of the nation," " The army of to-morrow," Mussolini calls his Balillas, or militarized youth movement. Each boy is given a rifle to mark his entrance into full Fascist membership. He is promised it in the Balilla booklet : " Youthful conscripts of the Fascist revolution receive the rifle as the youth of ancient Rome received the toga of virility. It is one of the most beautiful celebrations of the party, and most significant."

At the age of eight Italian boys are taken into the Balilla and militarized until the age of fourteen, when the Avanguardisti take them up to eighteen. It was to fill the gap eighteen to twenty that the Fascists Grand Council made its 1930 law which begins army training on Sundays and holidays for that period. The official figures for Balilla vary from 800,000 to 950,000 ; Avanguardisti from 300,000 to 400,000 ; there are, in short, more than a million of them being militarized and a little less than a million girls and young women, in two similar organizations, Piccole Italiane and Giovani Italiane, who also receive some military training.

Having thus militarized the national culture of the future, the " enlightened tyrant-Prince," with one of those grandiose gestures for which he is now famous, one day devoted his thoughts to culture. Contributing to *L'Arte Fascista*, he wrote this manifesto : " Let us not waste the patrimony that has come down to us from the past, and let us further and create a new patrimony which shall be the peer of that past. Let us create a new art, an art of our own, a Fascist art."

He then placed the future of painting in the hands of his companion in early prisons and his colleague in the original fascio, that same rebel artist Marinetti who in writing the Futurist Manifesto, began with these revolutionary words :

We intend to destroy the museums and burn the libraries !

We hate unto death vulgarity, academic mediocrity, pedantry, and the cult of antique and worm-eaten art !

We intend to raise love to the sphere of danger !

We shall sing the songs of war !

In 1930 Fascism was ready to show the world what it had accomplished : it held its first exposition in Paris, where a hundred canvases, reeking with paint in cubes and circles, with words written across them, were shown an expectant art world : the show was a decided black eye for perspective, a swift kick to harmony in colours, and a " morte " for composition, a thumbed nose to significant form, altogether a dizzying spectacle, a cry for Fascist freedom.

It was also a complete return to the modern art—of the spring of 1914. It was Marinetti's Futurists back to the very day they dropped art for war. On the canvases the Futurist corpse of 1914 was stretched gaudily dead, with the signatures and dates of the living moment.

In 1933 modern Fascist art repeated its show in the Kronprinzenpalast in Berlin. The noted critic, Walter Mehring, saw nothing modern nor Fascist in it. " Severini, who once painted a turbulent *chef-d'œuvre* in his ' Bal Tabarin,' " he reported, " shows us to-day a still life in the pure French tradition of Braque. Carra, co-founder of the *Valori plastici* and Futurism, has returned to Impressionism, and the canvases of Montarini have nothing modern about them but the date 1932. Chirico, in the portrait of his brother, ' The Black Shirt,' alone recalls Fascism in its effect on colour. This canvas was painted in . . . 1910 ! Chirico, Carra, Funi have become the first in Italy in the tradition of classicism. I repeat : the first in Italy. Because modern Italian painting has done nothing but imitate Picasso, the pioneer in all new styles and also in neo-classicism. ' *Ils pissent sur mes talons*,' he says of all his young imitators. And, in fact, it is he who has revolutionized classicism."

But in Italy laws, decrees, orders can be issued regulating art. Painters, sculptors, architects, in order to participate in exhibitions, work on government orders, and produce statues for the cemeteries, the important lucrative outlet for the sculptors, must belong to a Fascist syndicate, and must therefore imbibe Fascist politics and culture, translate them into their work. At the Venice International and the Monza decorative arts salons Fascisti are given the prominent place and almost all the prizes, and the only pictures and statues taken by the government are those of syndicate members. The jury in all cases receives orders from Rome ; the commission of the ministries likewise sees to it that only members of the Fascist Academy and the party organization are honoured by prizes and purchase.

But the Duce's latest stroke of genius concerned the 1930 Venice exposition, when he gave the order that all the painters must symbolize Fascism in some manner, if only by the title to their canvas. Most of the pictures were illustrations ; many were symbolic concoctions of the spirit of Fascism ; there were numerous military scenes —the Black Shirts charging—could it have been unarmed civilians ?—with the bayonet, or Mussolini on a white or black or red horse, riding into Rome. (Somehow no one thought of painting him entering the Eternal City in a Pullman sleeper.)

In defence, the authorities offer the fact that from primitives to present-day portrait painters, artists took orders from popes, princes, and patrons ; Titian and Michelangelo and the greatest painter of all time, El Greco, not excepted. They also hint that the Soviets influence writers

and painters, but it is nevertheless true that the enforce-
ment of politics upon æsthetics in Italy is unique in the
history of the world. Up to now the results, too, are
unique. They are mostly propaganda and make nice
railroad posters.

Of the making of books there is no end : Fascist books
dealing with party politics and party philosophy, if such a
term can be used, although the fiction produced in the past
thirteen years outside of the works of the old writers has not
been worth while translating or reading. The leaders of the
march on Rome, De Bono, De Vecchi, and Italo Balbo,
have written prefaces to books on poetry, and one of the
new authors, Virgilio Fiorentino of Florence, is called the
equal of Virgil and Homer, the master of Milton.

His great Fascist epic is called *Le 27 Cantate della
Rivoluzione*, the twenty-seven songs of the revolution, in
twenty-seven volumes, each illustrated in modern art,
each bound in sumptuous leather, the total costing some
£120. Once a month, the lucky subscriber receives this
reminder of Fascist creative genius, richer and thicker
than has yet come from the mind of mortal man.

This is the story in Fiorentino's masterpriece : At the
beginning there is a divine intervention of the Trinity
against Satan, who is seeking to destroy Holy Rome by
means of Russian Bolshevism. The Unknown Soldier,
Dante, and the Virgin Mary appear before Almighty God
—this writer has no intention of being sacrilegious, he is
merely reporting the facts—and ask for aid. God decides
to invest Benito Mussolini with supernatural power, and in
consequence sends the Archangel Gabriel to visit the
offices of the *Popolo d'Italia* in Milan to present to the
future Duce the lictor's emblem, the fascio, as a symbol of
Divine Will.

Hell becomes alarmed, and Satan sends one of his
worst devils to the Versailles Peace Conference, the devil
enters into the soul of President Woodrow Wilson, takes
on the body of Wilson, and sends Wilson to the infernal
regions. At Versailles, the devil, replacing Wilson,
persuades the plenipotentiaries to steal the Roman

23

goddess of victory and to deliver her enchained to Yugoslavia.

This action infuriates Mussolini, who immediately forms the Fascist Party and burns the Socialist newspapers of Milan ; then begins a continual battle with the Radical forces, which, however, at the general elections of 1919, are able to capture the goddess of victory and place her on a rock in Dalmatia, for delivery to Lenin !

In the nick of time d'Annunzio, with the eagles of his aviation, flies to the aid of Mussolini, and even Satan cannot stop him, although he has the aid of Premier Giolitti. Nevertheless, God believes that the goddess of victory is still in danger, and sends the angels to save her, and to place her, for permanent safety, in the offices of Benito Mussolini in Milan. Mussolini, in a noble strophe, then swears to protect her with his life and until his death and to transport her to Rome, where she will rest eternally as the defender of the grandeur of Latinity.

There follows a bloody battle, the angels of the Lord and the Black Shirts on one side, the devils and the Communists on the other, and as the former begin to scent victory, Mussolini, like Saint Paul, is carried to heaven by the angels, where God points out the beautiful future of Fascism.

In the last chant the doors of the *Popolo d'Italia* are burst open by the heavenly host and the goddess of victory, alive and in resplendent armour, is led by the Duce into the Eternal City. God descends from his throne to contemplate the spectacle, as the chief of the Black Shirts presents the goddess to the King. The gates of Saint Peter's open and the Sovereign Pontiff advances to bless the goddess, and the epic poem terminates with a touching scene in which the Pope, the King, and the Duce embrace each other fraternally.

The author, being poet and politician, does not miss an opportunity of saying nasty things about America, Britain, Protestantism, and ex-Premier Nitti. The great work was chosen from several hundreds submitted in response to an appeal addressed to " the poets of Fascist Italy." Fiorentino compares his style to that of the " Chanson de

Roland " ; he has written 20,000 verses and expressed his purpose as that of aiding in the love feast of the Roman Catholic Church and the Fascist Party. (But that was before the break with the Vatican in the summer of 1931.)

The censorship of books was established with the following order : " From now on the publishing houses are invited to submit the proofs of all works which have a political character or content, to the Fascist federations, in order to permit a close censorship. In case of doubt, uncertainty, or controversy, the federations must transmit the proofs to the press office of the National Fascist Party, whose decision shall be final." [1] In addition, an index expurgatorius is sent to all book-dealers. Italy almost alone among civilized nations banned *All Quiet on the Western Front*. This book was considered dangerous to the spirit of militarism.

Under the circumstances, therefore, of censorship and supernationalism, which Mussolini thought would create an atmosphere similar to that in Athens in the time of Plato, culture, instead of prospering in Italy, has, in the opinion of most foreign critics, gone to its grave. Even Italians admit it is moribund. Similar to the Nazi leader's declaration, " When I hear talk about culture, I want to draw my revolver," is the explanation the noted theoretician of Fascism, Signor Ugo Ojetti, gives of the decrease in book publication in Italy, " Reader," he says in his newspaper, " let not the small number of books under review amaze you. Ours is an era of action, when not books but deeds matter. Instead of reading superfluous books, read rather —and re-read—the speeches of the leaders."

Ernest Boyd, reviewing *The Times* 1935 special Italian literary supplement number, calls it " a frank confession of intellectual sterility ; no name of any original distinction is mentioned belonging to a newcomer. Many fine writers are ignored, others are mentioned and praised in the precise degree of their acceptance of Fascism. . . . Italian culture, under Fascism, has nothing to offer the world. This may,

[1] January 29, 1929. Circular issued by the Fascist National Party, signed by Augusto Turati.

as every one assures us, make the trains run to time, but it does not interest those of us who heard of Italy before Mussolini invented this expensive way of advertising that not altogether obscure country."

In the preparation of the new Italian Encyclopædia the two Senators in charge reported that there was not a single savant among the Fascisti, not a single man of letters, not a single intellectual capable of carrying on the great work, so they employed non- or anti-Fascist talent.

When the party press discovered this act of treason it let loose its polemical tirades. Senators replied there would be no encyclopædia unless the right men were employed, regardless of politics. The semi-official *Il Tevere* answered that " if there is penury of competence in the Fascist camp, if Fascism has little in common with culture, it is of no great matter. The Fascisti have done and are doing more important things than making encyclopædias. The matter might just as well be dropped."

At the end of the first half-decade of Fascism the Under-Secretary of State, Giuseppe Bottai, admitted that " the sympathies of all those who in the academic field still occupy the first places are neutral or opposed to us."

As the years went on and the leaders of Italian culture still refused to accept dictatorships, the régime tightened its laws and decrees and deported a larger number of intellectuals to the Liparian Islands. On May 15, 1935, mass arrests of intellectuals took place in Turin, Milan, and other cities. Among the victims are noted university professors, including Professors Martinetti, Solari, Cosmo, Salvatorelli, and Giuas the scientist, whose wife also is in prison. The crime of the Giuas, however, is not intellectual opposition to Fascism, but being the parents of a political enemy.[1]

Returning from a visit to Italy, Anthony M. Turano wrote that " the atmosphere itself is so depressing that no outstanding writer has arisen here since the advent of the Dark Age of Fascism. Even the novelist is inevitably cramped and self-conscious, for fear he picture contem-

[1] *Manchester Guardian*, June 7, 1935. Arrest of intellectuals was apparently not of enough importance for the American press.

LET THERE BE CULTURE! 343

porary life in a manner unsuitable to the Fascist idea.
The consequence might be imprisonment or exile. . . .
Furthermore, the psychological emphasis has been so
completely switched on to patriotic stupidities, that there
is no longer a reading public in the older sense. There is
only the State and its trembling subjects." [1]

Angel Flores found that the young Fascist intellectuals
have at last got round to transcendental quarrels over
Form *versus* Content, furious hunts for the *mot juste*, and
an attempt to surpass " the perfect beauty of their idol,
the fairy-like Wilde," while the " revolutionary " writers
in 1935 discovered James Joyce and immediately issued
books with interior monologue as their feature. Critics
ballyhooed Ettori Settani's *Who Killed Giovanni Bandone ?*
as a Fascist triumph. It is one of history's present ironies
that the only important novel out of Italy under Fascism
is an anti-Fascist novel. Of *Fontamara*, by Ignazio Silone,
one of the large group of intellectuals either in prison or
exile, Clifton Fadiman says it is Italy's most valuable
export for some years, and adds that Fascism has " destroyed the simple, deep-rooted, and organic culture of
agricultural Italy."

The collapse or death of culture under Fascism is probably a great surprise to Mussolini. He has willed otherwise. Early in his dictatorial career he made the following
prediction : " The Italian school will again take its deserved
place in the world. From our university chairs true
scientists and poets will again illuminate Italian thought.
. . . *I have willed* that in collaboration with the universities, departments of Fascist economics, of corporative law,
and a whole series of fruitful institutes of Fascist culture,
should be created. Thus a purely scholastic and academic
world is being permeated by Fascism, which is creating a
new culture through the fervid and complex activity of
real, of theoretical, and of spiritual experiences."

But there is an apparent discrepancy between the will
and the deed. Mussolini wills art, he wills Fascist economics,
he brilliantly recognizes that civilization perishes without

[1] *American Mercury.*

art, and in practice his assistants militarize and stultify the national mind. To the Duce's glittering generalities must be added the more practical expression of the president of the National Fascist Confederation of Intellectuals, who announced a goal for the membership : " Of journalists and writers we have requested that they engage in what may be called ' spiritual imperialism,' in the theatre, the book, the newspaper, and by means of lectures."

The figurative donning of the black shirt by Italian culture was literally exemplified in November 1934, when the corps of teachers of the nation, by order of the Ministry of Education, put itself into Fascist Balilla or Fascist militia uniforms consisting of black top boots, riding-breeches, tunic, black shirt, black fez. At the same time (November 7) army officers in uniform took the places of the professors of the country and began in high schools and colleges the compulsory military culture courses announced two months earlier by Mussolini. No high school or college student can now pass from grade to grade unless he has a qualifying mark in militarism.

Under these circumstances the " liberation of the spirit " has no future in Italy ; the present is best summed up by Professor Horace M. Kallen, who made a study of cultural conditions in Italy and reported that " What I saw and heard and read there left me with the feeling that where art and thought are concerned, Fascist Italy is not alive, but drugged and dead. . . . In the world of art nothing is happening : only the Futurists whipping a dead horse and calling him Pegasus."

CHAPTER XXIX

THE IMPERIALIST ROAD TO WAR

WE have now seen Mussolini triumphant, if only temporarily, in his dealings with the Vatican, totally victorious in suppressing opposition parties and press, totally unsuccessful in his attempt to create art and culture.

Economically, the evidence is incontrovertible. Fascism has been a failure, and the lowering of the standard of living has been an inevitable result. The Fascist hierarchy, the manufacturers, big-business men, the bureaucracy, and army may be better off in Italy than before the war, but the masses of people, workmen and middle-class, are decidedly worse off.

Certain Fascist claims have already been disposed of in the preceding chapters, notably that " Bolshevism and social disorder have been abolished," that " Industry and commerce have revived," or that " employment has increased," a claim which was justified in 1925, but which was made in 1927 and 1928, when it was untrue, and which is ridiculous to-day. But there are still propagandists who claim that " wages and the cost of living have been balanced," and that the budget has been balanced, and many things which official Fascist statistics themselves deny.

The most important of the achievements which Mussolini and philo-Fascists have listed, in addition to those discussed previously, are the following :

The trains run to time.
The marshes have been drained.
Public works.

Restoration of the prestige of Italy.
Rebirth and intensification of Nationalism.
" Order, Discipline, Hierarchy " (The Fascist slogan).
The Authoritarian State.

Celebrating the first decade of Fascism, Mussolini in a
public oration recounted all the material achievements.
" And furthermore," he continued, " I say that we have
accomplished even grander things. Because the Fascist
idea has become part of the Italian nation, has become the
Italian nation itself, and is destined to live in the generations
which follow.

" Ten years of Fascism have created, as I have said, an
epoch. The material gains constitute only a part of the
work. . . . Fascism is destined to live. Fascism is a
living spirit, and that spirit will live even after the death of
the pioneers who created it.

" The great movements which have survived are those
which are animated with spirit. . . . Ten years of power
have given to Fascism a spirit which, above the material
things which it has constructed, is destined to live like the
other great movements of the past. The material realiza-
tions are useful for the nation for years. . . . The spirit
which created material things will live and will continue
even after these things themselves have disappeared.

" Already other nations begin to study us. The people
of the entire world demand of us : ' What have you accomplished ? ' The spirit of Fascism to-day is penetrating
other nations outside our frontiers and will live under other
suns.

" It is not a matter of the simple functioning of a
system nor of mechanical organizations of a government.
Fascism regards itself as a living organism, it believes in
and develops itself in a measure which the years augment
in vibrant vitality. . . . In ten years its virility has been
infused into the very existence and the life of the Italian
people. Fascism has fortified this virility and has given it
a plenitude of the kind which all nations require in order to
survive, and it has given to all humanity its spirit and its
benediction. . . . Ten years have created a living organism,

full of ardent life, promising us eternity. Fascism will transmit to posterity its heritage of Power and Will."

Fascism's achievements, according to Mr. Marcosson, " ranged all the way from purging the streets of beggars and the elimination of the once-dreaded Mafia to the stimulation of production, the reorganization of governmental departments, the transfer of public utilities to private ownership, the conversion of the railway deficit to a profit, the checking of currency gambling, and the restoration of Italian prestige abroad." According to Mr. Cortesi [1] " whatever opinions any one may hold concerning the spiritual and doctrinal content of Fascism, it is almost universally conceded that from a purely material standpoint Italy has made great strides under the present régime." He then proceeds to sum up the gains under Mussolini :

" The technical equipment of the nation has been greatly improved.

" The reclamation work covers an area of about 10,000,000,000 [sic] acres, involving the construction of 830 miles of drainage canals, 700 miles of irrigation canals, 2000 miles of new roads, 105 rural aqueducts, and 3500 farmhouses.

" Five thousand miles of road resurfaced in 1932 ; 3500 miles of new roads built.

" Great improvements in State railroads ; 350 new miles opened to traffic in ten years ; 300 miles under construction.

" Especially important is the new Florence-Bologna line, which has cost more than $70,000,000 and will soon be opened to traffic."

The gospel of Fascism, according to Howard R. Marraro of the Italian Department of Columbia University : [2]

The Italian to-day is much better fed than he was.

The standards of living have improved from 1913 to the

---

[1] *New York Times*, August 12, 1933.

[2] Columbia University's president, Nicholas Murray Butler, is generally regarded as the ace of liberalism in America. With equal thunders President Butler wars against Communism and Fascism, while he upholds the best traditions of American democracy. At least so he claims.

present. This improvement is particularly marked during the twelve years of the Fascist régime.

Thanks to the labour legislation of the Fascist régime, there has been no important strike or lock-out in Italy since 1926.

The *Opera Nazionale Dopolavoro* supplies entertainment, education, physical exercise, health, and welfare work.

Increased wheat production.

Hydro-electric power tells another story of progress under the Fascist régime.

Unemployment kept down by public works . . . costing 24,708,509,497·12 lire, or about £429,714,440, to August 31, 1932 . . . ; road building ; land reclamation.

Gold reserve rose from 5,626,300,000 lire on December 31, 1931, to 6,838,500,000 in April 1934.

Fascism in Italy has thus made genuine progress toward solving a series of fundamental economic problems. . . . The economic and social achievements of Fascism are truly impressive. . . . A more prosperous and happy nation.

Least important and most quoted is the argument that the trains run to time. The vast American tourist class, which includes bankers, editors, senators and representatives, mayors and mayoresses, army officers and just plain " folks," returned to its native land, where railroading is an accepted institution but not necessarily a yardstick for patriotism, and roared in unison, " Great is the Duce ; the trains now run to time ! " A poor simple, naïve minority which protested that some abstract and old-fashioned American things such as liberty of the press, freedom of the individual, equal justice, and the spread of culture were being slaughtered by the Corporate State, where an institution known as the O.V.R.A. exercised dictatorial terrorism, was squelched with the complete answer, " But the trains run to time." When the unruly minority timidly suggested that the Authoritarian State

Despite the fact that convincing proof has been given that Fascism flourishes at Columbia, that the Casa Italiana is a Fascist agency, directed by Fascists, or philo-Fascists, spreading propaganda for a policy opposed to the American liberal tradition and in violation of academic freedom, nothing has been done by President Butler to remedy this situation.

was the complete antithesis of the Magna Charta, the Declaration of Independence, and the Rights of Man, millions of tourists would leap up to chant the litany, " The trains run to time." The official press agents and the official philosophers of the Fascist régime explained to the world that the running of trains was the symbol of the restoration of law and order — Order, Discipline, Hierarchy.

No one has bothered to explain that the short period of railroad disorganization occurred just after the war, when Italy, in order to keep the troop and supply trains running, tore up the rails in many parts of the kingdom, and was forced to neglect road-beds and repair work everywhere ; and that immediately after the war she engaged upon a railroad reconstruction programme of five years, which resulted in June 1922, with enough success to make " the trains run to time," a claim of the liberal régime. (The liberal régime thoughtlessly hired no press agent, and no international bankers to advertise itself.)

No one ever denied that there have been disruptions of the Italian railroads due to strikes ; every one seems to have forgotten that not only did Mussolini advocate the ownership and control of the railroad system by the railroad working-men, but he editorially supported them when they struck.

Do the railroads always run to time under Fascist discipline ? An investigation during a fortnight in July 1930, made despite the fact that the press was forbidden to mention railroad accidents and delays, disclosed five cases : the Milan-Chiasso express was derailed at Seregano, two of the crew being injured ; two days later the train carrying the Hon. Minister of Justice Rocco was derailed and arrived many hours late ; on July 22nd the Rome-Milan Pullman was derailed at Targuinie ; on the 26th a locomotive and fourteen coaches fell into the Meduna River near Udine, and there was one other derailment of small importance. It is true that the majority of big expresses, those carrying eye-witnessing tourists, are usually put through to time, but on the smaller

lines bad rail and road-bed conditions frequently cause
delays.

Wrote M. Vandervelde, a noted Belgian Foreign
Minister, after a trip to Italy : " The time is no more when
Italian trains run to time. We always were kept waiting
for more than a quarter of an hour at the lever crossings
because the trains were never there at the times they should
have been passing." [1]

A word must be said about the great public works.
Mussolini has announced the completion of the aqueduct
of Pouilles, the Naples-Rome railroad, the Sila hydro-
electric works, and many others. Mussolini himself made
grand orations at the openings. He did not state, however,
that such public works take ten or fifteen years to finish,
that ex-Premier Nitti projected the Sila and other works,
that the aqueduct was begun in 1915, and that the Naples-
Rome railroad was all ready but for the oratory.

And take for another example the famous Florence-
Bologna line which Mr. Cortesi lists among Fascist triumphs.
On April 22, 1934, the Associated Press reported the
opening of the world's longest double-track railway
tunnel, " a high spot in Premier Mussolini's public works
programme," but after paying this homage, revealed the
fact that " work was started on the tunnel approximately
twenty years before " — *i.e.* in 1913, by a liberal
régime.

The case of land reclamation is a similar story. Mr.
Cortesi had reported that it " covers an area of about
10,000,000,000 acres," which is just about two thousand
times the area which Signor Mussolini claims, but this may
all be a typographical error or a wish-fulfilment betrayal
of the Fascist mentality.

Before the war the government announced that the
total of drained marshland was 700,000 hectares, the
hectare being 2·47 plus acres ; in 1928 the Fascist régime
announced that from 1918 to 1927 an additional 527,000
hectares had been put into cultivation by the Nitti, Giolitti,
and Mussolini governments, and that work was being done

[1] *Le Peuple*, Brussels, April 19, 1932 .

on 568,000 hectares by the Fascist government, leaving some 589,000 hectares for future operations.

In fact the work on the Roman Campagna began in 1911, when 9,585 hectares around Rome were reclaimed by government subsidy; in 1921 the total was 53,000 hectares, and the government passed an act for further increases. The company for the reclamation of the Pontine marshes was formed in 1919 and began operations on a twenty-year project on May 12, 1922. The Piscinara area operations also began in that part of 1922 which the Fascists call "chaos and anarchy"—*i.e.* a few months before they arrived.

Official statistics for electrification also reveal that the period 1913–14 produced 2·3 thousand million kilowatts, and that in 1918 it had been increased to 4 thousand million. From 1908 to 1915, according to *Fortune's* survey, Italy's hydro-electric capacity increased an average of 17 per cent. per annum; under Fascism, from 1922 to 1929, it increased 18 per cent. per annum, therefore " Fascist policy does not score a triumph." But the triumph—without statistics—is stressed in all emotional ballyhoo for the régime.

On the success side of the ledger must be written militarism. Here something new under the sun has been accomplished, and Sparta has been left behind : the Duce has finally militarized the cradles of the country.

From the day of birth until the child is capable of beginning his military training the Italian male will be under government supervision merely of a hygienic nature. But at the age of six he begins his service by joining the pre-Balilla military order. From now on his life belongs to the State. Here is the programme as finally completed in November 1934 :

Ages 6 to 8 : Sons of the Wolf.
Ages 8 to 14 : Balilla.
Ages 14 to 18 : Avanguardisti.
Ages 18 to 21 : Fascist militia.
Ages 21 to 34 : Regular army (18 months) service and active reserve.
Ages 34 to 55 : Reserves.

Fifty years of a man's life under militarization ; special training for women in the medical, chemical warfare, and allied fields ; mobilization of all citizens from sixteen to seventy in time of war—from babes in arms to a nation in arms—this is the undisputed accomplishment of the statesman who never tires of granting official interviews, in which he declares, " Our policy is peace," but who writes for the new encylopædia :

" Fascism rejects pacifism which implies renunciation of struggle and cowardice in the face of sacrifice. . . . Only war carries all human energies to the height of tension, and gives the seal of nobility to peoples who have the courage to confront it."

Weighing the fact that Italy cannot feed its present population, and the axiom that a superior population imposes itself, the Duce, on May 26, 1927, inaugurated the " battle of natality," to bring the Italian people up to 60,000,000. Birth control is a crime ; bachelors have been taxed and the taxes doubled ; exemptions in taxes and special privileges are given large families. As a result there have been " victorious " years in the Duce's baby war. In 1929, however, there was a nation-wide birth strike. Laws were proposed " against deserters from the good battle, to make them so strict that they are unbearable, that they will compel people to marry and have children out of sheer desperation." [1] In 1930, the 1927 mark was reached again. In 1931, however, the rate was 22·4 compared with 1927's 26·9. In 1932 the Duce ordered the idealization of the fat woman, the best breeder of children. But the battle is still on.

To " free the Italian people from the slavery of foreign bread " Mussolini announced the *Battaglia del grano*, and shortly afterwards his victory. That Italy has increased its wheat production cannot be questioned. But every year, when nature smiles, the crops of the whole world increase, and it is only the Fascist press (on instruction from the official bureau) which sings the praise of the divine Duce ; in those years, however, when the crops throughout

[1] The Fascist leader, Scorza, in *Lavoro Fascista*, December 31, 1929.

the world are bad, the Fascist press (on instruction) puts the blame on elements over which the Duce still has no control.

Thus in 1932, when Italy's wheat yield rose from 67 to 75 million quintals, Fascism rejoiced in its leader in the battle of the grain. It was an increase of 12 per cent. That same year, however, abundant nature gave neighbouring and still republican France an increase of 17, and Spain, which had just shaken off dictatorial tyranny, an increase of 13 million quintals respectively, 23 and 34 per cent. Of this, no mention in the Fascist press.

Patriotism, Prestige, Order, Discipline, Hierarchy, the Authoritarian State, remain to be considered.

Patriotism and Imperialism have been restored.

Italian prestige has been enhanced.

Order obtains. In the chapter on the Corporate State there have been noted various strikes and uprisings; in the chapter on journalism a revolt in Sardinia has been mentioned, but it must be admitted that nothing that has happened under Fascism has seriously affected the stability of the régime. Wherever men and women have tried to strike or even to speak against the régime, the Fascist militia has made short work of them. The prison islands are full of political and intellectual opponents.

Before the war there was a joke known to all the diplomats of Europe. It was simply this : " Order reigns in Warsaw." It was a reference to the periodical reports made to the Tsar of Russia by his governor in Poland, who, after listing the riots, battles, dead, and wounded, always concluded his optimistic message with the phrase, " Order reigns in Warsaw."

Order, Discipline, Hierarchy seem secure in Italy. On the last-named subject Mr. Percy Winner, one-time Rome correspondent and later foreign editor of the *New York Evening Post*, wrote : " To be a potential candidate for the Mussolinian toga is as much a political suicide in modern Italy as being a candidate for the Caesarean toga was on occasions in ancient Rome."

Which leaves for consideration the Authoritarian State.

Just when this conception sprang from the brain of the Duce cannot be determined. It was certainly not part of the original Fascist programme. In 1920, moreover, Mussolini took the occasion of Nitti's proposal of the *ora legale*, or daylight-saving time, to write a magnificent exposition of his philosophy of the State :

" The proletariat detests the *ora legale* because it is war-time hour. I, too, am against the *ora legale* because it represents in another form intervention and coercion by the State. I do not make it a question of politics, of nationalism or utilitarianism ; I take the part of the individual and against the State. Numerous individuals are in potential revolt against the State, not this nor that State, but against the State itself.

" The State is burdened with its enormous bureaucratic machinery, to the point of asphyxiation. The State is supportable so long as it sticks to soldiery and policing ; but to-day the State does everything, it is the banker, the usurer, the shipper, the insurer, the post-office, the railway, the impresario, the industrialist, the maestro, the professor, the tobacconist, and many other things, instead of providing, as it once did, the policing, the judiciary, and the agency for taxation.

" The State, Moloch with its horrible face, to-day does everything, sees everything, controls everything, and carries everything towards its ruin ; every function of the State is a disaster. Disaster, the art of the State, the school of the State, the post-office of the State, the navigation of the State, the food supply—alas, of the State this litany can be continued into infinity.

" If only mankind had a vague sense of the abyss which awaits them, the number of suicides would increase greatly, because it goes towards the complete annihilation of all individuality.

" This, this, is the great malediction which drives the human race back to its uncertain beginnings of history.

" The revolt against the legal hour is the supreme attempt of the individual against the coercion of the State, a ray of hope filtering into the spirit of our desperate indivudualists.

"Down with the State in all its forms of incarnation. The State of yesterday, of to-day, of to-morrow, the Bourgeois State and the Socialist State.

"To us who are about to perish as individualists there remains, in the present darkness or in the tenebrous to-morrow, but one religion, however absurd but always consoling, *Anarchism.*"

Within a few months Mussolini's entire "philosophy" of the State underwent a change. The State became a "hierarchy which must end in a pin-point," himself; several years of functioning as hierarch led him to the following conclusion :

"The sense of Stateship grows in the conscience of the Italians, who feel that the State alone forms the indispensable guarantee of their unity and independence ; that that State alone represents continuity in the future of their race and their history.

"The State is the central idea of our government ; it is the political and juridical organization of national societies, and evolves in a series of institutions of various kinds. Our formula is this : Everything in the State, nothing outside the State, nothing against the State.

"The government is the highest expression of the régime. Therefore everything which depends on and descends from government is Fascist. Fascists must be doubly disciplined, as Fascists and as citizens. It is wrong to conceive the grotesque and absurd anachronism that the Fascist State is an authority which it is possible to dispense with, thus falling into the foolish and anarchistic demagogy which cauterized us with fire and sword.

"The Fascist State is the Fascist government, and the head of the Fascist government is the head of the revolution."

(Or, "*l'État, c'est moi*" all over again.)

We do know that Mussolini, like Marx before him, studied Hegel, and just as he never hesitated to rewrite the one in the original Fascist manifesto, he helped himself to

24

the older philosopher in his remarkable *volte face*.   Not only
the idea, but the wording, is Hegel's :

Mussolini :	*Hegel :*
The State is a spiritual and moral fact. . . . incorporates the political, juristic and economic organization and such an organization is in its birth and development a manifestation of the spirit.	The State is in and for itself a moral whole. . . . and realizes itself consciously. The State is a spirit which arises in the world.
The State reaches beyond the short span of life of the individual.	. . . it self-consciously realizes its independent power, in which single individuals are only passing moments.

The announcement of this Hegelian State—which the
Pope was later to denounce as Statolatry—came many
years after the Fascist régime had already established itself.
Behind the announcement stands one fact : in August 1920,
the State was " Moloch with its horrible face . . . the great
malediction which drives the human race back to its uncertain beginnings in history " ;   in September 1920,
Mussolini made his bid to lead a socialistic or communistic
army into Rome and was rejected ; in 1922 the march was
made in the pay of the bankers and industrialists, and in
1923 Mussolini asked the philosophers of Italy to supply a
philosophy for Fascism.   Hegel was the only man out of the
past who fitted the present.

And so we have Mussolini's Authoritarian State, a
totalitarian dictatorship, facing the historical truth that
every autocracy such as his, from ancient times to that of
Napoleon III., has ended in revolution or war, and we have
a Duce who sits with a revolver on his desk, intent on out-
witting history.

Sometime recently Lloyd George, released from the
strictures of political office, said to an Argentine journalist
that " it will be on account of the errors and absurdities of
its economics that Fascism will reach its dissolution."
Mussolini replied by calling Lloyd George " only a second-
class little lawyer," but the balance-sheet of Fascism shows
one thing surely, and that is that Fascist economics have

been a record of errors and absurdities. They seem typical of all authoritarian dictatorships. They are or have caused :

Dangerous decline in the standard of living ;
Alarming increase in taxation :
Financial excesses relatively beyond those of any modern State, hidden from the public by budget manipulation and secrecy.
Disastrous financial-economic actions, such as stabilization, for purely prestige reasons.
Waste ; graft ; loss of billions through the necessary multi-police and espionage and militia systems.
Suppression of parliament, press, public assembly, and other critical or controlling factors.
War preparations which lead to war.

Autocratic dictatorships always begin in enthusiasm and end in corruption or bloodshed. Dictatorships which make use merely of the Hegelian phrases, refusing to consider the " idealistic philosophy " which accompanied them ; dictatorships which are imposed from above, refusing to alter the economic system either by bringing the masses of the people into co-operative ownership of the means of production or by providing economic security for the majority while guaranteeing the profit system of the ruling class, always face the revenge of social and economic and moral forces which attack the weaknesses of absolutism. Dictators in our own time have disappeared, or have been dismissed quietly, or have been driven out, or into exile, or been assassinated ; dictatorships have been dissolved, peacefully altered, or drowned in fraternal blood, and usually for the same reasons :

The financial ruin of the State :
The economic anæmia of the nation ;
The strangulation of the people by taxation and the public debt burden ;
The armament race.

" You can do anything with bayonets except sit on

them," said one of Mussolini's great predecessors, Cavour, and the Fascisti celebrating their first decade laughed at the phrase. But Cavour took the long view.

Dictatorships have always proved the most expensive form of government, and their few achievements have been overbalanced by their inefficiencies and errors. The democratic State can commit and admit its mistakes. The dictatorship of a class—Russia, for example—can and does admit its mistakes, as for example, Lenin's announcement of the New Economic Policy, which was a refutation of a great part of the Communist programme and which the Opposition called a reversal to pure capitalism. But the Authoritarian State does not err.

To hide its errors the Authoritarian State has absolutely refused to permit :

The approval or disapproval of the people by free election ;
The control of finances by the public ;
The controlling criticism by the press ;
Sharing responsibility with a freely elected parliament.

All of which, co-operating with a dictator would, while weakening the personal ego, the Will, the régime, at least prolong both the man and the system in power, and eventually lead to a normal free government without a violent interregnum. An example of the latter type of dictatorship was that of King Alexander of Yugoslavia and his successor. But it is difficult to imagine the magnificent ego, the transcendental will to power, of the Italian Duce bowing for a moment to criticism, control, or indeed any outside influence. This born proletarian, this real man of the people, more than any person living to-day, represents the socially and economically deaf, dumb, and blind ruling class, programmeless, unphilosophical, unideological and anti-ideological, but determined at any price, including the always logical and ultimate one, imperialistic war, to maintain its supremacy.

We have passed slowly through the centuries of village economy, serfdom, and the feudal overlords ; very quickly through the era of industrial and commercial expansion, the era of colonization, the opening of world markets, the exploitation of " inferior " peoples, and we have arrived at the most magnificent smash-up in history in the decade and a half of the World War and the economic débacle of 1929.

The rule of capital, big business, commercial penetration, and colonial expansion has been a time of democracy and social reform. But apparently, as Mussolini himself claims, liberalism is dead and the Goddess of Liberty is a rotten carcass : the ruling class can no longer make their profits and afford to grant democracy and social reforms. The various imperialisms which have divided the world have left no new markets to conquer, no inferior peoples to make into slaves and serfs to produce wealth and to absorb the production of the superior peoples.

In this world emergency Fascism arose to perpetuate the system of exploitation of its own people as well as of those which it could conquer. The Authoritarian State is also the Helot State, the Serf State, for the vast majority outside the reigning hierarchy. Year by year Italy has been returning to the time of serfdom and the feudal overlords.

The balance sheet of Fascism indicates it plainly. But while it must be admitted that the Authoritarian State is a complete success, it is also becoming apparent that the return to serfdom is not a complete solution of the ecomonic problem of Italy or any other State which has or may copy this successful plan. Big business imperialism in Italy has not been able to continue its rate of profit despite the tremendous increase in taxation, the dangerous decrease in wages, the most complete denial of the rights of man in post-bellum history.

Many years ago Mussolini wrote that " the proletariat should train for that great historic conflict when it will be able to settle accounts with its adversaries ; for the Italian proletariat needs a bath of blood for its force to be renewed." From 1922 on frequently he claimed that Fascism was a real revolution, a bloody revolution, that the blood bath was the *sine qua non* of a great revolutionary change. To-day the paralysis which has invaded Fascism, its finances, economics, culture, and spirit also demand a blood bath, and to forestall it in civil war and at the same time satisfy imperialism, which historically has advanced from one blood bath to another, Italy must take the road to a foreign war. Although black, the Fascist shirts have become very dirty, and must be washed in blood.

Those opponents of Fascism who have always maintained that it presented no new philosophy, no new ideology, but was merely a restatement of a medieval system, and that every step taken by Mussolini was a step backwards into a dead civilization, had proof of their view in the official reasons Italy gave to the League of Nations for war in Ethiopia.

The massacre of Ual-Ual was the first excuse given. But it was dropped even before the League's commission absolved both countries of guilt. Then came two new reasons : imperialism, or the necessity of expansion by powerful nations, and *Kultur*, or the right of a civilized country to take over a barbaric country where slavery still flourished.

Both reasons date from the eighteenth and nineteenth centuries ; it is true they were used by Britain in building her empire, and were advanced by Wilhelm in an attempt to rule the world, but no nation has been hypocritical enough to use them again in our time. As for slavery in Ethiopia, the League has taken action, the Emperor of Ethiopia has done his best, considering the fact the country is a loose confederation in which tribal chiefs frequently refuse to listen to Addis Ababa. But the hypocrisy of the whole matter is best shown in the fact that Fascist Italy has herself admitted that slavery in the form of economic servitude still flourishes in her African colony of Libya.

The road to war has been inevitable. Even before John Strachey wrote that " Fascism means war," an Italian writer, Mario Carli, predicted that " Fascism issued from the war and in war it must find its outlet." Fascism means war because imperialism means war, and no one has ever denied that Fascism is imperialistic.

" Imperialism is at the base of the life of every people which desires economic and spiritual expansion," Mussolini once wrote, and again, " We must have the courage to say that Italy cannot remain for ever penned up in one sea, even if it is the Adriatic," while in the famous June 5, 1923, speech against Yugoslavia, he said that " all Italians of my generation understand the lack of territory. It is not surprising, therefore, that our spirit is frequently excited as it turns towards imperialistic aspirations. This is an expression of immanent historic reality, because people who are progressing have their rights against people who are declining. These rights are marked with letters of fire in the pages of our destiny."

In justifying his imperialism Mussolini said in a recent speech : " Invasion of sovereign rights has been in progress for centuries. Where is the nation to-day which during its history has not invaded the sovereign rights of others ? Take the United States ! How did you push your frontiers back ? "

To Mussolini's credit it must be said that he did not, as other imperialist nations have done, resort to euphemism in announcing his imperialism, although diplomatic hypocrisy cloaked the Ethiopian apologia. Sordid and cold-blooded as a post-bellum world may consider his scheme to take by violence the only remaining unexploited piece of Africa, it must be admitted that the intention to seize and conquer land has been frankly stated for a decade.

Many of the preceding chapters contain the reasons for the Fascist road to war. The glorious period of 1922-25, when the industrialists, manufacturers, large employers, subsidizers of the party, were being repaid, was followed by an economic reaction which proved boom-times artificial. After 1925 it became impossible for the " new " system to enrich the few and continue to impoverish the many. One by one Mussolini's promises, which once brought thousands of liberals, radicals, and idealists into his party, were dropped, and instead a programme of ruthless taxation which took half the national income was enforced. And no nation could continue to flourish under that condition, even though the standard of living of the masses was reduced dangerously year after year.

Since the depression Fascism has come to a dead stop. All that it has had in the past four or five years is a record of broken promises, an unbearable debt burden, and the dynamic oratory of the Duce. But one cannot live on oratory alone.

We have seen the collapse of every financial and economic factor in Fascist Italy, exports, imports, emigrants' remittances, tourist trade; we have seen the debts grow mountainous, the national debt increase 15,000,000,000 in four years; we know that the international bankers have refused to issue loans, and we know that the tremendous population pressure has increased during the ten years which now mark the Italian depression. Every economist and every intelligent student has been aware of the forces which for a decade have been driving the dictator into either war or collapse; only in the *New York Times* (September 1, 1935, magazine section, page 2) is the opinion expressed that " Mussolini is the first ruler since Napoleon by his own will, without external provocation or internal propulsion, to lead his people into a campaign of conquest."

The internal propulsion has been progressive for years and it has now become headlong.

Like many a bankrupt business man who takes his last resources and plays them on a number in Monto Carlo, Mussolini, rather than take the other way out of his dilemma, the fulfilment of the social-economic programme which he wrote in 1919, must play the game of war.

The prediction of Mussolini's course was made twenty-three centuries before John Strachey. Aristotle, founder of political science, wrote : " The tyrant who, in order to hold his power, suppresses every superiority, does away with good men, forbids education and light, controls every movement of the citizens, and, keeping them under a perpetual servitude, wants them to grow accustomed to baseness and cowardice, has his spies everywhere to listen to what is said in the meetings, and spreads dissension and calumny among the citizens and impoverishes them, is obliged to make war in order to keep his subjects occupied and impose on them permanent need of a chief."

The word " chief " in Italian is " duce."

CHAPTER XXX

Ave Caesar!

WHATEVER the final outcome may be for Italy, for Mussolini the one thing he confesses has worried him most has now been won : he has made his mark in history.

There is, of course, nothing strange nor abnormal in the concern which a leader of men feels about posterity ; it is merely part of the problem of immortality which has confused and inspired mankind from its first intelligent beginnings. " I am obsessed with this wild desire—it consumes my whole being," said Mussolini to his Egeria ; " I want to make a mark on my era with my Will, like a lion with its claw." It has been made. The dictator may fall gloriously on an African battlefield or pass away peacefully in bed half a century from now, but Clio has already provided ample pages for the Duce's record.

For almost a quarter of a century he has wooed this muse, acting the Hero, posing before men and camera-men, and time and history, eagerly watching for the signs of his immortality. Even in his youthful soap-box speeches he was already conscious of what press and public would say, and as he grew to manhood he worked on his cutting-books with more enthusiasm than a Hollywood star, but always he kept looking ahead, to a place in the future where his name would shine on deathless bronze, when statues would be erected of his likeness side by side with the Napoleons, and better still, the Roman Caesars, and the gods and demi-gods of all recorded time.

At the Lausanne conference a group of diplomats on an upper floor, looking down an elevator shaft, beheld their newest colleague with his back to the operator, making

364

faces and gestures before the rear mirror. The Napoleonic attitudes were unmistakable.

In the history of the world no man has been more photographed. The paintings, sketches, and busts of the Duce surpass in number those of any being to whom deity has not been seriously attributed. A great part of the leader's day is spent reading the press of the whole world, where every item dealing with him and his activities has been marked by subordinates. He reads them with the air of a man seeking something.

Although he never tires of fatalistic remarks about his destiny in the stars, he has retained the peasant superstitions of his childhood. Twenty centuries earlier analogous rulers, dictators, leaders, tyrants, conquerors, strong kings and frightened kings, were sending to the Delphic oracle or looking at blood and entrails, watching the flights of birds and reading signs in thunder and lightning. Mussolini seeks sibylline warnings in the newspapers and the history books of other revolutions. With the same eagerness with which Lenin, Trotsky, and Stalin watched the Bolshevik revolution take the course of the traditional French Revolution, each acting in his own way to defeat the Brumaires and Thermidors and circumvent the Little Corporals, so Mussolini, warned that history takes an inexorable course, strives to impress his superior will upon it.

Curious, but not surprising to psychologists, is this mingling of the belief in free will, predestination, fatalism, and the commonest Forli superstitions. The village " witch," old Giovanna, taught Mussolini her " magic lore " ; he became " an adept in interpreting dreams and omens and telling fortune by cards." [1] He is quoted often saying, " My blood tells me " and " I must listen to my blood," and he once declared proudly, " *Que voulez-vous ? Je ressemble aux animaux, je renifle le temps qui vient, je suis mon instinct, et je ne me trompe jamais* " (" What would you ? I resemble the animals, I scent the times, I follow my instinct, and I never make a mistake ").

The Duce and the age of dictators have already been

[1] Sarfatti.

explained by the scientists. Freud has expressed his belief that nations, like human beings, can suffer a neurosis ; Adler believes that people like individuals suffer from inferiority, struggle hard to shake it off and to become superior, and in the case of Italy and Mussolini the world has its best example. More recently Stekel has presented his authority complex to explain the weakness of the masses and the power of the Mussolinis, the " father-substitutes." The millions of inferiorities of the people mass together to become a superiority ; the people identify themselves with the leader, partaking of his authority, and the leaders are usually neurotic, suffering from a " compulsion complex." " Dictators in general," continues my colleague, John Gunther, in expounding the Stekel theory, " are a sort of regression to childhood. Love of a leader is a reversion to infantilism." Stekel concludes that " for many generations men fought for democracy, liberty, the right of free assembly and free speech. Thousands of good men have died for these causes. But now one country after another gives up its free institutions, people even vote away their freedom. New dictatorial revolutions . . . are welcomed with relief, not opposed by force. There is a world scramble for authority, for the security of leadership. People everywhere, because their parental sense of authority has disappeared, are looking for a father substitute, for a strong and beloved parental hand."

Germany in 1933 and Italy in 1922 are the most excellent proofs of the contentions of all three psychologists. Although Italy was known as one of the victor nations in 1918, it was greatly humbled in the peace treaty of 1919, which divided the war spoils among the stronger powers and left little more than a dispute over Fiume in the lap of their colleague. The Italian people, who had for a while come through the shroud of inferiority when Garibaldi and his Red Shirts appeared, were therefore in the psychologically ripe stage to accept the man of promises, the man of violence, the demagogue who defied the oppressors, gratified the national yearning for superiority, and wore a black shirt.

One of the seeming paradoxes of the Italian situation which Italy has not yet discovered, although she could do so easily by reading the officially printed works of the Duce, is that the embodiment of their wish-fulfilment neither loves nor respects the masses who follow him. Time and again Mussolini has quoted Machiavelli's opinion of the common people as " mud " and sneered at public opinion. But the more the Duce shows that he despises his followers, the more they shout their love and loyalty. Unlike the bourgeois gentleman, Lenin, who really loved the world-filling proletariat, the oligarch of Italy, in origin plebeian, almost hates them. " I do not adore this new divinity— the masses," writes the Duce, thereby confirming Stalin's view that even revolutionary leaders at times despise their following, and that " an aristocratic attitude of the leaders towards the masses " frequently arises, an attitude which Lenin escaped because his faith in the nobility of the working-man was never shaken.

The greatness of Mussolini can only be measured by the lowness of his worshippers.

He stalks through the world like the one man who wears the mantle of Zarathustra, possesses the mind of Machiavelli, is the inheritor of the power of Caesar, while all the little minds, all the hundreds of millions of unimportant, un-thinking, weak, and ineffectual human beings (whom Sinclair Lewis has both immortalized and crucified with a new word) grovel at his feet, proclaiming him the conqueror. Emperor or Galilean ? The same hundreds of millions go to their churches on Sundays and proclaim an unarmed Man who was weak and humble, who preached humility and kindness and love and non-resistance. The other six days they arm for war and praise violence. The mob mind can worship both.

In all seriousness Mussolini has been compared by his idolators with every one, from Jesus Christ to Theodore Roosevelt.

After Farinacci's solemn declaration that Mussolini's only logical successor as Duce could be Jesus, the official Fascist press proclaimed the infallibility of its

SAWDUST CAESAR

leader, a political dogma meant also for the eyes of the
Pope.

No less a person than an American ambassador [1] wrote
that " the Duce is now the greatest figure of his sphere and
time. One closes the door when one leaves, feeling, as
when Roosevelt was left, that one could squeeze something
of him out of one's clothes."

Inasmuch as the Duce himself permits painters to draw
a lock of hair over the forehead in the Napoleonic manner,
busts made very Caesarean, and a large proportion of the
millions of photographs show him *à la* Bonaparte on horse-
back, or assuming other heroic poses, it is obvious he invites
comparison with the world-conquerors.

Mussolini would like to uphold the tradition of the
" strong, silent man," but his passion for oratory prevents
him from complete achievement. But that he should assume,
consciously or unconsciously, the traditions of the world-
conquerors, Caesar, Alexander, and Napoleon, is quite
natural. All men arriving at similar heights, even the
catch-penny Central American dictators, have been known
to succumb to the rôle ; Mussolini steps into it as an actor
into his make-up.

The Caesar pose was most obvious to those who in April
1926 accompanied the Duce to Tripoli—to that very same
colony the annexation of which caused the same Mussolini
to attempt an armed uprising two decades earlier. Now he
had mobilized more warships for himself than Giolitti had
used for the war on Turkey ; on the prow of the *Cavour* he
strutted and took attitudes which every motion-picture
operator worth his pay recorded deathlessly, or he
sat with folded arms looking dreamily across the
Mediterranean.

He disembarked, he stepped into Africa like a conqueror.
The Tripolitans—at least those who were not at the time in
rebellion—the native troops, the Italian army, the civilians
and officialdom, made a grand uproar.

An American journalist, overcome with the sense of
historic emotion, raised his hand and cried, " Ave Caesar ! "

[1] The late Richard Washburn Child.

To the Duce he said : " It is like the old days when a Roman emperor landed."

Mussolini, delighted, said " Yes."

Others took up the cry. The sun-baked streets of a small African port in an important African colony echoed with the shout of " Caesar," and that very evening numerous red, white, and green posters with the words " Ave Caesar," followed by Mussolini's speech, published by the Fascist officials, were placarded throughout the colony as the expression of its greeting.

Julius, the divider of Gaul, shines over Mussolini ; the Duce looks into those cold pupil-less eyes every day, while his press reminds him that he is the pure Roman emperor type in face and will, the true successor to the thrice-crown-refusing political ancestor. Even the textbooks of Italy have been changed so that to-day all the Caesars are unblemished heroes, and the tyranny, corruption, and weaknesses of that ruler " who fell an easy victim to the cheap devices of the lewd Cleopatra " have been eliminated by the censor. To make their own hero greater, the idol of comparison has been cleaned and polished.

In the year of the Tripoli voyage Mussolini ordered that " within five years Rome must be restored to the grandeur of the Caesars " ; and within a few months he told an interviewer that " we are in the process of renewing the glory of the Caesars. I have a bust of Julius Caesar always before me." And although neither glory nor grandeur was completely renewed by 1931, in September of the next year Mussolini ordered the prefect of his native district to change the name of the Fiumincino River to " Rubicon." " Foreign visitors ask me where the Rubicon is, and we cannot show them," explained Caesar's successor ; " Let us find our river." But he had already ordered the event. Thus it was shown to the world that a problem which harried historians and geographers had disputed violently from medieval times could be settled only through an act of dictatorship.

A year later, at ancient Arminium, where Julius Caesar supposedly harangued the legions for *his*—or, as it is now called, the *first*— march on Rome, a statue donated by the successor was unveiled to " the great patron of Fascism, the first Black Shirt," whose " mighty conception which he gave to Rome and the world exists again in the blood of the race," and in Mussolini " the heir to the legacy which he bequeathed to Italy."

So the orators. To the podestá of Rimini Mussolini telegraphed : " The statue of Julius Caesar, which I have decided to give to your city, is similar to the statue in bronze which adorns the Route of Empire [Via dell Impero, in Rome]. If possible, you will place high on the column the words which Julius Caesar spoke to the militia men of the Thirteenth Legion, when, the die having been cast and the Rubicon having been crossed, he decided upon his march on Rome. Every year, on the Ides of March, you will take care to beflower the statue of the founder of the Roman Empire."

Four times in his talks with Ludwig the Duce mentioned the man whose bust broods over him : once he confessed that " Jesus was greater " ; another time that Shakespeare's play about the hero was " a great school for rulers "; again, in thrilling tones, " Julius Caesar, the greatest man that ever lived. . . . Yes, I have a tremendous admiration for Caesar. Still . . . I myself belong rather to the class of the Bismarcks," and finally, " The assassination of Caesar was a misfortune for mankind. I love Caesar. He was unique in that he combined the will of the warrior with the genius of the sage. At bottom he was a philosopher who saw everything *sub specie æternitatis*. It is true he had a passion for fame, but his ambition did not cut him off from the human kind."

Finally, in the summer of 1935, addressing several thousand former grenadiers, at the time of the mobilization for the Italo-Ethiopian conflict, he reminded them that " Julius Caesar once dominated the world, and that every stone surrounding them should recall the fact." (They were crowded into the ruins of the Temple of Venus.) " Nothing forbids us from believing that what was our destiny yesterday may again become our destiny to-morrow."

From Alexander the Great, who sighed for new lands to conquer, and from the time of every prophet and messiah, men have wanted to rule the whole world, or to make the whole world bow to their one idea. The men of power and egotism want to be king of kings, and many modern rulers use that title. The Ethiopian is not bashful. Caesar, Kaiser, and Tsar are variations on the theme. The idea of world conquest will probably remain for ever, even if it is to be eventually democratized into a sort of figurehead, a man of straw and sawdust, a super-secretary of a future super-League of Nations, and appear to this individual only in his serenest daydream of desire.

The last man to seize a large part of the world, Napoleon, called by Wells, an adventurer, a wrecker, a man of egotism and vanity, a personality archaic, hard, capable, unscrupulous, imitative, and neatly vulgar, is still the hero of the mob. Mussolini has at least this much in common with the Corsican : they were both well-whipped children, therefore destined to a rebellious manhood. Bonaparte was whipped by his mother, Mussolini by his father ; the one used a birch rod, the other a leather belt.

The mediocrity of the two minds is amazing. The Code Napoleon, which he claimed was a greater monument than his forty victories, was written by other men. The plan of the Corporate State is not Mussolini's. The " totally uncreative imagination " of Napoleon was influenced by Plutarch towards a revival of the Roman Empire ; Mussolini in all his words and deeds has shown the influence of the latest book he has been reading, the last strong-minded politician who has been advising him.

Napoleon was not above issuing contradictory and lying statements, as, for example, proclaiming to Italy that he was coming to free it from tyranny, while he told his soldiers to loot the country and wrote to Paris he was going to make the newly conquered State pay an indemnity of twenty millions.

When Napoleon faced the Council of Five Hundred he was as frightened as Mussolini the day he stammered about Matteotti and promised to " return to legality."

25

Yet both men prided themselves on physical courage.

The Napoleonic plan by which the First Consul had under him an *appointed* Council of State, which had under it a legislative body and Tribunate, a Senate, etc., is very much the Mussolinian idea of a " hierarchy ending in a pinhead."

When Napoleon became First Consul the whole world was at his feet, there was peace, and any ruler with a first-rate mind would have done something creative to astound the centuries. (When Mussolini took office, he had the support of all parties, there was peace, and a man whose mind was not warped by egotism and lust for personal power could have given Europe a lead in governing well.) Napoleon, says Wells, could do no more than " strut upon the crest of this great mountain of opportunity like a cockerel on a dunghill. The figure he makes in history is one of almost incredible self-conceit, of vanity, greed, and a grandiose aping of Caesar, Alexander, and Charlemagne, which would be purely comic if it were not caked over with human blood." If Bonaparte's aping of Caesar was so ludicrous and so tragic, what can one say of Mussolini's aping of Bonaparte ? Perhaps that, while he had not a thousandth of Napoleon's success, he has shed but comparatively few drops of human blood.

Both men denounced religion as " opium for the people," Mussolini, actually quoting Marx's phrase, Napoleon in making the famous Concordat, saying it was necessary to give the people religion to keep them quiet : " how can you have order in a State without religion ? "

Whether either dictator ever felt remorse is debated by historians and chroniclers. It is said that Napoleon, during his fits in St. Helena, regretted his order to murder the Duc d'Enghien, and sometimes wept for the dead. Only one person records a sign of regret in Mussolini. " The dead weigh heavily," he once said. On the occasion of the banquet which Italy tendered Ras Taffari, king of Ethiopia, the King and Mussolini found two beautiful envelopes in their napkins. Mussolini opened his and read :

" You are Matteotti's murderer ; prepare for the hand-cuffs."

The King opened his and read :

" Majesty, Matteotti's murderer sits next to you. Give him up to justice."

The King turned pale, but it is reported that Mussolini hid under a small laugh whatever emotions this dramatic reminder provoked.

It is also said that Mussolini sometimes has fits of terror and plans to escape from Italy in an airplane or a yacht.   But there is no actual evidence that the conqueror regrets anything.

Napoleon betrayed the French Revolution.   Future historians may well say that Mussolini betrayed, or at least delayed, the Italian revolution.

Much more appropriate is a comparison between the Duce and Louis Napoleon, who, like his uncle, also betrayed his republic.   For the *décret-loi* of Louis there are the royal decrees which Mussolini forces the King to sign and issues at leisure ;   there is the same perversion of justice, the liberal magistrates suffering the same fate as the French republicans, expulsion ;   university professors in the Third Napoleon's time were made to obey the political wind, too, and the press was censored and corrupted.   Louis placed government largely in the hands of the omnipotent prefects, and Mussolini appoints sub-dictators called podestás. Hierarchy is similarly established.   The pageants, exhibitions, and sports in France which preceded Sedan are duplicated in Rome.

Louis Napoleon was vain, empty, trivial.   His writings show small culture.   He was, like Mussolini, mixed up in liberalism, socialism, and Napoleonism, and likewise preached nationalist superpatriotism.

The similarity between the Italian Dux and the last German Rex, especially in egotistic oratory, has already been noted.

Of the men who make history to-day, especially of dictators, one expects great, rich personalities.   But Stalin is known for his metallic colourless voice, the absence of flourish, for the tendency to remain inconspicuous, and his

inability to sweep an audience with enthusiasm.[1] Like
Lenin, he was " a sense of compressed energy, of reserved
will power. He is not magnetic." Lenin and Trotsky I saw
at the height of their fame ; both surprised me because
they had nothing of the Communist-Socialist-Radical
speaker so well known throughout the world. Lenin
reasoned as Socrates once reasoned in the house of Cephalus.
The only dictator who answers conventional anticipations
is Mussolini, who is magnetic and dynamic, wild, histrionic,
who raises and lowers his voice as taught by the best
professors of drama, becomes cold, waxes hot, erupts like
his own Vesuvius, and uses his hands, eyes, shoulders, and
breath for the purpose of hypnotizing the mob.

Lenin was the only revolutionary who had a deep sense
of humour ; his successor, Stalin, makes jokes and laughs
over them ; frequently they are coarse jokes, and in this
Stalin and Mussolini are similar, except that at times Stalin
has been able to show a trace of objective humour, while
Mussolini has never betrayed it. Intolerance is one of the
secrets of Mussolini's success.

In almost every sentence of his speeches, in almost every
page of his writings, Mussolini curses his opponents. He is
always shouting " scoundrel," " traitor," " egotist " at
some one ; his enemies are " soft-brained cowards,"
" swelled frogs," and " a base and pernicious crew " ; he
never hesitates to call the man who differs from his opinions
a liar ; with the utmost contempt he speaks of political
enemies and those who have fought duels with him as weak-
lings, cowards; referring to foreign statesmen and journalists
who have said he threatens the peace of the world, he replies
" this is the accusation of fools " ; when he can find
nothing evil to say of those whom the world honours he
calls them " egocentric," he speaks of their " unbridled
egotism " ; he is always attacking those who " sell themselves for money, for power," whom he despises—and
frequently the word " turncoat " comes up, and " volte-face,"
which is Italian and needs no translation.[2]

[1] Isaac Don Levine, Stalin.
[2] All these beautiful phrases are culled from Mussolini's autobiography.

He fought a duel with a journalist named Scozzese ;
now that the latter cannot defend himself by challenging a
return duel, Mussolini gives himself the liberty, in writing,
of saying of his adversary that " among other various
imperfections, one might say he had that of physical
cowardice," adding, " I possess some qualities of courage."

The words of attack most frequently heard are " traitor "
and " physical coward " and " egotist " ; with them he
disposes of all who have met him on the field of honour or
who write works on philosophy which fail to include the
newest and greatest of all theories, Fascism ; every one
who has ideas not in comformity is an egotist, and any one
who acts non-conformingly is a traitor, while those who
oppose him are cowards.

Need one go to a psychologist for the explanation of
such behaviour, or is ordinary intelligence sufficient guide ?
Proust speaks of " that habit of denouncing in other people
defects precisely analogous to one's own." " For," he
says, " it is always of those defects that people speak, as
though it were a way of speaking about oneself, indirectly,
which added to the pleasure of absolution that of confession.
Besides, it seems that our attention, always attracted by
what is characteristic of ourself, notices that more than
anything else in other people . . . an unwashed man
speaks only of the baths that other people do not take . . .
a cuckold seeks cuckolds everywhere, a light woman light
women, a snob snobs." There can be no better explanation.

Again, when Mussolini declares : " I have annihilated
in myself all self-interest : I, like the most devoted of
citizens, place upon myself and on every beat of my heart,
service for the Italian people. I proclaim myself their
servant. I feel that all Italians understand and love me ;
I know that only he is loved who leads without weakness
without deviation, and with disinterestedness, and full
faith," a student of his character can find it the great self-
confession of what he lacks most.

One thing he has is a blazing hatred. " Not," as one of
his compatriots says, " the hatred of a social rebel which is
but another facet of love, like the hatred of Brutus for

Caesar, of Bruno for the Papacy, of Mazzini for the tyrants,"
or the hatred which inspired Milton and Byron and Shelley
sublimely, and which has made heroes and martyrs.
Mussolini's dominating hatred, which was important to
his success, was the drop of poison on the swift arrow of his
Will.

Of this man's amazing egotism much has been said. It
is the most natural trait in human beings who are failures
to shout down the successful man, no matter who he is or
what he does. Napoleon and Pericles are equally condemned.
No distinction is made between the ego which drives a man
to lead the world by developing all that is great and powerful within him, and the ego which leads another man to
rise high by destroying all others. Mussolini's ego is a
compound. Sometimes it exhibits itself in all its naïve
crudity.

Three days after he had seized the government his old
friend, Paolo Orlano, a comrade who could call him by his
first name, came into Benito's office, saying, jestingly, " I
want to see how you are preparing to rule Italy."

" Preparing ? I ? " replied Mussolini, as Orlano afterwards recounted. " Why, I'm already in the middle of it.
I am ruling. I'll show you how I rule."

Mussolini pressed a button, summoned a secretary,
asked that a telephone call be put through to one of the
leaders of the march and of Fascism.

" Hello. I am talking. Mussolini. Be—ni—to Mus—
so—li—ni. Listen. You are expecting to receive the
field-marshal's baton. Fine. But you are not going to get
it just yet. You—are—not—going—to—get—it—just—
yet. Get yourself a small cane. Good-bye."

" There," he said to Orlano. " I'm not here as a
tourist, but to give Italy a government and to govern it.
That never was before, but is now : a government. I am
it. And all, mind you, all Italians shall and will obey.
Italians have never obeyed. The Italians must be ruled
and shall be ruled."

Mussolini threw his head high, as if to snap it from his
neck and shoulders—a movement that Orlano saw for the

first time in this man, but which was to be immortalized
later in a million photographs and many films.

When *Piemonte*, a newspaper of Turin, printed a
questionnaire regarding Mussolini's greatness in history,
the dictator telegraphed to the prefect of police : " Call the
editor of *Piemonte* and ask him to stop the referendum.
Tell him that Mussolini himself does not know exactly
what he is, and therefore it is difficult for others to judge
him. The referendum can be resumed fifty years hence."

At another time he declared that " I am convinced that
I was destined to rule Italy some ten to fifteen years more.
My successor is not yet born."

The egotism of the ruler is transmitted to the youth of
Italy. The Fascist publication for the universities thus
informs the coming generation : " The Italian of to-
morrow, and that means the Balilla and the Avanguardista
of to-day, will be the natural heir of the Fascist mentality,
and will not need to discuss these four points :

" 1. That Italy deserves to be the biggest and strongest
         nation in the world.
" 2. That Italy will become the biggest and strongest
         nation in the world.
" 3. That the Italian laws are the finest in the world.
" 4. That the men who now rule are the best, and that
         we owe them honour and obedience."

Of the noble traits in Mussolini's character none stand
out more than his emancipation from the degenerate
desire for money, exceedingly rare in persons who are born
poor and who, on acquiring riches, frequently remain
miserly through the fear of ever being poor again. Mussolini
insists six separate times in his autobiography that " money
has no lure for me." " I ask nothing for myself, nor for
mine ; no material goods, no honours, no testimonials."
" I have annihilated in myself all self-interest." " In
politics I never gained a penny. I detest those who live
like parasites, sucking away at the edges of social struggles.
I hate men who grow rich in politics." " To me money is
detestable ; what it may do is sometimes beautiful and
sometimes noble."

His enemies say that if all this is true, why did the Fascist official press, boasting of the new income-tax law, congratulate the Duce on paying his the first day—the sum of 200,000 lire, which would indicate an income of 500,000 lire and a capital of 10,000,000. And why, ask enemies, does Mussolini insist so much on his contempt for the lure of money ? Why does he mention it at least six times in his autobiography ?

The truth is that Mussolini does not care for money— for himself. But he does not hesitate to use it as a means to power. The 1914 episode of the French funds for founding a newspaper, and the 1919 episode of the Fiume funds, and the 1920 episode of subventions from the employers, while exposing the ruthlessness of the man, are not, even in the charges of enemies, instances of personal greed. Money means power ; more so in Europe than in America. In Europe a man is born in a class, and imprisoned in that class as in a fortress. The peasant begets peasants, the proletarian proletarians, and rare is the case of the youth who breaks the caste lines. The workman's son does not go to college and graduate into the professions, and the rich man's daughter never marries the foreman—a fact that causes a wrong laugh over many an American film. Brains and talent and even genius are wasted in Continental Europe because of class distinction and lack of money. And Socialism flourishes for the same reasons. Mussolini, hating money philosophically, has never hesitated to get it and use it to break himself out of his class prison.

Strangely enough, there is a mental parallel. He suffers from claustrophobia. All his life he has felt himself tied down, hemmed in, suppressed by invisible forces. He hated the confines of the schoolroom. He fled. One of the reasons he escaped military service was the dreadful appearance of the prison-like military barracks of his province, and although he tried to forget the iron bars of frequent visits by reading philosophy and politics, prison cells have left their lines on his character.

He cannot stand locked rooms. In the Chigi Palace every interviewer has remarked the enormous chamber, some fifty or sixty feet long, which serves him as an office. His spirit requires vast spaces. He loves to fly in an airplane, enjoying the power, the superiority, and the freedom of an unpeopled infinity. He has refused to enter the Blue Grotto of Capri.

In exhibitionism he surpasses all the notable men of our age. Chicherin, the timid intellectual, once appeared in a uniform of the Red Army, and did not cut a brave figure. The Kaiser was magnificent in shining breast-plates, but Mussolini goes in for Central American splendour. The first time he addressed the Chamber he rigged himself in an operatic gold and spangles which gave the foreign ambassadors their first good laugh under Fascism. Short, stocky, bulgy, myopic, and fairly bald, he poses so well the world believes him heroically tall, with the most magnificent flashing eyes.

His literary judgments are sententious and weak. He is the author of such philosophical gems as " smoking is a distraction " and " the Will to Power is a cardinal point in the philosophy of Nietzsche " and " The hills and the sea give one the feeling of infinity." He has a college freshman's enthusiasm for Nietzsche's " blond beasts " and " the egotism which in men of power does not admit of restrictions " ; he is impressed with Nietzsche's quotation from the Arabian sect of Assassins, " To see men suffer is good, to make them suffer is better."

Few of Mussolini's admirers have anything to say about his twenty-year record of changing parties and ideals. Sarfatti, for instance, describes her hero as " impulsive and meditative, a realist and an idealist perfervid yet wise, a romantic in his aspirations, but a classic in his handling of public affairs, Mussolini has a groundwork of consistency in him underlying all these seeming incompatibilities." But a more worldly, less fascinated person, Mussolini's Cheka agent, Rossi, goes deeper into his employer's character. " How," asks Rossi, " can certain noble sentiments which Signor Mussolini expresses in his speeches be reconciled with facts which put such brave moral, political, and penal responsibility upon his shoulders ?

" His temperament, unstable by nature, as I am certainly not the only one to know full well, has, together with his mania for Machiavellianism, led him in the last few years into numberless acts of duplicity and changeableness.

" By turns he is cynical and sentimental, impulsive and cautious, irritable and calm, generous and cruel, quick to decide and slow to move, uncompromising and conciliatory.

" All the qualities of heart and mind have in him contradictory aspects, but in his activities as head of the government, and of the Fascist Party, the tendencies which predominate are duplicity, superficiality, and improvisation."

An explanation of the seeming incompatibilities in Mussolini's character is offered by Adolf Saager : " This is the deeper reason for Mussolini's betrayals : His Unconscious always decides in favour of his hunger for power and his ruler instinct serves the political reaction in the nation ; against which his Conscious is always still striving for some union with the Radicals. From that moment when his Unconscious (which is the unfalsified natural power of a man) becomes dominant, his actions gain certainty and continuity, such as would delight an æsthetic observer in the actions of a preying animal.

" This explains Mussolini's periods of trembling and anxiety, because his Conscious and Unconscious are at war.

" Nothing is more ignorant than to understand Mussolini's coat-turnings and contradictions, his 'hypocrisy' and his ' betrayals ' as signs of character weakness ; these things compose his very character, they are his destiny. This is his organic development."

There remains the question of greatness.

He is, for instance, a great journalist but a tenth-rate *littérateur*. His eloquence is marvellous—emotionally, not logically. He is a great politician, a great leader of the mob, but he is a demagogue and not a statesman.

He is a genius at assimilating the ideas of other persons and making them his own.

He is totally unscrupulous.

He has never done anything original.

He has a tremendous will but an inferior mind.

If achievement is to be measured by such qualifications as strong, well-conceived ambition ; difficult struggle to reach the gaol ; complete accomplishment of ambition ; and importance, human value of the success gained by the man, Mussolini easily passes the first three tests. His ambition has been superhuman, his struggle one of the most noteworthy in our time, and he has accomplished everything his heart desired. But whether there is any great significance in his work, or any human value whatever, cannot so soon be judged.

Mussolini may found an African empire. He may in a small way emulate Julius Caesar. Or he himself may be destroyed by the monstrous State he has created, but he no longer need worry about his place in history. He has made his lion's mark. Even Mr. Wells, who somehow prefers Jesus and Buddha and King Asoka to the Caesars and Napoleons and Wilhelm the Seconds, will some day have to give more space to the Fascist phenomenon.

History will say that Mussolini shows the triumph of the superiority complex, the triumph of Nietzschean catch-phrases, the triumph of the adapter of other people's ideas, the triumph of the book-made egotist.

Reactionary dictators are men of no element of greatness, men with no philosophy, no burning humanitarian ideal, nor even an economic programme of any value to their nation or to the world. Grand and imposing as they look in their flaming uniforms and shirts in nationalist colours on marching days, they are almost forgotten the hour a change is made. Who now remembers Valdemaras ? What country did he rule ? What became of Pangalos ? How many Bratianos were there, and what happened to them ? And how ignoble became that same Primo de Rivera who one day before had stood arm in arm with Mussolini, his treaty-friend, his proud disciple ? But it is not too fantastic to imagine a time after Mussolini's disappearance, when the commentators will say that, after all, he was only a renegade Socialist who could never be trusted, a puny, sententious imitator of Lenin, a rather foolish repeater of Kaiser Wilhelm's foolish phrases, a man mentally and physically ill, a megalomaniac who thought he could change the course of economic forces by the use of magnificent phrases taken from Karl Marx, Nietzsche, Hegel, Vilfredo, Pareto, and his former colleagues in the Socialist movement, and nevertheless a person worthy of statues. After all, he is the original Duce of Fascismo, and all the others are merely imitators.

All of Mussolini's monuments will be monuments to the strength of a weakling, monuments to the weakness of his opposition, to the cowardice of the masses, but, above all, monuments to an Ego and a Will.

Mussolini has made his mark in history, but history records the marks of warriors, suppressors, and vandals as well as saviours and liberators.

History and monuments will recall Benito Mussolini as a Caesar—not a Julius but perhaps a Caesar Borgia or perhaps a Kaiser Wilhelm. If not a Napoleon Bonaparte, then at least a Louis Napoleon.

Everywhere new statues appear of Benito Mussolini to-day, and more will be erected in his lifetime. The statues of Julius Caesar will probably remain for ever in Eternal Rome—but the day will surely come when in all the noble cities of Italy there will arise the statue of Giacomo Matteotti. A free people will then decide if there is to be room also for those of our Sawdust Caesar.

APPENDICES

The Fascist Decalogue

I. Know thou that the Fascist, and especially the militiaman, should not believe in perpetual peace.

II. Days spent in prison are always merited.

III. One serves his fatherland even by standing guard at a petrol tank.

IV. A companion must be a brother, first because he lives with you, and second because he thinks like you.

V. A rifle, the munitions belt, etc., are not entrusted to you to be worn at your ease, but to be preserved for war.

VI. Never say " the government will pay," because it is you who pay, and the government is the one you wished and for which you put on uniform.

VII. Discipline is the sun of the armies ; without it there are no soldiers, only confusion and defeat.

VIII. Mussolini is always right.

IX. The volunteer profits by no extenuating circumstances if he disobeys.

X. One thing must be dear to you above all—the life of the Duce.

The Fascist Ten Commandments [1]

1. God and country first : all other affections come after love for these.

2. He who is not ready to sacrifice body and soul to Italy and to serve Mussolini without question is unworthy to wear the black shirt, symbol of Fascism.

[1] Issued by Giovanni Guiriati, Secretary of the Fascist Party, October 1931.

383

3. Use all your intelligence to understand the orders you receive and all your enthusiasm to obey them and carry them out.

4. Discipline is not only a virtue for a soldier in the ranks. It should be a daily and hourly habit.

5. A bad son and a lazy scholar cannot be good Fascists.

6. Employ your time and talents so that work becomes a pleasure and pleasure becomes work.

7. Learn to suffer without grumbling, to be generous without expecting a reward.

8. Carry out good actions to their end ; do not leave them only half accomplished.

9. Be daring and courageous in moments of difficulty and desperation.

10. Thank God every day that he has made you an Italian Fascist.

THE FOREIGN POLICIES OF FASCISM

Speech by Premier Mussolini

" Do you remember my speeches last May at Leghorn, Florence, and Milan ? I will comment on them long after the event now that the tumult of others' comment appears to have abated. With these speeches I intended to *tear the mask from the face of hypocritical Europe, which stammers of peace at Geneva but prepares for war everywhere*.

" These speeches were regarded as declarations of war, while it was forgotten that the men, groups, parties, and sects to which I alluded at Florence have been waging war against Fascismo for the last eight years.

ACTS OF " MORAL WAR "

" Isn't killing Fascists merely because they are Fascists an act of hostility ? Isn't defaming the Fascist régime and impairing its credit an act of war ? What slander, however infamous, has been spared the Fascist régime ? Isn't what happened after the Trieste executions proof that war against the Fascist régime is already in full existence ?

For the present it is moral war, but it prepares for military war.

" Slanderous inventions are an act of war. Soon we also shall have cut off the hands of children, as was said of the Germans in 1914. All this is to increase hatred of *the Fascist régime which is now preached by millions upon millions of individuals.*

" We are fighting against a world in decline, but which is still powerful because it represents an enormous crystallization of interests. Let Fascists take good heed that anti-Fascism is not yet dead.

" A state of moral war against us already exists, but side by side with moral war preparations for material war are being hastened at our frontiers."

Then waving a thick bunch of papers, Premier Mussolini went on :

" Do you see this leaflet ? It contains the day-by-day military preparations made against Italy for the last four years, long before my speeches at Leghorn, Florence, and Milan. It is a list of the batteries placed in position, forts constructed, armaments ordered or delivered at our frontiers. Could I help sounding the alarm ?

" WILL DISARM WHEN ALL DO "

" Naturally, those whose mask was torn off tried to invert the situation by representing Italy as the only wolf amid a bleating flock of peaceful lambs. But that trick is puerile. *Italy arms relatively because others arm. She will disarm when all disarm.*

" I repeat that as long as there are cannon they will always be more beautiful than beautiful, but often false, words. When words will be sufficient to regulate relations between peoples then I will say that words are divine.

" Let it be clear, however, that we are arming ourselves spiritually and materially in order to defend ourselves, not in order to attack. Fascist Italy will never take the initiative of war.

" Even our policy of revision of the treaties—which is not new but was first advanced in 1928—aims at avoiding war. The revision of the peace treaties is not dominantly of Italian interest, but interests the whole of Europe and the whole world. Revision is not absurd or impossible, since the possibility of revision is contemplated in the Covenant of the League of Nations. The only absurd thing is to expect treaties to remain absolutely immobile.

" Who violates the League of Nations Covenant ? Those who at Geneva wish to perpetuate two categories of nations—armed ones and defenceless ones. What juridical or moral equality can exist between armed and defenceless nations ? How can one expect this comedy to last for ever when its very protagonists are beginning to show signs that they are tired of it ?

" As for Italy's policy on the Danube and in the East, it is dictated by reasons of life. We are trying to utilize the last square inch of our territory. What we are doing is gigantic. But soon our territory will be saturated by our growing population. We wish this and we are proud of this, because life produces life.

" By the year 1950 Italy will be the only *country of young people in Europe*, while the rest of Europe will be wrinkled and decrepit. People will come from over the frontier to see the phenomenon of this blooming spring of the Italian people.

" Only toward the East can our pacific expansion occur. This explains our friendships and our alliances. The dilemma propounded at Florence still holds good. It goes hard with our enemies already, but we are marching side by side with our friends.

UPHOLDS SINCERE POLICY

" Our foreign policy is sincere, without evasion or mental reservations. A written agreement is sacred for us whatever may happen. Nor do we know of any other means whereby a people can increase its prestige and the confidence others have in it.

" The longer our régime lasts the more the anti-Fascist coalition has recourse to expedients dictated by desperation. The struggle between the two worlds can permit no compromises. The new cycle which begins with the ninth year of the Fascist régime places the alternative in even greater relief—either we or they, either their ideas or ours, either our State or theirs !

" The new cycle must be of greater harshness, not of greater indulgence. Whoever has interpreted it differently has fallen into a grave error of interpretation. This explains why the struggle has now become world-wide and why Fascismo has become the subject of debate in all countries, here feared, there hated, elsewhere ardently desired.

" The phrase that Fascismo is not an article for exportation is not mine. It is too banal. It was adopted for the readers of newspapers who in order to understand anything need to have it translated into terms of commercial jargon. In any case it must now be amended.

" *To-day I affirm that the idea, doctrine, and spirit of Fascismo are universal.* It is Italian in its particular institutions, but it is universal in spirit ; nor could it be otherwise, for spirit is universal by its very nature. It is therefore possible to foresee a Fascist Europe which will model its institutions on Fascist doctrine and practice, a Europe which will solve in the Fascist way the problems of the modern State of the twentieth century, a State very different from the States which existed before 1789, or which were formed afterward.

" To-day even as yesterday the prestige of nations is determined absolutely by their military glories and armed power.

" *Fascism is an army on the march.* Its well-being, therefore, must be guaranteed by methods of safety. The Masons, who are sleeping, may reawaken. By eliminating them we can be sure that they will sleep for ever."

" Italy is an immense legion which marches under the
26

Fascist symbols toward a greater future.   Nobody can stop
her.   Nobody will stop her."

(Rome, Oct. 27, 1930, Palazzo Venegia, 8th anniversary
eve celebration.)

" DIEU N'EXISTE PAS " [1]

BY BENITO MUSSOLINI

When we claim that " God does not exist," we mean to
deny by this declaration the personal God of theology, the
God worshipped in various ways and divers modes by
believers the world over, that God who from nothing
created the universe, from chaos matter, that God of
absurd attributes who is an affront to human reason.

With each new discovery of chemistry, physics, biology,
the anthropological sciences, of the practical application of
found principles, dogma collapses.   It is a part of that old
edifice of religion which crumbles and falls in ruins.   The
continuous progress of the natural sciences now extending
from city to country, disperses the darkness of the Middle
Ages, and the multitudes desert the churches where from
generation to generation they betook themselves to pray
to God—that monstrous product of human ignorance.

Let us examine the nature of God.   We force ourselves,
therefore, to reason in a vacuum, the God of religious
being their own image of their mental vacuum, the proof of
the complete absence of any activity in reasoning.

How can the idea of a creator be reconciled with the
existence of dwarfed and atrophied organs, with anomalies
and monstrosities, with the existence of pain, perpetual
and universal, with the struggle and the inequalities among
human beings ?

Epicurus, the philosopher who lived in Rome in the time

[1] " God Does Not Exist," from *L'Homme et la Divinité*, par Mussolini,
Benito ; Bibliothèque Internationale de propagande rationaliste ; Chêne-
Bourg, Genève ; Juillet, 1904.   This is Mussolini's first published work ;
the translation, such as it is, is my own.

of the decadence of the Republic, posed the following questions :

" Either God wishes to do away with evil in this world and cannot succeed ; or he can do away with it and does not wish to ; or he cannot and does not wish to ; or finally, he wishes to and can. If he wishes to but has not the power, he is not all-powerful. If he has the power to do away with evil and does not wish to, he is not infinitely good. If, as affirm the deists, he can and wants to, tell me, then, why does evil exist on earth, and why does not God make it impossible ? "

That which affronts human reason most is the inconceivable fact of the creative power of a God who from nothingness created everything, from chaos the universe. . . .

One would have to be completely without knowledge of physiology, botany, and psychology to claim to-day the existence of a " soul " independent of the body ; on the contrary, one which does not form one of the two distinct aspects of the unique human nature.

Dogma is absurd because it presupposes immobility and the absolute. Nothing in the world is absolute, everything is relative. Nothing is entirely changeless, but there is a continual transformation, a perpetual movement of forces.

Dogma presents to human reason an obstacle to progress because it imposes limitations to the painful but salutary impulses towards the search for truth, because it checks the free expansion of all intellectual energy.

Science is now in the process of destroying religious dogma. The dogma of the divine creation is recognized as absurd.

" Religion is the opium of the people."—KARL MARX.

It being demonstrated that religious dogma presents itself to the human spirit and to rational criticism as " the absolute consecration of the absurd," let us see why moral religion is " immoral."

The evangelists are ridiculous when, instead of studying the Bible as a document of a certain historic interest, they try to credit it with real life and bring to the masses the principles of Christ (who perhaps never existed) as the

ethical principles of a morality everlastingly young, permanent, modern, in complete accord with the present age.
The Bible and morals called Christian are two cadavers
which the evangelists attempt to galvanize into life with,
it must be agreed, small enough success.

It is, therefore, clear that religious morality is one of
resignation and sacrifice, a morality which may be dear to
the weak, to the degenerate, to slaves, but which results
in the diminution of reason and human personality. It
bends man towards the earth, making him a slave to
divinity. It favours the conservation of those primitive
sentiments which belong to that period of animal life long
left behind, and transforms the " thinking being " into a
" passive sheep " who lives in the fear of the universal
judgment.

Religious morality shows the original stigmata of
authoritarianism precisely because it pretends to be the
revelation of divine authority. In order to translate this
authoritarianism into action and impose it upon humanity,
the priestly caste of revealers has sprung up, and with it
the most atrocious intolerance.

Certain it is that religion is a psychic disease of the
brain, a contraction, a tightening up of the individual who,
if he is profoundly religious, appears to us as abnormal.

The history of many saints, beatified by the Church, is
repugnant. It shows nothing more than a profound
aberration of the human spirit in search of ultra-terrestrial
chimeras ; it is a delirium which can attain the state of
spasms of passion and which ends in madness.

Therefore, many of those who to-day hover over the
altars of the Catholic Church are pathological cases,
hysterics, *déomanes*, and demonomaniacs.

Even to-day in the more remote parts of Italy and
Spain we can witness similar phenomena, Saint January
for the people of Naples, and the Madonna of Lourdes for
French bigotry. Are they not analogous aberrations ?

If we read the history of religions, we find that it deals
with the pathology of the human brain. If to-day the
Middle Ages are retiring into the thick shadows of convents,

it is due to triumphant scepticism ; and if the epidemic disease of religion no longer appears with the terrible intensity of former times, it is due to the diminution of the political power of the Church which formerly placed on the heads of people its cap of lead.

Religion presents itself to our eyes in another characteristic : the atrophy of reason. The faculty by which man is differentiated from the lower animals is his reasoning power. But the devout believer renounces reason, refuses to explain the things which surround him, the innumerable natural phenomena, because his religious faith is enough for him. The brain loses the habit of thinking ; and this religious sottishness hurls mankind back into animalism.

In concluding we say that " religious man " is an abnormality, and that " religion " is the certain cause of epidemic diseases of the mind which require the care of alienists.

Religion has shown itself in the open as the institution whose aim is political power by which to externalize the exploitation and the ignorance of the people.

BIBLIOGRAPHY

Balabanoff, Angelica	*Erinnerungen und Erlebnisse.*
,, ,,	*Wesen und Werdegang des Italianischen Fascismus.*
Barnes, Major J. S.	*Fascism.*
Beals, Carleton	*Rome or Death.*
Béraud, Henri	*Ce qui j'ai vu à Rome.*
Bolitho, William	*Italy under Mussolini.*
Bordeux, Jeanne	*Benito Mussolini the Man.*
Borghi, Armando	*Mussolini in camicia.*
Buozzi, Bruno and Nitti, Vincenzo	*Fascisme et Syndicalisme, Paris, 1930.*
Chiesa, Eugene	*The Political, Financial, and Economic Situation in Italy, Paris, 1929.*
Child, Richard Washburn	*A Diplomat Looks at Europe.*
Einzig, Paul	*Economic Foundations of Fascism.*
Elwin, William	*Fascism at Work.*
Ferrero, Guglielmo	*Four Years of Fascism.*
Fiori, Vittorio	*Mussolini the Man of Destiny.*
Garibaldi, Ricciotti	*Le Fascisme et l'Italie.*
Gentile, Giovanni	*The Philosophic Basis of Fascism, Foreign Affairs, January 1928.*
Goad, H. E.	*The Making of the Corporate State.*
Gorgolini, Pietro	*Le Fascisme.*
Haider, Carmen	*Capital and Labour under Fascism.*
,, ,,	*Do We Want Fascism?*
Kemechey, L.	*Il Duce.*
King, Bolton	*Fascism in Italy.*
Ludwig, Emil	*Talks with Mussolini.*
McGuire, Constantine E.	*Italy's International Economic Position (Institute of Economics, 1926).*
Machiavelli	*Le Prince. Preface de Benito Mussolini.*
Malaparte, Curzio	*L'Art de Coup d'État.*

Matteotti, G. . . . *The Fascisti Exposed, London,*
1924.

Mowrer, Edgar Ansell . *Immortal Italy.*

Mussolini, Benito . . *Campo di Maggio (with G. Forzano).*

,, ,, . . *"Dieu n'existe pas" (1904).*

,, ,, . . *John Huss.*

,, ,, . . *Mussolini as revealed in his Political*
Speeches.

,, ,, . . *My Autobiography.*

,, ,, . . *My Way Diary.*

,, ,, . . *Socialismo e difesta armata.*

,, ,, . . *The Cardinal's Mistress.*

Nenni, P. . . . *La Lutte des classes en Italie, Paris,*
1930.

Nitti, F. F. . . . *Nos prisons et notre evasion, Paris,*
1930 *(translated and published*
in abridged edition in the United
States under the title " Escape ").

Nitti, Francesco . . *Bolshevism, Fascism, and Democ-*
racy.

Nomad, Max . . . *Rebels and Renegades.*

Page, Kirby (editor) . *A New Economic Order.*

Phillips, Sir Percival. . *The Red Dragon and the Black*
Shirts.

Por, Ödön . . . *Fascism.*

Prezzolini, Giuseppe . *Fascism.*

Roberts, Kenneth L. . *Black Magic.*

Ronin, Paul . . . *L'Ombre sur Rome.*

Salvemini, Gaetano . . *Mussolini Diplomate, Paris,* 1932.

,, ,, . . *The Fascist Dictatorship,* 1927.

Sarfatti, Margherita G. . *The Life of Benito Mussolini.*

Schneider, Herbert W. . *Making Fascists.*

,, ,, . *Making the Fascist State.*

Sforza, Carlo . . . *Makers of Modern Europe.*

,, ,, . . . *European Dictatorships.*

Strachey, John . . *The Menace of Fascism.*

Sturzo, Don Luigi . . *Italy and Fascismo.*

Suckert (Malaparte), Curzio *Social, Moral and Economic Con-*
flicts of Fascism.

Survey, The . . . *Fascism, a Symposium, March* 1,
1927.

Trentin, Sylvio   .   .   *L'Aventure Italienne.*
Turati, Augusto   .   .   *A Revolution and its Leader.*
Valois, George .   .   .   *Finances Italiennes, Paris,* 1930.
Villari, Luigi .   .   .   *The Awakening of Italy, London,*
                                 1924.
    „   „   .   .   .   *The Fascist Experiment, London,*
                                 1926.

INDEX

A

Albertini, 168, 169.
Alessandro (Papa), 12–13, 236.
Amendola, Giovanni, 156, 168–172.
d'Annunzio, Gabriele, 60–69, 72, 73, 86, 104, 275, 329–330.
Aristotle quoted, 362–363.
Arpinati, Leandro, 214, 215.
Azzione Cattolica, 247, 249, 252, 253.

B

Bacci, Giovanni, 21.
Balabanoff, Angelica, 4, 36–39, 40, 124, 132.
Balbo, Italo, 209–211, 215, 221.
Battaglia Facisti, quoted, 180.
Battisti, Cesare, 2.
Berneri, Camillo, 206.
Bianchi, Michele, 209.
Bird, William, quoted, 185–186.
Bissolati, 19, 44.
Bolitho, William, 154 n., 164–165, 217 n., 223.
Bond, John, quoted, 186.
Bonomi, 19, 21.
Bonomini, trial of, 49.
Bordeux, Mme, quoted, 165 ; 299.
Bottai, Giuseppe, quoted, 276–277.
Bottazzi, Professor, 285.
Bovone, Domenico, 224.
Boyd, Ernest, quoted, 341.
Briffault, Robert, quoted, 289.
Brubaker, Howard, quoted, 246, 294.
Buozzi, Signor, 79, 83, 124, 277.

C

Cabrini, 19.
Cachin, Marcel, 46, 48.
Cadorna, General, 59, 60.

" Ceca," the (or Cheka, or Ovra) 122, 154, 193–208, 228.
Censorship of books, order for, 341.
Ceva, Umberto, 205.
Chamberlain, Sir Austen, 258.
Child, Richard Washburn, quoted, 368 n.
Citrine, Walter M., quoted, 290.
Cittadini, General, 113, 133.
Clayton, John, writing on censorship, 164.
Corporate State announced as completed, 270.
Corriere della Sera, the, 135–136,
Cortesi, Mr., of the *New York Times*, 281, 282 ; quoted, 347, 350.
Croce, the Italian philosopher, quoted, 153–154.
Curzon, Lord, 122.
Corfu bombarded by the Italian navy, 255–256.

D

Darrah, David, his expulsion from Italy, 325.
De Ambris, Alceste, 66, 68, 70, 73, 275.
De Bono, General, 150, 163, 169, 170, 197, 209.
De Bosis, Signora, 204.
De Carnezza, 190, 191.
De Santo, 107.
De Vecchi, General, 89, 93, 115, 209, 211.
Decrees issued, 270.
Del Re, Carlo, 205, 206.
Demetrio, V., quoted, 258.
Dollfuss, 265, 266, 319.
Donati, Dr., quoted, 197–198.
Dumas, Charles, 49, 50.
Dumini, Amerigo, 142–143, 146, 152 ; trial of, 159–162, 181, 195, 212, 213.

E

Elliott, Professor W. Y., quoted, 290.
Examples of Fascist dismissals, 334.
Eyre, Mr. Lincoln, 86.

F

Facta, Premier, 109.
Farinacci, Roberto, 154, 159, 212, 214, 215, 367.
Fascio di Combattimento, programme of the, 123, 124.
Fascio di Resistenza, the, 60.
Fascismo, first mention of, 86.
Fascist Party publishes its list of achievements, 235.
Fascist publication for the universities, 377.
Federzoni, 44, 150, 200, 215, 240.
Filippelli, Filippo, 149, 150, 214.
Fiorentino, Virgilio, his great Fascist epic, Le 27 Cantate della Rivoluzione, 339–341.
Florence Freemasons, massacre of, 180–181.
Fortune, quoted, 306, 307.
Freemasonry, attack on, and purge of, 176–188, 228.

G

Galbiati, Don, 288.
Garibaldi, G., quoted, 178, 188, 227.
Garibaldi, Ricciotti, 199–202, 205.
Gautrand, Maître, 49, 50.
Gentile, his reform, quoted, 330.
Giannini, Alberto, 173–174.
Gibson, Honourable Violet, 218–219.
Giolitti, 69, 70, 73, 79.
Giurati, 89.
Gobetti, Professor, 172, 173.
Grandi, Dino, 115, 213, 215, 255.
Griffith, Sanford, quoted, 272.

H

Haven, Consul Joseph Emerson, shot at, 86.

Hegel, quoted, 275 ; compared with Mussolini, 356.
Hitler, 319.

I

Italian Press censorized, prohibited, and suppressed, 311–313.

J

Julius Caesar and Mussolini compared, 369–370.

K

Kallen, Professor Horace M., quoted, 344.

L

Labour Charter, the, 276.
Le Peuple of Brussels, quoted, describing interview of Mussolini and the Pope, 250–251.
Lucetti, Gino, 200, 220.

M

Machiavelli, quoted, 175 ; the modern, 294.
Macia, Colonel Francesco, 199, 201.
MacLean, H. C., quoted, 297–298.
Maffi, Cardinal, his anathema of Fascism, 239–240.
Mafia organization, 189–192.
Marconi, Guglielmo, quoted, 330.
Marcosson, Isaac, quoted, 273 n., 274, 291, 299, 347.
Marinetti's Futurist Manifesto, quoted, 331.
Marraro, Howard R., quoted, 282, 347–348.
Marx, Karl, ideas of, 123, 124, 127.
Massacre of Turin, 211.

Matteotti, Giacomo, 120, 121, 123 ; exposes Mussolini, 137–141 ; assassinated, 142–143 ; 145, 149, 150, 151, 155, 156, 157–159 ; quoted, 335.
Matteotti, Signora, 144.
McGuire, Constantine E., quoted, 284, 286.
Misuri, Cesare, 156 ; attacked and beaten up, 196.
Mitchell, Mowatt M., quoted, 298.
Mehring, Walter, quoted, 337.
Militarization programme of 1934 in Italy, 351–352.
Modigliani, 168.
Mori, Cesare, 190.
Mosconi, Minister, 303.
Motherwell, Hiram Kelly, journalist, 105.
Murphy, James, quoted, 196–197, 299, 300.
Murray, Professor Gilbert, quoted, 164, 191.
Mussolini, Benito, *passim*. See also Chronology, pp. vii–xiii.
Mussolini's " Notes and Recommendations," 314–315.

N

Naldi, editor of *Resto del Carlino*, 46, 47, 48.
Napoleon and Mussolini compared, 372, 373.
Nenni, Pietro, 17 ; dialogue with Mussolini, 102–103.
New York Times extract quoted and compared, 324.
New York World, quoted, 327.
Nitti, 129, 130, 133, 168, 190, 340.
Nietzsche, 14, 379.
Nobile, Polar explorer, 318–319.

O

Odier, M., Minister of State, 33–34.
Ojetti, Signor Ugo, quoted, 341.
Orlano, Paolo, calls on Mussolini, 376.
O.V.R.A., 203–206, 348. See also Ceca.

P

Palermi, Commendatore Raoul, stabbed, 186.
Parri, Ferruccio, 206.
Pericles, Mussolini wishes to emulate, 329.
Perroni, Adjutant-Major Vico, his confession, 169.
Pilati, Socialist Deputy Gaetano, assassinated, 181–184.
Pittaluga, General, 61, 62.
Pope, the, his contentions with Mussolini, 235–253 ; publishes his 1931 encyclical, 247–249.
Popolo d'Italia, journal, founded, 3–4 ; 48, 50 ; barricaded, 111, 112, 114 ; 168 n., 172, 272, 319, 339, 340.
Pressolini, 195–196, 213, 272.
Proust, quoted, 375.

Q

Quaglia, Carlo, 217, 218.

R

Railroads and trains in Italy, 348–349.
Ricci, Hon. R., quoted, 240.
Rivera, General Miguel Primo de, 259, 260, 261, 263, 381.
Roberts, Kenneth L., 273 n., 274.
Rossetti, Raffaele, 60, 61, 174–175.
Rossi, Cesare, 89, 91, 129, 133, 141, 143, 144, 147, 148, 150–151, 161, 162, 163 ; quoted, 174 ; 195.
Roya, Louis, quoted, 166–167.
Rumeley, Dr., 45, 51, 211 ; quoted, 379–380.

S

Saager, Adolf, quoted, 380.
Salvemini, Professor Gaetano, 165, 304, 305, 308.
Sarfatti, Mme, 56, 111, 126, 134 ; quoted, 166, 379.

Schirru, Michele, 223.
Schopenhauer, 14.
Serrati, Giacinto Menotti, Mussolini's friend and teacher, 5, 6, 25–26, 40, 128, 129, 168.
Service Orders, 314–318.
Settimána Rossa, the, or Red Week, 42, 43.
Sforza, Count, 205 ; quoted, 296–297.
Shardellotto, Angelo, 223, 224.
Shaw, Bernard, compares Mussolini with Napoleon, 165.
Slocombe, George, journalist, quoted, 321–323.
Smuggling of rifles and machine guns, 265, 266.
Sorel, George, 21.
Spingardi, General Count, 53.
Stahremberg, Prince, 265, 266.
Stefani press bureau, 320, 324.
Stories as to Mussolini's war wounds, 55–57.
Sturzo, Don Luigi, 94, 95–99, 168, 191.

T

Tagore's visit to Rome, 312, 313 ; quoted, 313–314.
Tancredi, Libero, his two articles, 46.
Taxation, 287.
Times, the, quoted, 252, 324.
Torrès, Maître, 49.
Treaty of Nettuno, 71.
Treaty of Rapallo, 71.

Treves, Claudio, 21, 52, 168.
Turano, Anthony M., quoted, 342.
Turati, Augusto, 168, 214, 215, 334.

U

Uniform for new academicians established by Mussolini, 330.

V

Valera, Paolo, quoted, 195.
Vandervelde, M., quoted, 350.
Villari, Luigi, quoted, 165, 199.
Violence made legal in 1925, 233.
Volpi, Albino, 159, 162.
Volpi, Count, 301, 302, 303.

W

War in Ethiopia, official reasons Italy gave for, 360.
Wells, H. G., quoted, 175.
Wilson, President Woodrow, 72, 73, 135, 257.
Winner, Percy, quoted, 353.

Z

Zamboni, Anteo, 221–222.
Zaniboni, Tito, 199, 217–218.
Zibordi, Giovanni, quoted, 158.

4